TED
DEXTER
85 NOT OUT

TED
DEXTER
85 NOT OUT

Quiller

First published in the UK in 2020 by Quiller,
an imprint of Quiller Publishing Ltd.

British Library Cataloguing-in-Publication Data
A catalogue record for this book is available from the British Library.

ISBN 978 1 84689 330 8

Jacket designed by Guy Callaby

Printed in Malta

Quiller

An imprint of Quiller Publishing Ltd
Wykey House, Wykey, Shrewsbury, SY4 1JA
Tel: 01939 261616
Email: info@quillerbooks.com
Website: www.quillerpublishing.com

CONTENTS

FOREWORD

For those of us old enough to have seen a bit of the 1960s it was a fun and liberal time: a time of optimistic deregulation and one in which heroes emerged alongside the popular culture that inspired them. You were for the Beatles or the Stones, or both; James Bond, of course; the Cambridge Footlights; Jean Shrimpton, Twiggy and the miniskirts; Muhammad Ali; Bobby Moore and George Best; Ted Dexter and John Snow. Well, I was. It was a wonderful time to arrive on the planet and begin the circle of life.

Much of this movement was about rebellion, revolution even, in response to the age of austerity. After the long and mainly drab post-war years, the young simply broke free and changed pretty much anything they could get their hands on. Music and fashion led the way, leaving sport's establishment to stutter in their wake. Only a few precious players could transcend the inertia, using both their talent and expression to delight the crowds and influence the young. Cricket was my thing, Dexter and Snow were the wind beneath my wings.

In Snow's case, there truly was rebellion against authority and the system it supported. This was not so with Ted though his free-spirit and somewhat cavalier approach to responsibility gave the impression of one determined to ruffle feathers. Not so. From the outset he adored sport, worked harder than some might think at his books and embraced diversions with the enthusiasm of a man who had more to do than could ever be done.

In truth, Ted is a contradiction: at once a conformist, as shaped by the early years of his life at home and school; and a modernist, whose lateral thinking did much to reform the structure of English cricket during his time as Chairman of Selectors. Richie Benaud observed that Ted's imagination and drive 'will be of great benefit to English cricket in years to come. Equally, I'm in no doubt that others will take the credit for it.' Yes, the rebellion in Ted was to challenge conservative thinking, take risks and invest in his life as an adventure. Both on and off the field, this has made for a terrific watch.

Tall, handsome and impossibly glamorous, Edward Ralph Dexter caught everyone's eye – it was just that he didn't always catch theirs. With the golden Susan on his arm, they cut quite a dash and cared little for the sniping that came from those less blessed. The enigma in him – and how! – was often confused with indifference and though cricket has remained his other great love, it hasn't been the be-all and end-all – a fact, by the way, that made his appearances all the more cherished and makes his company all the more engaging. It is remarkable to think that he first retired as far back as 1965, before returning briefly in 1968 to make a double hundred at Hastings against Kent and be immediately recalled to the England team for the Ashes. In the brilliant photograph of the moment when Derek Underwood claims the final wicket at the Oval, Ted is caught spinning to appeal for LBW with a face that smacks of a lifelong instinct for competition and achievement.

It was John Snow who said Ted was a man of moods, often caught up in theories, keen when the action was hot, seemingly uninterested when the game was dull...a big-time player, one who responded to atmosphere, liked action and enjoyed the chase and gamble. Maybe this was the reason he was drawn to horse racing; a dull day stalking the covers might be enlivened by thoughts of how his money was faring on the 3:15 at Ascot or Goodwood.'

Not that a five year-old boy knows any of this. I fell for the aura, and for the flair in those back foot assaults on fast bowlers. I don't suppose I saw the 70 in 75 balls against Wes Hall and Charlie Griffith at Lord's in 1963 but I feel as if I did – the power, the poise, the sheer gall of it. Nothing, not even the Beatles, could drag me from the television screen when he walked to the wicket, seemingly changing the picture from black and white to colour as he took guard. Frankly, much of the Test cricket of the time was pretty dull but there was a frisson, an expectation, with Ted just as there is when Ben Stokes is on his way today. It was all too brief; he had packed it in before I started proper school.

The last thing my father did with me before he died so young was take me to see the 1968 Gillette Cup Final at Lord's. This was during Ted's short comeback and when the great man strode to the wicket, I leapt about in excitement, cheering his name for all I was worth. He didn't get many but no matter, I had seen him live. That evening Dad bowled to me in the garden as I imitated every Dexter mannerism and stroke I had seen just a few hours before.

Later, I came to know him, first as Chairman of Selectors and then as a fellow member of Sunningdale Golf Club. He asked me to captain the England A team in Zimbabwe and then threw to me at the Harare Sports Club, urging me to hit through the line of the ball in my back-foot strokes before, exasperated at my hopelessness, taking off his jacket, rolling up his sleeves and showing me how it was done with all the sparkle and style of yesteryear.

I saw him climb off his 1000cc Norton, peel off his leathers and shoot 67 round Sunningdale in deep winter conditions. Last year, he played with us on a mid-summer's day and knocked it round in 84 to beat his age by a shot. Gary Player says that Ted is the best amateur striker of a golf ball he has seen. This hand/eye thing; this Dexter co-ordination with a ball is really something and everyone who has played anything with him picks up on it. Colin Cowdrey used to say that Ted was far and away the most natural games player of them all – 62 Test matches and an average of 47.9 in the era of uncovered pitches and no helmets proves the point. What's more, a criticism levelled at him was that he gave his wicket away more often than was reasonable. Well, I guess you can only please some of the people some of the time.

He has a blog, by the way, and it's worth a glance. I like this paragraph: 'In my last term at Radley College I had a hard game of rackets in the morning, scored three tries with two conversions for the 1st XV in the afternoon, was heard listening to operatic voices in the early evening – before repairing to the Grand Piano in the Mansion and knocking off a couple of Chopin preludes. "Quite the Renaissance man it seems" said my Social Tutor and I admit I liked the sound of it, if not quite knowing what it meant.'

Here is the story then, uncut. It fills gaps and creates gasps – after all, who would fly his own fixed wing Aztec BPA-23 to Australia in 1970, stopping twenty-four times en route, with his wife and two young children as passengers? Edward Ralph Dexter, of course! Over to you Ted ...

Mark Nicholas
August 2020

PROLOGUE

Nice, Côte d'Azur 2003

I'd always liked Nice. There was a strong family connection; my parents had left a pair of suitcases in the Hotel Negresco while fleeing from Italy via a ship from Marseilles in June 1940; the hotel obligingly agreed to look after the cases and, when my parents returned in 1946, decorously handed them back. Not long after I'd got my private pilot's licence in 1968, I flew myself there in my less then pristine Beagle Airedale for no other reason than I could. I remember stepping off the plane and inhaling a long delicious draught of maritime air with an instant quiver of anticipation. After decades of travelling I've found that wherever you land always has its particular aroma that will linger in the back of your memory forever – Barbados, Brisbane, Delhi all have their own distinctive overtones. The air in Nice is especially fragrant in spring; it must be the flowers and the herbs that clad the hillside where the Maritime Alps tumble down towards the glitter of the Mediterranean Sea. Since then I've always associated that scent with wonderful long lunches on jacaranda terraces, days lolling around on boats bobbing on a shimmering, gently lapping blue-green sea, days of relaxed golf, laughter, bottles of chilled rosé, nights in the casino.

Early in the new millennium, when my wife, Susan, and I made up our minds to spend the next phase of our life away from England – somewhere warm, a little exotic and easy on the eye – that corner of the Mediterranean beckoned strongly. Susan's priority was that we should be near the sea; she had happy memories of schooldays on the coast in Hastings, while my first instincts favoured Italy, where I had strong attachments. I was born in Milan and spent much of my childhood and my youth in that region – when Hitler wasn't on the rampage across Europe. Predictably, then, our initial searches for a new home had been along the Ligurian coast.

There was a tenuous Dexter family connection with San Remo. My dad had played golf there; the fairways were visible from the autostrada with the sea not far beyond. An attractive, grown-up sort of resort, it had a lot to recommend it; but then we realised how close it was to Nice and I'd never forgotten my first excited impressions of that vibrant city.

Susan and I had lived in London since we were married in 1959, up until a short spell in Ascot which hadn't really suited us. Even so close to the capital we'd found that we missed the bustle and amenities of the big city. We happened to know that Nice, being a busy port with a raison d'être beyond merely satisfying the sybaritic demands of rich tourists, was a year-round city, unlike, say, Cannes or San Remo which are more seasonal. The clincher for us was the French health system which people had told us was excellent. We hadn't heard anything to the contrary about Italy but, swayed, too, by the fact that Susan spoke more French than Italian, in the end, France it was.

**

It was with an almost youthful enthusiasm that we watched our sturdy Audi estate car being loaded onto the overnight train from Paris to Nice – sadly not the glamorous *Train Bleu* on which my brother and I had shuttled back and forth to Milan as schoolboys on holiday. This was a more prosaic conveyance which bumbled rather than sped towards the Côte d'Azur. But that didn't stop me bubbling with expectations of a new life where I wouldn't simply be Ted Dexter, remembered for cricketing centuries scored against great pace bowlers forty years before or, more recently and less flatteringly, for a four-year stint as chairman of the England Committee, whom some of the pundits had vigorously blamed when the game wasn't going so well for England.

**

More specifically, the first seeds of my disenchantment with life in England were sown on 11 September 2001. On that day I was sitting in a small anteroom at the headquarters of the Lord's Taverners, awaiting my turn for a scheduled meeting with their CEO. The door opened; I was already rising to my feet, when the young woman who had shown me in popped her head into the room. 'It seems a light aircraft has crashed into a tower block in New York,' she burbled with the excitement of passing on bad news. 'It's on the TV now.'

**

Most people remember where they were when they first heard news of momentous world events – the assassination of President Kennedy, Princess Diana's fatal crash in the tunnel beside the Seine, the tsunami that swept through the Indian Ocean in 2004 – but it's only afterwards that they can look back and see how those events impinged on their own lives.

I was certainly hit hard by 9/11. First, of course, by the shock of a human tragedy on such a massive, horribly callous scale, with the death of some three thousand innocent individuals; I struggled to comprehend the extraordinary sight of two of the world's most famous skyscrapers collapsing in vast billows of dust like burst balloons into an amorphous heap of rubble. Then after that, on a personal level, I was badly struck by the damage it caused to my business, Ted Dexter & Associates Sports PR, and the knock-on effect this had on my own life. The business had in any case recently suffered a setback through the loss of a couple of key clients, although I'd still been confident I had an ace up my sleeve – a scheme that looked as if it could be the best promotion I'd yet devised, and a major firm of City accountants were making very positive noises about sponsoring the project.

It involved the diversity of nationalities of players on the European Golf Tour. Each country would nominate three representative players as their national team, each month playing against all the other countries for the sponsor's 'charity prize' – a large sum of money to be paid to a charity of the players' own choice. The European Tour had liked the idea, taking the view that it would be an interesting addition to the purely individual nature of the weekly tournaments. The final meeting at Wentworth to clinch the deal was planned for 12 September!

Inevitably, that meeting was cancelled, and it soon emerged that several of the City firm's New York employees were among the thousands who had perished. Not surprisingly, my tentative and somewhat guilt-tinged efforts to reconvene the meeting hit a brick wall.

* *

After that, I found myself without the inspiration to start all over again; there wasn't quite enough fat on the body of the business to sustain it through a lean patch. Besides, I was sixty-six by then, still inconvenienced by several injuries sustained through sport and my own foolhardiness, and anyway, feeling like a change of scene. It was with a little sadness that I put in motion the gloomy process of winding up the company, as well as my remaining commercial interests. I was proud of what I had achieved, certainly – seeing through several initiatives that had changed the way cricket is played and how it's broadcast. However, the truth was, I was fairly bored with doing business for its own sake; I'd come to the conclusion that I wasn't one of life's natural businessmen for whom commerce was an ongoing sport. This was described to me by an inveterate and potent businessman as a game in which winning was even more important than profit; the size of profit was simply how you kept the score against the competition.

I understood the joy of gambling and had witnessed a lot of wagers shuffle off into the bookies' bag as my selections were beaten by a short head. But I'd gone into business for the mundane reason that I had a wife and family to support, and because, much as I had as captain of a cricket team, I loved devising original ideas, and I was optimistic that some of them might turn a profit. In the years since I'd stopped playing cricket (for which in the old-fashioned spirit of British sportsmen, I'd received little direct financial reward), I'd had several ideas, entirely my own, relating to the game I'd played and loved. As it turned out, I was able to breathe life into these projects and see them take their place and become essential tools in the reporting of world cricket.

Fortuitously, around the time I was thinking of dissolving my PR business, I had concluded negotiations with the International Cricket Council for the sale of the intellectual property behind the World Cricketer Ratings system that I'd devised twenty-five years before, and still owned. It made sense to me to cease my other commercial activities at the same time and bow out with good grace. Acknowledging that my active commitment to the world of cricket was coming to an end, I'd already announced that I wouldn't stand for a third term as chairman of the Cricket Committee at the MCC, although I believed that they would have gone along with another term. But I was beginning to feel slightly out of place – not anachronistic, but aware that younger members were talking a different language, with different attitudes to mine, and I'd recognised that it was time to move on. Thus, with the winding down of my business activities, I found myself at something of a loose end as far as occupation was concerned, while poor health had discouraged me from playing golf all through the winter.

Susan and I sat down to discuss how we should respond to this clear breakpoint in our lives and considered what options we had. The bad timing of the demise of my business had left me worse off than I had planned – by no means destitute, but without quite as fat a cushion against life's vicissitudes as I'd hoped for. After we'd discussed in detail with our children, Tom and Genevieve, the best deployment of what we were going to leave in England, ensuring that we would always have visiting rights (and grandparently duties) for a few months each year, we agreed that the most appealing solution was to move south, where the sun shone and I could put the whole 'cricket' thing behind me, once and for all.

It was with this resolve that we had set off on our Mediterranean recce, like a pair of migrating birds seeking a new roost, until we settled for the Côte d'Azur. Here, we thought, we could become M. & Mme Edouard Dexter, comparatively anonymous expat English and members of the Church of England community in Nice. Dramatically, though, before we had even arrived in Nice, our happy optimism suffered a severe kicking.

* *

On the train, lumbering south towards the Mediterranean in the middle of the night, in what was obviously a well-planned raid on our sleeper cabin, we had evidently been disabled by some kind of gas before being comprehensively looted. A short time later, becoming groggily aware of what had happened, we found we had lost pretty much all our cash and credit cards. Susan's handbag was taken, then thrown back through the door – empty.

The door to our cabin had not been forced and could only have been opened with a key held by the attendant. Susan had caught a glimpse of a face as her bag was hurled back and later recognised it as belonging to the attendant in the next carriage. Our own attendant claimed no knowledge of the incident and we were pulling into Nice before we had a chance to alert any higher official.

Now in an utterly parlous state, we had to get on with the business of finding our estate agent and moving in to the rented flat where we had decided to spend a six-month trial, before making a long-term commitment to Nice. We let ourselves into a plain and functional apartment in a large block a few streets from the seafront and the Promenade des Anglais. There was no view of the sea, though, and most of the windows gave on to a large enclosed central courtyard – a battered looking space which any futile attempts to beautify had long been abandoned. Indeed, we soon discovered that this echoing brick well was most enjoyed by skateboarding kids, hurtling down the marble balustrades, whooping and crashing.

We sat down in the plain chairs and looked at each other, feeling for a few moments as miserable as hell and close to defeat. With no ready money to buy food or wine, or Visa card to pay for dinner, we spent the first night of our new exile in a state of stress and doubt about our decision. We knew there would be light at the end of a short tunnel, but just then, tired and temporarily boracic, it was hard not to view the events of our journey south as a bad omen.

But came the dawn for the righteous, crisp and bright – a peaceful Sunday. We managed to find the Holy Trinity Anglican Church nearby, arriving there just after the start of 11 o'clock Sung Eucharist. We slid quietly into a pew at the back of the nave, enjoying the familiar nineteenth century neo-Gothic feel of the place, with dusty sunbeams lancing through richly hued stained-glass windows. We had planned to slip out a little early to avoid having to explain ourselves and our ghastly predicament to any strangers, but before we could leave, I felt a tap on my shoulder. I turned to face an older man who immediately identified me. 'Aren't you the cricketer?' he muttered with some surprise and, thank God, approval.

So much for trying to leave my old identity behind in England, I thought.

Our new friend insisted on ushering us through into the church hall where we soon met more of the locals. It was only later that I recognised the importance of this gentle social introduction to life in Nice.

The following day, we went to take advantage of a 'free' car wash included in the price of the train ticket. Anyone who has used the car-train service will know that vehicles tend to come off the train looking a lot rougher than when they went on. I recalled coming down from Scotland once, when my prized Bentley arrived in London with a smashed windscreen which had been thrashed by a heavy loose-chain carriage link while the paintwork was peppered with tiny dents by flying chips from the track ballast on which the sleepers lay. This elicited not a hint of remorse from British Rail, beyond a minimal payment in settlement.

After its much-needed wash the Audi emerged sleek and gleaming, which cheered us a little. We were taking on petrol at the adjoining pumps when, to save time, Susan was already walking the short distance to pay at the kiosk with a few euros she'd discovered in a pocket in her bag. All of a sudden, on the way back, she was flat on her face – mugged in a flash by two juvenile hoodlums on a scooter who had roared up, ripped her handbag from her shoulder and skidded off, taking what little money she had left in it, and all her jewellery which the previous night's thieves had missed.

Shell-shocked, I rushed to where she lay. At first, she seemed more bruised than battered and managed a slow hobble to the kiosk where she'd paid. The swarthy Niçoise behind the till had witnessed the whole episode, but displayed no sympathy. She shrugged her shoulders with a surly downturn of her mouth as if to say, 'It's not my problem.' We wondered if she knew the little shits who'd rammed Susan.

Stifling our indignation, we continued painfully to the nearest police station. Two gendarmes appeared at the door but brushed us aside with a disinterested flick of the wrist. They couldn't deal with us now, they said, it was their lunch hour. Brusquely, despite Susan's obvious injuries, they told us to come back later.

'Aha! Welcome to France,' we said to ourselves and wandered back to our flat, utterly dispirited and feeling we had completely lost control of events. Susan's face was starting to look black and blue, and one arm was throbbing. Back in our unfamiliar new home, I tried to bring some sense of normality to the scene. I asked Susan how much money she still had on her. It was less than ten euros; this, I soon found, was more than I had. I was completely flummoxed; I couldn't pretend that things weren't looking pretty desperate.

At that moment the phone tinkled. The call was from one of the men we'd met at church the day before. He'd rung, he said, to apologise for telling us the wrong opening times of the nearest big supermarket. I listened abjectly, thinking that, as things were, this was fairly academic, until he added casually, 'By the way, how are you?'

My answer was brief, but long enough to explain that we were in the shit, good and deep.

Later, we would recognise that we had just ridden over the low point of our troubles, and without that act of friendship, we might easily have cut and run. As it was, this kind intervention by an almost total stranger marked the start of twelve happy and stress-free years living by the Mediterranean, until in 2015, Susan and I reluctantly took the decision to return finally to England.

PART ONE

The First Thirty Years

Chapter One

CHILDHOOD

Although I've always had a passion for the Mediterranean, especially the corner where France and Italy meet, I don't clearly remember when I first set eyes on that magical sea. It was probably when I was an infant, visiting the Ligurian coast in north-west Italy with my parents, as they often did from their home in Milan. Scarcely a summer passed without a seaside week at Varazze.

I'd come into this world in that great Northern Italian city on 5 May 1935, at Via Sardegna No. 5. I was the second son of Ralph and Elise Dexter. Soon after that, probably as a result of my arrival, the family moved to a palatial apartment in the Piazza Repubblica, where I lived for the next four and a half years.

My father, whom I grew to know only slowly, was undeniably an unusual character. Physically, an athletic man with strong firm features, wavy silver hair and clear blue eyes, he was someone who generally kept his own counsel and spoke only when he had to. To his children and stepchildren he was always affectionate, seldom raised his voice and never raised a hand, however unruly my brother, John, and I might have been. The only time I heard him swear was when he was playing golf. Despite his reticence, he was relentlessly encouraging. I admired him immensely, and have tried to emulate him throughout my life, though not always with complete success.

Whereas I was always eagerly seeking new experiences, however unpromising, he had held a steady course throughout his life, despite the disruption caused by two world wars. In a rare moment of candour, he told me once that he could have forgiven the Germans for the first blight they'd imposed on his life, but not for the second. He never knowingly bought a single German product between the end of the Second World War and the day he died.

**

My father was born in 1891, the son of a prosperous City accountant, Edward Ralph Dexter of Crouch End, North London. With his two brothers, he was sent to the nearby public school, Mill Hill. Here he excelled as an athlete, still celebrated in handsome silver trophies proclaiming him the one-mile champion in 1909, and then, remarkably, champion of both the 100 yards and the half-mile in 1910. After Mill Hill, he and his brothers went up to Jesus College, Cambridge.

At Cambridge, sport became less important in Ralph's life, overtaken by his enthusiasm for drama with the Footlights, where he appeared alongside Jack Hulbert, a future star in London theatre. Years later, my brother and I found a clue to another aspect of Ralph's young persona in the form of an unpaid account from one of the smarter tailors in town.

At the very start of the First World War in 1914, like both of his brothers and most able-bodied young men, Ralph enlisted and was commissioned as second lieutenant in an Artillery Battalion. We still have a letter from him to his mother, written soon after he reached France. He told her how happy he was to have had a fleeting visit in those early days from his younger brother, Norman. His older brother, Eric, was also sent to France but was quickly repatriated at the first sign of tuberculosis, which was ultimately responsible for shortening his life. With great good fortune and against the odds, the two younger Dexters survived when the life expectancy of a subaltern in any of the infantry regiments on the front line was measured in hours rather than days. Perhaps the gunners were a little less at risk.

Nevertheless, Ralph was certainly exposed to danger, and the account of his bravery in winning a Military Cross, as recorded in the family archive, officially confirms it. Astonishingly, and uniquely, he was also the only officer commissioned on the first day of the war to come through those four hellish years alive and uninjured. The high mortality rate for young officers is implicit in the fact that by the Armistice, second lieutenant Dexter had risen through the ranks to Major Dexter, having briefly held the rank of Acting Colonel.

His lifelong love of horses must have developed during this time. On the rare occasions when he was willing to talk about the war, he often expressed his admiration for the strength, loyalty and courage of the horses that had pulled the guns. Even in his last years when short-term memory was failing, he could still recall the names of his favourites. Rummaging around in a gallery in the 1960s, I came across a print of a Snaffles watercolour of eight horses' heads, entitled *Remounts*, which I bought and gave to Dad. He named all the animals after his favourites, and on the mount below is a pencil drawing of a horse being lifted on board a supply ship, signed by Snaffles himself. The picture now hangs on my bedroom wall.

After he was released from the army in 1919, the changes in Ralph's life must have seemed extraordinary when he started his commercial career in the City offices of an insurance agency, Bevington, Vaizey and Foster. A long way from the shattering noise of the guns and the stench of mud and death, the sudden switch to a sedentary routine of paper-pushing would have been a shock to his system. No doubt seeking some replacement activity, he made sure he found time to ride horses and to become a good mid-handicap golfer.

Luckily for him, or perhaps inevitably, early in his career he was offered a chance that would entirely alter the course of his life. Bevingtons at the time had an underwriting agent in Milan. They had to do business this way as British insurance companies were forbidden to trade directly in Italy. The incumbent, an Australian, wasn't producing enough business to justify his existence. Ralph was sent down to see what was going on. As a result of his subsequent report of chronic drunkenness and bad behaviour, the Australian's agency was terminated, and Ralph was offered the franchise. He jumped at the chance of a little excitement, and moved to Milan in 1921, aged thirty, to take up the running of Bevington Assicurazione, writing Italian business for some of the largest British companies – Eagle Star, Royal Insurance, Liverpool, London & Globe, and Commercial Union.

He made a great success of the job, happily integrating with Milanese society, and astutely taking on a local partner, Pepino Sozzani. Pepino was a clever man who understood the business well. He was also completely loyal and became a close friend of my father's over three decades. There's no record of why a handsome, successful man in his thirties should have remained unmarried in Milan over the next ten years, or what he did for female companionship, but we do know that by 1930, he had met and fallen in love with Elise, Mrs Reginald Taylor, who was already living in Milan with Mr Taylor and their three daughters.

According to family tradition, Reginald Taylor was a hard man, not much of a husband or father, making Elise receptive to the attentions of a suave English bachelor with twinkling blue eyes. However, in those times, separation and divorce weren't an easy option and it's possible Ralph's love for her may have been unrequited for some time.

As children, my brother and I, and our three elder stepsisters, were told that they'd first met near the third green on the Menaggio and Cadenabbia golf course (near Lake Como) as Elise was crossing from the old fourteenth green to the fifteenth tee. My mother, then only thirty, always cut a neat figure on a golf course and I can easily imagine how she might have first caught my father's eye.

Years later, on a crisp winter's day, my brother and I with all our issue were on a bracing walk across the snow-covered course. We stopped and amused ourselves by etching a large heart and Cupid's arrow in the snow with a red flower to mark the spot where all our lives had begun.

A genuine, lifelong love match had been born there. Elise was able to obtain a divorce from her husband, and returned with her three daughters to England, where they lived in a rented house, always referred to in family legend as the 'hole-in-the-wall'. My father soon followed her back and went with her to Southampton to be presented to her parents, Mr and Mrs Harold Dartnall.

The Dartnalls were used to this kind of thing; they'd had eight children, of whom Elise was the sixth, and the elder of two daughters. She'd been born in 1900, and when her younger sister, Doreen, arrived, soon found herself acting as reluctant nursery maid to the much-spoiled baby of the family, which led to a determination to leave home as soon as possible. Her parents made it clear that they weren't happy when, just eighteen, she met and married Reg Taylor, who had recently been invalided out of the Royal Army Flying Corps.

When she turned up now, with three daughters and no husband, if they didn't say it, they must have thought, 'We told you so.' But the appearance of handsome, prosperous Ralph Dexter as replacement would have cheered them a good deal.

Harold Dartnall, with a near Olympian background of sporting prowess as oarsman and pugilist, and a national record in the gymnastic oddity of rope climbing, happily spotted similar characteristics in Ralph. Behind the house he had his own gym and a boathouse, where he invited Ralph to join him to discuss his daughter's prospects. He raised no objections and in 1931, at a local registry office, Elise married 'Uncle Dekker', as the girls already called him; soon after the marriage, they were calling him Dad, and loved him greatly for the rest of their lives.

My father and mother must have been thrilled when their own first child, John, was born just before Christmas 1932. John wasn't always robust as an infant, picking up several childhood illnesses that were severe, even life-threatening, in those pre-antibiotic days. However, these early setbacks didn't prevent him developing into an athletic young man of six feet two, who comfortably earned his first-team colours in rugby and cricket at Radley.

When I entered the world, three years after John, I was luckier as a baby and evidently more bouncy. I gathered this from my father's account of a 1936 car journey from Sussex to Milan which he made with my mother, my brother, me and a nanny. 'Little Edward has been very good and certainly likes to get his nosebag on!' he observed.

I'm sorry to say I don't remember anything of the first few years of life I spent in Milan up until the start of the Second World War and before the turmoil this created for an English family living in Italy. A few weeks before Prime Minister Chamberlain had declared war with Germany in September 1939, my father, who by then considered my half-sisters completely his own, brought his wife and five children back to England. Italy hadn't at that stage confirmed its own role in the conflict and as my parents had left a number of things unfinished there, Dad returned briefly to sign various papers relating to the business. He and Mum subsequently decided to make one last flying visit to close up the flat in Milan and do what they could with the help of Pepino to secure a future for the insurance business. While they were still here, the cut-off point was approaching fast; they had to make a rapid exit via San Remo to catch a ship out of Nice.

When they reached the dock, there was no ship. My father, rising to the challenge with his usual optimism, left their luggage at the Hotel Negresco and they sped on west to Marseilles, where they'd been told there would be a ship sailing for England. They didn't have anywhere to stay while they waited to leave, but, with that strange capacity of Englishmen abroad, my father bumped into an old friend, Teddy DeHaan, who knew a woman who was the madame of one of the city's smarter brothels. When we were old enough to know what a brothel was, my father told us that the place had been getting a bit rowdy as they were shown up to a room by this hospitable woman, who paused on the way up to yell at her girls: 'We have nice guests in the house tonight, so keep the noise down.'

The next day they boarded a cargo ship about to sail out of the Mediterranean via Gibraltar, up and across the Bay of Biscay to war-locked England. It took more than a week to get there.

* *

Dad was forty-eight by then, well beyond combat age, and could have expected a peaceful war, but because he was keen to do his bit, and spoke respectable Italian, he was called up to postings in the north and west of England within the RAF Intelligence Unit, Bomber Command, trailing his family around behind him like camp followers. My mother, living without staff for the first time in her married life, with five children to nurture, was just about coping, but was horrified when her husband told her he was being sent to Cairo to interrogate Italian prisoners as they were extracted from the North African campaign. From what he told us, it was a comfortable posting; we still have photographs of his colleagues, tanned, fit men wearing razor-creased shorts and toting tennis rackets in the surprisingly chic Gezira Sporting Club, evidently his home from home. In the end he was away for three years, leaving my poor mother on her own to deal with her many shortcomings in domestic skills.

John and I were happily unaware of whatever struggles she had for the first year or so, as we shuttled around Britain behind my father from Glasgow, to Northern Ireland, to Pembrokeshire, finding ourselves in different schools every few months. In Glasgow, the other boys couldn't understand our Italian-accented English; they called us Eyeties – especially unflattering during the war – and found us distinctly foreign; we could barely understand them either. This was the first inkling I had of some kind of apartness between us and children born in Britain. In South Wales, where I was sent to a school in Tenby, I got off to a bad start. On my first day, I arrived on my own, and found that I couldn't push the front door open. I simply turned around and walked home. Inevitably, our education was sporadic and not sticking much, but we didn't care. Finally, once my father had gone abroad, we settled in the Home Counties, in the village of Emberton, close to what is now Milton Keynes.

The youngest of my three sisters, Ann, was finishing her schooling as head girl of her evacuated school in Aberdovey. The elder two, Pammy and Peggy, were already signed up as part of the war effort, working day and night at the code-breaking unit at Bletchley Park.

While with hindsight I realise that life for my mother must have been pretty good hell, we kids didn't know any better and life in a two-up two-down cottage in Emberton suited us well enough. Over the course of a year or so, only once were we invited by the squire, Captain Trevor, up to the manor house, from where the captain's son and heir would disappear each term to Eton College. We didn't care; we were far more interested in getting a ride on farmer Robinson's carthorse, bombarding the next-door neighbours' house with squishy old apples or daring each other to cross the road for a peek through the grimy windows of a tumbledown cottage belonging to an old crone, widely (and in our view, credibly) alleged to be a witch. From a distance of eighty odd years, my six- and seven-year-old memories are of long, carefree, innocent summer days.

Once I found John and the rector's daughter, Lilla, perched close side by side on a branch of an ancient apple tree. Puzzled, I asked John what they were doing; he explained that they were 'flirting'. No wiser, and wondering what on earth they found to talk about, I willingly withdrew as requested.

Generally, though, despite our two-and-a-half-year age gap, John and I were always close. We enjoyed the same things, and we were both – then and for the rest of our lives – inclined to compete with one another. I'm reminded that the only present I can recall being sent by our father during those war years was a punchball perched on a spring stand, with two pairs of boxing gloves – perhaps to put our scrapping on a more ordered basis; perhaps responding to my mother's laments that we wouldn't stop hitting each other.

After a year or so in the tiny, overflowing cottage, our next move was to a larger place, Orchard House near Penn in Buckinghamshire. This was followed on my father's return from Egypt around Christmas 1943, by Potash Farm, Puttenham, near Tring.

This lovely period of boyhood is still vivid in my memory, as John and I roamed the local countryside at will, eager, for some reason, to make contact with a gang of Italian prisoners of war working on the farm (like many thousands at the time, happy to be here rather than on some splintering battlefront). John wanted to see how they would react to his own rudimentary Italian. They were sympathetic and offered to share their ration of fresh bread and bully beef with us. As a special treat, once per school holidays, we were allowed to cycle into Tring to go to the flicks – Laurel & Hardy, Buster Keaton – that sort of thing. Even more exciting was joining the regular rat hunts that took place on the farm next door. As the corn crop was taken from the main barn, starting from the top of the stack, the rats who occupied it as if it were a block of high-rise flats were forced ever downwards until finally they broke cover to race for fresh shelter, only to meet a wall of ravening terriers backed up by a cohort of farmworkers wielding sticks and shovels – the most legitimate of blood sports.

We also had two ponies to look after. Sugar, a classic naughty Welsh pony, was used to pull a trap (as a solution to petrol rationing) as well as to provide somewhat unpredictable transport for two boys. The other, Lady Alice, was a mare of almost thoroughbred lineage – a present to my sister, Ann, from her doting father. Ann, then at her most horsy stage, was constantly grooming the mare to present her at local shows and gymkhanas. John and I also enjoyed the gymkhanas, although we were less diligent in preparation and not always welcome. We would turn up with Sugar ungroomed and shaggy, with sweaty trace marks on her withers from pulling the trap to the show, while we were in our ordinary trousers, stuffed into socks and wellies.

On a typical occasion, we were entered in a simple fetch and carry race. The other ponies and riders were immaculately turned out by doting, competitive mothers who had been clipping coats, polishing boots, plaiting manes and tying ties for hours before delivering the mounts in horseboxes. The regular commentator on the public address was familiar with the shortcomings of the Dexter boys; his disapproval was manifest as he rolled out disparaging remarks: 'Here we go again!' or, 'Good heavens – not another refusal!' It was as clear to us as it was to them that we were never going to be accomplished horsemen, which must have been a disappointment to Dad, who had always retained his love of horses since his time in the artillery.

It seems extraordinary now, seventy-five years on, that the English were so ready and able to carry on their country sports throughout the war. These traditional activities, devised over the centuries to speed the passing of long rural winters, were perhaps recognised as doing the same for the long, dark periods of war.

**

Towards the end of the war there were three more arrivals in the household – first of all, our new baby brother, David, along with a tiny nanny, Bournie, who came to look after him and remained with the family even when we returned to Italy. David was born with Down's syndrome, with the soft round face and characteristic eyes of that condition. In his case, he also suffered from a slight squint. My parents loved him the more for his handicap, as we all did, and he repaid us handsomely over the many years he lived, with the innocent warmth and affection that he brought to our relationship.

We were all joined, too, by an affable and energetic white terrier called Bonnie, who feared nothing, bar the squadrons of American B57 bombers that took off every day from a nearby airfield, so heavily laden on the way to their targets in the German industrial cities that they barely cleared the tall Victorian chimneys of the farmhouse.

**

Early in 1946, my father returned to Milan to reopen the flat in Piazza Repubblica, and to take charge of Bevington Assicurazione again. He was gratefully aware that his decision in the 1930s to take on Pepino Sozzani as a partner had been wisely made when he saw that Pepino had done everything possible to preserve our family's belongings, as well as the viability of the business. Dad soon settled back into his work and the important function of providing insurance cover in the London market to Italian industry during the great post-war boom in construction. That summer, we all went out there for the first time since 1939, when I was now old enough to appreciate the difference of life in Italy.

Milan in the muggy summer months was no place for a family and my father had already decided to rent a country property on a permanent basis. It was under snow for five months every year but it was within driving distance of the fierce summer heat and polluted air of the city. The Villa Lugarna, which became an important part of all our lives, was surrounded by elegant, colourful formal gardens, shrubberies and ponds with an unforgettable view to the north up the full length of Lake Como.

The house belonged to the descendant of an Englishman, a Mr Alfred Wyatt, who, with a colleague, Henry Mylius, had created an eighteen-hole golf course four hundred yards up the slope on the western side of the lake. The course was opened at the turn of the century, soon followed by the creation of a railway line which zigzagged up from the lake into the higher valley so that holidaymakers – mostly English – staying in the grand lakeside hotels could come up and enjoy a knock round the spectacular new course, toting narrow canvas bags with just a handful of hickory-shafted clubs.

Up until the war, the Menaggio and Cadenabbia Golf Club had prospered and become a home from home to my parents and many others of the British/American community in Milan. However, the Italians had barely embraced the game by 1939, and with no players, the campus quickly reverted to grassland for the grazing of cattle and the production of winter hay over the six years of the European war. It was said that there were troops, possibly German, billeted at the club for part of the war and a few bullet holes in the old office clock face seemed to confirm that.

That it is now a jewel of the golfing world, sited precariously on the lower slopes of Monte Croce, overlooking one of the most beautiful lakes in Europe, ready to delight anyone with the good fortune to stumble on it by chance or the practical sense to seek it out, is largely due to the post-war care bestowed on it by three men – my father, Sir James Henderson and Christian Schmidt – who took it on in its involuntarily rewilded state after the war. Mainly for their own amusement, these three benefactors commissioned the resident farmer, Giacomo, to get out his scythe and swing it across the neglected acres, allowing the first, second, seventeenth and eighteenth holes to be reopened within a year. The second summer saw another three holes added: the third, the fifteenth and the sixteenth. It took a few more years to revive all eighteen of the original holes, while the expense of maintaining a full-scale, private course must have been substantial during that time. It was a major feat, and one of which the three men could be justly proud.

** **

While Dad was re-establishing the family homes, reclaiming the golf course and rebuilding his business, John and I spent two thirds of our time at school in England. In 1947, when I was eleven, I was sent to board at a long since defunct prep school called Norfolk House in the small Buckinghamshire village of Penn. It was here, on the tiny pitch, that I had the first inkling of my lifelong love of cricket. I had a vague notion of the game beforehand, not entirely positive, from an incident when my brother John and I were playing with a bat and ball in the garden at Orchard House. I was about eight and John eleven when he swung the bat and clouted me fairly forcefully on the forehead. There was blood and there were tears, and a very sore head, but no long-lasting damage, as far as I know (dementia hasn't set in yet) – though I have the scar to this day.

** **

The headmaster of Norfolk House, Cyril Glover, was a great cricket enthusiast who considered it his duty to instil his own love of the game in the boys under his charge. It was he who first showed me how to hold a bat and use my feet, keeping them together while waiting for the ball, then always going forward or back according to length, but never retreating. He would stand behind a boy batting with an iron-spiked stump against his bottom.

'Bowl up, bowl up,' he would call up the wicket.

For the batter, stepping away to leg was not an option. It was a lesson I didn't forget. And it was there, aged nine, that I hit my first six. It seemed to me then that it kept on going forever. Thirty years later when I went back to the school (by then morphed into some kind of institution) I was amazed and somewhat deflated to find that the cricket ground was no bigger than two tennis courts.

Among my musty archive I still have a school report from Norfolk House, thoughtfully preserved by my mother: 'He shows promise at cricket but he must remember he still has much – in fact almost everything – to learn, and is not yet in a position to control and give instructions to his fellows, who quite rightly resent it.'

I don't doubt that this was a fair summary at the time, nor that there are those who might think that judgement still holds good.

* *

Norfolk House suffered a change in fortune in my second year there when Mr Glover contracted a severe bout of shingles and sold the school. The man who bought it assumed a joint headmastership with another of the masters, Mr Barnes, who was responsible for all sports other than cricket. The boys were much relieved to be free of the despotic Glover regime, which had involved regular caning for the slightest misdemeanour. However, this respite was cut short one night when we boys were woken by a noisy bell-ringing ambulance and the clattering feet of stretcher-bearers echoing through the building. We learned in the morning that the new principal had tried to take his own life. He might even have succeeded; we were never told.

However, we soon learned that there was absolutely no money left in the school's bank account; it emerged that the hapless headmaster suffered from a serious gambling habit and had helped himself to all the school fees to fund it. Most of the pupils were day boys and they simply didn't reappear again, leaving the handful of boarders, mostly, like me, with parents abroad, to exist on a diet of powdered egg for almost a week before arrangements could be made to get us home. This provided a short, carefree interlude, during which the French master stayed on, without pay, to look after the six of us still there, exploring the local woods, building shelters, making campfires and having fun.

Mr Barnes, who presumably had received no money for his term's work, came to find me to tell me that he had to get to Devon to take up a new post, and if he were able to buy a train ticket, it would save him a long bicycle ride. Looking understandably sheepish, he asked if he could borrow the remains of my pocket money (about twelve shillings) to cover his travelling costs. Accepting his promise of swift reimbursement, and because I liked him, I agreed. He took the train and sent me back a pound.

I subsequently discovered that my father had been deeply offended by one aspect of this period of limbo at Norfolk House. One of the directors of Bevington's in London, General Liardet, lived right next door to the school; he knew that I was a pupil there, and he must have known about the place's debacle. Dad never forgave him for not rallying round and taking me in.

With my parents a few thousand miles away in Milan, I was on the move yet again, this time to stay with Uncle John and Auntie Doreen Kington. Doreen was my mother's baby sister, whom she'd been looking after when she first met and married Reg Taylor. John Kington was the kindest of men and a hard worker, often bringing his work home and slogging away at his desk, not to be interrupted. Doreen was always affectionate, though generally thought by the family to be a bit dotty, as a result of her claims to hear voices. They lived in Romsey, in a small, comfortable house where, with their own children having left home, they made me very welcome. I travelled every day to a modest private crammer just outside the town to prepare for my Common Entrance exam. Although I missed my parents, I had by that stage in my life moved homes so often that I took this new situation in my stride. In any case, it wasn't to last long.

My brother John was already in his third year at Radley, a less well-known public school in those days, near Oxford, to which my father had decided to send us both. He chose Radley over his own school, Mill Hill, because it was out in the country, more secure and surrounded by acres of playing fields, in fact one of the greatest expanses of level mown grass in the country. It was used at least once, like the vast meadows of Runnymede, for the national archery championships. John was quite bright and as far as I know had been admitted to the school on his academic merits. Somehow my father persuaded the school to take me without passing a Common Entrance exam, and a term earlier than normal, at the beginning of summer 1948, and a few weeks before my thirteenth birthday.

Chapter Two

SCHOOLBOY

I arrived at Radley with the advantage of being the younger brother of an established figure halfway up the school who was already recognised for his sporting talents. From the start of my first term, I threw myself into the higher level of cricket that was being played there. I wasn't as academically bright as John, but I was nevertheless conscientious about my studies. However, there was no question that they always took second place to my love of sport. For me Radley provided a cornucopia of sporting delights: besides cricket, I could play rugby, hockey, rackets, squash and golf, as well as trying athletics (including discus and shot-put). I even had a few goes at fishing!

I was lucky, too, that there were masters with a true dedication to passing on their own knowledge. I don't suppose this was for entirely selfless reasons; a games master could gain kudos by producing good performers, as well as the vicarious enjoyment of seeing them succeed, but on the whole I always felt their knowledge was given in a spirit of generosity.

**

John and I travelled back and forth to Italy for at least two of our school holidays in each year, taking the Simplon Express train across Europe which provided an early taste of an experience I loved and repeated many times over the next fifty years. There's no doubt, although I didn't realise it at the time, that this binational existence did lend John and I an air of sophistication that was evidently noticed and remarked on at school. We were always well kitted out in smart Italian clothes that must have contrasted noticeably with the dowdy tweed and flannels that were standard menswear in fifties England where food and clothes were still subject to rationing. My mother and father were always stylishly turned out, and they made sure we were too. We even wore monogrammed silk shirts and I arrived at school with a small travelling iron which our maid in Milan had taught me to use. Luckily, I was big for my age and I had a big brother looking out for me, or I might have suffered more than a little ridicule and bullying.

John and I went home to Italy for the Christmas and summer holidays – summer on Lake Como; winter in Milan. In the Easter holidays, Mum and Dad usually came to England and took us to top hotels. Milan in winter was tough and, being so close to the Alps, often freezing, with snow and filthy slush underfoot. There was no TV to watch, nor newspapers to keep us up to date with sports, though sometimes, if we were lucky, we could pick up the BBC on the radiogram. To compound our boredom, we didn't have any friends of our own age. I recall those winters as thoroughly tedious. A highlight on a weekday could be going with my dad and Pepino for their midday aperitif at a local bar. Afterwards Dad would take a siesta while I waited impatiently for him to take me to the trotting races held at the San Siro, the AC Milan stadium. I loved watching the trotters which I thought provided a better spectator sport than ridden races. It gave me a love of that un-English version of racing that I still retain. In time, as it happened, I also developed a taste – some might say too strong a taste – for British horse racing. Apart from the trotters, there were not very exciting walks in the nearby Giardini Pubblici, and more memorably, musical sessions, standing with my siblings, ranged behind my father as he sat at the piano and sight-read the latest songs from the London shows, while we sang along enthusiastically.

It was the summers on Lake Como that I remember best. The setting of the lake is spectacular, lined for its full length by majestic two thousand-metre mountains whose slopes run right down to the shore, sometimes broken by a ledge where a village or a single homestead had been planted, sometimes plunging sheer into the dark waters. John always loved water sports more than I did; he was noticeably better at swimming, waterskiing and sailing. He also loved long, rambling climbs up the mountainsides, and skinny-dipping in icy pools when he came across them. He was, far more than I, a real country boy, though I was happy enough to tag along, as much for his company as for the activity. My heart wasn't really in it the way his was – which was reflected in his being buried on the hillside above Cadenabbia, with the epitaph on his gravestone: *I will lift up mine eyes unto the hills, from whence cometh my help.*

It was inevitable that I should grow to love this uplifting and invigorating place and I still love returning there. However, my true appreciation of it lies in its endowing in me an everlasting love of golf. Although, in time, my father would undoubtedly have introduced us to the game, it was by lucky chance that John and I discovered for ourselves what joys it can provide.

During our first summer there in 1946, he and I were hanging around the

Villa Lugarna, probably looking bored, when Roger Francis, one of Dad's oldest friends, produced a couple of old hickory-shafted golf clubs and a few ancient practice balls from somewhere in the house. He showed us the rudiments of a golf swing, then pointed us up the hill.

'There's an old golf course up the road there; it's been abandoned since before the war, but if you can find a stretch with some short grass on it, you might be able to get in a bit of practice.'

Our first session on what we learned was the old Menaggio & Cadenabbia golf course didn't last long. We either lost the balls, or they were cut to shreds by the sharp edges of the old iron club heads. The balls were made of wound elastic over a small lead core, with a vulnerable thin skin on the outside, not much like the golf balls of today.

Most of the shots that we did manage were either skied or topped along the ground. However, we did occasionally connect, and discovered that there are few sweeter sporting sensations than striking a ball squarely on the club face and watching it rocket away in a beautiful parabola in the direction you intended. Both John and I were truly hooked from that day forward. We carried on wandering through the wilderness of neglected fairways and bunkers barely discernible under the crop of fine hay that covered the ground. We had no idea of what a proper golf course should look like, not imagining that this overgrown, neglected tract would be resurrected, little by little, each summer. It was somewhat like an archaeological dig, as piece by piece, hole by hole, my father and his co-restorers persevered over five years, until every hole was reopened and playable.

John and I were exceptionally lucky in the early stages of our game. From my first trip back to Lake Como in 1946, aged eleven, when we were staying in the Villa Lugarna, I was able to play golf all day if I wanted – which I did. More often than not, I played with an old golf pro, Signor Prete, who lived nearby. He was short of work at that point as a result of the lack of interest in golf in Italy since the British had left in 1939, and he used to come up and hang around the clubhouse, just for somewhere to go. I presume my father slipped a bit of money his way and there was no doubt that he got John and me off to a tremendous start in a game we continued to love for the rest of our lives. Even now I still sometimes think of Signor Prete as I'm driving off the first tee at my local club in South Staffordshire.

* *

Radley in the 1950s, like most other English boarding public schools, was tough enough and retained an almost Victorian ethos. We weren't allowed to eat outdoors or go into Oxford, just three miles away. Discipline was strict, not like these days when a master may think twice about questioning a boy's ability for fear of a backlash from parents paying vast fees. Boys were regularly beaten, not by masters but by their senior peers, sometimes for trivial misdemeanours like spitting or walking on the grass. Usually I managed to avoid this kind of thing. I think I was already learning that getting into trouble was usually more trouble than it was worth. During the first couple of years at Radley, prep was done in a communal study – the Social Hall – and each boy had a little cubicle with a desk and cupboard. You would work your way up the hall and when you reached the end, you went into a study.

At the end of a new boy's first term, it was a rite of passage that they were ceremoniously beaten up by the older boys and pushed head first into a dustbin, or some such humiliation. I didn't think much of this and with what might have been foolhardy braggadocio proposed that we younger ones should make a stand. I volunteered to take on the leader if the others would do their best with the rest of them. I was already big for my age, and years of scrapping with my older brother had made me fairly adept. I managed to deal with him and when the room went quiet, we knew that that particular rite of passage was concluded. As it happened, I was then invited to join a small study. Both John and I were both in 'F' Social, known as Southams. 'Tiny' Southam, our Social Tutor, was a huge former oarsman whose relaxed attitude easily earned the respect of the boys.

Disgraceful as it now sounds, ragging and bullying were everyday activities among the boys, behaving, I suppose, like young dogs who constantly scrap with their siblings in what is perceived as preparation for life. Thankfully, I was never a victim of this, although, from somewhere, I seemed to have acquired a sense of duty and decorum, which, if too obvious, can have a detrimental effect on a boy's popularity.

As it happened, I wasn't looking for popularity for its own sake and, in any case, I can see, looking back, that my enthusiasm for all ball games, and a lucky talent in playing them was an effective counterbalance to what people perceived as my 'serious' side.

It may be a failing, but I don't think I ever considered it that important to be liked by everyone; I can also say that in many decisions I've taken in later life I have quite deliberately ignored this as a factor. At school I certainly didn't go out of my way to court that kind of acceptance, beside which, my disposition, while not introverted, was to maintain a good level of privacy; this was, I think, often mistaken for shyness. Nevertheless, I made friends at Radley who were important to me, became part of my total persona and subsequently cropped up regularly over the next sixty or seventy years: Michael Martin, who taught me how to cast a fly, and who, forty years later, insisted on taking me out to dinner shortly after I stepped down as chairman of England; Tim Holcroft, whose family had me to stay at their place, Northbrook Park, near Farnham, when I wasn't spending my holidays in Italy. I remember the joy of pottering around their estate with Tim, sniffing in the English country at close quarters and sometimes doing a little rough shooting with 410 shotguns; Kit Hood, who shared the study and was a likeable, straightforward boy who never dropped his Yorkshire accent the whole time he was at Radley. I never met his father – a bluff north country tycoon, I gathered – anyway rich enough to send his son a new MG sports car for his eighteenth birthday (looked down on by another boy whose father had sent him a thoroughbred horse); Chris Walton, who married into the McLachlan family and went to live in Australia; Clive Carr – brilliant all-rounder at rugby, cricket, athletics and boxing. Under the keen eye of one of the sports masters, 'Scottie' Birks, we learned to shot-put together, and Clive went on to win the schools' meeting at White City with a record throw; and John Scott, who was capped for England at rugby.

**

For the first five years of my life, I'd been surrounded by people, speaking Italian, and had inevitably learned a little, which I'd quickly revived once the family had moved back to Italy. This propensity for foreign languages helped in my studying French, which I loved speaking. At the same time, I enjoyed music and drama – even playing the lead in Molière's *Le Bourgeois Gentilhomme* in French! It was produced al fresco in front of the Mansion (which was what the original building in the school was called). The show was going well enough, with most people remembering their lines, until a cue was repeated, and a whole scene played again. The audience were too polite to react – or, more likely, their French wasn't good enough for them to have noticed.

For my first two summers, I played cricket for the Midgets (U-14s), and the Junior Colts, keeping wicket and getting plenty of runs. I didn't get much coaching in those first two years, though I must have been seen doing something right because at the start of my third summer term, in 1950, just before I turned fifteen, I was selected to play for the Radley First XI, joining my brother, two and a half years older. This was when I first came into contact with Bert Robinson, Radley's professional coach, and games master, Ivor Gilliat, who had a long-lasting effect on my playing of the game. There was already a good wicketkeeper in the First XI, so I was encouraged to develop my reasonably accurate delivery of medium-paced off-cutters, helped by Bert who had himself been a reliable medium-pace bowler for Northamptonshire. He also gave up a lot of his own time to coach us, even on Sundays, when some of us would be in the nets all day.

Ivor Gilliat had come to teach at Radley although he had private income and didn't need the salary. He was a confirmed bachelor and an avid bon viveur. He had become a dominant member of the staff – a committed, old-fashioned sort of a schoolmaster – erudite, highly educated and with a strong sense of decorum. He had played cricket for Oxford University, where he'd performed as an outstanding wicketkeeper, despite his eighteen-stone bulk. He had also, astonishingly for a man of his size, played rackets at Oxford.

Having taken on responsibility for First XI cricket his forte was to encourage his young batsmen always to play an attacking game and to gain mental superiority over their opponents. 'You've got to get on top of them,' he would say. Another of his traits was an insistence that nothing 'that might sully the etiquette or beauty of the game would be tolerated'. He instructed us always to be waiting to greet visiting teams when they arrived and to carry their bags to the pavilion, suppressing any shyness or youthful lack of savoir faire.

Good manners were to him almost as important as the execution of a stroke. He even took us to the Café de Paris in London and, when we were playing away against Eastbourne College, to the Grand Hotel there, to coach us on table manners, and how to deal with waiters (not very compassionately, it seemed). In fact, the records show that Gilliat and Robinson produced unbeaten sides at Radley for three consecutive seasons, from 1950 to 1953. Many years after that, in 2007, I was happy to be asked back to Radley to propose Bert Robinson's health at his ninetieth birthday celebrations. It was only then that he revealed to me something that I would love to have known before – that down in the beagle kennels he had always kept a couple of greyhounds which he used to take to flapping races.

In my first season, I played fifteen First XI matches against other schools, Oxford colleges and various touring teams in which I took 26 wickets and had a batting average of 31.9 runs. Radley was in any case a good side, which included Christopher Walton, who later played for Middlesex, and Clive

Carr, who played with me at Cambridge. We were very lucky – privileged, you could say – to have played against legends like the great Trinidadian, Sir Learie Constantine, who joked, 'Hey boys, I wonder if I could get one into that score box?', and hit the next ball straight into the open front where the scorers sat. Hopper Reed, who hurtled the ball at us while we quivered in our boots, and Gubby Allen, fifty by then but still keen on getting runs, both turned up with touring teams.

**

I was still fourteen in May 1950 when I started playing for the First XI, and was awarded my colours shortly after my fifteenth birthday. While I was rummaging around for material for this book, I was amazed to find a diary I'd kept for that year – the only year for which I've kept a daily record of events for any continuous period of time. Thus I can see from a distance of seventy years just how seriously I took my game, and how self-critical I could be; I wasn't complacent then, and, truthfully, I never was afterwards, even in the most purple patch of my career, and especially not, years later when I stuck my head far above the parapet as chairman of the England Committee.

1950 diary entries for the first year (of four) in First XI:

10 May	*Bowled 15 overs. Very Tired. Jolly good in-swingers.*
11 May	*Got out for 5 runs. Must do better for First XI.*
27 May	*v MCC. Took 5 for 58.*
11 June	*Awarded First XI Colours.*
13 June	*v Stowe. Out to very bad shot.*
19 June	*Awful Hay Fever. Frightful.*
22 June	*Net with John (Dexter) and Bert (Robinson – coach).*
	Batted quite well. Bowling was a bit better.
24 June	*v Radley Rangers (Old Boys). Took 5 for 49!*
28 June	*Umpired Social (House) match. Gave a bad decision.*
20 July	*v Shipton (Village XI). Had wonderful innings.*
	66 not out with three sixes.
Term Results:	*15 innings. 5 not outs, 319 runs, av: 32*
	26 wickets, 565 runs, av: 22

There is a less creditable entry…

9 June   *Cocks (Head of Social) gave me one hell of a talking to about betting and the company I keep.*

I must have been a little shocked by this as I added…

I cried like a baby.

I regret to say that I ignored the reprimand over betting for many years after that.

**

My father in his understated way expressed his pride in what I was doing on the cricket field and made the effort when he was over from Italy to come and see me play. On the first few occasions, I didn't do well, and got out cheaply. I was remorseful that he'd taken the trouble and I'd failed to perform. Divining that this might have been due to his own presence, he came, without telling me, to watch me play an away match against Bradfield. He found a vantage point out of sight in the school chapel cemetery. Here he was accosted by the Bradfield headmaster, who suspiciously demanded to know why he was lurking in this clandestine way. After a somewhat embarrassed explanation, he was allowed to carry on watching from there. Conceivably the tactic had worked; there's no doubt that it doesn't take much to put a batsman on edge or out of kilter. In any event, without being aware of his presence I scored a hundred, and he gave me a new watch to commemorate the event.

**

My second season in the Radley XI in 1951 was overshadowed by my brother John's performance. While I scored an average of just 29 an innings, John, who was the team's strike bowler in his last season, took 54 wickets at 13 runs apiece. It must have been something of a relief to him not to have his younger brother snapping at his heels in competition.

Off the field, despite the wigging I'd had from my Head of Social over gambling, it was a habit which took a hold on me from quite early in my time at Radley, and which I never really shook off for many decades. My gambling activity at school was for the most part restricted to horse racing, either in placing bets myself or, perhaps more cannily, laying other people's bets. Of course, this didn't always work out, especially if I'd taken several bets for a winning favourite, but in the back of my 1950 diary there are lists of names of boys with the sums of money they owed, though never more than a few shillings.

In the winter terms, I was enjoying rugby, developing my place-kicking and playing at fly half, a position I enjoyed for the influence it allowed me to exert over the direction and style of play. I was lucky to have Leo Cooper as my scrum half; he was bigger than most who play in that position and his strong passes out gave me a few extra yards to play with. Even at that stage I was discovering my interest in the tactics of a game, as much as the playing of it. I was picked for the First XV in my third season. Once again, my brother John was already in the team, and we enjoyed playing together.

In the spring of 1952, not long after King George VI had died and Queen Elizabeth had acceded (while she and the Duke of Edinburgh were touring in Kenya) John and I were invited to go out to Italy and play against a team in Milan. Rugby in Italy was still a niche activity, although the game had been played in and around the Veneto since the 1920s.

I'd also had a growing interest in the game of rackets – which you could call a posh version of squash, but much much faster. I was encouraged in this by Ivor Gilliat, who had excelled at the game himself. He understood the benefit to a batsman in experiencing the extra pace and learning how to deal with it.

But my main sporting focus was now firmly on cricket. In the summer of 52 I was beginning to feel that I knew what I was doing, learning how to pace myself, and how to read the opposition's bowling more acutely. I scored 581 runs for Radley that season and my first century. I also played for the All England Public Schools team in a two-day game against the Combined Services XI at Lord's. In an unspectacular debut, I scored 8 and 43, but I did meet two players in the forces team whom I came to know a lot better: Michael Stewart, who some forty years later was England team manager when I took over as chairman, and Fred Titmus, who became an England teammate.

It was during this season that I sustained an injury to a knee cartilage that turned out to be a bit of a swine and, in spite of several operations and a lot of manipulation, continued to trouble me for the next seventy years. Even now I can feel it every time I drive off a tee.

* *

That same summer, I was saddled for the first time with the handle, 'Lord Ted', which has stuck to me like an indestructible Post-it note ever since. It was first bestowed on me, in the spirit of his customary irony, by Ivor Gilliat. One of my jobs as secretary of the school side was to ring through our cricket results to the sports pages of the newspapers. I was having dinner with friends on a Saturday evening when I suddenly remembered that I hadn't performed this chore. I blithely rang Ivor Gilliat, who was having a bath at the time, to ask if he could do it for me. He seemed to take it well enough, but suggested that my attitude was somewhat high-handed. He referred to me as 'Lord Edward' from then on. And it stuck.

In the course of my life I've come to see that once an individual is perceived by his friends and acquaintances in a certain way, it's damned hard to shake it off. Indeed, in a curious process, a nickname, or what it suggests, can go some way to forming the individual. Certainly this 'lordly' tag has stuck with me; it's been applied with envy, malice and sarcasm, though usually, thank God, with good humour.

* *

Having wielded a golf club with enthusiasm and a lot of help from Signor Prete since the age of eleven, it was inevitable that I should want to carry on with the game amidst the wonderful surroundings of Radley's playing fields. The first Radley golf course was built many years later when I contributed and was present at the formal opening. However, John and I had plenty of encouragement, largely from one of the masters, Neil Fisher, who still played for the Oxford and Cambridge Golfing Society, and we were allowed to play on Sundays at Frilford Heath. I generally restricted my golf to the non-cricket terms, so this meant an eight-mile cycle ride, with a bag of clubs clumping on one's back, through whatever weather was being chucked at us. A few of us hardcore golfers stuck it out, though from time to time, we caved in and hired a taxi, until my brother got his first motorcycle, an Ariel 350cc Red Hunter, a birthday present from our dad. I now had to suffer the terrors of riding pillion behind him if I wanted to play. More often than not, John and I played our golf together, although to his disgust, I nearly always beat him.

John's bike was eventually replaced by a vintage French Salmson sports car which provided one of the most explosive events in my time at Radley. On the last day of term there was a tradition that we were allowed to drive away in our own transport, so, needing no prompting from me, John drove the Salmson up to the clock tower with a flourish. Most of the boys and masters gathered around, keen to get a good look at it.

John was happy to respond to his captive audience. 'Just listen to this!' he bellowed over the rumble of the idling motor as he rammed his foot on the throttle to rev the engine.

We listened alright, until we all collapsed with laughter when the engine exploded with a deafening bang. The connecting rods piled through the sides of the sump, the oil trays were smashed, and when we tentatively opened the bonnet to have a look, only two of the four pistons were still there; the other two had been blown out of the exhaust by the force of the blast.

** **

There was, I concede, a certain amount of predictability about my appointment as senior prefect at Radley in my final year. Although, if I'd had any choice in the matter, I would probably have turned it down; the sense of duty that my father, and to some extent my older brother, had instilled in me convinced me that I must play the role willingly. I had to come back to school the day before the rest of the school returned. The purpose of this was to give the warden, John Wilkes, a chance to see something of me and presumably to get to know his new senior prefect a little better.

When I presented myself in his study, he didn't look up for several seconds, apparently engrossed in some papers on his desk. When, finally, he did raise his head, he made absolutely no eye contact with me. Looking absently at a point some way to my right, he spoke quietly. 'Ah, Edward. Can you tell what exactly is your relationship with the Almighty at the moment?'

I gulped. I didn't have a ready answer to this. I cleared my throat, and told him that I went to school chapel most Sundays.

He gave no indication whether or not this satisfied him. He nodded and resumed his perusal of the papers on his desk. The interview, it seemed, was over.

** **

There weren't many useful perks to the job of senior prefect, but I did think I'd identified one when we were holding a school dance versus a local girls' school. Astonishingly enough, this was the first time I'd really experienced that frisson of excitement that the unaccustomed proximity and possible complicity of girls could create. Heady with expectancy I thought I might use my position to take the head girl outside on to the terrace for a kiss and a little exploration;

I was firmly put in my place and learned an early, useful lesson in the use of discretion in liaising with women.

**

Outside of school, the major event of 1953 was the coronation of Queen Elizabeth II. I had the privilege of seeing it all, at least a section of the circuitous procession returning from Westminster Abbey to Buckingham Place, from seats my father had managed to book overlooking Hyde Park Corner. Sitting with my parents, the big excitement for the Dexter family was that my brother John, now doing his stint as a National Serviceman, was not only in the procession, but carrying the colours of his regiment, the Royal Inniskilling Fusiliers. Those old enough will recall that it was a squally, blustery day, and John's standard was blowing around like a kite in a gale. To our horror, we watched as it knocked his beret clean off, leaving him bareheaded, while a soldier behind him managed to capture the hat, and return it to him later. Despite this, it was a proud moment for me and my parents, and I still feel honoured that I was there, never remotely imagining that sixty-eight years on, Her Majesty would still be in situ.

**

In my last term, with perhaps more predictability than making head prefect, I was made captain of the XI. I took the captaincy seriously and enjoyed the responsibility of it. I learned to retain my calm in the face of most provocation, having observed how counterproductive losing one's rag could be in keeping discipline within a team. I did once or twice succumb to chagrin, but, I believe, only when mistakes that had been made were my own and could have been avoided.

My last school match, played at Lord's for the Public Schools against the Combined Services was something of an anticlimax, when I scored 2 and 0, which may perhaps have been responsible for a waning of my interest in cricket over the next couple of years while I was doing my enforced stint of National Service.

Chapter Three

SOLDIER

Within a few weeks of leaving Radley, like most other able-bodied eighteen-year-old males in the country I joined the British Armed Forces to become a soldier for two years. It was my view that National Service was what I assumed to be a necessary nuisance. It was probably easier to accept in the early fifties when notions of serving king and country were fresher and stronger than they are now. It was plainly a nuisance because it lengthened by two years the time spent between education and getting on with real life. At the same time, although I had no plans to make a career in the army, frankly, at that stage, I didn't have much idea of what I wanted to do. After my two years in the army, I hoped to go up to Cambridge, like my brother, and my father before him. Beyond that, I had only a sketchy plan that I might follow my dad into the insurance business, on the grounds that it had clearly provided him with a comfortable life and enough leisure time to play as much golf as he wanted.

My introduction to the army was as tough as it is designed to be. Even five years in a 1950s English public school hadn't fully prepared me for it, although disciplined schooldays helped me cope better than most of a mixed bag of recruits at the 67th Training Regiment, Royal Armoured Corp at Carlisle. We had our hair cut off the day we arrived, slept on cast-iron beds in dormitories, were yelled at from morning to night, marched all over the place at the double in hideously uncomfortable boots with packs on our backs, shunted back and forth, fed on revolting stodge and generally abused. Our main protagonist, Corporal of Horse Bashforth was a seriously tough character who stood no nonsense and undoubtedly licked us into potentially serviceable soldiers. One of the functions of this course was to crush the individual men to the point where any kind of leadership qualities might become evident. Even those with the right social credentials were by no means automatically awarded commissions. Looking back on the process from a distance of sixty-five years, it seems pretty unfair that no man had a chance of a commission if he hadn't been at a public school or, at least, a top grammar school. But that's how it was then.

These were ten weeks of total incarceration from which there was virtually no escape. The only route to the outside world was via a single, two-hour pass which could be earned through the outstanding performance of the unbelievably fatuous chores we were set. Luckily, I'd found a friend, Todhunter, who had a similar outlook and decided with him that we would make sure we excelled in the tidiness of our personal space in quarters – something which the army is obsessive about. We did the best, as we had somewhat arrogantly assumed we would, and were granted our two hours of freedom. It wasn't much but it felt like the current equivalent of a trip to Barbados. We were nodded through the gates in our pristine uniforms, with trouser creases like sabre edges and boots as spit and polished as black snooker balls. We marched off down the road, heading out through the glum Carlisle suburbs, with no particular destination in mind and as chirpy as sparrows in a blackberry bush.

The first passing car pulled in, and a smiling face beamed from a window. 'Hello, boys. Broken out of prison, have we? How about a nice cup of tea in front of the fire?' It felt like an invitation to dine at the Ritz, and was not to be refused.

They were a chatty old couple, who seemed to understand completely what a horrible time we were having at the camp. Over tea and toast, the time flew by until they drove us back and dropped us off at the barracks. It was a simple, timely act of kindness which meant a great deal to us then, and it has always lingered in my memory. I do hope that somewhere along the way, I've done the same for someone else.

Having survived ten weeks of basic training, I found myself on the War Office Selection Board List, the initial filtering process for prospective officers. The first stage was a short practical assessment of leadership skills at a camp in Oswestry. I was put in charge of four chaps and given the task of crossing a river with a couple of barrels and some planks. I made a rotten job of it, and assumed I'd failed. It occurred to me afterwards, though, that the materials provided were deliberately inadequate, the task was unachievable anyway and they just wanted to see how far I would get.

Evidently I'd done enough as I was selected and dispatched to the comparative luxury of the Officer Cadet Training Unit at Mons in Aldershot. The Unit specialised in training officer cadets in the Royal Artillery and the Royal Armoured Corps, of which the 11th Hussars, my regimental destination, was part – originally a cavalry regiment, who had swapped their horses for armoured cars in the 1920s. The 11th Hussars, known as the 'Cherry Pickers', or 'Cherry Bums', depending on how you saw these things, had played a major role in that most inglorious of British military adventures, the Charge of the

Light Brigade under the despotic command of Lord Cardigan. This had not discouraged me from being accepted by this smart, if not downright toffee-nosed, regiment through my Radley friend, Tim Holcroft. His parents had a connection with the regiment and, although I had no background in huntin', shootin' and fishin' and hadn't put my leg over a horse since the war years in Penn, they offered to put a word in for me with the Colonel of the Regiment, Major-General Boyce, whom they knew. The General consented to come down to Farnham and have a look at me; he came, grunted a couple of times, and agreed to accept me as an officer in the regiment if I passed through OCTU satisfactorily.

After my stint at Carlisle, my months at Mons provided a much more light-hearted posting, especially with London in easy reach. By this time, I'd managed to find a girlfriend – the twin of my new friend, David Scholey's current squeeze. With David, I soon got used to a punishing regime, finishing a day's hard training at six, in London by seven, back at all hours for a start at sparrow fart next morning. For me and a lot of others, memories of Mons will always be associated with lack of sleep. I was useless in my gunnery course, which evoked a harsh rebuke from my father, who pointed out that doing the rest of my National Service in the ranks would be even less fun. I took this on board and came out top in the wireless course two days later. Two days after this, Scholey and Dexter were going up in the ranks: I was scheduled to be Senior Under Officer for the passing out parade, and David, Junior Under Officer.

Inevitably, however, there were further lapses. A trip to London, and zero hours sleep before getting back to quarters, led to my dozing off when I was supposed to be in command of a convoy of armoured cars on Salisbury Plain and failed to respond to wireless signals. I was quite rightly blamed for the resulting fiasco caused by no one telling the drivers where to go. Somehow, though, I survived without being flung off the course, and received my commission. But the Dexter/Scholey passing out parade roles were reversed. That presaged our roles in later life. Both successful in our respective careers (he was a banker), he was knighted, while I scraped by with a CBE.

After my passing out parade in the spring of 1954, with my father looking on in relieved disbelief, I was posted to the 11th Hussars who were currently stationed in Malaya. Before embarking on a troop ship for the journey, I took my girlfriend out for a last fling, when I wrote a big cheque to a London restaurant, which I carelessly forgot to sign, and which afterwards followed me doggedly all the way to Malaya.

Getting to Singapore was a serious, old-fashioned troop movement, stopping at Valletta, Nicosia, Bahrain, Karachi, Calcutta and Bangkok. I celebrated my nineteenth birthday en route with a bottle of beer as the sun rose over Bangkok. Two days later, we heard that Sir Anthony Eden, who'd recently replaced Winston Churchill as leader of the Conservatives, had increased his party's majority at the general election. This heralded his fateful term as PM and led to Britain's debacle over Suez and the ultimate crumbling of the old Empire. When I first set foot on it, Singapore was still a British colony, under a shaky local government, which had recently been subjected to some serious rioting. This sadly deprived me of the chance to wander up the hill to Raffles Hotel and sample one of their famous gin slings, or to take in any of the other delights the city had to offer, although, at least for the time being.

The last leg of our journey from Singapore to Seremban, 180 miles to the north, was by slow train through steaming jungle. There was a real threat of ambush by the terrorists we had come to subdue, but this didn't materialise. Soon after we had arrived at the small town, we were sitting down to tea in the mess, a British military home from home, with the difference that most of the day-to-day chores were carried out by some local Malayan boys but more often Chinese.

As I settled in I began to learn what was expected of an officer of the 11th Hussars – a first-class performance of his job at all times with the appearance of having made little effort, and an obligation to entertain and be entertained as often as possible. Meanwhile the other ranks had to know their vehicles inside out and keep them spick and span. National Service 2nd Lieutenants were required to be even more proficient. The army were fully aware of the need to keep their troops fit and happy, and generally provided superb sporting facilities. They also knew the value of regular competitive sporting contests with whatever opponents may have been available locally. There was all the cricket, golf, tennis, swimming and athletics I could have wanted, and within weeks I was picked to play cricket for the state side, Negeri Sembilan. I made a few runs – enough to be included in the North v South match, perhaps the most important event in the Malayan cricketing calendar. I didn't do well but wrote home criticising the captain for not putting me on to bowl.

My Malayan tour was divided between time spent in camp, with regular all-day food convoys to be policed, and periods 'on detachment', taking my troop into the jungle, seeking out ambush positions, patrolling remote roads in our armoured cars and looking for any sign of terrorists. One of these detachments saw us billeted with a Gurkha regiment, officers' mess included, and far better fare than the Hussars enjoyed. I could happily have stayed there for the rest of my tour.

The enemy was a rag-tag group of armed communist rebels known as the Malayan National Liberation Army, which British and Commonwealth forces had joined the official Malayan army to put down. The British tactic devised by General Templer was to starve out the terrorists by cutting off supplies of food.

As it happened, and I suppose I should be grateful for it, my troop never had any serious encounter with the enemy, although there was one self-inflicted fatality. The lead APC of a returning patrol clipped hubs with the outbound one in front of me. By luck, as they reared onto their outside wheels, there was just enough space for me to pass between them before they crashed down and rolled into opposite side ditches, landing upside down. One of the drivers wasn't responding, and it was my duty to wriggle through the mud and water to check him out. When I reached him, I knew at once that his injuries were severe and, very regrettably, he died. As the officer in charge, I was ultimately responsible for what had happened, and the sense of shame that caused was a long time dissipating.

I was more affected by this traumatic event than I realised at the time. I certainly lost my nerve for a while, repeatedly ordering my armoured car driver to slow down. It was evident that my superior officers recognised my malaise went deeper than that, effectively putting me out to grass for the remainder of my service. I later concluded that I'd suffered from what's now known as post-traumatic stress disorder, or PTSD.

In a previous incident during a rare live ammunition firing exercise, I'd been peppered with a hail of small iron shards when a machine gun badly malfunctioned. Dozens of tiny metal splinters lodged under the skin of my chest and forearms and only came to the surface slowly over the next half-dozen years. Luckily, I was looking through binoculars at the time which certainly saved my eyes from serious damage.

Other than these two incidents, our Malayan tour was routine, uneventful and uncomfortable, with the almost constant irritation of being bitten by uncountable species of insects. My letters home recorded this, and the utter absence of any suitable or, indeed, any girls at all – in my experience, rarer than terrorists. However, the climate suited me well, with no hay fever; I enjoyed the even temperature and high humidity, even the daily soakings in the afternoon downpour, and I never had a day's illness. Meanwhile I tried to keep in touch with the rest of the world through outdated copies of *The Times*, the *Spectator* and the *New Yorker*. 'Although,' I wrote home, 'it would be nice to have a serious conversation with an intelligent man or woman on some subject other than the food, the weather or sex.'

If the monotony of the company was oppressive, the monotony of the jungle was absolute – an endless vista of green broccoli tops broken only by sporadic clearings of neat linear groves of rubber trees. The jungle nevertheless did possess a certain awe-inspiring beauty, and it was permanently alive with animal sounds and activity. Hordes of monkeys chattered incessantly, and we had regular sightings of pythons, coral snakes, cobras, wild pigs and huge boars. Elephants of the smaller, Indian variety also wandered freely through the less dense jungle growth. I imagine, in hindsight, that I was really quite lucky to have seen something of the virgin jungle and its fauna when I did; by now, much of that habitat has been cleared for rubber and palm oil cultivation.

During the muggy winter of 1954, I played a few games of rugby, mostly with and against Fijian soldiers of the Commonwealth Forces who were helping British and Malayan government troops in resisting the MNLA. I quickly came to know and admire the Fijians, many of them huge men, weighing in at sixteen stone and standing over six feet, contagiously jovial and great beer drinkers. They were also formidable rugby players. I don't think the Cherry Pickers had ever fielded a rugby side, until an order from the Colonel put me in charge of selection and training.

'Is there a fixture date, sir?' I asked.

'Ah, yes. Tomorrow; on the *padang*; against the Fijians.'

It was the first of two encounters. They slaughtered us, 76-0, and we thought we'd got off lightly. The return match was only marginally better, 74-3, and, as it happened, I was responsible for kicking the 3.

* *

The rugby season ended and by the spring of 1955, the despondency caused by my feeble batting performance at Lord's the previous year returned. I must have taken it seriously as I wrote about it in a letter to my parents. 'I'm afraid I'm beginning to think life's too short to spend days at a time playing cricket in the same unattractive place. Rugger, squash, even golf, leave room for a hundred other pursuits during the day but cricket is all-powerful and lets nothing interrupt it. Apart from that I feel as inept with the bat as I did last year and I am beginning to think that the little something that makes fifty instead of five has eluded me.'

Coming from a previously committed cricketer this was grim stuff, but fortunately within weeks the depression had lifted. Another letter home identified the cure. 'I got bored with using battered old regimental and club cricket gear and bought a whole new set of my own. It promoted immediate success and I made 183 runs for Negri Sembalan State against Johor on Saturday. You can't imagine what fun it was to make some runs again. I almost got the real feel of a bat back again!'

Although delighted to find my love for cricket still alive, I nevertheless turned down the chance of a ten-day visit to play in Hong Kong. It was getting close to my return to England and I was becoming a little 'boat happy' – a curious condition suffered by most of the men that sets in as their departure date approaches. Sufferers tended to be written off as useless to the regiment or the squadron. It was something I recognised years later when I was playing away on tours with the England cricket team, who often showed signs of the same syndrome towards the end of a long tour. I turned down the Hong Kong trip because I feared that the plane home would leave without me. As it turned out, it was three weeks late and I'd missed a great opportunity.

* *

I arrived home a few months after my twentieth birthday, to find that my father had made most of the necessary arrangements for me to join my brother John at Cambridge in the autumn. It must be said that getting into our finest universities in those post-war years was a hell of a lot easier than it is now. Intellectual prowess was not a prerequisite; a strong family connection, a clear source of fees and a good schoolboy sporting record were all it took. My father happily provided the first two of these.

My last flourish as a soldier came when I was awarded the Malaya Campaign medal, which I felt I'd done little to earn. It arrived without ceremony through the post, and was eventually placed in the Dexter trophy cabinet alongside my dad's MC. It was subsequently stolen, at the same time as the MC, and not replaced, although I do have a miniature.

Chapter Four

CAMBRIDGE STUDENT

In October 1955 I became a member of Jesus College, Cambridge. I knew none of the new intake, although, of course, John was already there. From this distance in time, I realise I had no idea how tremendously privileged I was to be there. Jesus is an ancient and venerable institution with many great men (though no women) among its alumni. It is an extraordinarily beautiful place, and I do sometimes castigate myself when I return there for not appreciating it more than I did.

Like most freshmen, for my first year I lived in college, in plain but spacious rooms, not much changed for a hundred years. Normally undergraduates were supposed to find digs in the town in their second year, but when I was appointed secretary of the cricket club for that year, I earned the right to stay put for another two years.

Looking back, it's obvious that I didn't intend to do any more work than I had to. I joined a couple of fairly fatuous clubs. I don't recall that The Natives did anything more than swallow oysters and champagne in large quantities and in any available swish surroundings. The Rhadegunds, named after the wife of an abusive Thuringian king, required members to have a double college colour. As far as I recall, it just did drinking – port rather than champagne – perhaps with food.

As for studies, it made sense to continue what I'd studied in my final years at Radley, so I opted to read Modern Languages: French and Italian. I'm ashamed to say that I abused the privilege of being a member of one of the world's oldest universities by failing to attend a single lecture all the time I was there. Nevertheless, I realised I would have to do *some* work. I had the option to read the first part of my Tripos in either one or two years and it seemed to me that if I could do it in one year and get my Part One, I'd be fairly safe for the next two. With this end in mind, for the three weeks prior to the exams in May 1956 I got my head down, ignored all social distractions and worked like hell. But it was tough because by this stage I'd also committed myself to cricket, and I wasn't going to neglect that either. I established a regime in which I was up before seven, worked until ten, played cricket for the rest of the day, and was back at work for the rest of the evening: six hours' study, six hours' cricket. In order to disguise any gaping lacunae in my knowledge, I made a point of achieving some freshness in my written answers. I avoided the old clichés – the wit in Molière and lack of it in Racine – and came away with a third in the Part One Tripos. For the time being I felt secure in my tenure.

Although I didn't appreciate it at the time, I was probably somewhat spoiled by an allowance from my father of £600 a year, a lot more than most of my contemporaries. John and I wondered how this compared with the £200 a year he'd been allowed forty-five years before. Out of curiosity, we investigated the ledgers of our tailor, Pratt Manning, and found that my father still owed three and ninepence. My brother paid this and sent my father a receipt. We also discovered that he had three suits made to our one and pointed this out to him. Showing some forbearance, he not only tolerated this teasing, but also gave us a car – first a convertible Austin, followed by a Rover 90 – which we used continuously until I cannoned it from one side to the other down Jesus Lane, narrowly missing two dons and whacking my head on the windscreen.

When I'd first arrived at the university, with the idea of pleasing my father and knowing how keen he was that I should play some rugby, I put my name down for the early college games and on a frosty autumn day walked out for the first practice. I was out of training, but that was to be expected. As I ran onto the field a little creakily, a ball rolled towards me. I gave it a gentle hoof which produced a sharp pain in the back of my leg. I ignored it for a few days, but the pain wouldn't go. Physio departments didn't exist in those days and the treatment of injuries was still rudimentary. I went to a doctor who told me I'd pulled a hamstring. He gave it a bit of a rub, told me to take an aspirin and lay off for a couple of weeks. The pain persisted for the rest of the season; I kept missing games, making my chances of getting into the university side remote. Besides, at school I'd played fly half, but there were already two international fly halves at the university; as a result I never made it into the First XV. I did, though, manage to get selected for the 60 Club, effectively the Second XV, playing on the wing, where I didn't really know what I was doing. However, I hoped I had satisfied my father's rugby interest by getting my 60 Club colours and playing against the Oxford University Greyhounds. (We lost.)

* *

In 1956, as my first summer at the university approached after a not especially noteworthy rugby season, and memories of some unenjoyable games in

Malaya, I was feeling inclined to eschew cricket and concentrate on my social life and golf, leaving a little time for academic focus. I had almost made it into the golf team in the spring term, and might well have settled for that, but this laissez-faire attitude was soon derailed by finding my name on the application board for freshmen's trials up at Fenners, the university's legendary cricket ground. This turned out to have been an initiative of my brother's, whose excuse for interfering was that he thought my father (who was after all paying for this wonderful interlude) would be disappointed if I didn't at least try to play cricket at Cambridge. I knew he was right and felt obliged, at least, to put in an appearance. Freshmen's nets led to freshmen's trials. In Melluish's XI v. Goonesena's XI, I made 55 retired and 65 not out. This was duly noted; and when I made some more runs in the final trial, Michael Melluish, the Cambridge skipper, invited me to play in the first three county matches. Despite my original lack of enthusiasm, I found myself committed enough to the idea of playing for the university and I accepted with more than a hint of the thrill I used to feel before a match at Radley.

I approached my early games at the university with a light-hearted flourish; my simple aim was to hit the ball hard and enjoy myself. But I was soon as hooked on cricket as I'd been before National Service intruded. At that time, Oxford and Cambridge fielded strong sides, at least good enough to take on a major county side, and both universities were established members of the first-class circuit. My first three matches were against the counties of Surrey, Yorkshire and Lancashire, at a time when Surrey were almost unbeatable, while Yorkshire and Lancashire were used to being in the top six, and formidable opponents. I batted against some of the best-ever England bowlers: Appleyard and Trueman, Laker and Lock, possibly Statham, too. I got runs against them all but it was clear that I'd taken a big step up in class. In six innings I had three noughts, two of them yorked, with my high backlift spotted at once; Trueman and Loader both got through me very soon. But I also made three forties against those counties and I never lost my place for the university from then on.

Melluish didn't offer me any bowling in that first year, which prompted me one evening in the nets, just for the hell of it, to bowl to him as fast as I could. I thundered up to the wicket and knocked his middle stump out twice, thinking that would be enough to convince him that I knew how to get the ball down to the other end. But I still wasn't put on to bowl that season. Melluish never told me why not, and I never asked.

* *

In the early part of the 1956 season, I celebrated my twenty-first birthday. My father was absolutely delighted with my performance in my first few games for the university and with characteristic generosity came over from Milan to throw a very smart party for me at my favourite London hotel, The Connaught. All my family were invited, and I was allowed to ask a crowd of Cambridge friends, including a number of fellow cricketers; I was beginning to feel like a real presence in the world of cricket.

In my fourth county match, against Sussex, I scored a duck in the first innings, but managed to keep my composure enough to go out for the second and hit two sixes, a five, and eleven fours for a total of 118. The pundits at Wisden were generous enough to notice. The Sussex captain, Robin Marlar, who'd also captained Cambridge a few years before, asked me afterwards if I was planning to play county cricket, and which counties I was qualified for. As I'd been born in Milan, I wasn't tied to any county. I did have overtures from Worcester and Warwickshire. The Worcestershire chairman, Sir George Dowty, of Dowty Engineering, invited me down to stay at his home, Arles Court, a Victorian monstrosity near Cheltenham where he'd built his aircraft component factory in the garden. I think he wanted to have a closer look at me, and see what I was made of before offering me an amateur place in the Worcestershire side. Besides a lot of hard and – in my view – irrelevant questioning, this also involved a tour of the Dowty works, when I was asked to put on overalls. Already well into my more snooty Cambridge cricketer phase, I didn't think much of that idea, and in the evening after dinner at the great Dowty mansion, when I was invited to play billiards, I considered the choice between playing tactfully or playing for real. I played for real; this did not please Sir George. There was an awkward lull in conversation at breakfast next morning, and I never heard from him again. Without giving it a great deal more thought, I happily agreed to play for Sussex, perhaps not entirely appreciating the significance of that promise.

By the end of my first university season, with a county to go to, as well as two more years playing for the university, I was pretty much committed to cricket, but I hadn't allowed it to deflect me entirely from my deeply entrenched love of golf. I abandoned rugby in the autumn term while I became a regular at the Royal Worlington Golf Club on the far side of Newmarket. I managed to play often enough to be included in the university team, of which I was made secretary in my second year, leading automatically to captaincy in the third.

I did play in the Oxford–Cambridge match at Lord's that year, where the inescapable excitement was almost eclipsed by the much worse, stomach-churning sensation I experienced when, before we went on, I was delivered a letter by hand, which, far from wishing me well, informed me that it was all over between me and Shirley Bowden, who had been the love of my life thus far, and for the last four years since I'd met her in my early days at Mons.

She was the same age as me, but like most young women in those pre-feminist times, her priority was to get married, and she'd found an ideal older man in Trevor Guy, scion of the once great Guy Motor Company. I met him and liked him from the start, and later accepted that he was the perfect husband for her. Nevertheless, I wished she'd waited at least until the match was over before delivering her 'Dear John' letter.

Once the university term was over, I was invited to play a couple of games for Sussex towards the end of the season, but I didn't present myself at their ground quite as soon as they were expecting me. In June, not long after I'd turned twenty-one, Melluish invited me to join a Cambridge cricket tour of Denmark. I don't recall much of the cricket, but towards the end of the tour, in Copenhagen, I met a Danish girl, Lisa Arendup, so lovely that I really didn't want to leave Denmark for a while. I scribbled a note on a picture postcard to Sussex saying I was sorry, but I couldn't play for them as arranged. At the time I thought this was a perfectly reasonable thing to do and anyway, I was doing them a good turn by agreeing to turn out at all. When I look back on this deplorable, cavalier action, which, I fear, must have reflected a regrettably bumptious demeanour at the time, I shudder with shame. It was only later in my career that I understood the complex factors, the arguments that went on over asking amateurs to play mid-season, the matter of the vested interests of the professionals, of the whole complex and delicate business of running a county side. I learned afterwards that, not surprisingly, Robin Marlar hadn't thought much of this casual attitude, although he evidently decided to overlook it for the time being and said they would be expecting me for the 1957 season.

* *

I was back in Cambridge that autumn, when British and French forces were dispatched by Prime Minister Anthony Eden to face down Egyptian troops acting on the orders of President Gamal Abdel Nasser. Nasser had declared his intention of taking control of the Suez Canal which ran through his country from its former imperial owners. In my naivety, I probably thought Eden was right, although as an expat Brit my feelings were not as strong as some of my fellow students. Meanwhile I maintained my primary focus on sport, and my policy of minimum attendance at lectures.

Having made my mark in the university golf match versus Oxford at Formby, I'd been appointed secretary to the university golf team, which pushed rugby off the agenda for good. Now I was committed to cricket in summer, and golf for the other two terms. I wasn't spending much time on girls either, still smarting as I was from the 'Dear John' note Shirley Bowden had delivered to Lord's, while the Copenhagen adventure had quickly fizzled out. At that stage, surprisingly perhaps, given my later fascination with racehorses, and even though I drove through Newmarket almost weekly on my way to play golf at Royal Worlington, racing's HQ was never a draw for me while I was at Cambridge. As I was already spending somewhat over my generous allowance, this was probably a very good thing.

* *

My second season in the Cambridge XI opened well. Gamini Goonesena was captain of Cambridge that year, and a very fine captain, too. An impressive all-rounder – leg-spinner and prolific batsman – he had already played for the country of his birth, Ceylon (now Sri Lanka), as well as Nottinghamshire. As Cambridge skipper, the fitness of his team was a priority. Before our first game he gathered the players for a pep talk about eating and drinking in moderation. He was relaxed about girlfriends, though, telling us, 'Now, I don't mind you going out on a Friday night if there's a match on the Saturday, but for God's sake, don't make bloody pigs of yourselves.' Still, as it were, a virgin at the time, I was a little shocked.

Gami, as we all called him, was a strong, early influence on me where captaincy was concerned. As I'd been made cricket secretary, I was destined for captaincy the following year and I was glad of the opportunity to learn by observation how to go about this demanding, often unappreciated role. Despite my burgeoning confidence, I knew there was always room for increased knowledge. Early in the season I was given an undeniable opportunity to learn a great deal more.

I got into the habit of getting up in time for early sessions in the nets, and one morning, as I was finishing a spell, someone tapped me on the shoulder. I turned to find the Fenners groundsman, a legendary Cambridge cricketing figure, former minor county player, skilled exponent of squash and tennis as well as a first-class shot and fisherman.

'My name is Cyril Coote,' he said. 'I watched you batting last year, and you're a fine front-foot player. But if you ever want to play for England you must be able to play off the back foot as well. Come up to the ground half an hour early every match day and I'll teach you.'

A friend from Jesus, an affable Australian called Ian McLachlan, had been in the nets with me. Hearing this offer and aware of its value, he hastily asked if he could come too.

Cyril Coote was a stocky man, whose lower half was foreshortened by damage done to a leg as a fifteen-year-old footballer. His large head and strong features heightened the sense of authority and considerable knowledge of every aspect of cricket that emanated from him. He knew as much about the nurture of greensward as anyone in the country. It was from him that I received my first insight into the value and vulnerability of a cricket outfield – knowledge that I put to good use thirty-five years later when I was reordering the outfield at Lord's. He had specially nurtured the Fenners pitch to suit young, less experienced batsmen, not to favour wily bowlers. He had himself played for Cambridgeshire, skippering the side for eight years, and he had studied many great players over his years as custodian at Fenners, where he had seen a lot of outstanding players go through their Cambridge years: May, Sheppard, Dewes, Doggart, among others.

Once he was sure of my aptitude and enthusiasm he was prepared to come out for hours, throwing balls short of a length outside the off stump, inviting me to try to hit them off the back foot, often with specific guidance; I remember him warning me, for instance, not to pull at Fenners because the ball was inclined to keep low. Lessons learned those mornings formed the basis of my batting style from then on.

I got Ian to come up with me as often as possible, dragging him away from his studies which he took much more seriously than I did. He was two years younger than me, not having done any National Service. Both naturally competitive, we threw balls harder and harder at each other, developing our game together with Cyril Coote's guidance. Ian only just missed a Baggy Green cap in his subsequent cricketing career, and made a great success of his life beyond that, in business and politically, becoming Australian Minister of Defence, and more latterly, the driving force behind the huge redevelopment of the Adelaide Oval.

I recognised that the coaching I was getting at Cambridge, as good as the Radley coaches had been, was bringing me up to a whole new level of the game. At a time when no players wore helmets, learning to avoid a whack on the head was critical. I was taught the paramount importance of keeping an eye glued to the ball – especially a short one – so that, as soon as it bounced, there was a fraction of a second in which to take evasive action, with a small lateral step and a sway of the head, allowing the ball to whistle by harmlessly. This, and later, watching Cassius Clay's feet in the boxing ring, taught me the value of nimbleness. These days, when most players wear helmets all the time, they don't need to be so careful; as a result, they stand with their feet apart, making swift foot adjustment more difficult. They all get hit from time to time, but generally without too much harm.

It was in this second year that my game and my relationship with cricket began to blossom. I made a hundred before lunch against Lancashire and finished with 185 runs, admittedly without Statham and Tattersall bowling. I'd quickly recognised just how good the pitch was, and how important good pitches were to the budding batsman. I'd learned on two superb grounds – Radley, then Fenners – an advantage denied to many young county batsmen. There is an old saying: 'you can't learn much about batting, sitting in the pavilion'.

One of the big moments for me in my second season at Cambridge was playing against the touring West Indies. I still vividly recall my first impression of their mighty players whose team I came to admire and enjoy more than any other during my career. I was fielding on the boundary near the pavilion; the West Indians were batting. After the first two wickets had fallen the legendary Frank Worrell stepped out though the pavilion door. He was very dark and very handsome – upright and masterful, his cricket whites immaculate, with pristine new gloves – carrying a brand-new bat as he strode across the rich greensward of the Fenners ground towards the wicket. It was a great entrance, and I aspired, then and there, to emulate his presence and the aura it created. Sadly, I don't believe I ever came close. And the West Indians proceeded to whack the ball about the ground like a team of Chinese ping-pong players. However, I was pleased that in my first crack in the face of some very quick West Indian bowling, I scored a 46 and 37.

That summer I was also invited to play for the MCC in a centenary match against Lancashire at Old Trafford. This fixture conflicted directly with my college exams. I thought I'd better talk to my tutor, Mr Fisher, about the few days' absence this would involve, and how the match was a big opportunity for me.

'Ah, Dexter!' he half-sighed. 'A couple of days away, eh? On the basis that your studies seem to be suffering already, perhaps it'd be for the best if you did go. Your examination results might well reveal how little work you've done.'

There probably was a case for sending me down immediately, but I had worked hard to pass my Part One Tripos in my first year, because, frankly, that traditionally meant securing my place at the university for the next two years. Besides, I was also secretary to two university sports teams – cricket and golf – which offered additional security. Nevertheless, I was very grateful to my tutor for not pressing the issue.

I went up to Manchester where the match was spoiled by rain, though I managed 22 in the first innings and 61 in the second. I did get the chance to hit a back-foot screamer past the quickly withdrawn hand of Lancashire legend, Cyril Washbrook. When the next wicket fell, out walked my great boyhood hero, Len Hutton. Like a small boy, I was all in a fluster and there was nothing I could do about it. I couldn't think what I should say if he spoke to me. He walked up to me, getting closer and closer until his face was very near to mine. He'd obviously noticed my shaking; he spoke huskily in broad Yorkshire. 'Are you alright?' he asked solicitously.

I was out almost immediately.

More significantly, in July I played for the Gentlemen against the Players at Lord's. I caused a stir (and surprised myself a little) by turning in what turned out to be my best-ever bowling performance. In the Players' first innings I bowled five overs, two maidens and took 5 for 8: Don Smith, Denis Compton, Dick Richardson, Godfrey Evans and Frank Tyson. I took three more wickets in the second innings, and was splashed all over the back pages. As a result, with some doubts about Trevor Bailey's fitness being raised, I was canvassed as a candidate for the fourth Test against the West Indies at Leeds. When it was confirmed that Bailey was definitely unfit, the England selectors called me in Peterborough. I was playing there against Northants in one of the three indifferent performances I put in for Sussex that season. They wanted to select me for what would be my first-ever appearance for England.

Unhappily, I was injured; I'd turned my ankle over bowling just that day. Robin Marlar was almost as upset as I was, but there it was, I was unfit and I knew I couldn't possibly play. If I'd been asked today how I felt about this, I might even have said I was 'gutted'!

* *

Two years after I'd come back from Malaya, I was still in touch with a number of friends from the 11th Hussars and it didn't take much persuasion to get me to the Cherry Pickers Ball at The Hyde Park Hotel in the autumn of 1957.

This event was a welcome home beano to celebrate a low-key but highly effective campaign in Malaya. We all turned out in our best mess kit: Cherry Bum trousers, spurs and immaculately tailored blue serge tunics, complete with chainmail epaulettes. There was no doubt that we really fancied ourselves. The full title of our regiment, bestowed after providing the escort to Prince Albert at his wedding to Queen Victoria, was Prince Albert's Own. The right to wear our cherry breeches had also been a gift from the Prince. We had worn lightweight tropical kit only in Malaya; I was delighted to have the chance to wear the full uniform, which had cost my dad a packet at the regimental tailors in Jermyn Street. Bizarrely, my wife still sometimes wears the trousers (the red ones, not metaphorical ones) sixty years on, but always complains about the prickliness. The Ball brought me back into contact with a number of fellow officers, especially Michael Cooper-Evans (who went on to be head of the JWT advertising agency) and Tim Forster, who for many years trained winning jump horses not far from where I now live. It was fun to see them all again, and it was Michael who kindly asked me to a party he was giving in a basement flat in Sussex Gardens a few weeks later.

We were already in the early grips of winter and I came from Cambridge with my golfing foursome partner, John Churchill, in his neat MG Saloon, as I'd just had a smash in my (technically my father's) Rover 90. I turned up looking somewhat battered, as a result of the crash, with a cut on my forehead, where I'd been through the windscreen, and wearing my very expensive British Warm officers' coat. Michael had also asked a girlfriend – his current girlfriend, he thought. She was the first and really the only girl I saw from the moment I walked into the room.

Susan Longfield was a striking, lovely looking young woman of nineteen – the house model for the famous Mayfair couturier, Hardy Amies, I learned afterwards from a not very gruntled Michael. The flat where the party was taking place was packed, with nowhere much to sit, and when Susan came over to where I'd managed to bag a seat, she simply sat on the floor, introduced herself and leaned against my knees. Still on the lookout for a girl since Shirley had given me the elbow, I couldn't ignore a warm tingle of anticipation when she seemed quite happy to stay and chat with me for a while; I certainly did nothing to discourage her. She was funny, vivacious and obviously widely admired. We talked happily with lots of teasing and joking for most of the party, without knowing much about each other. I didn't talk about cricket and she didn't talk about modelling, but by the time the party was petering out, without even taking mutual phone numbers, we'd established an easy, exciting rapport. When it came to leaving, somebody, without bothering to ask me, had taken my British Warm from the bedroom where I'd left it and I was impressed by the way Susan gamely scrabbled around under the bed trying to find it.

Outside, three or four of us men had hailed a taxi; one squealed to a halt and we all piled in. We hadn't slammed the door shut when we heard a female voice outside. 'Hang on a minute… Is there room for a small one?' We made room; it was none other than Miss Longfield, who managed to land neatly in my lap. I could hardly believe my luck, although it didn't last long. Just around the corner, she jumped out near her flat in Baker Street. At least I knew roughly where she lived, while I went on in the taxi to stay at a friend's place nearby. When I woke in the morning, the first thing I remembered about the party was that we hadn't swapped phone numbers.

A few days later she was having breakfast with her father, Tom Longfield. When he asked her what she'd been doing and who she'd been seeing, she mentioned that she'd met a chap called Ted Dexter, though she didn't know anything about him.

Her father, she told me later, nearly dropped his coffee cup. Anyone who regularly read the back pages of the newspapers would have seen reports of the first-class games in which Cambridge had played. Tom was a true cricket aficionado and a fine player in his own right.

He had played for Cambridge, as well as Kent, and had been captain of State of Bengal cricket team before the war. Here he had fielded one of the first Indian State XIs to include Indian players. Tom had found himself working in Calcutta as a result of the recommendation of a friend who worked for Morgan Grenfell Bank. The bank had an interest in a company called Andrew Yule & Co, a major dealer in Indian tea and jute. After a stint upcountry, Tom was appointed No. 2 in the Calcutta office, although he still spent a lot of time up in the plantations in Assam. He also spent almost as much time on the cricket field.

A few years after the party in Sussex Gardens, I was playing for England on the revered turf of Eden Gardens, the famous and historic Calcutta ground which lies near the old Government House. Half a century later when Susan and I were in Calcutta we found a portrait of her grandfather, Frank Garnett, in the ground floor of the club house; on the first floor was a portrait of her father. Her grandpa had been the first president of the Calcutta Cricket Club. He had worked for Royal Insurance in Liverpool, from where he was sent to Burma, where Susan's mother, Heath, was born. The family then moved to Calcutta when he took over the office there, and indulged his love of cricket, which was how she met the young Tom Longfield. Born in Calcutta in 1938, Susan's first years were spent in India, throughout the war, before being dispatched to an English boarding school, St Margaret's in Hastings, in 1946. There had been only two trips back to India for holidays with her family in India, and from then on Susan's life had been based in England, latterly in London, which was how, very luckily, I'd met her.

**

After a little pestering, Michael Cooper-Evans accepted the inevitable and gave me Susan's phone number. I was able to reciprocate when he asked me for the number of the girl I'd taken to the Cherry Pickers Ball. So I rang Susan to suggest a date; she sounded interested – a good start. I told her that the BBC had invited a group of us from Cambridge to their studios in Maida Vale to be part of a live audience at a recording of The Goon Show, the radio show that was roughly the fifties equivalent of Monty Python. She said she would come, and she seemed to enjoy it; my Cambridge friends were obviously impressed. Encouraged, I followed this up with an invitation to the theatre; Susan wanted to go to a production of Dylan Thomas' *Under Milkwood*, which was a hot ticket at the time. After the show we went on to the Royal Court in Sloane Square, where we could have dinner and dance upstairs. We dined well and danced afterwards for a blissful few hours, until the band packed up.

We had talked over dinner when I learned that Susan knew Michael through a friend she'd met sailing on Chichester Harbour from the village of Bosham, where her parents had rented a small holiday cottage for a number of years. She'd come with her mother to London to get ready for Queen Charlotte's Ball, a major shindig in the London debutante season. She hadn't had a 'coming out' party of her own but one of her closest friends had arranged for her to come to the ball. By tradition, all the girls wore white dresses, in which they processed into the ballroom, pushing an oversized trolley bearing a vast white cake. Susan's mother, perhaps feeling a little sorry that she hadn't been able to give her daughter a dance of her own, was ready to push the boat out in buying a suitable outfit. They went to Fortnum & Mason in Piccadilly, and up to the ladies' fashion department on the first floor, where the garments were stored discretely in closed cupboards. While they were being served, Susan was approached by Evelyn Whiteside, a beautifully elegant woman who ran the fashion floor. She asked Susan if she was planning a career. A little puzzled by the question, Susan told her that she was about to start a shorthand and typing course. Evelyn Whiteside had other ideas. She proposed that Susan become the house model in Fortnum's gown department. And so she did.

After a few months at Fortnum's, which Susan found a little boring, she was invited to do the same job at the far more glamorous Savile Row showrooms of royal dressmaker, Hardy Amies, where she was paid the royal salary of seven pounds per week. Her rent was only two pounds a week, so she was doing OK.

She would have liked to cross the Channel to the distinctly more glamorous fashion scene in Paris, to where her friend Françoise Garrigue, who'd worked at Simpsons, had recently returned. But the wages there were lower, and the only way the girls could survive was to acquire a sugar daddy (*un papa sucre?*) and she didn't want to do that.

In the meantime, working at Hardy Amies did offer its moments. The Queen, still in her late twenties, was a client and regular visitor. Susan observed that Her Majesty didn't have a great deal of interest in fashion and would bring along her former nanny to help. On one occasion, Susan told me, while modelling a dress for the Queen's inspection, they were discussing a recent burglary at the London house of the Woolworth heiress, Barbara Hutton, in which a large haul of jewellery had been stolen, including a number of sapphires.

'Oh well,' the Queen said lightly, 'Barbara doesn't really like sapphires,' which put the tragedy into perspective.

Susan, following correct protocol, left the room walking backwards, and promptly tripped over the back hem of the gown she was modelling.

* *

From then on, Susan and I started to see a lot of one another. When I returned to Cambridge after Christmas 57, we carried on going out together as often as I could get to London, or she to Cambridge. They were joyously innocent times when nice boys did not leap into bed with nice girls, making friendship possible without complications. I always enjoyed seeing her; we always had fun, we enjoyed the same jokes and our thoughts seemed mostly to run along the same lines. As sophisticated as we could be, we told ourselves that we could spend as much time with each other as we wanted, knowing that our lives might go off in different directions at some point, and that fun and friendship needn't necessarily lead to marriage.

I didn't really think this, though; I didn't know, but I hoped Susan didn't think that either, and in an attempt to create a watershed to find out which way our feelings really flowed, I threw down a challenge. I suggested that maybe it was time to move on, and that maybe we'd already said all we had to say to each other.

The words were barely out of my mouth when I realised there was one more thing I wanted to say to her, which was, 'Will you marry me?'

But coward that I was, I didn't say it. I went away and sweated for a week or two, until I couldn't keep up the pretence any longer, and I finally asked her.

'Yes,' she said, and that was that. Sixty-two years ago.

However, we decided not to publicise our intentions right away. We talked about how we should approach parents. I knew mine would be taken aback by my wanting to marry so young, with my living precarious, and my future completely undecided.

Susan was doubtful about her parents' reaction too. Her mother had been a cricket widow all her married life and had expended a lot of effort and ingenuity in keeping her daughter away from cricketers. When Susan first took me home, her mother looked as if she might explode. In time, though, especially with Tom Longfield's undoubted bias in favour of a fellow cricketer, we made our peace.

* *

My turn as captain of the university XI that season can best be called disappointing, which was exactly how Wisden described it. I had the excellent Ossie Wheatley, an accurate fast-medium bowler, to back me up but not much else besides. I didn't have such a bad season myself, scoring 92 and 109 not out against Lancashire, and a couple more centuries against some good opposition. But the university team had a disastrous encounter with the New Zealand touring side. The weather generally didn't help our efforts either that summer; pitches were wrecked by rain, and several games were curtailed or rained off.

I did experience a minor triumph on my college's ground when halfway through my last term at Jesus I was eating supper in the hall. Someone sat down beside me. I was concentrating on what I was reading; I didn't look up until I heard a voice beside. 'You're a nice fella, I don't think.'

'And who might you be?' I asked, snottily.

He said he was captain of the college cricket team. 'You've never played for the college,' he said reprovingly.

'Maybe because I've never been selected,' I protested.

As a result, I played my first college game against the Gentlemen of

Norfolk. They went in to bat first, and I was given the new ball. I knocked over the first three cheaply, thanked the captain and moved away.

'No! No!' he said excitedly. 'Keep going! We've never beaten these chaps.' I took nine wickets, all clean bowled for a handful of runs.

Asked to open the batting too, I went in and hit two sixes and the winning run in half a dozen overs. The game was all done in an hour and a half. I was never asked to play for the college again.

I was given another unlooked-for opportunity to perform for my college in the field of athletics, in which I'd barely participated since I'd left Radley. One of the less attractive aspects of Fenners cricket ground was that it was ringed around the outside, beyond the boundary, by a cinder running track. I was walking off after a long day in the field when a young man dressed for athletics panted up to me. 'Jesus has a match starting in a few minutes,' he gasped urgently, 'and we've lost a sprinter. Would *you* run for us?' He sounded desperate.

I'd barely done any athletics since leaving Radley, but I felt I ought to rise to the challenge, for the honour of my college. There wasn't time even to change, so I headed off to the start as I was, still in my boots and flannels. However, honour was served; I won the race.

Once I'd left Cambridge for the last time, uncertain about what I should do next, I simply went on playing cricket, as an amateur, hoping that something would turn up. My dad continued to support me with six hundred pounds a year – not far off the national average wage. I'd played four Championship matches for Sussex scoring an unspectacular 111, with a highest score of 32. I was wondering where to turn to next when I was awarded my first England cap to play against New Zealand in the fourth Test at Old Trafford. Susan lent me her little Ford, and I drove up the A6 to Manchester in a state of high excitement. After nets on Wednesday, I walked out of the ground with the ever-affable Godfrey Evans. He nodded at my modest little Ford Anglia in the car park.

'Is that yours?' he asked.

I owned up. 'Tell you what,' he said. 'Leave it there and come with me in the Bentley.'

We stopped at the first pub – a stone's throw from the ground. There were more pubs – possibly many more – between the ground and our hotel. Godfrey, I discovered, was indefatigable in his quest for drinks and people to talk to while he drank. When I staggered down to breakfast the following morning, I remembered virtually nothing of what happened the previous evening. I'd barely poured myself a cup of coffee before I was accosted by the England skipper, Peter May.

'I want a word with you, young man,' he said, giving his best impression of a headmaster. He pointed to a row of autograph books, neatly lined up ready for team signatures. 'What's this?' he asked, opening the first book. Filling the first page I recognised a scrawled *Edward Ralph Dexter*. He opened the next, and the next; I'd done it on every single one. Not one of my proudest moments.

**

England were in control of the New Zealand series by then, and the selectors were taking the opportunity to try out three new caps. Halfway through the game they were going to announce the touring party for Australia and New Zealand that winter.

For the first two days in Manchester, it rained most of the time, but on the Saturday I got my chance to bat, making a brisk 50. My captain Peter May was at the other end and gave me useful encouragement.

On the Sunday I played golf at Mere with my new pal Godfrey Evans and we hurried back to the Bentley to hear the touring party selection. 'Don't you worry Ted, they will pick you for sure.' But he was wrong. I wasn't in it.

My absence caused a minor controversy among the pundits. Indeed, it was one of the most influential, Raymond Robertson, who described the selectors as 'thrice-blinded moles for failing to recognise quality when they saw it'. I was certainly disappointed but it was true to say that at that stage, I hadn't played much county cricket, and several of the recent outstanding university players hadn't gone on to do well in Test cricket. Stoically, I took a deep breath and carried on, weighing up career plans but still playing cricket.

Remembering my encounter with Len Hutton, I had another Yorkshire experience after I'd come down from the university when I was asked to play at the Scarborough Festival, an end-of-season celebration first held in 1876, with such a fine tradition that many Test players were in the mix. At a prematch dinner, I found myself sitting next to the legendary Bill Edrich, a member of an extraordinary family of Norfolk cricketers. In his forties by then, he hadn't played Test cricket for a few years, since the 54/55 Ashes tour, but he was still a formidable player, with some remarkable records to his name.

I composed myself, took a deep breath and, plucking up courage, opened the conversation. 'You have a reputation as a fine player of fast bowling. Could you give me a few tips?'

He looked at me sideways. 'Have you ever been hit on the head by a fast bowler? No? Don't worry. It doesn't hurt a bit.'

I didn't believe him, but I didn't ever find out if he was telling the truth; I never was hit on the head in a match, even though some of the world's finest and fastest bowlers did their damnedest to get me, and I'd stopped playing a long time before helmets appeared.

Chapter Five

TEST CRICKETER

I came down from Cambridge in June, shortly after a gang of gung-ho engineering students at Gonville and Caius had managed to park an Austin Seven van on the apex of the Senate House roof, causing great bafflement and chagrin for the police and university authorities, while the papers had a field day. I'd left without sitting my finals, which would be a disgraceful way to behave these days, and I'm not proud of that at all; there have been times when I've thought that a degree, even a second in Modern Languages, might have been useful. Realistically, I don't know how I could have achieved that, given that I'm not a genius, and the amount of time I'd been spending on cricket, golf and Susan Longfield. So, I'd left with a sporting record that pleased my father no end, and an academic performance that did not.

Susan and I still hadn't announced our plans to marry when I took her to Italy to meet my parents at the family villa on Lake Como. They evidently liked her (how could they not) so we told them the good news. They didn't react as we'd hoped.

My mother took Susan for a long walk and a talk in the serene surroundings of the gardens overlooking the lake. 'We like you very much,' she told her, 'and of course we can see why Teddy wants to marry you, but you're both far too young.'

My parents had married fairly late in life, after my mother's first, early marriage had been a disaster. Mum was fifty-eight herself by now, Susan was just twenty and I was twenty-three. Mum and Dad were convinced that we were much too young to marry, especially as I was a long way from starting a career.

I understood her reasoning but it still really hurt. I wanted Susan and I to be married as much as ever, and I felt that my own mother should have trusted my judgement. I could have pointed out that she was on slightly shaky ground having eloped herself, aged only nineteen.

On that negative note, we came back to London, where I was determined to get a career going in the hope that this would deal with most of my parents' reservations about our marriage plans. My father wanted to help, and put me in touch with an old friend of his, Mr Bob Sprinks, of H R Sprinks & Company, Paris, which did more or less what Bevington Assicurazione SA did in Milan. Mr Sprinks' first idea was to introduce me to C E Heath & Company, a London insurance brokers, but when he heard that there was a strong possibility I might yet get called up to join the MCC cricket tour in Australia, if one of the party – as often happens – should fall ill or get injured, he felt it would be wrong for me to make a start in the London firm, only to find I might be packing my bags at any moment.

For the time being, I moved to Paris with the intention of gaining some business experience in Mr Sprinks' office. To start with I stayed in the Oxford & Cambridge Hotel in Rue d'Alger, on the corner of the highly fashionable Rue St Honoré (which suited Susan when she came to stay), and a short walk from the Jardin des Tuileries – très chic. After a short while I moved into a flat belonging to the family of one of my work colleagues, which was cramped but a lot more fun.

My duties in the office weren't demanding and I had time to play some golf at my boss's club at St Cloud. I also took the opportunity to have a good look around Paris – far more glamorous then than it is now. Susan came over for a few romantic weekends, when we would wander up and down beside the Seine, and up the Champs-Élysées, having our portraits badly painted in Montmartre, dropping into little bistros and night spots or jazz clubs, feeling quite the cosmopolitans.

* *

Meanwhile, in Australia, Freddie Brown, MCC touring manager, was having problems. John Mortimore of Gloucestershire had already been flown out to take some of the workload off Laker and Lock, and Willie Watson was having knee trouble. In early December, after Raman Subba Row, England's opening batsman, had broken a bone in his right hand, I had a call to fly out and join Peter May's team in Australia as soon as I could get there. That turned out to be a lot trickier than it sounded. Simply getting from Paris to London was delayed for two days by an old-fashioned pea-soup fog. But I made it in time to talk to Susan. In order to deter predators in my absence, and with her full complicity, I announced our engagement, packed my bags and set off for Sydney.

The lingering fog in London still hampered my departure, but, feeling pretty special, I finally found myself in a first-class cabin of the latest BOAC prop jet, the long-haul turbo-prop Type 175 Brittania, known as the *Whispering*

Giant. When I was served dinner at a table with damask napery and cut glass to drink from, with a senior pilot of the airline sitting next to me, I thought I'd really arrived. However, this experience didn't last. We stopped first in Bahrein, with engine trouble. I sensed that there was something indefinite about this pause and I was feeling under pressure to get on. When we heard that a Super G Constellation passing through had a single seat available, I proposed playing cards for the right to the seat. I won. I almost wished I hadn't, as I sat crammed in economy for the next four days with a group of loudly chattering Arabs. I arrived in Australia exhausted and almost speechless from laryngitis and fatigue. Meanwhile the press, with characteristic perversity and inventiveness, made much of what was perceived as my dashing Parisian existence and engagement to a glamorous fashion model. The playboy tag they hung round my neck then was to stay with me for years.

Susan was disappointed she wouldn't see me for a few months, but at least we'd committed ourselves to getting married the following spring, whatever anyone's parents thought. She took our temporary separation in her stride, and for the next few months we wrote back and forth to one another, by return of post, on those flimsy blue tissue paper airmail missives; I looked forward to each one, and they never failed to cheer me, such is the power of love.

As for the cricket, my first full immersion in an overseas tour was a bruising experience. I arrived in the middle of the first Test in Brisbane and it took me time to acclimatise and get fit again. On top of that, the pitches were hard, the light fierce and dazzling, and several of the Australian bowlers were throwing the ball, making it unpredictable and extra hard to play. With only a little county experience, I didn't know many of the players and had no real idea what I should be doing as twelfth man for the second and fourth Tests. With hindsight I'd say I protected myself in a carapace of languid, entirely bogus self-confidence, which would have done nothing to improve my popularity among the players. I was told, a few years later, that I'd been thought of as offhand, moody and ungrateful to those who were trying to help me, and, to ease the pain, I was doing a lot more partying than I should, which made things worse.

When I'd arrived, I found that the tour was already mired in quite ugly controversy about the bowling style of some of the Australian pace bowlers. Meckiff was one, Gordon Rorke was another. The list grew longer, including Slater, and two who played at Adelaide, Hitchcock and Trethewey. We instantly renamed them Pitchcock and Tethrowy, but we were reluctant to complain too loudly, with two suspected throwers on our own side, Tony Lock and Peter

Loader. At practice before the Sydney Test, Peter May asked Loader to 'throw him a few' to acclimatise. The first ball hit May on his right big toe before he could move; and that was the end of the practice.

** **

I spent Christmas 58 in Adelaide, sad that Susan wasn't with me, and jittery about playing against what looked like a tough, unpredictable opposition. I was twelfth man for the second Test; I did nothing of note in the third Test at Sydney but I wasn't happy to be made twelfth man once again in the fourth Test at Adelaide.

The first match in which I scored anything worth noticing, though not a Test, was in Tasmania, on the cooler, more verdant and familiar-feeling grounds of Hobart and Launceston. I had a nice little stand with Peter May in Hobart, scoring 38, before we headed back to Melbourne for the fifth Test. I didn't know what to feel when I was selected to play in the final Test, by which time we were irrecoverably 3-0 down in the series. I didn't want to let the side down again, especially as I had the impression that people had thought, 'What the hell! We've got nothing to lose – stick him in and see what he does.'

I didn't do good. One of the throwers, Meckiff, had me caught by the ageing Ray Lindwall diving one-handed at third slip. In the second innings, I did manage to stay around a bit longer, getting some kind of measure of Rorke's highly questionable bowling style, but after about an hour, I was caught off Davidson for a paltry six runs. In the two Tests in which I'd played, I'd done nothing to justify my selection; I'd scored a total of 18 runs and I hadn't bowled at all. Somehow my natural aptitude for clean ball striking had totally deserted me, and I had no idea why. The British press were predictably grumpy, and I came in for some pen-lashing, even being described by one pundit as having given one of the worst batting performances by an Englishman in Australia for forty years.

On the evidence of the scorecard, I couldn't disagree, and yet I knew for certain that I could have done better. We had still to head across the Tasman Sea to New Zealand, and with more players lost through injury and, in Statham and Loader's case, through a car crash, I was bound to play.

However, I was deeply downcast by then. I had, it seemed, completely mislaid my mojo and I just longed to get back doing what I knew I could: hitting the ball hard and hitting it sweetly. I was supremely lucky that John Mortimore, a fine bowler and Gloucestershire captain, came to my rescue.

When we arrived in New Zealand he offered to look at me in the nets. After he'd bowled a few balls, he stopped.

'Why,' he asked, 'are you standing with the face of your bat open?'

I didn't know what he was talking about. 'I'm not,' I protested. 'I'm just trying to keep it square to the line.'

John shrugged a shoulder in disbelief. 'You may think it's square. But I can assure you it's open.'

Doubtfully, I twisted the bat a few degrees in my hands, convinced that I would simply end up hitting the ball with the side of my bat. I played a few more balls from John, and within minutes – literally minutes – I started to time them sweetly and was hitting them hard.

I couldn't understand how I'd allowed my grip to pivot in the way it had. But I was struck by two obvious truths: I was a twenty-three-year-old, raw recruit at Test standard, unready for the pressure that can bring, and I could do again what I knew I was good at. From that moment on, my bruised self-confidence began to mend and I was sure I would redeem myself before I went home.

Our touring party had dwindled to twelve by the time we reached the green and temperate surroundings of Christchurch. With my new-found self-belief I was down at the nets as often as I could be, begging anyone to bowl at me. The lesson I'd had from John Mortimore had really got home; I was consistently hitting the ball clean and hard. There were only two Tests to be played in New Zealand. The first was on a fair wicket, but a turner, and the early batsmen were quickly removed. I came in to join Peter May, who helped me over the first half hour with practical advice and words of encouragement. I was beginning to feel comfortable in my stance, moving my feet well and swinging the bat. Most importantly, I felt I was earning my colleague's respect. I was making runs, and making them when they were needed. When Tony Lock came in, batting down the order, he came to my end. 'Don't worry,' he said. 'I'll stay with you. You just keep going.'

This gesture meant a lot to me; it expressed the attitude of the senior professional, accepting me at last, ready to work with me, rather than just putting up with me. I dared to hope that my pathetic performance in Australia would become just a dim memory – something past. In the end, I made 141, including twenty-four fours, in four and three-quarter hours. In the second innings I added nothing, but I had proved my point, at least to my own satisfaction, and in the second Test, I took my first three Test wickets.

* *

I flew back with the MCC party feeling mightily relieved that I'd redeemed my reputation. It had taken just the one good innings to give people a real idea of what I could do. In the end I'd enjoyed my first tour, fraught though it was at times, I'd learned a lot, and I'd made a number of new friends who were to recur regularly throughout my life. One of these was the formidable Australian spinner, Richie Benaud, who'd taken me out a couple of times in the series. I liked and respected him from the start, and we carried on swapping ideas, and bad jokes, for decades afterwards.

Arriving back in England in the middle of March, I was feeling so cock-a-hoop I was ready to take on anyone who might try to get in the way of my plans to marry Susan. As it happened, there was no opposition; Susan's parents were all for it, and mine had come round, or perhaps had just yielded to the inevitable. A date was fixed, 2 May, and a venue had been identified for the reception, the lovely Monkey Island on the River Thames at Bray. In the hands of industrious women, wedding arrangements were soon at full speed, and I found that the nearer the day came, the more I liked the idea.

Before that happened, we celebrated Susan's twenty-first birthday on 23 April. Her father had given her some money for a party and she asked some friends round for drinks. Afterwards just the two of us went to see *Irma la Douce*, a super musical playing in the West End, then on to a club at the bottom of Park Lane run by Hélène Cordet. Hélène was a glamorous woman of Greek origin, famous for compèring the TV show, *Café International*, and for being a childhood friend of Prince Phillip's. Her club was one of the smartest in London at the time. As my dinner jacket was still at the cleaners after my long campaign in the Antipodes, I decided – not without a dash of irony – that I would wear my white tie and tails instead. This was a little over the top, even for that distant epoch, but when we arrived at her club, Hélène loved it. She came over to our table. 'You're both so well dressed and look so lovely, I can't possibly charge you anything,' she said. 'It's a pleasure to have you here.'

**

Our wedding took place in St Michael's Church in Bray, a village on the Thames a few miles downstream from Maidenhead. It's a pretty place, best known these days for two outstanding restaurants, the Roux Brothers' Waterside Inn and Heston Blumenthal's Fat Duck. I haven't risked my pocket book at either of them. The marriage service was conducted by the Vicar of Bray, assisted, rather grandly, by the Bishop of Gibraltar, in whose scattered diocese lay the Anglican parish of Milan, to which my parents belonged. The stone-towered mediaeval church was packed with relations and old family friends. A touch of glamour was added by Susan's friends from the fashion world (including Hardy Amies who had designed her wedding gown) and, of course, by Susan herself who looked serenely lovely, and made me feel very proud. A clutch of my cricketing colleagues, some of them well known, provided a counterbalance to all the glamour on the bride's side of the church.

The vicar gave a touching sermon, of which I remember very little, before the whole party moved in a colourful crocodile along the short walk from the church and over a picturesque footbridge across a narrow channel to Monkey Island. Originally Monk's Eyot, this was an elongated curve of land lying in the meandering Thames, where, in the early eighteenth century, the third Duke of Marlborough had commissioned the building of two pavilions as a fishing retreat. It was a peaceful place of seven acres, landscaped with broad lawns fringed by weeping willows. During the twenties and thirties, it had become known as a venue for romantic trysts – some might say dirty weekends – for the better-heeled. Post-war it was less racy but still wore an air of faintly rackety sophistication which appealed to Susan and me.

It was an enchanting reception, on a perfect day in early May, and when the time came for us to leave, we were having such fun that we didn't want to go. However, a small launch had been booked to pick us up from the island's jetty to ferry us downstream while everyone waved us off. We didn't go far in the boat; as soon as we were out of sight round the first bend in the river, we hove to and jumped onto dry land to retrieve a small car Susan had borrowed from a friend, and we set off gleefully on the first leg of our honeymoon.

We'd been driving for about half an hour when Susan suddenly gasped. 'My passport!'

'Oh God,' I groaned. 'What about it?'

'I left it in the vestry when we were signing the register,' she admitted in a small voice. At that time, brides were obliged to lodge their new passport with their married name in the care of the vicar, only to be released once the vows were made and witnessed.

Feeling somewhat deflated, we drove back to the church in Bray. As we approached the village, Susan ducked below the dashboard and I kept my head down as carloads of jolly guests leaving our reception drove past us, going the other way.

I safely recovered the passport and we restarted our honeymoon, heading for the small Kent town of Rye. We had been there the year before, when Susan had come to support me in my last varsity golf match (which Cambridge had won by a single point). We stayed in a pretty oak-beamed inn before setting off for France next morning. We enjoyed our drive across northern France along the straight, flat, poplar-lined roads, with a few stops at little bars en route to Paris. We had booked a room in the Oxford and Cambridge Hotel in Rue d'Alger, where we'd spent a few happy nights the previous summer while I was working for Bob Sprinks. We planned to stay a week on a budget of £100, which, while it was worth a great deal more then, still wasn't very much. That didn't stop us having a wonderful first week of marriage.

Arriving back in London was a bit of a comedown. We had, at least, somewhere to live – a brand new, smart little flat in a block on the corner of Bourne Street and Ebury Street, where Daylesford farm shop is now. The block, Venner House, had been built by Don Gosling, an ex-naval man who was also in the car park business, and had just taken over National Car Parks. We were able to get a good deal on it as Don had just married Susan's flatmate, Elizabeth Ingram. My father, entirely aware of the state of my finances, didn't like the idea of Susan and me shivering in a garret somewhere and had generously bought the flat for us. We didn't have much furniture, beyond a bed and a cooker, and after a few weeks spent perching on traditional orange boxes, our nest-building instincts kicked in and we cheerfully set about putting it all together. However, when I brought in the suitcases that contained everything I owned, and poured out my old shoes, rugby boots, cricket bats and all the classic gear of a bachelor sporting life, Susan was horrified. 'I thought I was going to have a pretty little London home,' she cried, 'and now look what you're doing to it!'

Not long after we were back from Paris, we arranged a day at Royal Ascot with new friends Charlie and Carol Benson. We were determined to do it in style with a champagne picnic in the Ascot car park. Susan and Carol were looking great in stylish hats, Susan's probably on loan from Carol. Charlie and I were in morning suits and top hats, easy for me having worn them for our wedding the month before. At that stage I hadn't been racing much. When I'd been at Radley, I studied the form and posted off tiny bets to the local bookie with an 'enclosed postal order for three and ninepence'. Now, standing by the Ascot paddock in the dappled sunlight under the beech trees, with the sweet aroma of the horses striding by, looking at the cocky jockeys in their bright silks and the famous big-time trainers oozing knowledge and authority, I began to feel in tune with the whole game. I began to admire the horses for their physical beauty, their athleticism, for their courage and determination. I started to watch them more closely and follow their careers. At this stage, though, I wasn't betting heavily – a ten bob note or a quid was about the norm.

We had a good day, drank too much champagne and made some enjoyable new friends. Sally Crichton-Stuart was there, too, whom Susan knew well through their fashion connections and who had introduced us to the Bensons. The same age as me, Charlie was a truly colourful individual, an old Etonian and young racing journalist who scribbled and provided tips under the AKA, first, of 'Bendix', then 'The Scout' on the Daily Express. His tips won as infrequently as any other Fleet Street tipsters' but he did have a deep knowledge of racehorses. Charlie was witty, perceptive and possessed great charm, as a result of which he seemed to have connections with everyone notable in racing, in fact, anyone notable for anything. In time he became a ferocious punter, though his biggest bet that first year was ten shillings. The second year he was betting in hundreds and was owing a thousand pounds before the last race. He had a hundred pounds each way on an 8/1 outsider which won by a nose. The third year he got the bit between his teeth and went on an amazing winning spree running into many thousands – enough to buy a house in the Boltons and a lot of diamonds and emeralds for Carol. He had become a regular presence in our lives over the years, but when, in the 1970s, he became Robert Sangster's court jester, he was moving in social echelons beyond our range. He was one of the famous gang of friends who rallied round the disappeared Earl of Lucan after the Lucan's nanny, Sandra Rivett, had been murdered in the place of the Countess.

* *

Back at home, I was beginning to appreciate that being married was not quite the same as being single, and I was determined to play my part properly. The problem was that I had no money, and little prospect of accumulating much; Susan, on the other hand, was more than earning her keep. She had decided to leave Hardy Amies before we were married and had gone freelance, signing up to London's most successful model agent, Peter Lumley. Soon her image in a shot by top photographer, John Adrian, from the John French Studio could be seen all over the place as Pond's face cream's Angel Face. And this led on to her appearance in a number of other ad campaigns.

I was committed to playing for Sussex, still as an amateur, but, despite my last flourish in the New Zealand Tests, there were no signs of imminent reselection for the England team. It wasn't easy. Playing for Sussex was unpaid, although all my expenses were paid. In any case, in the still old-fashioned snobby fifties, it was still considered ungentlemanly to be paid to practise a sport you loved; a gentleman player was expected to have his own means, other sources of income; and this gentleman had neither, but I did have a generous dad.

Nevertheless, for the time being, I was quite happy to be playing for Sussex that summer. I was getting to know more of the players and more about them. I respected Robin Marlar's somewhat capricious captaincy. He wasn't nicknamed Mad Marlar for nothing.

Our new home in Ebury Street was ideal for the job. During the season I walked to Victoria Station and took the 9am Brighton Belle (first class) with my regular corner seat, a newspaper and my own pot of marmalade. I could sit back for an hour, do the crossword, and be at the Sussex county ground at Hove by 10.10am. After the day's play, I would take the 7pm train back to London and be home in time for dinner.

Sometimes, if things had gone on longer than normal, or we'd been playing away, or on one of our alternative grounds at Eastbourne, Hastings or Horsham, I'd stay down, which was no hardship as I enjoyed Brighton. This was without doubt a good era for me, before the full-scale circus of international cricket had taken me over.

This was when I acquired the first of a long tally of what I would call interesting motors – the beginning of an unceasing fascination with bizarre or extravagant cars. I sold my dull little Ford Anglia to Susan and replaced it with a red Borgward, kindly supplied by Sussex County Cricket Club. This was a potentially expensive hobby, especially when I started having to buy the cars myself, but in the main, it usually washed its face for me, and occasionally even yielded a heart-warming profit.

* *

I found my form for Sussex quite quickly. By the end of May, I had made what turned out to be the fastest hundred of the season against Worcester on a sodden wicket at Dudley (not far from where I live now). It was my first hundred in the Championship and my first real breakthrough in the county games. The magazine *Sporting Record* informed me that this fast hundred had won me their weekly award. I received a smart lighter inscribed '*Sporting Record*, performance of the week, May 1959.' I told Susan it was to commemorate our memorable wedding night. It turned out to be the fastest century of the season, and that earned a one hundred-pound prize, which covered the cost of our honeymoon.

Apart from a couple of interruptions, I played a whole season for Sussex and began to appreciate the demands and rigours of a six-day week county cricket season, combined with a lot of travelling.

On the international scene, England were hosting a Test series against India that summer. After my big score in New Zealand at the beginning of the year, I was hoping for a call, but I wasn't asked to play until the fourth Test, by which time the series was already won. I scored a decent 45 in my second innings and took a wicket. In the fifth Test, in August, I scored a duck, but took 2 wickets. On the whole, I didn't feel I'd contributed much to England's clean sweep. There was, though, an England tour of the West Indies scheduled for winter 59/60, for which my performance in the last Indian Test at the Oval had proved crucial. Before it was under way, Gubby Allen, chairman of the MCC Cricket Committee, had sought me out and confided in me.

'The only thing between you and the winter tour of West Indies is your bowling. When you're given a bowl in the Oval game, don't try to do too much with the ball. Just relax, try to keep it straight if you possibly can – and you have a fair chance of making the trip.'

I followed this advice, bowled just respectably enough and hoped for the best. Eventually, to my great relief, I was told that I would be included in the tour.

That was something to look forward to, but at the end of the county season, it seemed like years away, while my financial predicament was as uncomfortable as ever. I also had to face up to the hard truth that, whatever happened in the West Indies, I might have to look outside cricket for a career.

Without a degree to open any other doors, I still thought my best option was to follow my father into the insurance business and, thanks to Bob Sprinks' influence, the opportunity originally offered to me by him was still open. What made it even better was the agreement with my employers, C E Heath & Co, that I could continue to take time off to play for Sussex.

When the cricket season ended, my routine changed. Instead of catching the Brighton Belle, I jammed on my bowler hat, walked up to Sloane Square and rattled round the Circle line each morning to C E Heath's offices in Houndsditch.

After all the excitement, highs and lows of international cricket, I found the daily grind deeply uninspiring. I was nevertheless keen enough to make a go of this possible career and settled down sufficiently to sit and pass the first part of the insurance industry exams. It was about this time, probably out of sheer boredom, that the studying of form and petty punting on horse races I'd done as a schoolboy became a daily preoccupation.

There is a plethora of theories about what drives a gambler. Nobody can quite identify it (although these days the big online gaming companies have become very sophisticated in knowing which buttons to press). One theory is that the gambler becomes addicted to his own, self-generated adrenalin. I certainly knew all about adrenalin; I was quite accustomed to the way a big surge could produce and drive a sustained sporting performance. I've observed that in my own case, a good shot of the stuff could increase my hitting power by ten to fifteen per cent.

I should put my hand up and admit that from then on and for the next forty years, I did become something of a punting addict. I began to read the racing pages avidly and, being a glutton for theory, devised my own systems to process the flood of information available. As a boy, I'd loved going to the trotting races with my father in Milan, where he always had a bet. But, where he was a rich man who only placed small bets, I was exactly the opposite. In my defence, I can also say that I did respect obvious limits; I never, as it were, gambled the house; nevertheless, it was a problem and more than a mere irritant to my long-suffering wife. I did not quite fit the normal profile of the addicted gambler. I seldom, if ever, went to casinos. I liked to play for a few pounds on the golf course but on nothing like the scale of a few of my friends.

I became increasingly depressed as the underlying worry of my situation was relieved only to a small extent by the prospect of the West Indies tour, although I was still conscious of my lacklustre performance in Australia the previous year, and an unstellar appearance against the Indians that summer. Anyway, the tour didn't start until just before Christmas and in the meantime, I was beginning to feel quite ill. My depression grew worse, my eyes started to ache and I lost my appetite, After a week of this I went to see a doctor. He told me that I was suffering from jaundice and, worse, there was a serious possibility that I wouldn't recover from it in time for the West Indies tour. This made my depression worse as I endured a regime of weekly blood tests, before I began slowly to recover my strength.

I was lucky enough to have the continuing support and confidence of Gubby Allen, chairman of selectors. He assured me that he had me pencilled in for the trip, provided I could get myself fit. He took me to see a specialist who gave me more effective remedies and – as important – confidence. A week or so before the team was due to depart, I was told I could go too, but I would have to take things easy for the first two or three weeks of the tour.

Chapter Six

THE WEST INDIES
AND THE COUNTY GAME

We set sail from Bristol docks on 8 December on the *SS Camito*, a banana boat returning unladen to Barbados. It pitched and rolled for most of the ten-day voyage, and some of the team never left their cabins. My doctor had thoughtfully given me an injection of some magic potion against seasickness, and I didn't miss a meal. Sea transport on the way out to a tour was preferred because it allowed players to acclimatise gradually, to adapt to the changes in temperature, humidity and light that they would find on the cricket field.

It also gave the captain, Peter May, the opportunity to talk to his team, which he had described as 'young and experimental'. He could discuss the options in a relaxed, unpressured atmosphere, which was important on this tour because it was a very different group to that which had set out in 1958 to the Antipodes, with the notable absence of Bailey, Evans, Laker and Tyson. For myself, I was still smarting over my failure in that tour, and privately wasn't at all sure that I deserved to be on this one. This self-doubt wasn't helped by a lot of the pundits who were saying precisely that, implying that I was altogether too dilettante an individual to be taken seriously. If they'd been writing these days they would have said that my career so far had been all hype and not much substance. Peter May, thank God, didn't take the same view – not surprisingly as he must have had a hand in selecting me. Sitting on the rear deck of the ship, watching our wake widen as we headed south from the chilly North Atlantic, he talked to me on my own.

'We've been thinking over the side and it looks almost certain that you'll be in the team for the first Test at Barbados. There just won't be time for anyone to play themselves into the side and so we must make decisions now. We would like to see you batting at No. 6 and we'll put you into the covers and let you stay there.'

He showed no signs of uncertainty, which bucked me up, and I settled down to enjoy the cruise. With the lingering jaundice, I wasn't supposed to exercise, which meant that I just had to lie around in the sun. I was happy; it felt a lot better than crouching behind a desk in Houndsditch, looking out of the window at the rain pissing down. As each day passed, I felt my spirits rise like a well-made soufflé. Surprisingly I never once missed my regular betting escapades. I don't think I had a single bet for the whole of the tour.

Arriving in Barbados for the first of many joyous visits, I had been ordered by the doctor not to do anything strenuous for the first ten days – an order with which I was more than happy to comply. Before the first Test at Bridgetown, we had a game against the island's team, which included some of the West Indies star players: Hunte, Nurse, Sobers, Weekes and Griffith. It was a hard match on hard-baked ground, in the unrelenting blaze of the tropical sun; hard on the ribs too, when one of those big, loose-limbed bowlers got into his stride. When they batted, Nurse and Sobers made 367 between them. They beat us by ten wickets, to great rejoicing from the whole West Indian side. Without doubt Barbados had for some years been quite capable of taking on the world single-handed, but this was the first time they had defeated the MCC since 1926. Not a great start to the tour, although as it turned out, it was the only game we lost. A few years later, in 1967, Barbados had the audacity to take on a Rest of the World XI; they received a good hiding for their hubris!

However, while we waited for the first Test to begin on 6 January, there were wonderful beaches to lie on, warm, blue-green sea to swim in and some of the friendliest people in the world to talk to, especially about cricket.

As I had hoped, I was picked to play in the first Test. Peter May won the toss and chose to bat. Geoff Pullar and Colin Cowdrey walked out to open the innings. I recall vividly the first few minutes of that game. All the talk had been about the speed of Wes Hall's bowling. Our only English experience of him had been as a lanky teenager in the 57 tour, when some senior West Indies players said he was lucky to be on the trip at all, that he had only come along for the ride. He was lively enough then but had seemed no more than another medium-pace bowler with a short run.

I pursued my own research by asking Denis Atkinson, former great West Indian all-rounder, about this new, awesome reputation Hall had acquired.

'Tell me, just how fast is Hall now?' I asked Atkinson. 'Is he just fast, like Trueman or Statham, for instance?'

Atkinson answered with ominous obscurity. 'No, no. Wes Hall has plenty of pace.'

At the start of the first over, Wes Hall took the ball. He walked back slowly for forty yards, as a deep silence fell on the England dressing room. He ran up with a mighty roar from the crowd. The ball pitched, lifted and flew past the off stump at shoulder height. I shook my head, and pitied Pullar and Cowdrey. What I'd witnessed was that Wes Hall was ridiculously fast, faster than any bowler I'd ever seen. Maybe not faster than Rorke from sixteen yards, but Rorke and his school weren't exactly playing cricket. However, there was nothing suspect about Wes Hall's bowling. He had a beautiful, pure action, with a step up in pace beyond anything that any of us had encountered.

I went in at No. 6 and had made just 28 when I experienced what may have been the major turning point in my career. I had managed to hang on against the fast bowlers, had a taste of Ramadhin and then faced Sobers' off breaks and Chinamen, left arm over the wicket. I drove one back half-heartedly, carelessly, straight at him. It was a foot off the ground, and I can see Sobers smiling now, as he leaned down to take this easy catch. But he put it on the floor, and I stayed in – lucky man!

I carried on to make my first major Test hundred. I faced Hall, Watson and Sobers (in his lively medium-pace style), followed by Ramadhin and Sobers again – in his slow style. It was a varied attack which wasn't easy to handle, made harder by the fact that I batted for half the time with lower-order players, which didn't help. The best of it was that when they took the new ball, my eye was in; that bright red cherry was just asking to be hit, and I hit it into every quarter of the field.

At the end of the innings, I was on 136 not out. I rejoiced at the clamour of a most wonderful reception, especially from my parents who'd come over to watch the game. I think I knew then that it was this innings which had truly established me as a Test cricketer. The match ended, drawn, before I got a second innings.

The next Test in Port of Spain, Trinidad, was one of the most rambunctious matches in which I've ever taken part. There were riots over umpire's decisions, combined with internal clashes within the West Indian team due to island loyalties. I happened to be the trigger to the main eruption by the crowd. The home team was already taking a beating. They were 94 for 7, while Trueman and Statham were just carving them up – Sobers had been caught off Trueman for a duck. I had just run out Singh, the obligatory local island selection, comfortably – by at least two yards; the umpire's decision was unequivocal, and simply not open to question. But there was already a tricky, restless mood in one section of the crowd contained by high, chain-link fencing and angle-iron posts. Already frustrated by what they thought were other bad decisions, when Singh walked off (readily enough), they went berserk.

Over the fence came a torrent of empty Coke bottles, followed by more and more which smashed onto those already on the ground, creating a sea of glass splinters. The police came out to hustle the protesters from the stadium; the fire brigade were called and an ancient hose unravelled, with a view, perhaps, to dispersing the crowd without injury. A dribble of water spluttered from the spout until they got the pressure up, when water squirted from dozens of slits in the seldom deployed and degraded hose. One of the firemen, attempting to get onto the field, got himself impaled on one of the fence stanchions. The mayor of Port of Spain came in to quell the noisy mob. Play had been stopped for the day and eventually the crowd, reverting to their habitual joviality, went home. Luckily the next day was Sunday, with no play, and an army of men and women came into clear the field of bottles and thousands of glass shards.

Despite this interruption, in our first innings I'd managed a gratifying 77 before I was caught and bowled by Singh, in the spirit of cricket irony. In the second I was cleaned bowled for 0 by Wes Hall. But I did take 2 wickets for 7 runs in the West Indies second innings which made a useful contribution to the only match we won. This game, with the other four games drawn, won us the series, the first time the MCC had ever beaten the West Indies on their own territory. There had been four previous tours, starting in 1929, with two drawn series and two losses.

* *

From the start of the tour Peter May had warned us that some of the cricket we were going to play might be slow going. He feared correctly that the West Indian over rate would be anything between slow and snail pace.

'We will simply match their rate,' he said, 'and not an over more.'

It was not a concept that appealed to me at all. When it came to my turn to make these decisions as captain, I consistently made a point of a good over rate, whatever the circumstances. But enjoying a one-up lead, May thought there was no good reason to alter his tactics.

The third Test was at Sabina Park in Kingston where my mum and dad joined us, and Susan too. We were all staying at the Courtly Manor Hotel with its colonial-looking chalet rooms ranged around a swimming pool. When we arrived in our rooms, smiling maids bustled in to take our washing, bring us towels and turn down the beds. This was luxury, we thought.

Raymond Illingworth had other ideas, putting his head round the door. 'Rooms are a bit bloody small, eh?' he opined. Before long the whole team was sitting out by the pool for a couple of beers before dinner when Susan glided serenely by on the first-floor balcony. The group around the pool fell silent, until the hush was broken by an unmistakeable Yorkshire drawl. 'Eh, ducks. Goin' to see mother-in-law for a bit of advice, are we?' There was, as usual, a hint of a leer in Freddie Trueman's voice.

God bless my lovely Susan for taking it in her stride and responding with a smile and a wave.

There were no rules about wives joining the tour in those days, but few professional cricketers could have afforded it anyway. I was lucky; I had a rich dad; he paid for Susan's flight and a nice double room for us. Inevitably there was a hint of envy, perhaps even resentment, but in any case, I let the Dexter family down somewhat by making two low scores in the match that followed. Not surprisingly, everyone blamed my poor performance on Susan's appearance. The real problem for most of us was that the Sabina Park pitch, which was inherently rock hard and grassless, glinted like a mirrored floor. The groundsman had developed a way of spinning the light roller until you could see your face in it. For a player not used to it, it could be quite disconcerting – although not, it seemed, for Colin Cowdrey, who played two of his finest innings, of 114 and 97.

We started the fifth Test one up, with one to play back in Port of Spain, where we advanced with very deliberate slowness towards the draw which would win the series. Walter Robins, our tour manager, whose mantra throughout the tour had been that we were all lazy and no good for anything, was disgusted by the tactic, but those of us who had fought a tough campaign and come out on top were happy to have achieved it by whatever means. For me personally, this series was the key watershed in my career, when whatever remaining doubts selectors may have had about my usefulness were clearly dispelled. I played in all five games and, in the fourth Test in Georgetown (in what was then British Guiana) with Peter May injured and Ken Barrington getting badly hit by Wes Hall in the first innings, I was promoted to bat at No. 3 in the second innings. From here I scored 110, which effectively neutralised the West Indies first innings lead of 100+ and we drew the match. From that point on, I always batted first wicket down for England and never lost my place. For me, No. 3 was the best place in the batting order. Naturally, this hinged on how long the openers had hung around, but if the first wicket fell quickly, the ball would still be new, and the bowlers fresh, needing a good technique and a cool head. I knew I had the technique if not the coolest head.

When the series came to an end, I had topped the English batting, with 526 runs from nine innings, at an average of 68.75. More surprising, I was even third in the Test bowling averages. I flew back to England at the start of April 1960, feeling that I had truly arrived at Test level, with a firm and justifiable place in the England side.

I had landed in the West Indies determined to prove myself, and to prove the critics wrong. This was the start of a happier time when the critics were disposed to say nice things about me. The revered cricket writer E. W. Swanton flatteringly compared me to Walter Hammond. Even Alan Ross, *The Observer*'s man, hitherto no Dexter fan (and still not rating me as a bowler while Trevor Bailey was still around), did relent to the extent of hailing, 'a potentially great batsman – and a vindictive cover point, too.' The fielding comment was well earned as a result of my early resolve to hunt down every shot that came my way, whether they were looking for a run or not. It had resulted in at least one crucial run-out and a lot of runs saved.

All my grim depression of the previous autumn was well behind me now.

**

The MCC tour party returned to England by air, not banana boat, perhaps in recognition of our achievement. It was a triumphant homecoming, London was bright with cherry blossom and crocuses, and it was wonderful to be back at home with Susan. When she hadn't been in the West Indies over the winter, she'd been working on her own career, and was enjoying the freedom of being a freelance. She had made friends with a number of other glamorous, fun-loving models who were with Peter Lumley's agency. Susan had introduced Peter to her friend Sally Croker-Poole, who was a great success and went on to marry Lord James Crichton-Stuart and, later, the Aga Khan. She also saw a lot of one of the great models of the era, Bronwen Pugh (who married Lord Astor), and Jean Shrimpton, the first big face of the sixties, whom Susan described as 'like a little pony'. Some pony!

It wasn't quite the 'sixties' yet, but London was beginning to wake up and, with new-found confidence from my winter Test performance, Susan and I threw ourselves into the spirit of it. Susan had a growing circle of friends who worked like her in the world of fashion, and I was still keeping up with old friends from Radley, the Hussars and Cambridge. There was a good cluster of those with whom I'd lived in a large flat in Hereford Square in South Kensington, where we arrived down from Cambridge in regular succession for generations it seemed. For the most part, they were good company and keen to make the most of life. My friend from Mons, David Scholey, was often around, and notorious bad boy, Mikey Taylor, was always ready to pinch another man's girl, given half a chance. We held a few small gatherings at our flat, with my brother John (now preparing to take over the Italian business from Dad) making the most of them when he was over here. All sorts of lively people would come, while Susan and I loved the entertaining.

At the same time, I had a new cricketing job (prestigious but unpaid) at Sussex County Cricket Club where Robin Marlar had handed over the captaincy to me. He'd wanted to do it the previous year but the big cheeses in the Sussex cricket hierarchy weren't so sure about me; they were still a little twitchy about what they considered my cavalier attitude. I think, probably, the Copenhagen incident still rankled. Now that the appointment had been confirmed, I had the impression that they were agreeing to it despite their lingering misgivings. That didn't worry me too much – I sort of understood, and anyway, I'd soon show them what I could do.

There was, frankly, plenty of scope for improvement on recent performance. In 1953 Sussex, under David Sheppard as captain, had been runners-up in the Championship, but since then they had been floundering somewhat in the bottom half of the table; they'd come fifteenth out of seventeen in 1959.

When Robin Marlar handed over to me, he didn't pretend that he hadn't been struggling and was hoping I would come in and shake the place up a bit. Although Sussex had a fine history, with several great names linked to it, when I arrived the mood was a long way from being that of a potential contender for the county title. Strong sides – Yorkshire, Surrey, Middlesex and Worcester – had been slugging it out at the top for the last few years, and Surrey, our northern neighbours, hadn't lost to us in over a decade.

Hove was a lovely but sleepy ground in a somnolent town, where the older members, dozing in their deckchairs, had become used to not winning. However, when I accepted the job (in fact, grabbed it with both hands), I made up my mind that there was no point in doing it if I simply believed, like them, that we didn't have a chance of winning. This thought fuelled my ambition as Sussex skipper for the next three years and I happily got down to the task.

I loved my few years in charge at Hove. I was by then an enthusiastic analyst and strategist of the game; I had really come to enjoy the chess-like subtleties and imponderables that informed the decisions that had to be made. I made a lot of friends among players and supporters, and came to appreciate the distinctive old-fashioned English way in which the club was run. During my time there, as player then as captain, racing between London, Hove and the county's other grounds, I came to know every mile of road and railway. I loved driving, especially then when the roads were emptier than they are now and the M23 didn't exist. As captain, I'd graduated from my red Borgward to the pale blue SS Jaguar which I judged a fitting conveyance; I was, after all, twenty-four years old.

I have warm memories of arriving promptly at the Hove ground at 10.40am on a match day, with a wave to the gatekeeper, and a quick word to some of the members trundling in with their wicker lunch baskets before I headed straight to the pitch for a look, a quick prod and a chat with the groundsman. From there I would walk on to the pavilion, newly spruced with rails and woodwork in Sussex blue, and drop in to see the club secretary, Col. Grimston, in his office. He was responsible for the whole operation of the club, with a large staff, a bunch of young, fractious cricketers to keep in order, and a pile of paperwork in the office, while I ran the games.

Already turning over the options in my mind, I would make my way up to the captain's dressing room and bathroom, a smart little suite on the top of the stand on the second floor. Since being captain at Radley and Cambridge, I'd always enjoyed the dilemmas posed by the toss. Making the right decision, I'd learned, called for a knowledge of meteorology, human psychology, horticulture and historical precedent, as well as a true gambler's nerve. I never saw any point in asking the rest of the side what to do – especially at Hove. The bowlers said we should bat and the batsmen said we should bowl. The pitch before lunch was notorious for its freshness from the persistent sea breeze and maritime dampness before the sun got up to take some of the moisture from it. In the first hour, despite a pale colour and with the sun already bright, every ball would leave a short skid mark, with some movement, which the always consistent Ian Thompson used to relish. When, almost as if on a fixed cue, the marks disappeared, Ian would take his sweater without being asked. Every captain has problems reading a pitch, but I soon learned that they were particularly tricky at this idiosyncratic ground.

**

Having played for the county for three seasons, I already had a good idea of our strengths and weaknesses in the field. The most obvious shortcoming in the team (excluding Alan Oakman) was our poor close catching. I decided to deal with this from the outset and thought I'd keep it simple. I drafted in Alan as consultant. There would be a lot more catching practice preseason and then before play each day. This is pretty much standard practice now, but then it wasn't; and it worked.

Our first Championship game under my captaincy was against Warwickshire at Edgbaston. They had finished fourth the previous year and the bookies wouldn't have rated Sussex's chances at all. Their skipper was M. J. K. Smith and my old university colleague Ossie Wheatley was bowling for them. In a display of perhaps justifiable complacency after a first innings lead, they declared before lunch on the third day, leaving us to make 255 in just under three hours.

Batting at No. 3 as usual, well fired up and with my eye in, I hit 93 in fifty-one minutes. We went on to win by 6 wickets. The old boys listening to John Arlott back in Hove must have been ecstatic, if they hadn't had a heart attack.

When Yorkshire, the reigning champions, arrived at Hove with Illingworth, Trueman and Close on the team, I felt that a new optimism and expectation among the deckchair brigade had replaced the usual resignation.

We batted. I made 96 out of a total of 280 which Yorkshire passed without even losing a wicket; with a dash of hubris they immediately declared. We went back in; I scored 76, when, with my gambler's spirit in charge, I declared, leaving them to make 250 in 155 minutes. This shocked them; they weren't used to seeing Sussex captains trying to win. I was bursting with pride as I watched my team bowl out the best in England for 217. The Sussex fans were almost poleaxed by excitement, while the rest of the cricket world was simply stunned. A few corks popped that evening.

Looking back on my own batting performance for Sussex, it's always Hove I remember best – Hove and Jim Parks. It isn't coincidence that I made more runs and had more productive partnerships with Jim Parks than any other cricketer. Generally, I found that you could have a partner whom you dominated; you took the bowling when you wanted it, probably refused his runs but made him take yours. Or you may have had to deal with the opposite, when you played second fiddle and let him make the running. I did both many times. However, my partnerships with Jim were always on an equal footing, where ascendancy was regularly passed from one to the other. Against subtle spin bowling Jim easily had the edge; against downright fast stuff, I had the advantage. But there was always complete accord; we were both timers of the ball, both quick enough between the wickets, and both sharply attuned to the other's mood and style of play. For me, this had a wider purpose, after I'd come back from the West Indies determined to show the people at home that I had turned the corner in my batting. At the start of the season, Jim Parks and I were both in the running for one thousand runs in May. By 11 May, a 97 and a 76 off Yorkshire took me to 429. I had hooked Fred Trueman and survived, for which he gave me a friendly clap; I also hammered Ray Illingworth off the back foot through the covers.

'My word,' he'd grunted, 'they've taught you a thing or two out there in the West Indies.'

By 18 May I'd reached 721, taking 151 off Glamorgan and 100 off Surrey. But although I was the first to 1,000 that year (including five 100s), I didn't make it in May. Jim didn't quite get there either, but we went out in grand style on the last day of the month with a third-wicket stand of 222 against Surrey at Hove.

By the end of May, we had seen off Glamorgan and Notts and, in a blaze of glory, beat Surrey for the first time since 1947: Dexter 135; Parks 155. By then we'd played seven Championship matches, drawing two and winning the rest. I could scarcely believe it, though I didn't pretend that I hadn't made a difference. However, this put a great deal of pressure on me and the team, and I knew we'd be lucky to keep it up. Meanwhile, the chaps in the deckchairs in Hove didn't know what had hit them, and more supporters were signing up every day to join them. By the end of the season, we had 1,200 new members, and takings at the gate had increased by £2,000 (around £40,000 in today's money).

After this tremendous start to my first season as Sussex skipper, I had to turn my focus on the Test series against the touring South Africans. The first match started at Edgbaston on 9 June. I was now first choice for the No. 3 slot for England, and I played nine innings over the five Tests. Despite the relative weakness of the South African batting, which led to us comfortably winning the first three games, there was nothing wrong with their attack, led by the outstanding Neil Adcock. As a result, we produced, with one exception, a series of low-scoring matches. Although I felt that I never got into my stride, I didn't do too badly with a couple of fifties.

Initially we'd all had to contend with the very suspect action of South African fast bowler, Geoff Griffin. Geoff was a nice chap, but he was a thrower. In the second Test at Lord's he clean bowled me with a ball I simply didn't see; with no sight screen at the pavilion end, it came from the wrong place at the wrong time. However, after he'd taken a hat-trick, he was no-balled for throwing. It was the last Test match he ever played, while we drew the fourth and fifth Tests and won the series.

Back in the county game, after my blazing start, my batting didn't continue in such great style. There were excuses. It was a soggy summer; there were some bad wickets, but I stayed fresh, keen, full of vim and loving my job. I kept up the pressure on my team throughout the season, using all the energy I could muster, racing about the field, encouraging, trying to lead by good example, as we rose from fifteenth out of seventeen to a point where we were making a real bid for the Championship. We played thirty-two Championship matches, winning twelve of them, and finishing in fourth place, the highest position since 1934. In the twenty matches I played in, I made 1,771 runs at an average of 55, and took 33 wickets.

However, towards the end of the season I was beginning to understand just what a tremendously draining process the grind of the county game was – six days of cricket (two three-day games) in almost every week of the season, with virtually no time to rest properly. I began to appreciate that a player like our fastest bowler, Ian Thomson, with an awful lot of work to do, simply couldn't be expected to perform at the peak of his abilities, in pace or technique, week after week; nor could the key batsmen, with the additional psychological pressures they were under.

Having approached the task with unquestioning enthusiasm, I was beginning to ask myself if this really was the best way to deliver attractive and quality cricket. I'd already started thinking of four-day cricket as a better way of achieving that, but as a raw new boy, I didn't think I was in a position to do much to alter things. That privilege and related responsibility were to come twenty-five years later. Nevertheless, although the Test series had left me a little flat and in serious need of a rest, by the end of 1960 I was generally happy.

I took the time for a trip back to see my mum and dad in Italy, where we were able to celebrate a huge improvement in Dad's health. When he and Mum had crossed the Atlantic to follow the MCC tour around the West Indies for the Test series earlier in the year, he'd occupied the time in between with long periods of sun-soaking and gentle aquatic exercise. As a result of this three-month holiday, a cycle of severe bouts of bronchitis from which he'd been suffering for some years was now well and truly broken. I'd been aware for some time that whenever he came up to the lake from Milan, he would take a few days to recover from the pollution in his lungs. And when John and I visited him in Milan, he would always prefer to have any kind of financial discussions in the morning when, he admitted, he was still functioning properly. Now his unhurried sojourn in the tropics had left him visibly rejuvenated and full of beans as he approached his seventieth birthday. I was doubly thrilled that not only had he loved witnessing a watershed in my own cricketing career, he'd also had this tremendous boost to his health.

Chapter Seven

A-TOUR TO INDIA

I was frankly relieved that there was no tour in the winter of 1960/61. This offered a welcome respite from a continuous round of cricket after the 58/59 tour in the Antipodes followed by the 59/60 Test series in the Caribbean. And it came after a very full-on year captaining Sussex when I'd given everything I had to the job. Even the dry and undemonstrative writers of Wisden had acknowledged my efforts there, naming me one of their five cricketers of the year. Robin Marlar, in a not entirely unbiased tribute he was asked to write, compared by bowling, with considerable flattery, to that of the great Australian, Keith Miller. With a dash of purple prose for which he later became known in the pages of *The Sunday Times*, he described it as 'speed unleashed in a final orgy of muscular activity'.

This hiatus also gave Susan and me the longest period that we'd been able to spend together since voicing our vows before the Vicar of Bray eighteen months previously. No baby had yet appeared, leaving us relatively free of commitments, except to each other. Nevertheless, we were both working. I was back in Houndsditch, labouring in the engine room of C E Heath insurance brokers, and Susan was making the most of a successful modelling career. It gave us the time to renew friendships that had suffered from my almost permanent absences. It also allowed me to indulge my other sporting passion, with some regular golf at Sunningdale.

The air of change that was already palpable in Britain at that time was heightened by other major changes in the wider world. In America, John Kennedy was voted in to be the first young, post-war president, generating excitement and optimism that could even be felt in London. Susan and I sensed that we were lucky to be young and alive and together. I had a year full of challenges to look forward to, with the possibility of taking my county to the top of the Championship, and the Australians coming over to give us a chance to grab back the Ashes.

However, during a day at the races that autumn, I was befriended by a man called David Hough, who turned out, regrettably, to be a factor in letting loose the latent gambler in me. I didn't encourage him particularly, but he stuck to me; I don't believe he saw me as a source of funds or as a potential mark for a con, but he was often at the races when I was, and always wanted to hang around and chat. Generally, I liked going to the outer-London tracks which were easy to get to: Hurst Park, Sandown, Kempton, Ascot – even the odd Monday evening at the famously trappy Frying Pan in Alexandra Park.

At that stage I would have described myself as a small-time punter; I enjoyed the frisson of a bet that was no more than a painless flutter. But I was ready to crank up the tension a bit and when David told me that he picked up a few useful tips from some of the northern stables, near where he came from, I thought that might give me a bit of the edge a gambler needs. He started passing on a few tips – some won, some didn't, but I was in a frame of mind where I was prepared to believe he was helping. I hadn't known him long when he told me about a two-year-old, Fine Yield, entered in a minor race on one of the northern tracks. I was ready by then to have a bigger bet than usual but I didn't have an account with any of the big London bookmakers. I thought the only way I could get the money on was to seek out an on-course bookie at the main meeting of the day in Newmarket. I had to drive there with my fifty quid in cash to get it on at the nerve-tingling price of 20/1. I was even more excited when just before the off, it had shortened to favourite.

And it won; I took a thousand quid off a grumpy-looking bookie, ran to the car with my pockets bulging, jumped in, locked the doors and raced back to London in a state of high glee. Susan wasn't so happy; she didn't think I needed that kind of encouragement. But it was inevitable that this big win – a thousand pounds was a very useful sum in 1961 – got me more heavily hooked on betting. I'm sorry to say that I didn't heed Susan's fears and began to spend more time at home with my nose in the form book.

In the meantime, with no cricket to play for a few months, I took advantage of the free time to take in a season's jump racing. I always preferred jumping to the flat; it attracted a more enjoyable set of people. For one thing, you didn't have to be super-rich to owner a steeplechaser; a horse with sporting chance could be bought for as little as a thousand pounds in those days – less if you knew where to look. There was a more genuinely amateurish air to the sport as a result and I relished the atmosphere and excitement of it all. The Old Bath Road to Newbury soon became a regular run.

**

In early 1961, the world's eyes were on the new US president, John F. Kennedy. The inauguration of the first young, post-war American leader seemed to herald great feelings of hope around the Western world and the start of a new phase of history. This sense of optimism was severely shaken a few months into Kennedy's presidency when he ordered an invasion force to take back control of Cuba from the revolutionary leader, Fidel Castro. This ended in a humiliating disaster at the Bay of Pigs and prepared the ground for far more alarming problems down the line.

Meanwhile the cricket world's focus was on an exciting series that was being played between the West Indies and their Australian hosts. Although the Australians won the series 3-1, there was some very attractive cricket being played. This had the effect of putting future pressure on England to produce a colourful and lively performance when the Australians arrived in England that summer.

The pressure was on me, too, as it was being suggested by some of the English press that the most likely source of attractive, exciting cricket was me. I didn't object; by that point, I'd formed the view that playing cricket was as much for the enjoyment of the spectators as anything else. During the course of my career, this attitude didn't always work for me, but in some areas, specifically limited-over cricket – when it was finally allowed to flourish – the notion that cricket had to deliver as a spectator sport rather than a serious game of chivalry that dare not break any of its scared codes was ultimately seen to be vital for the future health of the game.

* *

For me, 1961 was dominated by the touring Australians. Naturally I was pursuing my ambitions for the Sussex team, and I was pleased to see that the changes I'd introduced in my first season as skipper were now seen as normal. However, my own contribution in the early part of the season, before the Australians arrived, was regularly hampered by chronic knee trouble. I'd played only five matches for Sussex before the first Test opened at Edgbaston on 8 June.

I was, not surprisingly, feeling a lot more confident about playing against the Australians than I had been in my first disastrous tour in 58/59. Although I hadn't achieved anything spectacular against the South Africans, the previous year's success with Sussex – and my own batting for them – had built my confidence. My recurring knee trouble seemed under control, and I looked forward to the series. Richie Benaud, although undoubtedly one of the finest of cricket captains, was bringing over a band of Australians who were not particularly outstanding; England weren't without a chance of regaining the Ashes from them.

On the first gloomy day in the Birmingham ground, I went in to bat with a scoreboard showing 36 for 1. I whacked a 4 off Alan Davidson, but got caught off him soon afterwards, leaving the wicket with just ten runs to my name. I was interested to see how Benaud, who was suffering from an intermittent injury to his shoulder, deployed his bowlers, and his own bowling. I was beginning to understand what a masterful skipper he was. They bowled us out for 195. When they came in, we had our first sight of Bill Lawry, who was to become one of Australia's most consistent batsmen over the next decade. We couldn't make much of a dent in the Australian innings and Benaud was able to declare at 596 for 9, leaving us with a shortfall of 321. I arrived at the wicket for the second time at 93 for 1, with a long hill to climb. Benaud put himself on to bowl against me, but Raman Subba Row was smart; he kept me down the other end while I found my feet. By close of play at 106 for 1, Benaud had appealed against me twice and I'd been dropped by Mackay.

The next morning was brighter, and I went out with a bit of a bounce in my stride. I took a couple of fours off Richie on my way to making 29 runs in twenty-nine minutes. Subba Row then Cowdrey were both seen off at 239 for 3 when Ken Barrington joined me after lunch.

By 3pm, I'd completed my first-ever 100 against Australia with my seventeenth four. We had caught up with their score by 3.45, which at least secured a draw; we couldn't declare because we simply wouldn't have had time to bowl the other side out. After tea, at eighteen runs ahead, I thought I could take a few risks and let it rip. In the last quarter of an hour of my innings, I scored 32 more, giving me 180 on the board with one over to go.

Richie put on Bobby Simpson, an occasional leg-spinner. I was greedy for 200 – quite possible with a six or two, or three. When I was stumped halfway down the pitch, it was Mike Smith's turn to come in and face the rest of the over. He didn't look pleased.

I wasn't unhappy as I walked off, if a little embarrassed at the manner of my dismissal. But at least I had nullified some of the criticism I'd earned on the 58/59 tour. But I made sure I made myself scarce when Mike Smith came back to the dressing room.

In the Lord's Test, Colin Cowdrey won the toss on a dry, if cloudy, morning, and confidently decided to bat. He was a lot less confident after a few overs, when it was clear that there was something very wrong with the pitch – a manifestation of a regular mystery at Lord's. There was an elusive ridge in the wicket about which the groundsmen could do nothing and which no one could explain. It was always there, but on some occasions, like this one, more so than on others. Bowlers from the pavilion end enjoyed a double advantage. To a ball just short of a length, it gave extra bounce; a little further up and it could keep low. There was an additional disadvantage for a right-hand bat, who would already be standing a couple of inches on the low side, due to the inherent slope of the ground, a fall of nine feet overall.

Batting in these circumstances could be hellishly unpredictable, and when I went in, I took the view that I must take the runs when I saw them. As a result, I was quickly out for 27. However, I did bowl quite effectively towards the pavilion, without the advantage of the ridge. With a bit of luck, I got Lawry out, but not before he'd made 130 and had effectively won the match for Australia.

I didn't do much to help in England's only victory over the Australians at Headingley, but I did take six wickets at Old Trafford, and made 76 in eighty-four minutes in a run chase that looked as if it might give us a win, instead of the expected draw. Perversely, my efforts prompted Richie into calling a drinks break so that he could give his team a quick pep talk, then put himself on to bowl, despite the sharp pain this caused his shoulder. He admitted afterwards that throughout the match, before each session and during every break in the dressing room, he was having treatment from Dr Bass, the Arsenal doctor who had travelled up to Manchester expressly to do the job. Bowling round the wicket – unusual for a leg-spinner in those days – Richie proceeded to take five wickets for 12 runs in 25 balls. That was that, and Australia won. I had to give Richie the credit he was due for a great tactical manoeuvre by a superb captain. But there was one unpublicised, less laudable incident in that game instigated by the often irascible chairman of selectors, Walter Robins.

Robbie, as he was familiarly known, had found a drinking companion at lunch one day and had not seen any of the afternoon's cricket as England were slowly but surely batting their way towards an invincible position. The ever-reliable Ken Barrington had doggedly made his way past 50 and was not out at the tea interval. Robbie, taking notice now, had become exasperated at England's slow progress. He stormed into the dressing room to shout at Barrington, telling him to 'Get a bloody move on!' After that, and as a result, wickets fell quickly, offering Australia a squeak of a chance they should never have had.

The final, drawn Test at the Oval left them 2-1 up in the series, and as I watched the Australians depart, my feelings generally were deflated. Naturally

I was pleased with my big score in the first Test, and a decent innings at Old Trafford. Nevertheless, I'd learned something from their visit by closely following Richie Benaud's handling of his team. I concluded that it was his leadership of a moderate squad – on paper, weaker than ours – that ultimately won the series for them. It wasn't so much the minutiae of his captaincy on the field, but his aura of assurance and calm which was impressive. Naturally this is more easily achieved in a winning team, but by no means every captain has this talent. In the modern era, Eoin Morgan, captaining the World Cup-winning team, has it. I know Joe Root admires him, and perhaps, in time, he will emulate him.

**

I didn't have many answers for those who were looking at Sussex's performance as the season drew to a close. After the great turnaround of 1960, when supporters had even begun to talk breathlessly about the possibility of winning the Championship, we simply hadn't sustained our progress. Of the thirty-two games we'd played, we'd won eleven, lost ten and drawn eleven – one win fewer and four more defeats than the previous year. This saw us fall from fourth to eighth place, which was still a lot higher than where we'd been before I took over as captain. Wisden pointed out that the main reason for the slide was my own lack of form. Only twice had I scored over 50 for the county, and I made 1,200 runs less for them than in 1960. They were kind enough to attribute this to the knee problem. At the same time, Alan Oakman had scored more than 2,000 runs, backed up by Don Smith, Jim Parks, Richard Langridge and Ken Suttle, while Ian Thomson took at least 100 wickets for the ninth successive season. Despite Thomson's performance, overall, it was our bowling that seemed to be our weakness, while our catching had improved. In batting we'd made 28.16 runs per wicket, third in the Championship. Our bowling average of 28.62 runs per wicket placed us fourteenth out of seventeen. I had to admit that I hadn't been charging around the field, chivvying everyone, or focussing as sharply as I had in my first year. I was realising that it took a lot out of a man – physically and mentally – to keep up that pace for six months at a time.

In the meantime, as the domestic season wound down, the MCC were preparing for a winter tour to Asia – taking in India, Pakistan and Ceylon (now Sri Lanka). In early September I was rung by Gubby Allen – effectively chief selector – who told me that I was to take on the tour captaincy. I was told that neither of the former captains, Peter May nor Colin Cowdrey, wanted to go on what looked as if it would be a gruelling tour, with eight Tests, and over twenty first-class games spread over nearly five months. Several other key players had also said they wouldn't go: Subba Row, Edrich, Flavell, Trueman, Close and Statham, which meant that, in reality, we would be fielding an 'A' XI. In my view, the MCC were showing a risky lack of resolve by allowing leading players to cry off international games simply because it didn't suit their personal agenda. (This was a selectors' problem for many years, which I made an effort to tackle when I was made chairman of England thirty years later.) Back then, while I was inclined to deplore this lack of commitment on the part of these senior players, I was aware that it was giving me the chance to captain the tour. Ideally, I would have liked to have made my captain's debut in a home series, with a full complement of players. But having played in the Antipodes and the Caribbean, I was keen to travel to India too. Of course, I said 'Yes, please' to the captaincy.

Some commentators had reservations, though. There were still those who thought I was a flash in the pan, and I was, after all, only twenty-six. On the plus side, as captain of Radley, Cambridge and Sussex I'd had a good record. The university match had been won at Lord's, and Sussex had raced up to fourth place in the table in my first season as skipper. Nevertheless when, after only two years of captaining a county side, I was asked to lead the MCC in India and Pakistan, I couldn't help thinking it was a little premature.

Before we left, I made a promise to the press. 'I'm determined to aim at positive cricket and won't be put off by fear of being beaten. In the Tests I might sacrifice a batsman for an extra bowler – risky perhaps, but I shall insist on attack to achieve results; the last thing I want is a succession of stalemates.'

**

We landed in Lahore, Pakistan, on 8 October. It was my first visit to the Indian subcontinent, and as soon as we'd landed I was enthralled by what I found: the vivid colours, the odours and the cacophony of the place. We were billeted in the less than luxurious Airport Hotel, as it turned out, one of the few hotels we stayed in, and just about the best. While we acclimatised I went exploring in the crammed and bustling streets of the city. I was struck forcefully by the shocking poverty that I was to find frequently all over India and Pakistan. You'd have to be a hard man to ignore this kind of deprivation. At the same time, I discovered that what the people lacked in modern facilities and diet, they made up for in their enthusiasm not only for the game of cricket but for life in general despite their poverty. This was a time when interest in cricket was burgeoning all over the subcontinent, now that there were emerging national stars. I soon learned that the Indians enjoyed cricket for the same esoteric reasons as the British, as well as for their long cultural association with it through the British presence in India for the past two hundred years. I was impressed by the great pride they took in their local players and it was exhilarating to play in front of such vast enthusiastic crowds. By the end of the tour, we'd been watched by some two million spectators.

The first of the three Tests we were to play against Pakistan started on 21 October in Lahore. In advance of my first match as skipper, I took the initiative to do a little subtle preparation by taking all the opposition management out to dinner beforehand and making sure their glasses were topped up. I wanted to pre-empt the recurring problem of local umpires at the matches displaying any national bias. They took it on board.

**

I lost the toss for the first of seven times out of eight in the Tests we played. Naturally the Pakistan captain, Imtiaz Ahmed, put his team in to bat first. Before the wicket had deteriorated into the customary wispy concrete slab it would be after a day or so, they scored a solid 387 for 9 and declared. We replied with 380 all out (after I'd hit my wicket for 20). In the second innings, on an increasingly wearing pitch, they fell apart. I bowled their captain for 12 – a good move, one captain versus the other – and we bowled them all out for 200. In our second innings, our opener, seasoned campaigner Peter Richardson, got us going with a 48, while I went in at No. 5 and added 66. We reached 209 for 5, winning my first Test as captain by five wickets. As it turned out, it was the only Test match we won on the tour. The umpiring had been completely fair – perhaps as a result of my wining and dining the management – but this was a rare moment of umpiring parity among all the matches over the months that followed.

However, we weren't scheduled to complete the Pakistan three-match series straight away because, somewhat carelessly, the Indian team were booked to tour in the West Indies from February to April. After Lahore, we had to head south for the first of our five Test matches against India that would be played between early November and mid-January. We travelled first to Mumbai (then Bombay) to play the first Test. This was the start of a hectic timetable, crisscrossing India with a series of first-class games to be squeezed in between the Tests. The Indians were living up to their reputation for hospitality but large formal gatherings with lengthy speeches were the norm, which could be hard to take after long days in the field under the Indian sun. Personally, as captain, I had a role to play at these gatherings, giving speeches and shaking hands with dozens of local dignitaries, all of which I enjoyed well enough, but I was conscious that some of the players were finding it a strain. Some were suffering from intermittent gastric troubles from the curries and other unfamiliar cuisine, as well as from the unaccustomed climate and a lack of facilities for dealing with it.

Travelling by road and staying in somewhat rudimentary guest houses was exhausting, although our hosts did their best to look after us, often in the most primitive conditions. On one occasion we arrived tired out from a long day's travel and were billeted in a charming but basic bungalow; we sat down to dinner either side of a narrow trestle table, all ravenously hungry. Our host appeared and bowed with a namaste, obviously respectful of the cream of English cricket.

'You are very welcome,' he said gravely, 'and soon we will serve you a nice omelette and you will all be very happy.' He bowed again and left. A while later, a serving wallah appeared and with great deference, placed a plate with a single omelette on it in front of one of the party, before scooting off to get the next – or so we thought. There was a long hiatus before anything else appeared; we could all hear each other's stomachs rumbling, and as with any gathering of fit, hungry men, there was a sense of mutiny in the air. Feeling responsible for my team, with my military officer's training to settle the men first, I thought I'd better seek out the chef to move things on a little. I found my way behind the scenes to where the food was being cooked in a bamboo lean-to. A single small chap, looking anxious, was leaning over a tiny coal brazier with a frying pan, cooking the omelettes one by one. If he'd had another frying pan, I'd have cooked a few myself. In the end, they all arrived and were quite delicious. We thanked our hosts with real feeling, albeit with unspoken reservations.

**

We played three Tests before Christmas, in Bombay, Kanpur (in Uttar Pradesh) and Delhi – where I took some time off to look around. I found a great rackety city of extremes of grandeur and squalor, and a fascinating contrast between the great Mughal buildings of the Jama Masjid and the Red Fort, and Edwin

Lutyens' grandiose British government buildings of the 1920s and 1930s.

I was also entertained by some of the Indian players, including the Indian skipper, Nari Contractor, a brave and stylish left-handed bat who always opened for his side. Brave because famously, three years before when he was playing against England at Lord's and facing Brian Statham, he was hit very hard on the chest. Although he batted on and made 81 runs, it was discovered afterwards that he had broken two ribs, and he even went on to bat a second innings in plaster. Keith Miller, who was commentating for the Australian media, declared that Contractor deserved a Victoria Cross for his bravery.

In this series he was trying to encourage his team to play a more attacking game of cricket, and to some extent he succeeded. He didn't have a particularly great hand to play in his team, but he had shrewd judgement, helped, it should be said, by winning four out of five tosses in the series.

Another of the Indian players who showed me something of local life was my own Sussex colleague, Mansoor 'Tiger' Pataudi. Tiger was, in fact, an Indian Nawab, titular ruler of Pataudi and Bhopal, and son of the only man to have played Test cricket for both England and India. He was an extraordinary cricketer, a prodigy who had broken all batting records at Winchester College and debuted for Sussex the same year that I did, when he was just sixteen. He was also the first Indian captain of the Oxford XI. A sophisticated, witty and handsome man, he had a characteristic cool calmness about him, never displaying any kind of doubt or anxiety. He'd been in a nasty car accident in Hove earlier in 1961, which had resulted in his losing most of the sight in one of his eyes. It was generally thought that he would never play again. Determined and brave as he was, he went straight back into the nets and somehow managed to train his single good eye to function without binocular vision, to the extent that he was selected, aged just twenty, to play for India against England in the last three Test matches of our tour.

**

After Christmas and before the fourth Test had been played, I got an unpleasant shock in a telegram from Ladbrokes, the London bookmakers. For convenience, before I'd left England for Pakistan, I'd opened an account with Ladbrokes, which I held jointly with David Hough so that he could get bets on for me while I was away on tour. They were writing to tell me that the account was £1,000 in debit. Furious at David, and at myself for trusting him, I replied by return. 'Please close this account. I will settle on my return.'

After that, I had no contact with David Hough, until forty years later when, out of the blue, I received a cheque from him for £2,400. With it was a note from him, saying that he'd always felt bad about what he'd done, but until now he'd never had funds to repay me. With forty years of inflation, his payment was worth a fraction of what he'd taken from me, but I appreciated the gesture, and a few months later, when I was hosting a lunch for friends at Ascot racecourse, I asked him to join us. He declined the invitation; his arthritis wouldn't allow him to travel from Lancashire. He mentioned, though, that he had become a member of the prestigious Lytham St Anne's Golf Club, which suggested that he had now managed to overcome his gambling habit, as, indeed, had I.

* *

In the last match in Madras (now Chennai), capital of Tamil Nadu, in front of a vast, cheering crowd, Pataudi produced a dashing performance, taking only two and a half hours to score his debut Test century. In the first hour after lunch he and Contractor added 82, their stand in all producing 104 in ninety-five minutes. Pataudi's 103 also included sixteen fours. This led to India winning by 128 runs, which won them the series 2-0.

I've always cherished a story of a keen fan of Pataudi's asking him when he had decided, despite the damage to his eye, that he could play Test cricket for India. He had replied, no doubt, with a laconic shrug of the shoulder: 'When I saw the England bowling line-up.'

It was probably a good thing that the tour schedule was so crowded that it left little time for the players to dwell on wives and girlfriends back in England, though some were more homesick than others. Christmas Day, for instance, was far from being a happy celebration with the family; it was spent travelling from Cuttack to Calcutta where we started a new match on Boxing Day. If we wanted entertainment, we usually had to make it ourselves. On Saturday nights we traditionally held a drinks party where our two fast bowlers would often get out of hand.

One evening we had been billeted in three separate houses in a small village compound. It was Barry Knight's idea that we should dress for dinner and Tony Lock, Surrey's celebrated left-arm spinner, decided to seat himself at the head of the table. He immediately started issuing orders like a Maharajah, appointing Barry as his official food taster. The Essex man took on the role with enthusiasm. When the first course arrived, he helped himself to a mouthful, grimaced extravagantly and flung the bowl out of the window, to the obvious alarm of the unfortunate food-wallah. Behaviour soon deteriorated, with four hefty cricketers bearing our self-appointed Maharajah, sitting cross-legged on a bed, through the streets of the village. To add authenticity, he started scattering largesse, in the form of low denomination coins, among the gathering of bemused villagers who had come to watch.

Our procession wound its way into one of the other houses, with the Maharaja bellowing his demands: 'Bring on the Nautch Girls!' – the Indian equivalent of Japanese geisha girls. Inevitably, the least likely candidate for the job – jug-eared redhead, Robert Barber – was chosen and had all his clothes pulled off, was painted with gaudy make-up like a pantomime dame and presented to the astonished Surrey spinner, who haughtily – and sensibly – decreed that was enough role-playing for one night.

**

I would have been disappointed if on my first visit to India, I hadn't encountered a genuine Maharaja. We got close to it when we met the Maharajkumar of Vizianagram. The younger brother of the Maharaja, he had set himself up in another of the family's estates near Benares and, known by everyone as 'Vizzy', he could not have been more authentic, or more welcoming.

He was, for one thing, a huge cricket aficionado. He was also absurdly rich, and a very generous patron of the game in his own state and across India. He had played cricket as a schoolboy in England and in his twenties he had harboured strong but entirely unrealistic ambitions to play the game at the highest level possible. He had a ground created within the precincts of his palace and had paid some top cricketers from around the world to play there.

In 1932 Vizzy bankrolled the Indian tour of England. Four years later his investment paid off and he was named captain for the second England trip. It was an embarrassing disaster. He fell out with a lot of players and batted hopelessly. He did reappear briefly on the Test scene as a guest commentator for the BBC during the Indian tour of England in 1959.

As captain of England, I was treated as a very honoured guest and was even presented with an almost lavish gift of a tiger skin, complete with a fearsome head, though somewhat marred by missing teeth and a few patches of mange. I accepted it gratefully, of course, and when it reached our home in London it soon became a favourite playground for our recently arrived son, Thomas.

**

The Indian team set off almost immediately for their tour of the West Indies, led by Nari Contractor. They won a couple of the tour games but lost the Test series unequivocally by 0 games to 5.

I was saddened by one ugly incident in an Indian tour match against Barbados when Nari was hit viciously on the head by a bouncing bomb of a ball hurled by Charlie Griffith. Wisden described the incident: 'Contractor did not duck into the ball. He got behind it to play at it. He probably wanted to fend it away towards short leg, but could not judge the height to which it would fly, bent back from the waist in a desperate, split-second attempt to avoid it and was hit just above the right ear.'

He slumped to his haunches, clutching his head. Within a minute he had started bleeding from his nose and ears and was helped from the middle by Ghulam Ahmed, the Indians' manager. In the pavilion, the bleeding didn't stop and he was rushed to hospital, where he started vomiting badly and losing movement on his left side. That evening Ahmed gave permission for an emergency operation to be carried out. In the course of the surgery that followed Nari lost a lot of blood and several players – including the West Indian captain, Frank Worrell – donated theirs to help him.

Nari was too injured to play in the fourth Test, and, indeed, although he recovered enough to carry on playing first-class cricket, he was never selected for a Test match again – a harsh blow to Indian cricket. I met up with him again when he and his wife were passing through London on their way back from the Caribbean. They dropped into our flat in Ebury Street and we had dinner together. An impressive and dignified man, he became a leading figure in the coaching of Indian cricketers. We met again half a century later to reminisce when I'd been invited from London and he came up from Mumbai for a fiftieth anniversary of the 61/62 series in Kolkata in 2012.

Nari's place on the 1962 West Indies tour was taken by his vice-captain, Tiger Pataudi, who at the age of twenty-one became the youngest-ever captain in Test cricket. Placing himself in the middle order, he managed only two forties in his six remaining innings as India were pounded in the next two Tests.

* *

The England team stayed on in the subcontinent and continued their tour with a few more first-class games in obscure corners of India before heading back up to Pakistan for the two Tests we had yet to play there to complete our three-match series. The first of them was in Dhaka, the old Mughal capital of Bengal in the middle of the flood plain of the Buriganga River in East Pakistan (now Bangladesh). The pitch was like rolled plasticine; nothing bounced higher than a few inches. At one stage in the game, we were reduced to trying 'Spedigue Droppers' – a high, looping delivery designed to come down directly on top of the bails – a technique supposed to have been perfected by an otherwise unheard of Mr Spedigue. This ended in an irritating draw; we had dominated the game, and were left needing just 171 to win, but could only manage 38 for no wicket in the time left. In early February we moved on for the final Test in Karachi, where we had another frustrating result. I lost the toss yet again, and Pakistan opened; and they were all out for 253, with my taking two of their wickets. Our first innings went well, and I made my highest-ever Test score of 205, out of a total of 503. The Pakistanis upped their game for their second innings, making 404 for 8 (of which I took three), leaving us no time to come back, which led to another draw.

At least we had clinched the series, the only time, incredibly, that an England team has ever done so in Pakistan. The tail end of our excursion to the subcontinent was a very enjoyable mini-tour of Ceylon, now Sri Lanka. We played a two-day game against the Ceylon Cricket Association in Colombo, another two-day game against Central Provinces in Kandy, and, back in Colombo, a final three-day first-class match against All Ceylon, which we won and where I took 4 wickets in their first innings and five in the second – guaranteed to provide happy memories. As a result, my bowling received its finest accolade, with a headline in the *Ceylon Daily News*: 'Not since Harold Larwood!' The standard of cricket in this small country was remarkably high, while the Sinhalese were not only charming and hospitable, but also committed and well-informed cricket fans. In the short time we were there, I was staggered by the lushness and beauty of the island, and the peculiar little corners of Englishness that still survived. Playing golf at six thousand feet in Nuwara Eliya, where the ball flew in the thin air, I was amused that the houses in the former tea planters' hill station looked like the Edwardian mock-Tudor villas of a Surrey town.

As we finally flew back to England, I couldn't say I was sorry the tour was over, and the rest of the team were thrilled to be going home. It had been a marathon of a tour, with thousands of miles travelled in ancient, lumbering trains and buses rattling over rutted and potholed roads, staying in accommodation that Mowgli might have recognised. We had been away for 136 days, including eighty-two days of cricket. It had been a gruelling schedule, as Peter May and the other refuseniks had guessed it would be.

I didn't feel that I was returning with my tail between my legs, but I did have to deal with the raw fact that notwithstanding our unique win over Pakistan, India had defeated England for the first time in history. India didn't feel as triumphant as they might have done, pointing out a little peevishly that they had never faced a full-strength England side. They were understandably resentful that some of England's star players chose to turn down the trip. Wisden in their summary did concede that there were extenuating factors behind the poor result of the first tour I had captained, not least my bad luck with the toss. At Calcutta and Madras the pitches favoured spin increasingly as the matches progressed and losing the toss had been a big handicap. India, to their credit, took their chances well, but the results might have been very different if England had batted first.

Wisden also noted – and I felt this was partly aimed at me – that not many batsmen had been prepared to take chances and despite my promises, a good deal of negative cricket resulted. Even in the games outside the Tests, the MCC players had found most of the pitches too lifeless to force many results in the fifteen hours allotted for each game.

Whatever the pundits said, I felt that, for what was in effect an 'A' team tour, we hadn't done badly, and almost all of the new caps went on to become important members of England sides over the next decade. Only G. Millman and the medium-paced bowler, D. R. Smith missed out. This clearly demonstrated the value of 'A' tours, which I insisted on sending out regularly later, in my administrative career.

Chapter Eight

ASHES IN AUSTRALIA

W e landed at Heathrow on 20 February to be greeted by a throng of families and press. It was wonderful to see Susan again after five months, looking as beautiful as ever, and very pregnant, with the baby due in early March. I was looking forward to fatherhood although I had only a vague notion of what it might entail. Susan was excited, but understandably nervous, like nearly all first-time mothers. I tried to appreciate what this might be like, but generally the male isn't wired to cope with it.

Our first child, Thomas, arrived on 10 March 1962, at St Bartholomew's Hospital by Smithfield Market. Susan was thrilled but exhausted. At home she'd prepared a room, filled with baby accoutrements and gifts from doting grandparents. The lad showed his appreciation by yelling enthusiastically every evening when he was put down in his smart new cot.

Resolutely we pretended we couldn't hear him but like any new parents we were full of qualms and misgivings about whether we were doing the right thing. Of course, in time, like most babies, he did quieten down and we were able to enjoy him. One morning, quite early on, I was allowed out alone with Thomas in his smart pram. As I was thoughtfully pushing him along beside the Royal Hospital gardens, I noticed other people – women mostly – looking dubiously at my child. I wondered what they thought was wrong with him, until one of them kindly told me I had put him into the pram the wrong way round, with his head at the pushing end, not under the canopy. These things, I told myself ruefully, just aren't instinctive in a man.

Apart from the unexpected emotions and excitement of suddenly being responsible for another, completely helpless member of the human race, I found that after the long Indian tour, it took me some time to reacclimatise. This had to be achieved while dealing with the press reaction to the tour – in the main negative – which I didn't enjoy. The Pakistanis were due in England for a full five-match series in the summer, and more significantly, at the end of the year, an England squad was due to head off for Australia.

I was by no means sure that I was a shoo-in as captain either for the Pakistan series, or the winter tour. This was made clear to me by Walter Robins, now chairman of selectors, in a speech he gave to the press in early April.

'We want a captain – above everything else a leader,' he said, 'who must answer every bid or challenge Australia make.'

Implicit in this was the view that I hadn't made my case for continuing captaincy while I'd been in India. I wasn't unaware of occasional shortcomings on that tour, but I also believed that any of the other possible contenders for the job would have had just the same difficulties and would have dealt with them in the same way that I had. And, I was prepared to admit, I had learned a hell of a lot. I realised that I was never going to be the warm, one-of-the-boys kind of leader that some seemed to think appropriate, but I felt – and could cite my opening success at Sussex – that I was quite capable of leading by example, and of creating winning strategies and mindsets. Meanwhile, although I would have liked very much to skipper the Australian tour, there were obvious names in contention.

Robins, along with the other selectors, Doug Insole, Alec Bedser and Willie Watson, were going to look long and hard at the likely candidates for captaincy in Australia. I would have the advantage of leading the forthcoming Test series against Pakistan. This, though, turned out not to be a sound basis for that kind of assessment; it was hopelessly one-sided, with a weak Pakistan team generally offering little resistance. I skippered the first two Tests, winning them by an innings and nine wickets respectively; however, in the second Test, at Lord's, I was guilty of what was perceived as a glaring faux pas. We had bowled the other side out for just over 100 in their first innings, without Tony Lock getting a bowl, then we'd run up a total of 370 in our own. In their second innings, Pakistan were 77 for 4 when a noisy group of English spectators started chanting: 'Put Locky on! Put Locky on!'

I understood, and played up to them a little, wheeling my left arm and getting a few cheers. I nodded cheerfully and threw the ball to the great Surrey spinner. I was less cheerful a few minutes later when a simple catch to short leg was dropped in Tony Lock's first over. With this simple boost to their morale, the two current batsmen, Javed Burki and Nasimul Ghani, staged a dramatic counter-attack, whacking Lock all over the place. As soon as this started to happen, I had to think about taking him off, but this was difficult; after all, Tony Lock was a senior, highly respected, almost revered bowler; I couldn't simply ask him to come off after a couple of overs. There was always the hope that he would start doing his magic any moment. But they had their eye in and their tails up, and soon settled down to take 78 runs off him in 14 overs. At the end of play, as Burki and Ghani walked off, with scores of 101 each, I was so

Above: An early photograph with brother John, and again at Radley College in 1949.

Left: Cambridge colours at Scarborough, 1956.

Below right: Army photograph.

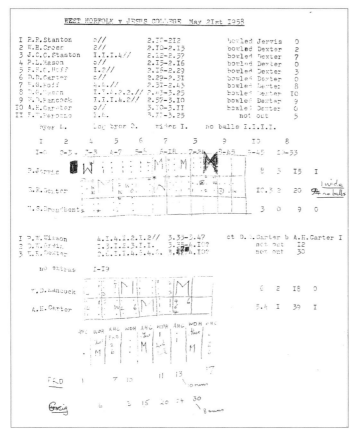

Above: Jesus College match scorecard, 1958. Ted took 9 for 20. All bowled.

Right: Cricket or golf?

Below: Rest and relaxation in Barbados, 1959.

Below right: With Jim Parks at Hove, 1961.

Clockwise: Susan during her World Modelling Tour in 1962.

Clockwise: Brothers, John and Edward; Susan; the happy couple; the whole family; with the bridesmaids and John.

Above: Boys and girls at Hove 1961. The Sussex cricket team.

Below left: England's best, Dexter and Barrington.

Below right: Huge crowds in India, 1961.

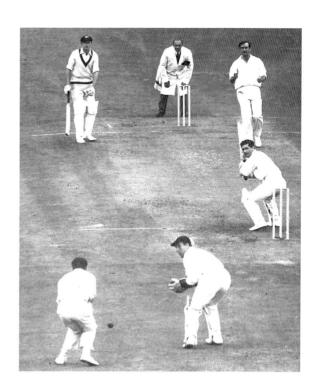

England v Australia at Edgbaston, 1961.

Above left: Hooking Sobers out of the ground, in the MCC v South Australia State Match in Adelaide, 1962.

Above right: Back foot drive, Adelaide, 1962.

Below: Dennis Lillee with Ted after hitting him on the head during a photoshoot which became too realistic.

Knock-out Cup Final, 1963 at Lord's Sussex v Worcester.

preoccupied and cursing myself for my own stupidity in letting them off the hook, that I forgot to clap them. It was careless of me, especially as skipper, but it was certainly not a deliberate slight to the batsmen.

The chairman, Walter Robins, thought otherwise. As soon as I was inside the pavilion he gave me a resounding bollocking for being 'unsportsmanlike'. He had clearly not taken it well, and as a result named Colin Cowdrey as captain for the next Test at Headingley. However, although I was able to make my mark in this match by taking 4 wickets for 10 in nine overs, Cowdrey might still have been named for the fourth or fifth Tests had he not developed a kidney complaint which kept him out of both of them. I was named captain for them, and, in the end, we won the series 4-0 with one match drawn. I felt I'd done more than enough to prove my worth, averaging 87 with the bat, including 172 in the fourth Test, but Robins would still make no firm pronouncement about the winter tour.

Colin Cowdrey still wasn't fit for his previously announced captaincy in the Gentlemen v. Players match, due to start at Lord's on 1 July. This high-profile match was also being viewed by the selectors as a trial for the Australian tour captaincy; I skippered the Gents in Cowdrey's place in what was the last ever staging of the match at Lord's.

The scrapping of this annual fixture which had been played since 1806 was a significant event in the final removal of the amateur status in first-class and Test cricket. By the late 1950s the distinction between amateurs and professionals had lost credibility and amateurs of sufficient ability were no longer presenting themselves in any numbers. The splitting of players into two distinct groups had been a fundamental part of the game since its inception up to the Second World War. In its simplest form, professionals were paid, while amateurs (referred to as 'gentlemen') were not. This, like the commissioning of army officers, was a hangover from a British class system that was becoming less relevant. Almost all amateurs were public school or at least upper middle class; the professionals were generally working class. Even then there were professionals who made a living from the game and those who were professional because they could not afford to be amateurs. Perhaps the way captaincy was handled was the most ridiculous aspect of it all. Professionals were deemed unable to take on the role and thus often found themselves playing under amateur captains who were barely of club standard. Counties often scratched round to find someone – anyone – willing to take charge. Some were so poor that they did little more than stand on the field while the senior professionals ran the show.

One by one the defining practices – separate dressing rooms, amateurs' initials on scorecards, with surnames only for the professionals, separate accommodation – were chipped away, although some reactionaries fought for the status quo, however fatuous the situation had become. Several county committees were expressing the view that it was time to treat all participants in the game simply as 'cricketers', but it was only in May 1962 that the Advisory County Committee put forward a proposal to scrap amateur status. Some counties had been employing 'amateur' captains as assistant secretaries, in some cases paying them more than the pros. It was clear that this shameful scam could not persist.

In November 1962 at a meeting of the seventeen first-class counties, this lingering anachronism was finally abolished when the distinction between amateurs and professionals was officially ended. We were all to be called 'cricketers' whether paid or not. The formal scrapping of amateur status came on 31 January 1963 when the MCC confirmed the earlier decision without dissent. Nobody was surprised when the news reached us on the grapevine in Australia.

Wisden, often a little behind the curve, took the view that, 'By doing away with the amateur, cricket is in danger of losing the spirit of freedom and gaiety which the best amateur players brought to the game.' I, on the other hand, was totally behind the decision, although it had no immediate impact on my own circumstances. I certainly had no plans to ask for payment halfway through the tour. In the wake of such forward-thinking, it also made possible a fresh, innovative version of the game like the Knockout Cup, which would be launched in 1963, of which I was a fervent and proactive supporter.

After this penultimate Gentlemen v. Players match (an absolute final, diluted version was played in Scarborough in September) I could have felt complacent about getting the captaincy in Australia, but from the sidelines, another unexpected, although more or less plausible, candidate had emerged: my Sussex colleague, David Sheppard. David wasn't playing a lot of cricket then, apart from a handful of matches for Sussex. The England cricket captain in 1954, he'd been ordained in 1955 to the evangelical church of St Mary's in Islington, North London. Through his curacy there, he'd become passionate about working in the inner City, a mission which he fulfilled as warden of the Mayflower Centre in Canning Town, East London. This inevitably took up a lot of his time, and he hadn't played in a Test match since 1957. However, perhaps seeing it as a way of broadening his ministry, he had unexpectedly declared himself available for Australia, and Walter Robins was giving strong signals that he favoured him over me as leader. When the Pakistan series was over, Sheppard had scored a century in the Gentlemen v. Players game, prompting a number of commentators to suggest that he had the captaincy in the bag.

Whatever Robins' view of Sheppard as a leader, he must, in the end, have had cold feet about sending a part-time cricketer, albeit a popular and respected individual, to lead such an important tour; and I was called into the committee room at Lord's to be given the job.

Although, of course, I did my best not to let it show, I was massively relieved. I'd found the tension created by Robins' selection process mentally and emotionally gruelling, complicated by the fact that I, too, had a lot of respect for David Sheppard, who subsequently, as I came to know him a lot better, became a significant influence in my wider life.

With an unexciting Test series, and no new heights being achieved by Sussex, my life at home had been dominated by new parenthood, and my own parents' decision to leave Italy and come back to live in England, in Chichester on the Sussex coast. They had chosen this pretty cathedral city because my three half-sisters now lived in the county. It was easy for Susan and me to get to, and very much on my beat as I plied the county playing cricket. Dad enjoyed the wonderful riding country up on the Downs and fulfilled his dream of having his own horse stabled nearby; the months that followed may have been the happiest of his life. The proximity of Fontwell Park, the local jumps course, also provided many afternoons of fun for the two of us. He loved coming to see me play when he could, and especially in the serene, noble surroundings of the cricket pitch at Arundel Castle.

Cricket at Arundel was an important part of the Sussex game, and was to become more so in the future; Arundel's owner, Bernard, 16th Duke of Norfolk, was a true aficionado, as well as being president of the county side. As a young player and as captain, I found that we had a shared interest in racing – he kept a number of good horses in training – and I'd got to know him well. More than once I was offered a bed at the castle during a match, saving me a round trip to London and back. It was a singular experience staying in a massive fortress as the guest of a duke, but I would usually be brought down to earth by a game of croquet on the castle lawns, a sport completely at odds with my particular skills.

Susan also knew him from her frequent trips as a loyal supporter to the various Sussex grounds. On one occasion she was going into the reserved enclosure on the top of the stand at Hove with a crowd of other Sussex wives. A droopy figure, sitting slouched in old coat and hat, leapt up as they came in through the gate. While the other wives fumbled for their tickets to show they had a right to go in, Susan fumbled for the words to introduce them to His Grace, the Duke of Norfolk.

The Duke was also a key figure in the MCC; indeed it had been announced to considerable amazement around the cricket world that he was going to manage the tour to Australia and New Zealand that winter. It was mooted, only partly in jest, that he'd been chosen because he was the only person thought capable of keeping the England captain in order, in which, I admit, there may have been some truth.

I was pleased about Mum and Dad's move for, although his health had improved significantly since the West Indies trip, he was seventy-two now, and had developed a few chronic problems. However, it was Susan's parents who wanted to help out over her plans to join me for part of the MCC tour to the Antipodes.

With the help of Peter Lumley's agency she was arranging a considerable Antipodean tour of her own, starting off with a number of modelling assignments in Australia for the mighty Myer Emporium, a long-established chain of prestigious department stores, the equivalent of Harrods, with branches in all the major cities. Her appearances would often, but not always, coincide geographically with the travels of the cricket tour. Afterwards, she had engagements in New Zealand, and had been invited to the US simply to wind down and enjoy some American hospitality on her way home. My brother-in-law, George Woodward, was European representative of *The New Yorker* magazine. He was based in London but still very well connected across the Atlantic, and he assured Susan that she would be well looked after.

Her parents, Tom and Heath Longfield, on their return from Calcutta in 1957 had bought a cottage in the small Berkshire town of Bracknell (now a hi-tech megapolis) which we often visited. They insisted that they were perfectly happy to care for the growing Dexter child there while Susan was away. We proposed that we should employ a full-time, live-in nanny to do the day-to-day childcare chores, so Susan could safely leave the boy with them, knowing that he would be well looked after in every way. I said goodbye to Thomas and Susan (who was going to join me in three months' time) and joined the England IX with the assistant team manager, Alec Bedser, on 27 September to set off for Australia, and my biggest tour as captain of England.

In order not to stretch a long tour of six months even further, we flew the first leg of the journey to Aden, from where we boarded the recently launched luxury liner, *SS Canberra*, on her regular voyage to Australia. It was comfortable and convivial, and I joined in the Marylebone Calypso Club which

Tom Graveney formed, for our own amusement and the other passengers'. Generally, though, I didn't see it as a captain's function to sit around in the bars drinking beer with the team. I was criticised for this, in the same way that I was criticised for not consulting enough with players on the field. I willingly admit to being prepared to be experimental in some of the options I chose. Inevitably, some experiments didn't achieve the desired result – that is what experiment means – but in my view, they have to be tried.

One of mine which met with mixed reception involved a plan to improve the team's fitness over the week and half of the voyage. On the ship with us was a British athlete, long-distance runner Gordon Pirie, who was on his way to the Commonwealth Games in Perth. Inevitably, early on, I found myself chatting with him. We discussed the lack of exercise my team were getting on their way to a prolonged sporting programme and as a result I persuaded him to give them 'keep fit' classes and oversee runs around the deck. Fred Trueman flatly refused to do any running and even jokingly threatened to throw Gordon Pirie overboard. He complained to Alec Bedser that he'd bowled more than a thousand overs for Yorkshire, he was the best fast bowler in the world and he didn't need extra training; so he was excused. Nor did Fred think much of Pirie's proposed diet of nuts and lettuce. He needed to eat steak to bowl like he did, he insisted, and that was that.

The *Canberra* paused in Ceylon just long enough for us to play a one-day game in Colombo, and for our team manager, the Duke of Norfolk, to join us with three of his daughters. 'You may dance with my daughters,' he told the team, 'you may take them out and wine them and dine them, but that is all you may do.' Curiously, twenty-two years after that, Colin Cowdrey married the Duke's eldest daughter, Lady Anne Fitzalan-Howard.

We landed at Fremantle, near Perth in Western Australia, on 9 October where we were joined by Brian Statham who had just flown in. Gordon Pirie somewhat sourly wrote a piece in one of the papers in which he described the England team as lazy, unfit and overweight, while Fred Trueman was quoted in *The Sydney Morning Herald* wondering if the MCC were playing under jockey club rules – referring to the Duke of Norfolk's and my own interest in horse racing – or were on a church mission, in view of the Rev David Sheppard's presence on the team. It was a standard display of Trueman's pantomime grumpy Yorkshireman.

We had a week to settle in and prepare ourselves for the first match of our tour which was against Western Australia. It was a short interlude when long sessions in the nets were strangely dominated by what was going on in the wider world, in the Caribbean – in Cuba, to be precise. The Americans had been nervous about what was happening there since the revolutionary leader, Fidel Castro, had taken control in 1959. On 14 October 1962, the Americans discovered missile sites on Cuba which brought every town in the US within range of Soviet nuclear weapons. President John F. Kennedy called a meeting of the National Security Council and issued the Russians an ultimatum over the removal of the weapons.

Meanwhile, at the end of the week, the tour bus headed deep into the outback to play at the gold mining town of Kalgoorlie, 370 miles north-east of Fremantle. A major purpose of the MCC tour was flying the flag and promoting the game as well as earning revenue for England county teams. This included playing 'bush games' against local league teams, good enough to get our team played-in before taking on the State sides and the Australian national XI.

We played and beat a Western Australia country team with the extraordinary events threatening from halfway across the world. We returned to Perth and were getting ready for our next game when, on 22 October, President Kennedy addressed the American people on TV to tell them about the threat they were under. It was an announcement that ricocheted around the globe, looking alarmingly like a detonator to a nuclear world war. For a few days most of the world seemed on tenterhooks, although, tens of thousands of miles away, I took the view that not even the most hawkish of Soviet leaders would seriously want to start something that would obviously lead to the destruction of his own country. Nevertheless, I was relieved on behalf of my six-month-old son when the Russians backed down and took their missiles away. Besides, in the long build-up to the start of a key Test series, these problems were superseded for us all by the far more pressing task of beating the Australians at cricket.

In Perth we beat Western Australia by 10 wickets, to be beaten by the same margin by a WA Combined XI, before heading off to Adelaide for a state match against South Australia. This resulted in a fairly even draw and we were given the chance to relax the next day as guests of the Victoria Racing Club at Flemington racecourse. We were able to watch the running of the Melbourne Cup, one of the richest two-mile handicaps in the racing world. It's a terrific day, part of the Melbourne Spring Festival, which is something like our own Royal Ascot, with women venturing out in their finest frocks and most flamboyant hats. About half a dozen of us went and watched from the committee box in great comfort. Naturally, our tour manager was there, and supplied us with a tip for a long shot in the big race. We all had a few dollars on the horse, ridden by 'Peanut' Pertwee, which got our hopes up by ranging alongside the leaders in the final straight. The yells of encouragement from the England cricketers was so loud that the Duke had to turn and look at us. 'Keep the noise down, please chaps,' he admonished.

The horse was, predictably, already dropping down the order, and the noise with it, as he came in fifth, and the favourite won.

**

After ten tour games of widely diverse calibre, the MCC arrived in Brisbane for the first Test which started on 30 November. The Gabba cricket ground in Brisbane was the closest to the equator that we played in Australia; it was high summer when we arrived, and hot as hell. Our team by now was feeling bullish, projecting far more positivity than that of the 58/59 tour, where I personally had fared so badly. The feeling was that, with a bit of luck, we had a side quite capable of taking enough matches off the Australians to bring back the little brown vase.

The first game, where performances turned out to be fairly evenly matched, ended in a draw. As captain, I thought I'd made most of the calls correctly, and contributed to our score with a frustrating 99 in the second innings.

**

In a country preoccupied with sport in general, and cricket especially, the Australian press were committed to intense scrutiny and far-ranging speculation, and not just about the cricket. They whipped up the public's interest in the unusual presence of a fully functioning Church of England vicar as a key member of the English batting attack, as well as his widely reported appearances in pulpits all over Australia. There was also a lot of coverage about the England tour manager, also hereditary Earl Marshall of England and the premier British duke, all of which was inexhaustibly fascinating in a country which still swore allegiance to our own queen.

The arrival of the England captain's wife to fulfil a number of high-profile modelling assignments added yet another dash of spice to their journalistic efforts.

Susan arrived in time for Christmas before the second Test, having had official permission from the MCC, as my wife, both to join the tour in Australia and to undertake some professional modelling while she was there.

We spent Christmas in Adelaide. The England team held a champagne party for the press in the morning before our Christmas lunch – always a little bizarre in the height of summer for us northern hemisphere folk. After lunch a golf match had been arranged with a betting sweep to add interest for the non-players. One of the local favourites to win was the legendary Sir Donald Bradman. He showed himself to be in great form, arriving on the seventeenth tee in a good winning position, until the BBC's commentator, Brian Johnston, intervened. Brian had a vested interest: he'd bought Sir Don's opponent, Ken Barrington, in the sweep. Bradman, with Barrington pressing hard behind him, was about to tee off, preparing to swing, eager to win, and showing all the determination and concentration which had made him the greatest batsman of all time.

Johnston swanned up behind him. 'My goodness, Don! You're doing well. Not so easy this one though – into the sun, and, say – that big bunker looks a little menacing. How are you doing, by the way? What's your score?'

I felt sorry for Sir Don as he hit straight into the bunker, took six to hole out, and another six down the home hole. Barrington won, and Brian Johnston happily trousered his winnings. I subsequently had a separate game with the Don on his home course, the Royal Adelaide. Years later John Woodcock, then of *The Times*, sent me a scorecard of the match. Bradman: 2 handicap; Dexter: 4 handicap. Par 73; The Don 75, and 77 for me. Honours even.

* *

The press took more interest in Susan's activities than even I had anticipated. They reported minutely on every job she did, taking the opportunity to lay into me for joining her on some of these jobs, especially where I was thought to be earning money from them. I was sorry to see that it was the former Australian cricket star, Keith Miller, who was the most prominent critic, writing in one of the big Australian papers, under the headline, 'CRICKET ROW OVER SUSAN'. There was no row, other than that being created by some of the press, but Miller wrote, 'Susan Dexter may unwittingly become the centre of the biggest rumpus of the MCC tour of Australia. Within five days of her arrival, cricket dignitaries are openly expressing fears that she is the innocent party to a commercial exploitation of the England captaincy. The diehard MCC authorities,' Miller went on, 'can scarcely approve of a store turning the English captaincy into a commercial gimmick.'

Miller was referring to a vast billboard which, to the amusement of most of the England team, had been put up outside the Myer Emporium, the most prestigious of Melbourne's department stores, urging the public to 'Come on in and meet the skipper's wife!'

It was harmless stuff, and I felt it was cheap of Keith Miller to use it to give me a kicking. Perhaps it did put me in a vulnerable position, but I was perfectly sure in my own mind that it wouldn't make any difference to the ultimate purpose of the tour which was to bring back the Ashes.

My only regret about all this was that Susan simply didn't know what had hit her when the criticisms started flowing. Why had she left her six-month-old son back in England with her parents, the press demanded. How could she be planning to stay away so long? Why was she cashing in on her husband's prominence in an entirely different field? She was in tears at one stage, regretting that she'd ever come.

I pointed out to her, gently but firmly, that these views were those of a small minority whose job it was to hold strong views in order to keep the readers reading, and the papers selling. Most of the Australian public, if they were aware of her presence at all, were fascinated and charmed by her.

In any case Susan might have been our lucky charm for the Test match that was set to be played over the new year at the vast Melbourne ground. Over a quarter of a million people came to watch, which would have given the Australian team a boost, no doubt, but also put enormous pressure on them to deliver. I was thrilled to be performing in front of such a crowd, however partisan.

We got off to a good start when we had the Australians all out for 316 in the first innings. In reply, Colin Cowdrey scored 113 and I added 93, in a stand of 175, to England's final total of 331. This small margin of 15 runs was enough to quicken the blood of an incorrigible optimist; we had only to bowl them out in a sensible amount of time, I dared to think, to have a good chance of winning the match. Overnight they were tottering with 105 for 4, two of them to Freddie Trueman.

At the start next day, we were pulling our boots on when I realised that Freddie wasn't with us, and nobody had seen him at the hotel. My heart sank; I really didn't need our number one bowler going AWOL at this critical stage in the game. With only minutes to go, and a substitute fielder getting ready to fill in, Freddie shambled into the dressing room. 'Sorry, skip,' he murmured. 'Overslept, skip. Be with you in a jiff.'

We tarried and he just made it onto the field with us. I threw him the still fairly new ball and tried to stay optimistic. I was alarmed to see that after bowling a few balls of his first over, he was already puffing and panting. I looked heavenwards, praying for better things. By halfway through the second (eight-ball) over, the ball was barely reaching the wicketkeeper. I shook my head, told Freddie to take his sweater and sent him to field in a shady part of the ground, where I would keep him until I thought he'd got his strength back.

We had Bill Lawry boxed in, scoring slowly, while the supremely consistent Brian Booth was looking set; as they settled in, it seemed that our attack was losing its sting. Nevertheless, I resisted the temptation to bring on Freddie just yet. I didn't even want to catch his eye. It was a big gamble holding him back and I was praying that when the new ball came, he would come up to scratch and deliver his best.

Late in the morning, on the last ball before lunch, I was bowling to the intractable Lawry, when I managed to give it more pace than he was expecting, and uprooted his middle stump. It was a key wicket.

In the afternoon, I carried on bowling at one end myself, until the moment came, and I chucked the new ball to Trueman; I could almost hear the relief of the England fans. He caught it with a nod and a faint conspiratorial grin as he ambled back to the start of his eighteen-yard run-up.

The tension must have got to the Australians too. Trueman piled into them; he had Mackay lbw for 9, Benaud caught at slip by Cowdrey in a superb rolling catch for 4, and clean bowled McKenzie for o. All out for 248.

Pullar and Sheppard went in for us half an hour before the close of play. Pullar, with a little bad luck, fell to McKenzie's first ball, a leg glance, which Jarman dived and caught. Pullar had scored just 5 runs. In this situation, the conventional course would have been to send in a nightwatchman; but I'd never had a nightwatchman in my career, and I certainly didn't want one now. I always feared having to bat the next day with a tailender, so I marched onto the pitch myself. Helpfully, bad light took us off a quarter of an hour early, with a score of 9 for 1.

In the morning, I was sure I'd made the right decision, and felt strong and confident walking out to bat with the always competitive David Sheppard. At that critical first phase of the day David may not have been feeling at his most confident. He'd been out for a duck in the first innings; he'd also dropped two critical catches from Richie Benaud and Bill Lawry. Whatever his inner thoughts, as we walked out, he showed what a natural reader of the game he was, as well as a good psychologist. 'Fifth day pitch, Ted,' he pondered. 'Probably not a day for big shots. Let's take the ones and twos for a while and see how we get on.'

We got on well! Within half an hour we had run them ragged. Bowlers were cursing the fielders as we pinched the singles. When they moved in closer, we could nudge the ball past them for twos and threes. Not surprisingly, given our strategy, I was run out for 52, while David came into his own, scoring 113, his third and last Test century, before he too was run out. Colin Cowdrey came in and hit a solid 58, and we reached our target with 7 wickets and seventy-five minutes to spare. It was a great and entirely decisive victory.

It was only when we were sitting in the coach outside the ground that it really hit me – that I was captain of England, and we had just beaten Australia on their own ground for the first time in quite a while. *And* we were one up in an Ashes series. It was the highest point in my Test career, and my innings of 52 that day became for me the most important that I'd ever played. I was euphoric, perhaps with a dash of gambler's joy, that the risks I'd taken had paid off so handsomely. It more than made up for the old humiliation of five years before, when I'd flown out from Paris to make an arse of myself on that terrible tour.

* *

The following day, I pulled my portable Remington typewriter from my case, rolled up my sleeves and sat down to write up my perspective of the match that had just finished for *The Observer* in London. Before I had left for Australia I'd already been commissioned by the Sunday paper to file a series of first-hand skipper's accounts of the tour. This arrangement, with a useful fee attached, had been negotiated for me by a singular behind-the-scenes operator called Bagenal Harvey. I'd first met Bagenal with Denis Compton in El Vino's, the Fleet Street wine bar which for years was the pivotal watering hole for many of the hacks who worked in the street. He was a distinctive looking chap who liked his champagne and always wore a dark red cravat. He and Denis had been introduced to one another by sports news agency owner, Reg Hayter.

Reg had been sailing with the England team, en route to a tour, when Denis Compton had turned up at his cabin with a suitcase full of correspondence —' much of it unopened. He asked Reg to have a look at it all, as he couldn't be bothered or didn't have the time. Reg opened the case and found it stuffed with fan mail and requests from people for Denis to do things or put his name to various products or newspaper articles. It looked as if there could be thousands of pounds' worth of offers among the unopened rumpled envelopes and dog-eared papers. Back in England, Reg tied up a couple of newspaper deals for Denis and suggested that he should hand the suitcase over to his friend, Bagenal Harvey, who would follow up the best of the commercial offers on Denis's behalf. Bagenal, a small-time specialist publisher with a nose for a deal, agreed to take away the case full of post and get his secretary to go through it all and they would see what deals could be done.

The first result of this was that Denis, who had played football for Arsenal as well as cricket for England, became the face of Brylcreem. A lot of other lucrative deals followed, all brokered by Bagenal, who had turned himself into Britain's first full-time sports agent, the forerunner to Mark McCormack and the hundreds of others who now ply that trade.

When I met him with Denis, he immediately scented a prospect and asked if he could help me with some extracurricular earnings. It sounded like a good idea to me; I agreed, and he started looking for opportunities. One of the first people to whom he introduced me was the sports editor on *The Observer*, Clifford Makins, who habitually consumed two bottles of Krug (at £2 a bottle) with his friends every day in El Vino's. I got on well with Clifford; indeed he remained a friend until he died some twenty-five years later.

Bagenal swiftly sewed up a deal for me to write on a regular basis for the paper. I'd already written a few pieces before I left for Australia that autumn and I was looking forward to doing the articles they'd asked for.

Out on the ground before the last day's play in the Melbourne Test, His Grace, the tour manager, came over to speak to me.

'Ah, Ted,' he said. 'I've received this telegram from Lord Nugent [president of the MCC].'

He thrust a piece of paper at me. It read:

'This is to advise you of concern here at Lord's that articles by Ted Dexter in The Observer may break the terms of his player agreement.'

Before I had a chance to react, the Duke handed me a second telegram. 'And this is my reply,' he said. It was short and pithy:

'Please don't bother us. We are trying to win a Test match. Norfolk.'

That was the last I heard from Lord's on the matter. In my next letter home to my dad, I mentioned the incident. My father replied, in the open knowledge that Lord Nugent was a keen botanist and a particular aficionado of desert plants, that he would like nothing more than to stick a cactus where Lord Nugent might not like it.

* *

We had a tour game to play in Tasmania, where Susan put in an appearance at the Myer Emporium in Hobart, before we flew back to Sydney for the third Test. As soon as we'd landed I was engulfed by a horde of reporters, hungry for fresh meat. Now we were the conquering heroes, and everyone wanted my version of events, particularly in the absence of our tour manager, the Duke of Norfolk, who had been recalled to London by the Queen. As Earl Marshall of England it was one of his responsibilities to oversee the planning of such events as state funerals. Ever since Sir Winston Churchill had suffered a stroke in 1953, Her Majesty had required the Duke to draw up minute plans for his funeral, on a scale 'befitting his place in history'. Known as 'Operation Hope Not', every time Sir Winston suffered another stroke, these arrangements had to be urgently reviewed and fully rehearsed, in readiness for any sudden change in circumstances. We missed His Grace and his authoritative but affable and encouraging presence – a bracing change from the irascible Walter Robins.

For a duke, he could be unexpectedly warm and down to earth. There was a well-reported instance of this when he was in the swimming pool with John Murray, who was rigidly obeying protocol by calling him, 'Your Grace'.

'In the swimming pool, Murray,' the Duke declared, 'you may call me Bernard.'

Another time, we were all staying in the Windsor Hotel in Melbourne when Ken Barrington had told the Duke about the trouble he had sleeping.

'You can call me for a sleeping tablet anytime,' the Duke offered generously, 'even in the middle of the night.'

Ken took him at his word and called him on the hotel phone after midnight. The Duke responded at once, and set out down a series of long corridors to find Ken's room. When he got there he knocked a few times, but with no reply. He put his ear to the keyhole, to be rewarded by the sound of Ken's loud, rhythmic snoring.

＊＊

Sadly, within a few days of our return to Sydney, once the third Test had got under way, our public standing had reverted to more normal levels. Bobby Simpson, spinning fiercely on the Sydney wicket, took four of our wickets in the first innings, then 5 for 25 when our batting utterly collapsed in the second, handing the match to the Australians, and levelling the series 1-1.

The fourth Test, despite an astonishing opening to our innings when Ken Barrington hit four fours in succession off Davidson's first four balls, making one of the most extraordinary first overs of any Test match, the game went nowhere and ended in a draw. It did, though, generate a much-repeated story, when David Sheppard dropped Neil Harvey off Freddie Trueman. The

Yorkshireman barracked David afterwards. 'The only time your hands are together are on Sunday.'

This is the story that grows and morphs over the retelling. Another version had Trueman saying, 'Pretend it's Sunday, Reverend, and keep your hands together.' Or it was Sheppard who had said, 'Sorry Fred, I should have kept my hands together.'

When an Australian couple met Mrs Sheppard, who had joined her husband on the tour, and asked her if the Reverend could christen their baby, she advised against it. 'He's bound to drop it,' she explained.

Both teams, and their captains, came in for some scorn for producing such negative play, when we had bravely forecast the opposite at the start of the series. Richie Benaud, on the whole, was better at handling it than I was; he was five years older, with that much more experience, and he'd become a canny manipulator of the media.

I had a lot of respect for Richie as my opposite number and despite the fact that we were prime rivals on this stage, we had quickly found a rapport. This was encouraged by an initiative that Richie had taken through his contacts in the Australian Broadcasting Corporation, who arranged that he and I should have regular ten-minute round-ups of the action at the end of a day's play.

I rose to the challenge like a salmon to a silver fly, and it became a feature of the tour. Because Richie and I were both interested in articulating our theories to justify our strategies, these exchanges were thought to have worked well. I have tried to get my hands on recordings of them; sadly, they must be buried very deep in the ABC archives.

* *

There was a hiatus of almost a fortnight before the final decisive Test match in Sydney. The MCC side spent the time playing a four-day fixture in Melbourne and three minor games in Canberra, Dubbo and Tamworth. Although they were scheduled as 'minor', the Canberra game, against the Prime Minister's XI, took on an inflated status with Sir Donald Bradman's agreement to play his first cricket in fourteen years. This was bound to fill the ground with spectators and unrealistic expectations; Bradman, generally deemed to have been the greatest Test batsman of all time, and was, after all, fifty-four by then, had taken his participation seriously enough to have several sessions in the nets in the days before the game.

I naturally understood that the crowd were keen to see him at the crease for a decent amount of time, if only for reasons of sentimental nostalgia. There was also the chance that once the adrenalin was flowing, he might well give us a glimpse or two of the master in his prime.

First, I put on Tom Graveney to bowl – I hoped gently enough to give the older man a chance to get used to being in front of the stumps once more. To a great cheer, Sir Don took a straight four off Graveney.

It would have been offensive and perhaps a little demeaning to the Don to have put on another obviously unchallenging bowler. With that in mind, and having considered the options, I put on Brian Statham, knowing that he would drop his pace and pitch it up. He bowled a good gentle delivery, outside the off stump, but as the Don covered up, the ball perversely trickled from his inside edge onto his pad, onto the wicket, and a bail fell off. It was his fifth ball. The spectators gasped at this summary dismissal of their greatest cricketing hero, and I with them.

* *

The last Test in Sydney was a fiasco, but not through any particular action of mine or Richie Benaud's. The Sydney Oval was sodden after days of heavy rain. It hadn't been mowed for weeks, leaving the turf on the outfield so long and lush, not a single ball reached the boundary when we batted on the first day. Although the groundsmen trimmed the grass as much as they could, the second day wasn't a great deal better. So although the pitch itself was alright, the game petered out in what might have looked like a grim, unsightly, defensive tussle on the part of both sides.

It was a disappointing end to the Test series, which had otherwise shown a lot of watchable cricket. Richie and I had achieved good over rates and the games had been played in a generous, sporting spirit. The last game left the series at 1-1, allowing the Ashes to remain in Australia, where they'd been since 1959, although, on balance and having started as underdogs, I believe England came out of the series slightly the better of the two.

Nevertheless, I was having to face a barrage of criticism, including some stinging assessments by Keith Miller in his newspaper column. And there was worse to come. In the aftermath of the series, and before we set off for New Zealand, Neil Harvey, Richie Benaud's vice-captain who had played throughout the series, had announced his retirement, and I spent a convivial evening with him, his wife and Richie Benaud. I sat next to Harvey and we had a wide-ranging chat about his future plans. On the field, Neil had been a highly competitive opponent, and I felt pleased that at the end of an intense series of matches, we could communicate with each other in a civilised and grown-up way. A few days later, I was reading a truly vitriolic piece about me in his column.

'Dexter,' he said, 'was the worst England captain I have met... Seldom have I seen a prominent visitor to this country appear to be at times, so ungracious to his hosts, the Australian team.'

It hurt, and it made no sense to me. I was thankful that a number of other Australian commentators were fair enough to say that Harvey's piece was way over the top. Among other examples of my superior attitude that Harvey cited was, 'an oath from England's captain that shocked wicketkeeper Wally Grout'.

The notion that a hard-bitten keeper from the land that invented sledging would be shocked by the odd four-letter word from a batsman in a moment of high concentration was ludicrous.

To my disappointment, our domestic press were not entirely forgiving either. They too picked up the theme of my 'haughtiness' and 'aloofness', with the old 'Lord Ted' sobriquet cropping up. I was beginning to understand by then the mixed motives of the media as a whole, and newspapers in particular, whose primary aim was to sell as many copies as possible. Hard-bitten old hacks know that what most excites their readers is controversy and iconoclasm. I refused to take it too personally, and had enough self-confidence to ride the punches.

I readily admit that there were occasions on the tour when I did go off to do my own thing, if, for instance, I'd been offered the chance of a fine day's racing or a special round of golf (on one occasion with Gary Player and Norman Von Nida at the wonderful Kooyonga Golf Club). But I also did a lot to encourage goodwill and camaraderie among the tour party as a group, along with the press and other camp followers. One of my initiatives which lasted for all the Antipodean tour was the Bowers Club, a Saturday night gathering with whoever cared to join. Members wore a bow tie emblazoned with a wine glass emblem for these occasions, which were strictly for fun and the source of a lot of memorable jokes and pranks. It was a chance to relax with a couple of gins, without any of the pressures of the game, and to build relationships with the journalists who, wishing to do their job properly, wanted to know us better. Brian Johnston was naturally always there – probably a founder member – John Woodcock too, and Michael Melford. We chose different venues for each occasion – a bar, a bizarre restaurant, somebody's room – and they always created a lot of merriment and – to use a word not used then – bonding. Despite the great disparity among the backgrounds of the players – socially, educationally, geographically – those divisions which were still evident in society in general in mid-century Britain were utterly irrelevant on the cricket field, and, in my experience, this generally applied to our downtime.

When we were back in England, later in the year, Susan and I invited the whole team to a party at our new house in Fulham (a move demanded by the growth of our family). They all made themselves quite at home, soon coming to the end of what I had thought was an inexhaustible supply of drink. When I went to look for the case I was holding in reserve, for just that emergency, I discovered that it had already been found, and consumed.

Things are clearly even less formal now, when anyone in the team can address the captain as Rootie, or our greatest cricketer as Stokesie. In my era, admittedly over half a century ago, the idea of addressing my captain, Peter May, as 'Pete', or even 'Maysie', was unthinkable.

If some of the pros did harbour a smouldering resentment about their status which had precluded them from captaincy, I wouldn't blame them, although I was never conscious that they treated me in a way that was antagonistic or remotely envious. And, of course, many professional players who were subsequently appointed captain of their county have made as great a success of it as any of the former 'gents' might have done. Initially others found the extra responsibilities beyond them and stood down.

**

I left New Zealand on 20 March 1963 at the end of the twenty-six-day, three-Test series which had followed the marathon Australian tour. We had won all three Tests there, as we had been expected to; we'd played well and I was satisfied with that result. One incidental aspect of the Kiwi tour which has stayed with me was a piece of captaincy of which I was quite proud.

By the time we reached Auckland on the North Island for the first Test at Eden Park, we had been on the road almost five months and there was barely a dozen of us left who were still fit and uninjured. Among us was David Larter, a great big Scots lad who played for Northants. He was twenty-two, a lanky six feet seven and, on a good day, a more then capable bowler. Up until now on the tour he hadn't played in a single match; he gave the impression that he simply didn't want to and had just come along for the ride. He always seemed to have some little niggle – an ankle, or a strain – and would sit in the dressing room with his feet on the balcony in a big pair of slippers. I'd tried to identify the reasons, although I knew he had a reputation for sporadic moodiness, sometimes just refusing to bowl. Now he had no option; he was in the team, like it or not. He looked as if it had come as a bit of a surprise to him, but I was glad I'd got him on the pitch at last. When the time came, I gave him the new ball not really knowing what to expect.

When I saw what he did with it, I wasn't at all happy. He was all over the place – full tosses, wides, halfway down the pitch...

I was at mid-off and before his next over, I spoke to him. 'OK David, relax, pitch it up. Just settle down.'

But his second over was as bad as the first.

'What are you trying to do?' I asked him, no doubt a little testily.

'I'm sorry skip, but I've tried my inswinger; I've tried my outswinger and I've tried my slow ball, and across the seam.'

I looked him in the eye – difficult at his height. 'OK, you listen to me,' I said carefully. 'You're going to bowl every ball with your fingers across the seam.'

I walked him down the pitch to a point just short of a length. 'I want every ball to hit this spot. You just whack them down there.'

He appeared to have taken in my simple instructions. For the rest of the game, he followed them and the improvement was almost miraculous.

John Reid, the Kiwi captain and a powerful batsman, whom I knew fairly well, faced David for a few overs, before he caught my attention. 'Hey, Ted. Where's this bloke come from?' he asked, obviously impressed. 'He's a bit off a handful.'

Larter took 3 wickets for 51 in their first innings, and 4 for 36 in the second. I was chuffed by what I saw as a useful piece of captaincy. I'd done him a favour, and I'd done the team a favour.

* *

On my way back from New Zealand, I took a detour to Southern Africa, to play in two matches organised by the International Cavaliers, an ad hoc team made up of well-known, presumed crowd-drawing players from all the Test cricket nations. It generally consisted of players who were between series, not required for one, had retired from Test cricket, or, sometimes, up and coming young players considered worth watching. It was, in the best sense of the word, a circus that entertained many huge crowds around the cricketing world during the fifties and sixties. This was the first time I'd played for them, but by no means the last. I found that it could be fun, it didn't take long and it was well paid. On this trip I played for the Cavaliers against Rhodesia, which still had a strong cricket tradition, and the Transvaal, in South Africa. One of the games was played on a pitch with stumps on springs, such as you might have found in Britain in an inner-city municipal park. My only recollection of the game was that after two balls, I heard behind me the dreaded twang of iron springs. I also discovered that a whack in the chest fielding in New Zealand was getting worse, not better. It turned out I had a broken rib.

I finally arrived back in London at the end of March, after being away for six months, knackered and looking forward to seeing my wife. Overall, though, I was pleased with the way the team had played on the Antipodean tour, and despite some carping from a few of the scribblers when we got back, on the whole their judgement on my captaincy was positive – some very much so. On a personal level, I'd also scored more Test runs than any other England captain had in an Ashes series. This augured well for my prospects for leading the England team in the next Test series against the visiting West Indians, due to kick off at Old Trafford in early June, in spite of the continuing presence of my old bête noire, Walter Robins, as chairman of selectors.

I had an interesting year to look forward to with Sussex, after we had finished seventh in the County Championship the year before. I felt we had a real prospect of doing better than that, a key element being the rapid improvement in our outstanding young bowler, John Snow. More important than this, though, was the small matter of five Test matches against the formidable West Indian side who were coming over to play us on our own turf.

Chapter Nine

THE WEST INDIES
AND THE KNOCKOUT CUP

Susan had arrived back from the States before me, just before Thomas' first birthday on 10 March. She had spent a terrific time in New York and New England. She was pleased to tell me that she'd been treated with outstanding hospitality – perhaps not surprisingly for a charming and beautiful English woman – but it was good to hear that there was still some old-fashioned courtesy alive and well in the former colony.

As soon as she landed she'd gone straight to Bracknell where Thomas had been staying with her parents. Reunited with her one-year-old son, Susan was thrilled to pick him up and hold him again. She was, though, suddenly distraught to find that he didn't have a clue who she was and hadn't recognised her at all. Before she understood that it was perfectly normal for a baby not to retain recognition for any length of time, she really started to wish she hadn't been away at all. Of course, it was only a matter of days before it was all on again, and Thomas knew exactly who his mother was, and her remorse was dispelled.

With the help of the live-in nanny we had employed, Tom and Heath had loved having him with them and they were adamant that it had been no trouble. It can't have been easy; the winter of 1962/63 had been one of the hardest on modern record, when the freeze was so severe and so persistent that not only did all the lakes in nearby Windsor Great Park freeze over, but stretches of the Thames itself had frozen so solid that people were skating on it in complete confidence that the ice wouldn't crack.

As soon as I got back to England, I drove down to Bracknell to pick them up in the neat Jaguar saloon provided for me by Sussex CC. Thomas himself looked as well as could be and, in the six months since I'd seen him, almost double the size and practically a different person. As we drove back to London up the A30, with Thomas in a carrycot lashed to the seat behind us and Susan sitting beside me on the pale grey leather upholstery, I was struck by how it suited her and how well she looked. It was marvellous for the three of us to be together back in London after a long five months away.

I was particularly happy that, despite Sue's early misgivings in Melbourne when people like Keith Miller had turned on us, her tour had been a great success. The Australians – people and press – had loved her, and this had done a lot to boost her confidence.

I found it didn't take long to reacclimatise to London and the English spring weather, although I was struck by events in the news which seemed to be heralding a new era. The radio waves were full of a group of Liverpudlian musicians, The Beatles, whose first LP, *Please, Please Me*, had come out in March and was already taking Britain, then the world, by storm. Who could have predicted the way these four young chaps would go on to dominate pop music all around the globe for the next few decades; I know that I didn't; I was still stuck with Sinatra's *Songs for Swingin' Lovers!*

Alongside this, in the spring of 63, another news story that carried on resounding for years to come was the revelation that John Profumo, Britain's Secretary of State for War, had been sleeping with a nineteen-year-old model from a poor family in the suburbs. The girl, Christine Keeler, had also had an affair with a Soviet attaché, a clear recipe for political explosion. Her mentor, Stephen Ward, osteopath, amateur artist and friend of a number of rich and powerful men, was investigated over procuring prostitutes for his friends. It was a story with all the salacious elements to keep it going for the whole summer, the first time this kind of activity had been so blatantly discussed in the media. It also spawned the famous courtroom riposte from one of the girls, Mandy Rice-Davies, on being told that Lord Astor (now married to Susan's friend Bronwen Pugh) denied having an affair with her or even knowing her: 'Well, he would, wouldn't he?' Ms Rice-Davies had giggled from the witness stand.

As these big stories, new music and changing attitudes were unfolding in the springtime, my own focus was on more important things – the summer's prospects for Sussex cricket, and the eagerly anticipated tour of England by the West Indies cricket team, against whom I fully expected to captain the England side. I was soon back in the routine of catching the 9am Brighton Belle from Victoria to arrive an hour or so later at the Sussex ground, where I was making preparations before the first game of the new season against Glamorgan at Hove on 1 May, and – more excitingly – the introduction of the Knockout Cup, a newly devised one-day, limited-over competition.

It was during an early season Championship match against Middlesex at Lord's that a sudden cloudburst caused a stop in play which led at last to decisive action being taken over a long-standing problem with the pitch there.

In 1963, movable pitch covers hadn't yet been introduced and the rain was sluicing down the square. From the dressing-room balcony I watched, fascinated, as I pondered the topography of the wicket, and its distinct bias. Looking harder, I noticed that the water was flowing across the whole square, with the exception of a dry strip at the Nursery End. This was, of course, the infamous 'ridge', which had been causing trouble for batsmen for years, certainly as long as I'd been playing at Lord's and which the grandees in the committee room refused to take seriously. I recognised at once that this was the perfect opportunity to point it out to those who made decisions; I raced down to the committee room where I knew I would find Gubby Allen.

Gubby existed at the very pinnacle of command in the MCC, but I knew I could talk to him. Since he'd first seen me playing at Radley, he had earmarked me as a future England player. He'd gone on to do a lot to encourage me while I was at Cambridge and to influence other selectors. He was, I knew, glad that I had confirmed his faith in me, and I was grateful for his continuing support. Our relationship was good enough for me to haul him out and up to balcony to witness for himself this strange, elusive phenomenon.

I found him. 'Gubby!' I blurted, out of breath. 'You know I've been going on about this ridge on the pitch for years?'

'Yes, yes,' he said, waving a dismissive hand. 'There is no ridge.'

'Gubby, will you please come and have a look.'

He stood up from his chair and walked reluctantly to the window to see for himself. He stared at the rainwashed pitch for a few moments, before nodding his head. 'Okay,' he conceded, 'I see what you mean; I hear what you're saying. Leave it with me.'

Within a couple of days, men with theodolites were out on the pitch, measuring angles. Soon after that, the hallowed turf was being dug out, and flattened.

I was delighted to have triggered a result, and so, probably, were a few other batsmen who, like Nari Contractor, had been injured directly as a result of the ridge. I recognised then what a danger it was to allow the status quo to get in the way of pragmatic decisions and, thirty years later, as chairman of the MCC Cricket Committee I had no hesitation in making essential, radical and far-reaching changes to the quality of the whole playing area, outfield included.

**

Far-reaching changes to the way the game was played, watched and, ultimately, remunerated would also take place that year, with the establishment of the new inter-counties knockout competition. I had watched with interest the previous year, when a series of three limited-overs matches played between four counties – the Midlands Knockout Cup – had been tried out. This event, involving Leicestershire, Northants, Derbyshire and Notts, was a precursor to a wider experiment that had been proposed at a meeting of the MCC's Advisory County Cricket Committee, where the possibility of a limited-overs knockout competition had been discussed.

Leicestershire's secretary, Mike Turner, who had taken the initiative with the Midlands competition, recognised that cricket's post-war boom had ended and unless significant changes were introduced to make the game more compellingly watchable, it might die altogether as a spectator sport.

Having captained a county side now for three years, I was in complete agreement with him. However, Turner's four counties Midlands experiment was a flop. It was too restricted in size, the weather for all three games was horrible and the crowds that turned up were negligible. Nevertheless, plans had been put in place for a wider experiment, involving all the major counties, and although a sponsor had not been found, the 1963 fixture calendar had been adjusted to include the sixteen games required.

I was more than excited by this development. I saw it as a real chance to shake things up in Hove and to apply my enthusiasm for strategy and tactical theorising. At the time, I had a few reservations about this style of play, as I felt there was a danger it would encourage monotonous bowling, when, after all, the art of bowling is as much a part of the game as the more obviously eye-catching art of batting. Being pragmatic though, and seeing this new competition offered my county an opportunity to steal a march on the rest, I recognised the advantage we had with four or five top-class medium-pace bowlers. My theory was that with tight, consistent bowling that was always going to hit the stumps, we would be able to pin down the opposition and restrict their scores.

Hard as it is to believe now, there were sixty-five overs per innings. On that basis, I didn't think that batting would differ much from a normal Championship match for at least half the overs, after which the run chase would begin in earnest, ideally with wickets in hand. Where I knew we had an edge was in our bowling, and I received complete co-operation from the bowlers on a simple set of tactics.

Every ball should be hitting the stumps.

Wide of the stumps was a bad ball.

Short and going over the top was a bad ball.

It would be my responsibility to set the field – not theirs – because batsmen are all different: left-handers, right-handers, each playing with a gamut of favourite strokes and shots.

We set two close fielders to stop the singles.

We always had a third man to cut off the edges.

But when wide balls were hit square for four, and the bowler asked for some cover, my answer was always: 'No! Pitch it up, bowl straighter, and you won't need it.'

These tactics were shown to work time and again, although it took a long time for our opponents to grasp what we were doing. I should say that in these days of supercharged bats, this might not work so well. At the same time, in any case, the advent of shorter and shorter matches has altered the whole game again, with the beneficial result being the increased importance of the leg-spinners.

After one preliminary round to bring the number of contenders down from seventeen to sixteen, all eight first round games were played on 22 May, with Sussex playing Kent at Tunbridge Wells. We won the toss, Colin Cowdrey set a friendly field and we made a big score. It all looked thoroughly sporting and obviously delighted the big crowd that had turned out to see this new version of the game. But when Kent went in, the picture changed dramatically. The only man who looked as if he might cause us trouble was Peter Richardson. However, it wasn't my game plan to get him out. I simply set the field back, allowed him to take a single, then bowled tight to the other batsman to force him to make the runs, not Richardson. There were boos and bellows from the crowd, making it clear they didn't like what we were doing. But importantly, there was a result and, by any standards, a good day's entertaining cricket. Richardson received the Player of the Match award, but Sussex had shown the spectators what could be done, and moved on to the quarter-finals.

* *

Three weeks later, the Championship contenders Yorkshire and Sussex were drawn against each other for our first knockout game at Hove. Our success against Kent at Tunbridge Wells had got the fans fired up, and the ground was packed. For the next eight and a half hours, nobody left their seat, and the spectators were rewarded with a memorable game.

Jim Parks put in a blistering, masterly performance, including two of the most spectacular sixes I ever saw – two remarkable cover-driven slashes outside the off stump by a batsman who revelled in this sort of cricket.

Yorkshire came in looking for runs, a little too quickly at first, until they were pulled together by the youngest member of the side, Geoff Boycott, already a bright new hope for Yorkshire and for England. We couldn't shift him, and he kept the innings going until he ran out of partners, just a few minutes from the end.

Sussex were through to the semi-finals.

**

In the meantime, the West Indian team had arrived at the end of April to an enthusiastic welcome from the large community of West Indians now living in Britain. I was delighted to see Frank Worrell, whom I'd admired since I'd first played against him at Cambridge and, of course, he had captained their side when England won the series against them in 1960. I also recognised that he'd brought a strong and experienced team with him and containing them would be a big challenge. Nevertheless, historically we had a good record against them, and I was confident that we were capable of winning the series.

At the England team dinner before the first Test at Old Trafford I ran through the qualities of each of the opposing batsmen, to derisory snorts from Freddie Trueman after each name. This confidence, however, didn't survive the first game.

The next day the West Indians piled up a first innings tally of 501 for 6, before bowling us all out for 205 and 297 with a follow-on. While I was pleased with my 73 in the first innings, I was frustrated that it hadn't done much to inspire the other batsmen. On a wicket that was taking spin, they'd made little headway against Sobers and the canny spinner, Lance Gibbs, who took 11 for 157. The tourists' usually destructive fast bowlers were having no effect. Even Charlie Griffith managed only one wicket, giving little hint of the pace that was to take him to thirty wickets in the course of the series. Nevertheless, I could see we might have a problem with the way he was bowling.

After I was out, I sat beside the legendary Lancashire and England batsman, Cyril Washbrook, and asked him what he thought of Charlie's action. As the first ball left his hand, Cyril started to discount it as a slower ball, but when it whistled through to the keeper, chest high and going like a rocket, he grunted. 'I see what you mean.'

Later that day, I found Gubby Allen, the ultimate authority, and registered my concern. He simply shrugged. 'There's nothing we can do unless the umpires call him, but I can assure you he won't come to England again.' These were empty words, though. Charlie did come to England again, still with the same action, but fortunately, a good deal slower. In 1963, though, Charlie Griffith was to be our nemesis.

The West Indians went in for their second innings needing just one run to win.

* *

A week later at the County Ground in Hove, the West Indians arrived for their scheduled tour match against Sussex. We got off to a pretty ignominious start when they bowled us all out for 59 in our first innings. They replied with 297 for 9, of which I took 3, before girding my loins and going on to make a gratifying 103 in two and a half hours. The West Indies team still won by 6 wickets, though, and I was left in no doubt that they were one of the most formidable teams in the world, and we had a major fight on our hands if we wanted to succeed in the Test series.

This led on to the second Test at Lord's, an extraordinary, tense cliffhanger of a classic, and one of the legendary matches of English Test history.

For this match, the selectors made a couple of important changes to the team. We felt the key quality in dealing with the West Indian bowlers was courage, and in my view, Brian Close was the most fearless batsman available; I wanted him to open. Although he may not have had the best technique against a moving, swinging ball, he knew how to defend himself against very quick bowling. I got him into the side, though I didn't manage to get him into the opening spot.

I also wanted an additional bowler, and thought that Derek Shackleton would be the most useful choice. Derek was thirty-eight by then, and he hadn't played in a Test match for eleven years. I had to push for him as he was deemed by some to be too mundane a bowler to take wickets in Test matches, although he'd taken an awful lot of county wickets for Hampshire. I wanted him now because he was uncannily accurate, always moved the ball off the seam and was capable of bowling forty overs a day at his medium pace in typical English conditions that suited him well. On the first day at Lord's he bowled thirty-eight overs and didn't take a wicket, but the next morning, he finished off the West Indies innings at 301 with three wickets in four balls.

Micky Stewart and John Edrich opened, and Edrich was out first ball, getting a touch down the leg side. At a score of 2 for 1, I walked out through the Long Room feeling calm and totally focussed, knowing exactly what I was going to do.

Out in the middle, Charlie Griffith and Wes Hall were both firing on all cylinders, each in their different, often devastating fashion. Of the two, Charlie was the more disconcerting, primarily because he was a 'thrower'. For the batsman, the difficulty with throwers is caused by the apparent delay in the release of the ball. Instead of the straight arm swinging in an arc, the trajectory is flattened, and when the ball leaves the bowler's hand it's like facing a bowling machine, when you never know quite when it's coming. The thrower has the additional advantage of surprise, in being able to vary his pace with no apparent change in action. Charlie also had good control and a deadly yorker.

Since then, I'm happy to say, the curse of the thrower has been effectively eliminated from the game, thanks to better TV coverage and slow-motion replay. A current guideline permits a degree of arm-straightening before releasing the ball, while umpires are no longer required to 'no-ball' for throwing on the field, they're supposed to make a report after the game. Under the present system, I believe umpires would have reported Charlie, and he would have been suspended, as Geoff Griffin had been on the South African's last tour.

In terms of wickets taken, Charlie was the more successful, but compared to Wes Hall's classical, flowing motion, his action was grotesque. In his delivery stride, he veered sharply to the left as he catapulted the ball down the other end. He didn't have much of a follow-through but what there was left him closer to extra cover than the batsman. By the end of the series, Hall had taken 16 wickets at 30 apiece; Charlie took 30 wickets at 16.

This was what I was preparing myself for as I took my guard. I was clear in my own mind about the innings I was going to play. There would be no stoical defence; I was going to strike back, full on, from the start. By what good chance, I can't say, but I immediately found my best form. Never had I been able to see the ball so early, nor had I ever found myself in quite such a confident, attacking vein.

Cricket writer Alan Ross in his book, *West Indies at Lord's*, a full and stirring account of this unique match, described my innings, with just a dash of purple. At the risk of evoking accusations of personal vanity (while admitting it still gives the heart a bit of a lift, even after fifty-seven years), I quote the passage:

Dexter came next, hurrying down the steps as if unable to contain himself. What nobody could suspect was that in the next hour they would be present at one of the greatest innings seen at Lord's since anyone could remember ... Dexter, all told, batted for only eighty minutes, receiving some seventy balls. Off these he scored 70 runs, being out to Sobers at 102, the scoreboard at his dismissal bearing a cock-eyed aspect ... It all happened so quickly that even watching it going on, the scale was difficult to comprehend. Suddenly Dexter was 50, the innings not in ruins, but classically erect, like pillars soaring with eagles... the applause, echoing round St John's Wood, did him justice. He held up his bat as if quieting it, an intimation that more was to come. Hall now trudged back without eagerness; Griffith was somnambulist, enveloped in fogs of disbelief...

My demise was not long in coming when Frank Worrell realised what had happened to his usually invincible brace of fast bowlers, and switched to the more subtle wiles of Sobers and Gibbs.

Sobers had me lbw. I thought it was marginal, and under the current DRS system, I would certainly have referred the decision to the cameras. But the umpire's finger was up and that was the end of my bit of fun.

I left the field with the scoreboard showing 102 for 3, but after me, Barrington, Parks and Titmus took England's final tally to 297, just four short of the West Indies. Once he had seen the back of me, Charlie Griffith appeared to revive, and went on to take 5 for 91.

Although he didn't get me out, I'd taken a bad whack on the knee from one of his thunderbolts. Once I was back in the pavilion, having soaked up some heart-warming applause on the way, I realised how bad it was. The damage was serious enough to keep me out of the game for the next day. In the meantime, Colin Cowdrey took over as captain.

For the West Indies' second innings, I could only watch from the pavilion with my leg up and my teeth gritted. Astonishingly, they made just 229 runs, of which Basil Butcher produced 133. Trueman took a blistering 5 for 52, while my man Shackleton took 4 for 72. I sat there amazed by England's performance and impressed by Cowdrey's decision-making. Without Butcher's input it would have been a rout.

As a result, we went in for our second innings needing 234 to win the match. It was a tall order, but doable, I dared to hope.

Not for long. Our second innings began as disastrously as our first. Edrich went for 8 to a lifter from Hall, which put me in. I walked onto the field with rather less swagger than my first inning, my dodgy knee wrapped up like an

Egyptian mummy and not at all comfortable. Micky Stewart made a few more runs before he was caught off Hall for 17. Ken Barrington came in looking solid and had made 55, including two sixes by the end of play.

I didn't do so well. I had scored a couple of runs when Frank Worrell brought on Lance Gibbs, with the fourth-day pitch offering a bit of turn. I went forward to drive him, but I couldn't get as close to the ball or bend my front knee as much as I wanted; it turned, the gate was open and I was bowled. Enter Colin Cowdrey. He and Barrington were settling down together when Cowdrey got into trouble defending a short ball from Wes which kicked up towards his face. He put his left arm forward to protect himself; the hideous crack of a ball hitting bone echoed around the field as Cowdrey's bat fell to the ground. That was him done for the day; he retired on nineteen and walked back to the pavilion clutching his arm. Victory was looking less plausible.

Nevertheless, my confidence revived at the sight of the tough, redoubtable Yorkshireman, Brian Close, striding in, ready to take whatever Hall and Griffith could fire at him. A short while later, he'd made his first 7 runs before the light was deemed too bad. Tea was taken early, when the Queen met the teams, but before play could resume, Close and Barrington appealed against the light. The day closed with England on 116 for 3.

There was news of Cowdrey from the hospital; he had a broken bone in his left forearm. Meanwhile, the nation was agog; the Test match at Lord's had even pushed Christine and Mandy off the front page of the morning papers.

* *

On the damp-smelling dawn of the final day of this epic match, the capricious weather was still in charge; to my intense frustration, drizzle delayed the start of play. When the players eventually walked onto the field, to win the match we needed 118, with six wickets in hand. I certainly knew that it could be done — so long as we had enough overs to do it.

Once play had started, my frustration turned to dismay as I saw what Frank Worrell was doing. Knowing by then that his chances of winning were dwindling, he was determinedly playing for a draw. He set a defensive field and had obviously instructed his fast bowlers to take their time. They were strolling back to the start of their long run-up for each ball as if they had all the time in the world, and on the field, once the ball had been stopped, it always took the long route back to the bowler. Fielders were dawdling between overs, while the captain was leisurely in field placing. All these ploys which Worrell coolly deployed led to an abysmal over rate. If a bowler was taking too long, the umpires had the right to suspend him for the rest of the innings. But it would have taken a brave man to intervene in such an already dramatic situation.

Barrington and Close settled in quickly, although Barrington looked as if he'd lost his spark since the day before. After adding just five more, he nicked one from Griffith, and was caught behind. Jim Parks, looking positive as usual, scored only 17 before he too fell to Griffith, lbw. Brian Close, still unflinching from the battering he was taking, batted on through the arrival and departure of Titmus and Trueman, both caught off Wesley Hall, scoring 11 and 0 respectively. England's score stood at 203 for 7.

The tension in the crowd was building all the time. We needed 31 runs to win. We had two wickets in hand. The light was looking as if it might get involved. Close was our last chance, and I knew that he would relish the challenge, and he knew he would get little help from the tailenders. He was walking down the pitch against the quicks, taking a few blows to the body. A truly brave and bold cricketer, he suddenly cracked three fours through the leg side. The crowd roared, then froze. He tried once more, snicked a ball from Griffith, and was caught behind. He'd scored 70 and walked back to a standing ovation in the pavilion. We were 219 for 8.

Shackleton came out and walked steadily to the wicket. Facing even the tiring West Indian whirlwinds wasn't going to be fun. But he scored a couple. Allen had managed 3. There was one over left to play; 8 runs needed to win.

Shackleton scored a single; Allen did the same.

Shackleton faced, hit and ran again, and was run out.

England were on 228. Nine wickets had fallen. The sense of a drama being played out was profound.

Allen was still at the wicket.

The question now was whether Colin Cowdrey, with a broken arm, would bat or not?

Suddenly he was there, walking down the pavilion steps and through the gate, his left arm in plaster and his head held high, prepared to bat one-handed.

Two balls remained of the final over, with 6 runs needed to win the match.

The crowd quivered and held its communal breath.

Allen had the strike. He blocked the first ball.

Now, off the last ball, there were four possible results.

A six would win us the match.

A wicket and West Indies would be the winners.

Five runs, perhaps from a panicky overthrow, would mean a tie.

Allen calmly blocked the ball, and the match was drawn.

Suddenly the ground was alive with joyful, ecstatic West Indians, racing up to celebrate with the men who had saved them from defeat. Lord's had never seen such a pitch invasion as the players ran for cover in the pavilion.

Meanwhile, inside the pavilion, I was bitterly disappointed; we had come so close, so near to victory in what must have been one of the most thrilling, drama-filled Test matches in years. I believe that, beyond what was going on in the field, this was partly due to the tremendous enthusiasm brought to the occasion by the British West Indians, so much more ready to show and express their passion than the more restrained Anglos.

Despite intense disappointment over a game which I truly thought we deserved to win, and my misgivings over some aspects of the West Indian game, with the throwing and the time-wasting, especially during our second innings, I acknowledged their skill and physical prowess, as well as the canny pragmatism of their captain. Remembering my manners, I hurried down the corridor at the back of the pavilion to congratulate Frank Worrell and his team for their part in an epic and memorable Test match.

Nine days later, we were in Birmingham to play the third Test in even nastier weather than we'd had for the Lord's Test. I was quietly pleased about that; I knew the West Indians loathed playing in cold soggy conditions even more than we did. And we had the advantage of being used to it. After the euphoria over the Lord's Test, this one had a lot to live up to. Sadly, as a spectacle, it did not. We batted first on an accommodating, easy-paced pitch which Hall and Griffith did not appreciate, taking only 7 wickets between them in the whole match. With no standout performances we crawled to a total of 216. We improved on this by bowling out the West Indians for 186, in which I had the satisfaction of taking 4 wickets for 38, including Frank Worrell for 1! But it was Freddie Trueman who gave us a winning chance with 5 for 75.

Our second innings produced a pleasing partnership of 101 between myself and Yorkshireman Philip Sharpe, making his Test debut, who made 85 not out (sound familiar?) and also confirmed his reputation as one of the best slip catchers in the English game. We wrapped up the game by bowling them out for 91, with Trueman bagging 7 for 44, a total of 12 wickets in the match. We had won the match by 217 runs and squared the series 1-1. Not one of their batsmen made a 50 but, pleasing as it was to win a game, I knew that not all the pitches would be as helpful as Edgbaston.

Before the next Test Sussex played a Knockout Cup semi-final versus Northants. We were all out for 292, with the lanky David Larter, my New

Zealand project, taking 4 for 68. But they had the formidable Ian Thompson to cope with in helpful conditions and were all out for 187. Thus we sailed into the first-ever limited-over final without having been seriously threatened.

Over in Worcester in the other semi, played below the graceful might of the cathedral on the Severn, Worcestershire beat Lancashire; we would meet them at Lord's on 7 September. The public, as I had predicted, were well fired up by the new knockout competition and were looking forward to its climax. So was I; for despite the gloomy forebodings of a number of the wrinklier pundits, these one-day games, by quickly delivering a clear result, were certainly proving more entertaining than the traditional three-day Championship matches. With the intrusion of the Test matches that summer, I'd missed quite a few county games; nevertheless, we were doing at least as well as we had in 1960, and I was hopeful for our chances of getting even closer to the top of the Championship.

Regrettably, the West Indian series didn't go so well. The sun shone at Headingley for the fourth Test and the tourists, quickly taking the upper hand, beat us by 221 runs.

Towards the end of August, we did better in the final Oval Test, but not better enough. Griffiths took six wickets in our first innings; new boy Philip Sharpe top-scored with 83 runs in our second. In the end the West Indies scored 255 for 2 to overtake us in their second innings, beating us by 8 wickets. Despite this disappointment, everyone was elated to see a capacity house of twenty-four thousand, two thirds of them West Indian supporters, marking a well-earned 3-1 series triumph for their team.

I accepted that we'd been beaten by a better team. I congratulated Frank, of course, but, much as I admired him, I couldn't stop myself from saying to him afterwards, 'Well done, Frank, you've won the series, but I didn't like the way you did it at Lord's. And as for Charlie, you know how I feel about his action.'

Frank kept cool, as was his way, and smiled. 'That's just the way it is, man.'

* *

Halfway through the final of the Knockout Cup at Lord's it wasn't looking good for Sussex. The pitch suited the Worcester spinners – three of them who all had Test experience. Despite a good fifty from Jim Parks, we made an unimpressive 168. Worcester came in to bat and, as normal for the one-day games, I deployed my clutch of reliable medium pacers. But it just didn't happen. As I had feared, conditions were all wrong for my kind of bowlers who were failing either to contain the batsmen or take wickets. I had to think of something different. It didn't take genius; I had only one option. I turned to Alan Oakman, the only spinner we'd brought with us that day. As I threw him the ball, I could not have hoped for what followed.

Alan bowled steadily and accurately to begin with; I prayed that he could keep it up. His amazing figures of 13 overs, 1 for 17, speak for themselves. Well backed up by John Snow, the pressure started to tell. They just couldn't get the ball away while Alan took a wonderful catch as well. This confirmed my view that in these competitions, there was a real advantage in batting first; if you got a big score on the board, you were invincible; if you got a middling or even a smallish score, the other side tended to adjust their scoring rate to your score. This could provide a chance to put the pressure back on them. We did that day, bowling them out for just 154. We had won the first Knockout Cup.

This had been an exciting journey for Sussex who had never previously won any trophies. In those early days, when the game consisted of sixty-five overs a side, it allowed time for some good quality cricket to be played. My tactical approach of bowling straight and full had been vindicated, and I was proud to have played a major part in bringing this new form of county cricket to a wider audience.

The cricket scribblers were almost unanimous in their view that the new competition had been a great success, and had pulled in full houses. They liked the fact that they consistently saw a lot of action, and there was always a result, where there was always a strong chance of a draw in Championship matches.

Chapter Ten

PRIME MINISTERS

A few days after winning the Knockout Cup Final – a landmark for Sussex, and for cricket – I climbed into the 3-litre, wire-wheeled Jaguar, an upgrade with which the county had recently presented me, and drove sixty miles from London down to Chequers, the Prime Minister's country residence in Buckinghamshire. I'd been invited by Mr Harold Macmillan to lunch there, along with Frank Worrell and a handful of cricketing and political figures. I guessed we had been asked in recognition of the great success of the West Indies tour which had transfixed the nation for most of the summer, especially the already legendary Lord's Test. I was flattered that someone had taken the trouble to find a date when Frank and I would both be free.

I pulled up, parked and gazed up at the impressive, surprisingly warm face of the Tudor mansion. Built about 1560 in mellow red brick with stone mullions and some nineteenth-century faux gothic trappings, it was a quintessentially grand English manor house and seemed to me to be absolutely right as a Prime Minister's country bolthole – being used, as I write this book, by Prime Minister Boris Johnson to recuperate from his dose of coronavirus.

As I strode up to the front door, I'll admit to a quick frisson of excitement and importance. A butler let me in and showed me to a handsome panelled room where the Prime Minister shook my hand warmly and offered me a drink. We discussed the success of the West Indies tour, and cricket in general. He was attentive, and obviously knew what he was talking about. He introduced me to some of the guests, an interesting mix of cricket and politics. A familiar face, the Duke of Norfolk, had a foot in both camps; I assumed the other politicians were known cricket buffs – indeed I'd seen them at Lord's from time to time. Frank Worrell was already there, obviously at ease, as well as the illustrious veteran of West Indian cricket, Sir Learie Constantine, then in his mid-sixties and high commissioner in London for Trinidad and Tobago.

I also met Iain Macleod, leader of the House of Commons, urbane, impressive and one of Harold Macmillan's senior lieutenants, and I gathered that we were to be joined by Christopher Soames, Winston Churchill's son-in-law and then Minister for Agriculture. I realised that lunch was being held up for him when I heard the Prime Minister ask, a little testily, 'Where is Soames?'

When the minister burst into the room, uttering fulsome apologies, Macmillan raised a droopy eyebrow. 'You're late, Soames. Now tell me, what's the current state of the national harvest?'

Soames, evidently caught on the hop, blustered. 'Oh, quite satisfactory, Prime Minister.'

'That's not what I've heard,' the PM replied acerbically. 'I understand grain yields are down by as much as thirty per cent. I'll have your full report on my desk on Monday?' He glanced around at the rest of his guests. 'Shall we go into lunch?'

The agricultural discussion carried on into lunch, with the Prime Minister revealing a thorough grasp of his minister's brief and the current problems. I'd never seen a top politician functioning at such close quarters and was fascinated to see a first-class mind engaged and able to focus so tightly on the minutiae of government. At the same time, although he gave no obvious sign of it, I thought he probably had more pressing political problems on his mind. I was more than dimly aware that the Profumo affair which had been playing out all summer had damaged the government and was approaching a climax. Lord Denning, Master of the Rolls, was due to present the findings of his inquiry into it all at the end of the month.

Iain Macleod didn't admit to any anxiety over Profumo, but he impressed me too. It was a new experience for me to hear political issues discussed with frankness and fluency in such a small gathering. For the short time I was at Chequers, I felt privileged to be so close and in such easy circumstances with those who ran the country. It was a memorable and enriching experience which stayed with me for a long time. I was reminded of it again over the following year, when I entered into my own brief dalliance with politics.

**

Three days later, I was welcoming the West Indian touring team to Hove for the second time that summer. On this occasion there were two notable absences, Frank Worrell, and Charlie Griffith. I can't recall if they were injured or it was a case of cricket politics, particularly in the case of Charlie G. The game was to be played in the one-day, sixty-five-over format of the Knockout Cup and had been arranged to take place before the team left England after their five-month sojourn; as far as I recall it was a bonus fixture for our winning the cup. It's one distinctive feature was that at the start of their innings we had them at

4 for 9. We won, we enjoyed the game and, more importantly, so did our fans, who were already delighted that we'd climbed back up to fourth place in the Championship.

In my fourth year of captaincy, Sussex had done well. As captain of England, overall it hadn't been a bad year. We'd left Australia on an even footing, we had won three Tests in New Zealand, and although we'd lost the series to the West Indies, we'd played some great cricket, and entertained millions. Personally, I felt I'd contributed some of my best performances – certainly the Lord's Test was going to stay with me; indeed, it still does.

* *

When the MCC sounded me out on how I felt about taking the England team on the forthcoming winter tour of India, my immediate instinct was to shake my head. The last Indian tour had been tough, and in the end, not hugely rewarding. On top of that, after the long Antipodean tour which had ended for me at the beginning of April, and a full-on cricket programme at home since then, I needed a break. For one thing I owed it to Susan and Thomas to spend some time with them and have Christmas at home. I consulted with Susan, who agreed with me wholeheartedly.

I declined the invitation and felt as if a load had been lifted off my back, although I did so with some self-reproach, having been critical of senior players pulling out of the previous Indian tour which I'd captained. M. J. K. Smith was given the job; I gave him a few tips about how things were done in India, and wished him good luck.

I was more than happy to turn my attention to my domestic life, and to developing some business activity to bolster my unreliable income from cricket spin-offs. As I was beginning to enjoy my sabbatical from cricket, I was a little taken aback by events that overtook Harold Macmillan, my attentive host of a month before.

In a bizarre climax, towards the end of September, the Master of the Rolls, Lord Denning, released his report on Profumo, which generally exonerated the government. Nevertheless, damage had been done by the affair and Macmillan was said to be plagued by concerns over his government's unpopularity after a safe Tory seat had been lost in a by-election. When he was taken into hospital in early October to have a benign prostate tumour removed, he used this as a pretext to stand down. The premiership was passed to Sir Alec Douglas-Home – a delightful human being who was simply not suited for the job. On one occasion, meeting him at a reception, I noticed that when conversation dried up, he simply looked down at his shoes for inspiration. Harold Macmillan would have just passed me by with a nod and smile. Sir Alec's tenure came to an end only a year later when a Labour government was elected and Harold Wilson moved into 10 Downing Street.

More immediately for Susan and me, the first thing we had to deal with was the increasingly obvious inadequacy of our accommodation. With Thomas growing and the relentless accumulation of paraphernalia that seemed to surround even an eighteen-month-old boy, we had come to the conclusion that there simply wasn't enough space for the three of us in our neat little Ebury Street flat.

We let it be known among our friends, and anyone else who might have been interested, that we wanted to sell the long lease on the flat. A friend of Susan's family soon showed an interest. Michael Marshall was an affable, if unusual, indeed slightly mysterious, figure who had no obvious full-time employment and enjoyed watching cricket. He wrote a bit and, from time to time, appeared to be involved in some other impenetrable business activity. There was in his demeanour and studied vagueness something that suggested to me that he might have been some kind of a spy. An intimate knowledge of cricket would have made excellent cover for clandestine activity in England. I'll admit that my jaundiced view may have been caused by his having known Susan before me, and his still being a little too friendly with her for my liking.

I learned later that Susan's parents had known him in the fifties, when he was running the Calcutta office of a British company, United Steel – which swiftly debunked my spy theory. When he bought the flat he was, in fact, still involved with United Steel, before joining a management consultancy, and in 1974, being elected Conservative MP for Arundel and ultimately knighted.

Once we knew for certain that Michael Marshall was going to buy the flat, we started looking for a larger place, which meant, for price reasons, looking further west. Luckily, my brother, John, had a friend who sold us a short lease on a maisonette in Finborough Road, SW10, for a modest £7,000. This was in the furthest margins of the Royal Borough of Kensington and Chelsea, on the border with Fulham and within a short distance of the Chelsea FC stadium at Stamford Bridge – so near, in fact, that if we were home on a Saturday afternoon, we could hear the fans bellowing in the old-fashioned Chelsea way from the Shed at the south end of the ground. In a handsome, early Victorian building, our new home occupied the first, second and third floors, with three bedrooms and a decent-sized drawing room (enough to accommodate most of the England team when they came to the party we gave for them). In one of the mezzanine floors, there was a playroom for young Master T. Dexter and all the baggage that came with him.

Not long after we'd moved and were settling in at Finborough Road, Susan announced, to our great excitement, that she was pregnant again; it was early days, with the baby not due until the beginning of June. I was more pleased than ever that I had turned down India. Meanwhile Susan was still much in demand for modelling and there had even been discussions about my doing a few television commercials with her. As usual, I was ready to try anything. 'Bring it on!' was my view.

In our new, bigger place, we found ourselves short of furniture. This prompted my first taste of scouring antique shops, an activity which I learned to enjoy, buying furniture at first and over the years all sorts of things that caught my eye. Every time I had a decent win on a horse or a greyhound, for example, I liked to spend a proportion of the winnings on some interesting object which with luck, would also appreciate in value and, more importantly, the funds wouldn't go straight back to the bookmaker.

I was a bit green to begin with and my trusting nature sometimes got in the way, so it didn't always work out. One of my brothers-in-law, Dick Prichard, older and more worldly wise (or so I thought), had moved out of London and was buying furniture for their larger house. He recommended an antique shop near his country home. Here was a rare dealer who promised to buy back any item at the price paid, at any time in the future. We slowly filled the house in a way that pleased us, but a year or so later, Susan and I decided that a fine cherrywood chest I'd bought didn't really work where we'd put it and we didn't have anywhere else for it. It was no problem, I told Susan; I would take it back to the dealer and he would give me my money back. When I went to see him about it, his urbane features took on a look of pained regret. Since I'd bought the piece, it seemed, cherrywood had gone out of fashion, he told me, shaking his head hopelessly. You could hardly give it away, he said, and my chest wasn't worth half what I'd given for it. He suggested I put it in an auction, where, I assumed, he would go and buy it back for a fraction of what I'd paid him. I left his premises having learned a useful lesson in antiques buying.

* *

We were glad to have the extra space at Finborough Road when my brother David came to live with us for a while. He was now twenty and had been living in a handicapped community close to the Sheiling School where he'd been happy for most of his childhood. I'd been incredibly impressed by the school and the ethos behind it. The practical application of its philosophy and its achievements have been stunning.

The Sheiling Curative School for Backward Boys and Girls at Thornbury in Gloucestershire was an offshoot of the Camphill Movement which had been founded in 1940 by Dr Karl König. König, a follower of human philosopher, Rudolf Steiner, described the thinking behind his foundation: 'The handicapped child is no longer looked upon as an imbecile person and a burden to the community. Their human abilities are recognised and great efforts are being made to treat and train, to teach and help these children.'

This kind of understanding and compassion was comparatively new. Until less than a century ago, the child with a damaged brain had been excluded from society without a qualm; if he was not simply tolerated as the village idiot, he was just put away, out of sight, out of mind. Even in the 1960s there were still many fearful and ignorant parents who were overwhelmed by the unexpected, undeserved tragedy of having a mentally handicapped child in the family. However, David was a deeply loved son to his parents and brother to his siblings and was capable of giving back as much love as he was given. My father and mother both doted on him and had diligently researched every possible option for his care and education, and we were delighted that the Sheiling School had been so good for him. Like his older brothers, he usually went back to Italy for the holidays, where he would play golf, or come to the restaurants my father liked, and as far as was possible, he was just another member of our family.

The transition from school age to adult life for a child with Down's tends to be difficult and when he had reached that point he was admitted to a charitable community not far from Thornbury which provided a natural extension to the Sheiling School. He was well cared for there and expected to work at simple tasks within his range. He was happy there too, until the two adults on whom he most relied left the community at the same time. On our next visit, Susan and I could see that this had been very tough on him. He'd become quite unsettled, feeling vulnerable, bereft and insecure. It seemed to us that he had reached a distinct watershed in his life.

We agreed that the best thing would be to have him living with us in London while we reviewed his needs and decided what to do next. We thought and hoped that living in our home, he would experience a bit of stability and security, as indeed, for a while, he did. He was undoubtedly happier, but now, hormonally, a young man, he was becoming more self-conscious about his handicap and was beginning to talk quite morosely about his future.

'Nobody's ever going to love me,' he said in a way that really moved us.

We understood that he was reaching a new phase of life that would need sensitive, specialist handling. He told us that this was his first home, aware, it seemed, that there was a difference to the community living he was used to.

However, in the end, he was missing that sense of community, and we were aware that we couldn't give him the full-time care and attention he needed. The problem we faced was that there were very few places that offered the high standards we wanted for him.

I had already done some homework in anticipation of this situation and had discovered a proposal for the creation of a new special village at Shangton, near Market Harborough, under the auspices of Cottage and Rural Enterprises, or CARE. The same organisation had already established a CARE village in Devon. This one was the initiative of a local businessman and farmer, Jack Townsend, who had donated the land, but was looking for funding for the development costs. I understood what he was trying to do and spent many hours with him working on fundraising ideas. Sadly, however, his health started to deteriorate fast and he died soon after his project had become a reality.

One of the first things I did, in November 1963, was to hold a fundraising lunch at the Tallow Chandlers' Hall in the City of London, to which I invited about a hundred wealthy Londoners, on the grounds that if one is going to ask people for money one might as well ask the richest. About twenty came, including the new Prime Minister, Sir Alec Douglas-Home. He arrived and was shown to his place next to me. As soon as the opening pleasantries had been exchanged, he started talking about his problems in the House. I listened closely, fascinated, having had lunch and talked with his predecessor only a couple of months before at Chequers. We talked a little about cricket, although he modestly made no reference to his own first-class record: ten matches played, for Middlesex and Oxford University among others; 147 runs in 15 innings, an average of 16.3 and 12 wickets taken and an average of 30.25. As far as I know he is the only British Prime Minister ever to have played any serious cricket. Despite his slightly fusty image which had been such a gift to the cartoonists of the time, I found Sir Alec a delightful, remarkably straightforward and unaffected man, although, perhaps, not tough enough for what is a very tough job.

Regrettably, as a fundraiser, it was not a success. One personal friend wrote a cheque for £1,000, but the rest barely contributed as much between them. I was disappointed, a little disgusted and, some weeks later, embarrassed when my friend asked what the total sum raised had been. However, with a lot more work, the money needed for the new CARE village. was found and David became one of the first members of the community. He had his own room and furniture there and happily worked in the print shop. There were few restrictions on the residents, and he was free to roam out of working hours. It was to be his home for the next forty years.

When my mother died, with my father very immobile and my brother John living in Italy, the entire responsibility for David's welfare fell on Susan and me, and inevitably with my own packed schedule of work and travel, the bulk of day-to-day caring for him fell on Susan. With characteristic good humour she undertook the task wonderfully. My side of the Dexter family owe her enormous thanks for the loving care she gave David for much of his life.

* *

Later in November, on the twenty-second, to be precise, I headed west from London on the newly opened first leg of the M4 on my way to a meeting in Bristol. My sister Pamela lived in Tetbury, near Cirencester, and had invited me for dinner and to stay the night on my way back. I didn't know how long my meeting would go on and had warned her I might be late.

'Just do your best, please, Teddy,' Pamela had said.

Inevitably I was late. I was still in the car driving from Bristol listening to the radio when I heard a shocking announcement that was to reverberate all around the world in a matter of hours. President John F. Kennedy had been shot dead by a sniper while driving in an open-topped car through the streets of Dallas, Texas.

Like everyone else who had heard the news, I was stunned, shaken and worried. By the time I arrived, dinner had started. I sat down at once, with my mind full of the news I had heard, which the rest of the party obviously had not.

I didn't mention it at first, though; I felt it would somehow be rude to announce it and ruin the dinner party. For a while I made myself join in the conversation carrying on around the table, acutely aware that I was the only person at the table who knew what had happened. As I talked, I was wondering what on earth I should do.

I made up my mind, took a deep breath and interrupted the conversation.

'Are any of you aware,' I asked portentously, 'that President Kennedy was assassinated in Dallas today?'

As I had thought it would, the dinner party stopped dead in its tracks.

Chapter Eleven

ASHES IN ENGLAND, HUSTINGS AND SOUTH AFRICA

Christmas at home in 1963 came as a welcome change for Susan and me. Having turned down the India tour, this was the first Christmas I had spent in England for five years, and I had forgotten how enjoyable it could be. We asked Susan's Auntie Rhoda and cousin Caroline to join us at Finborough Road, with Thomas, aged twenty-one months, at least vaguely aware that something festive was going on. A week or so later, the arrival of 1964 marked the start of an unexpected new phase of my life.

At 28, I couldn't claim ever to have been seriously politically engaged, but given my background, it was fairly inevitable that my political leanings were broadly Tory. I knew roughly what was going on; I read the papers like anyone else. I had also had lunch and discussed political issues with two Prime Ministers, both Conservative. From this I knew that the current government had a few problems; I thought they probably weren't feeling too bullish about the general election due to be held the following October. Nevertheless, until one evening shortly after Christmas, when Geevers Wynne-Jones, chairman of the Cardiff South East Conservative Party, knocked on my door, it never occurred to me that I might get involved.

What he and his colleagues in Cardiff South East wanted was for me to consider standing as the Conservative candidate for their constituency in the autumn election. Their previous man, Michael Roberts, had suddenly stood down. They hadn't the time to establish a new local candidate and wanted a name that voters would at least recognise on the ballot sheet.

When I learned that the incumbent MP was James Callaghan who had held the seat since 1945 and was Labour's Shadow Chancellor, even with my scant knowledge, I realised it would be a tough challenge. It also occurred to me that the thrashing Sussex CCC had just given Glamorgan CCC might be a hindrance.

I think the constituency selectors also felt that my regular appearances on TV screens in various advertisements, as well as playing cricket, had made me a familiar face, which, I was assured, would help in attracting votes. I doubted that, but I went along with it.

Perhaps to test the strength of their convictions, I told Mr Wynne-Jones that they should think again. I admitted that I knew more about Italian politics than English, and that the sum total of both wouldn't be enough to fill a five-minute speech to the Young Conservatives of Cardiff South East.

Despite my protests, they didn't back down. They persisted, and after a little demurring, I committed myself to standing for Parliament in ten months' time. Susan thought I had gone mad, but she was used to that.

The process got under way and once I had presented myself for inspection by the constituency party, I was formally adopted, and there was no turning back.

In an odd way, I relished the prospect. I loved new challenges, whatever they were. At the same time, I was still fully committed to playing cricket; I was by then writing regularly for *The Observer*; there was more television work coming up, but I felt there was still enough room in my life for this new activity. I may have been a little romantic about the prospect, but I went into it willingly with a genuine aspiration to make something of it, if only for the experience.

I wasn't surprised to find that there were those who saw it otherwise. On the eve of my adoption Neville Cardus, doyen of cricket writers, analysed this new departure of mine in the *Daily Express*:

> *Apparently Dexter is undecided at the age of twenty-eight, whether he is*
> *(a) a great batsman*
> *(b) an unpredictable bowler*
> *(c) a journalist*
> *(d) a television star [in Australia]*
> *(e) a potential golfer*
> *or (f) a future leader of the Tory Party.*
> *It is beyond me that Dexter, a young man with his talents as a great cricketer, should think for a moment of giving up any of his days or nights to Westminster and politics.*

Having had the rare pleasure of spending Christmas and the new year at home with my family, I hadn't played a game of cricket for three months when I had to get myself ready to depart for the West Indies. I was playing in a short series of first-class matches for the International Cavaliers. I'd played a couple of rough games with these nomadic mercenaries in Southern Africa on my way back from

Australia a year before. This was going to be my first 'tour' with them, albeit consisting of only four games to be played – three first-class matches against Jamaica and one against a local team, quaintly named, Combined Parishes. The whole trip would take less than three weeks, and Susan, only slightly pregnant, was coming with me. She was looking forward to the Caribbean in winter. We'd been invited along with Trevor Bailey, Peter Richardson and their wives to stay with Frank Worrell who, to the dismay of his fellow Barbadians, now lived in Jamaica. He put us all up on camp beds scattered around the house.

After a career lasting nearly twenty years Frank had retired from cricket at the end of the previous year's Test series in England. He was now a member of the Jamaican Senate, and a warden at the University of Jamaica. He was also involved in cricket administration and at the end of the year was manager of the West Indies team in Australia. In 1964 he received a well-deserved knighthood for his services to cricket – an impressive man who managed to combine gravitas with urbane charm. He was tremendously hospitable to us and staying with him added a lot to our enjoyment of the trip, which was in any case a far more informal affair than an MCC tour.

In the Caribbean winter sunshine and the lush Jamaican landscape we played some truly enjoyable cricket in front of big, appreciative crowds. In one particularly hard-fought game, Colin Ingleby-Mackenzie, one of our lower-order batsmen and old Etonian captain of Hampshire, came in to bat with me. The Jamaicans had put on a new young tearaway of a fast bowler, obviously keen to emulate the speed and fear-inducing properties of bowlers like Charlie Griffith. They had taken the new ball and I could see he was gearing up to do his worst. I didn't think my pal, Colin, was going to enjoy himself. I went to have a word with him.

'Colin, you won't like this. Just try and take a single and I'll handle him.'

Colin nodded and managed to do as I had requested. Once I was facing, I let a couple go. I was looking for a ball just the right length and line for my not so subtle intentions. When the right one came along, I whacked it straight at the young bowler, just like a one iron, into the wind at Rye. It was bang on line for his head, but he ducked just in time and hit the ground prostrate where he lay for a few moments before getting up, looking terrified. He didn't follow through much after that.

It was a good fortnight. Susan had a lovely time, and I was more than happy with two good personal scores of 176 and 120. The second of these was particularly gratifying when Jim Laker, who in my early days had not been a great supporter, told me it was the best innings he'd ever seen. We were grateful to Frank Worrell for having us, but concerned that he hadn't been entirely well and was receiving treatment. Indeed, three years later while he was with the West Indies team in India, he was diagnosed with leukaemia and died shortly afterwards, aged just forty-three. He was buried in Westminster Abbey, a measure of the regard in which he was held.

I had a brief rest from cricket again before the English season started, and took the opportunity to take up some of the offers I'd had to appear in a few TV advertisements. It had been proposed that I do one with Susan; together we would try to encourage the British viewing public to drink more Vermouth, in this case the trickily named French version, Noilly Prat.

This was a challenge indeed. Spoken quickly, without applying a French accent, 'I'll have a Noilly Prat, please' sounded like a somewhat obscene request. They wanted posh English voices to say it with a French accent – phonetically: 'I'd love a Noy-ee Prah.' I doubt that our amateurish efforts improved their sales one iota. The strange-sounding name was to prove an insurmountable handicap. They might have done better simply to create an entirely new brand.

I also advertised a number of strictly male products like Peter England shirts and Ingram's Shaving Cream. Susan joined me in the Ingram's ad, smiling and fussing about while a voice off asks enigmatically, 'Is it the built-in aftershave?'

To which I reply, 'Yes, it is', and Susan hands me a pair of batting gloves which looked disconcertingly like two bunches of bananas.

I wondered how this was going down among the voters of Cardiff South East.

* *

At the end of February Mike Smith arrived back in England following two months of a less gruelling MCC tour of India than I'd had in 1961/62, for which he was grateful. They had drawn all five Tests – disappointing for him although he had enjoyed the tour, where his opposite number on the Indian side had been Tiger Pataudi, like Mike, a former captain of the Oxford University XI. I had no regrets that I hadn't gone, especially as it would have meant missing the Jamaica trip. And by then I was looking forward to having another crack at the knockout competition, especially as it now had a good sponsor behind it and had become the Gillette Cup. It's said that when the executives from the Gillette company charged with discussing the deal with the MCC arrived at Lord's with a pragmatic budget in mind, they were pleasantly surprised to find that they could fund their commitment to the new event almost from petty cash. They committed and the Gillette Cup had arrived. This sponsorship would, I knew, ensure that the one-day game would maintain a high profile and, more importantly, continue to be played.

I was very optimistic about the attention this form of the game had attracted in its first year, especially with so many Test and first-class matches still producing something approaching two draws to every one result, a serious disincentive to the spectating public. This time around, the Sussex team already knew exactly how to play the one-day game, but over the five rounds of the previous year's tournament, our tactics had been endlessly examined, analysed and discussed in clubroom bars and the back pages of the newspapers. I was conscious that there were bound to be a few copyists among the other county captains.

Beyond the Gillette Cup prospects, there was the Championship to think about, although, frankly, by then I had lost some of my enthusiasm for that competition. In any case, dominating my hopes and aspirations was what would be my fourth encounter with the Australians, my second as captain.

Against Benaud in 1962/63 I had held them at bay in that famously exhausting series, but now, with Benaud, Harvey, Mackay and Davidson all retired, I would be facing Bobby Simpson with what was being described as one of the weakest sides ever to leave Australia. I'd heard this kind of talk before and had learned to treat it circumspectly, especially where Test series were involved. Nevertheless, I was hopeful that we could twist their tails in our own country.

When it came to it, though, it was a disappointing, rainwashed series, especially when compared to the gladiatorial combats with the West Indies the previous summer. The first Test in Nottingham was drawn.

The first day of the Lord's Test was lost to rain. On the morning of the second day, 19 June, I was rung and told it was still too wet, and there would be no play that day either. So, by great good fortune, I was able to race through the London traffic to St Bartholomew's Hospital, where Susan was, once again, about to give birth, this time to our second born. She was already in labour and the baby's arrival was very imminent when, just as with baby Tom, I was shooed from the room. I sat in a corridor and pulled out my copy of the *Sporting Life* but barely had time to look at the day's runners when I was called back in to gaze with pride at our first lovely daughter, Genevieve. I drove Susan back home with the baby and introduced her to Tom. A boy and a girl – a proper, neat little family, I thought, already aware that we had run out of space again. I was at Lord's the following morning, after two lost days, to commence the second Test. This too ended in a draw.

The only match that reached a decision was the third Test at Headingley, where, I regret to say, as a result of my bowling decisions in the Australians first innings, I left a deep footprint for the press to tread in for the rest of time.

England won the toss and after losing John Edrich for 3, I joined our new opener, Geoffrey Boycott (who had made his Test debut and 48 runs in the first match at Trent Bridge). He and I made the most of some unusually inaccurate bowling from Neil Hawke, but we didn't take as much advantage of it as we could have. Hawke and McKenzie, with the help of some fine catching, broke into our innings and we were all out for 268. This total didn't look so modest when Australia in reply stood at 178 for 7. This put me in mind of the Brisbane Test of 62, although this time there was no Benaud, Mackay or Davidson to fire up the lower-order batting. But Peter Burge, who had come in at No. 4 was still playing with impressive single-mindedness when, after Graham McKenzie had gone for nought, he was joined by Neil Hawke. England's spinners, Titmus and Gifford had been dominating the bowling. The new ball was due, while Burge and Hawke, ringed by close catchers, weren't playing a stroke. It looked like a stalemate. I knew that Trueman and Flavell were itching to get hold of a new ball and see off the tail. Less than half an hour earlier Trueman had made the old ball bounce and move, taking Cowper out with a perfect inswinger. Now with Burge and Hawke looking immutable, I sought the new ball. The umpire held it up; the crowd fell silent to witness the docking of Australia's tail.

If anyone on the ground at that moment was shocked by my decision to replace the spinners with the fast men, he must have been an oracle. It was a debatable choice with no obvious answer, although for me, with what I could see, it was straightforward. The spinners were getting nowhere now, and Peter Burge in form had shown he had as complete a mastery of spin as any other type of bowling. At Sydney in 1963 he had held out against Titmus and Allen for over two hours; at the Oval in 1961 he had hit them all round the ground. Hawke was an unknown quantity, but he seemed to be coping with spin, whereas Trueman had castled him at Lord's. I had to shift these men. A decision had to be taken. I took the new ball.

Trueman and Flavell had 42 runs scored off them in just 7 overs. It was inexplicable that they bowled short to Burge, one of the best hookers in the game. The pitch at Headingley was, and still is, well known as a feather bed for short balls. Whatever got into them that day, I never discovered. Wisden described the performance: 'Trueman fed Burge a generous supply of medium-paced long hops.' The batsmen had added 105 between them before Neil Hawke was finally caught off Trueman.

The keeper, Wally Grout, came in; he and Burge put on another 89 before Titmus, whom I'd put back on, had him lbw. He walked off with the score at 372. By the time Burge finally hooked a ball to a catch off Trueman — at last — he had scored 160.

There have been years of discussion about my handling of this innings, with no firm conclusions reached, but it did establish for a long time to come that the taking of the new ball is never a straightforward option.

* *

For the Old Trafford match, with Australia now one up, I found myself once again chasing them in a series. Bobby Simpson made it clear that he was playing a back game and handled it with great skill. Trueman had been dropped as a result of his abject performance in the Leeds Test, and Australia made 656 for 8, including a studious 311 by Simpson. However, thanks to a stand of 246 between Ken Barrington (256) and me (174), we reached a total of 611 and avoided defeat. It was the first time that two teams had made 600 runs in an innings in a Test, and for a brief few days the nation's cricket fans were gripped, until followed by the inevitable draw, which meant that whatever happened in the last Test, Australia had hung on to the little brown urn yet again.

The Oval Test started on 13 August and, although I didn't know it at the time, I captained England for what was to be the last time. The rain once again curtailed this final Test, resulting in the inevitable fourth draw of the series, and Australia's final tally of 1-0 was confirmed.

I was bitterly disappointed, of course, but I didn't feel I'd made many wrong decisions; we had produced some fine batting and bowling performances, but in the end, the weather had won.

One encounter during the Oval Test has stuck in the memory, although it had nothing to do with the match. Among the spectators in the pavilion was the Maharajkumar of Vizianagram, or Vizzy as he'd asked me to call him when I had enjoyed some of his lavish hospitality in India in 1961. When I was told that he was there, I sought him out for a chat. As soon as I saw him I was shocked by the change in his appearance. His thick mane of black hair had been replaced by a mop of pure white. His cheeks had hollowed into sunken dips, and there were dark wrinkled rings around his eyes. I couldn't avoid commenting on the dramatic change in his appearance and asked him what was wrong.

He returned my gaze with a mournful look and sighed. It was a result, he told me, of his other great passion which was tiger hunting. He had been out on a regular hunt, riding high in a howdah on his favourite elephant when a tiger had crept up and attacked without warning; the elephant, alarmed, staggered violently to one side, and the howdah slipped to the ground, spilling out a defenceless Vizzy.

His voice dropped to a whisper as he described the scene. 'I was face to face with this tiger – only inches away. I truly thought that was it, and I'd had it.'

At the last second, though, the tiger had been distracted from his intention of attacking and devouring Vizzy, and the Maharajkumar had survived. It was clear, nevertheless, that this close encounter with a possible savage death had taken a huge toll on him. The poor man died back in India not long after my seeing him at the Oval, literally, it seemed, frightened to death.

The last month of the season was taken up with the final rounds of the now excitingly popular Gillette Cup, which we won for the second time, and the last of the three-day matches of the Championship.

**

Once the cricket season was over, I was able to focus on preparations for my first foray into British politics. From the start, I'd taken the view that I was a long shot, but I was determined to do the best that was possible. Geevers Wynne-Jones, the local party chairman, had told me frankly, 'You're not going to win, but we must show our supporters that we're trying here. You'll be doing us a great favour.'

The last Conservative candidate, Michael Roberts, was a schoolmaster and well respected, with the kind of oratorical skills that are appreciated in Wales. He had spent ten years and two elections working on it and had sneaked up to within one thousand votes of Callaghan's share in 1959 before he had decided not to stand again.

I thought it would be a tough call to improve on that and I certainly wasn't tipped to win, so the downside was light. While I hadn't been politically active at university, I knew a few other Conservative politicians from my Cambridge days, including Tom King, who also had aspirations to sit in Parliament (and got a lot further than me). Beyond that, I was vaguely casting around for possible post-cricket careers.

As 15 October, election day, approached, it was beginning to dawn on me what I'd taken on. Now that I had seen more of my opponent Jim Callaghan, whom I instinctively liked, I realised what a major player he was within the Labour party. At the same time, nationally, there was an air of gloom among those Conservatives in the know. Harold Macmillan's slightly messy demise and Sir Alec's perceived detachment from the ordinary man, added to the lingering smell of John Profumo's public mendacity, were having a detrimental effect on their public image.

I was also aware that the new Labour leader, Harold Wilson, wasn't particularly attractive to the voters either and, sanguine as ever, I approached the election feeling that if I could get through to the voters, I had a chance.

I met Iain Macleod for the second time since seeing him at Chequers when I was among a gathering of Conservative candidates in Westminster in which he spoke eloquently and potently about the importance of winning this election for the Tories. I went off to South Wales feeling fired up and probably more confident than was reasonable, but I took the view that one never walked out to bat expecting to be out for a duck. I enthusiastically did my stint of electioneering, backed up by the ever-loyal Susan, as well as Thomas and Genevieve in her carrycot (although there is no chance whatsoever of Genevieve canvassing for the Tories these days).

I enjoyed myself, up to a point, although I didn't find it easy to engage with voters on their doorsteps in any meaningful way. However, I flattered myself I was going down alright, overlooking the fact that, on the whole, the people who came to our meetings were already committed to our cause.

As I expected the press picked up the ball and the cricket puns flowed. 'Dexter's Big Test.'

'Mr Dexter's Tricky Wicket.'

'Mr Callaghan, the demon bowler of Cardiff South East.'

Once, it was reported, when asked a question on the stump, presumably a bit of an off-spinner: 'Dexter wisely took his bat away.'

To be fair to Jim Callaghan in the same terms, he played a very calm game. One if his smarter tactics was to emphasise local problems, rather than avoiding them. For years housewives in the constituency had been complaining about the dust that billowed from a nearby cement works, ruining their washing. In his manifesto there was a photo of him standing with some of the housewives, next to their grey washing on the line. He never attacked me frontally, just one well-flighted googly on the spot a few days before the election, otherwise a concentrated campaign among the members of his own side. He did pay me the compliment of being seen around the constituency more than in previous elections, but that was about the extent of his counter-attack against the negligible threat that I posed, and he comfortably carried the day. I felt that my defeat wasn't totally without honour; I had at least managed to attract 22,288 votes to Callaghan's 30,129.

This evidently reflected the mood of the nation which voted in a Labour government for the first time in thirteen years. Twelve years later, Jim Callaghan himself became Prime Minister when Harold Wilson stood down during his third term as premier.

I had to admit to myself that the whole adventure had been something of a vain hope in two senses of the word. But I'd had a go, and undoubtedly I had learned something from the experience – not least, that politics was probably not my ideal metier.

**

One negative side effect of standing for Parliament was that the MCC-South Africa tour's departure date, 15 October, coincided directly with election day, where my presence was required in Cardiff South East. Naturally, I was dead keen to go on the tour – I'd scored a century against all the other Test-playing nations, and wanted to complete my full house. I was selected and given special permission to join the England tour three weeks late, although, of course, I was denied the captaincy, which reverted once more to Mike Smith.

Meanwhile, before I flew out to join them, I had to pick my way through another controversy, self-generated, of course, over a piece of déjà vu. I enjoyed writing my regular *Observer* column, particularly because I was free to choose what I wanted to write, on a variety of topics. I was lucky to have the platform and, having been subjected myself to much press comment, I took a special pleasure in developing my own voice. I knew I was no Cassandra but I liked the process of formulating views and trying to express them accurately. I tried not to be self-indulgent, and, in any case, Clifford Makins would have sat on me if I were, but it did mean that I could flex my pen over issues that I thought deserved airing. Reading the pieces on a Sunday morning, I realised that they didn't always come off; indeed, some of them didn't even make it into print.

It had been preying on my conscience since the previous summer that Charlie Griffith had been able to carry on bowling with an action which looked more than suspect to many others besides me – Tom Graveney, Ken Barrington and Colin Cowdrey among them. Griffith had not been called by the umpires, publicly criticised or reprimanded in any way, and I took a cue from the imminent West Indies tour of Australia to point out the deficiencies in Griffith's action, effectively to call him out for 'chucking'. I said that the result of the forthcoming contest would be meaningless if Griffith were permitted to bowl as he had done the summer before.

It was felt that within the piece were implicit criticisms of the umpires, the managers and the MCC committee. No doubt heads were shaking at Lord's.

**

I'd left it all behind me by the time I arrived in South Africa, where I found that not having that responsibility of captaincy suited me well. It allowed me to relax and enjoy some spectacular tourism, as well as having a few good innings. Basil Easterbrook in Wisden's tour report wrote, 'Dexter undoubtedly benefitted from being relieved of the burden of captaincy. He seemed more relaxed and at ease than at any previous time in his career and made a major contribution to what was always an excellent dressing-room atmosphere.' It was probably as well that the undercurrents of fractious dressing-room politics were kept under wraps.

When I'd caught up with the team, I soon saw that the youthful Yorkshireman, Geoffrey Boycott, was being well and truly boycotted by the other younger pros on the tour. When I asked them why, they told me that he was so self-centred and obnoxious that they didn't want anything to do with him. Michael Brearley was also suffering at their hands; they refused to bowl at him properly in the nets because, they said, 'he's so inept, we don't want to make him look worse'.

In Boycott's case, I thought he needed a leg-up and spent some time and trouble trying to rehabilitate him, with a little success. In retrospect, I might have served cricket better if I'd left him to suffer, and perhaps to learn to curb his selfishness at that formative stage in his career. I was more than a little irritated when, at Port Elizabeth, I became the first to be run out by him. His subsequent trail of at least *thirteen* run-out victims lasted throughout his career. Eventually, Ian Botham decided that enough was enough and intentionally returned the compliment. I wish I'd done the same years earlier. As for Michael Brearley, and indeed, the dreaded knight himself, I can only admire their tenacity in reaching the pinnacles of the game despite their distinctly shaky early experiences.

**

The first Test at Kingsmead started on 4 December, and we won convincingly by an innings and 104 runs. It was a big fillip at the start of the tour, although we could only draw the next four Tests. In the second Test at the Wanderers, I was 172 not out at the close on the first day. It was a perfect pitch with a fast outfield and as I walked out the next morning, I thought I would never have a better chance of beating Len Hutton's score of 364. I was out in the first over, but at least I had completed my set of centuries. But perhaps the best occasion for me was a run-out. I was nearly thirty years old, not as quick as I was, so found myself parked down at third man. Colin Bland, brilliant big-hitting batsman and a great run-out expert himself, was also fleet between wickets and twice stole a second run in my area. Surreptitiously I sidled in and next time, as he turned for a second run, I knew I had him in trouble with a throw-in that was rapid and on target, providing one of the most pleasing moments of the tour for me. Bland was a fine all-rounder, but, sad to say, his future was blighted by acute alcoholism and he died young in London, despite a lot of friends trying to help him.

England left South Africa in February, having won the series 1-0, the first overseas Test series we had won in five years. We didn't lose a single match on the tour, winning eleven and drawing eight. Mike Smith as captain had pulled it off by keeping calm and keeping spirits up. Praise was lavished on him, and my own captaincy compared unfavourably. I reminded myself that over four years I had led England in thirty Tests. Nine had been won, and only seven lost – but then, I hadn't won the Ashes. I had to shrug my shoulders and wonder how Mike would fare – if he was still in charge – in Australia the following winter.

Chapter Twelve

LEG BREAK

Back in England after the enjoyment of the South African tour, and conscious that my days as captain of England were over, I still couldn't whip up much enthusiasm for the county game. I'd loved winning the first two Knockout Cups, but by now Sussex would have lost its innovative edge as the others caught up. I found myself thinking less about cricket and more about what, ultimately, I was going to do to support my family. The television advertisements and, to a certain extent, my journalism I tended to treat as transitory activities, although I hoped to keep up the writing, if only as a sideline, for as long as any paper would publish me.

I had also been having ongoing discussions with Bagenal Harvey, with the idea, perhaps, of getting more involved in his business. I could see that the managing of sportsmen's careers and sporting events had a solid future, and both were areas in which I had a lot of knowledge and experience.

Over the previous couple of years with the support of his best and oldest client, Denis Compton, Bagenal had been developing the concept of the International Cavaliers. This loose collection of cricketing stars from around the world had existed for a while as a kind of peripatetic touring team. I'd played in a couple of matches with them in Southern Africa on my way back from New Zealand in 1963, as well as the four-match tour in Jamaica in early 1964, which had attracted big local attendances. I could certainly see the potential of it, especially as the players were receiving appreciably more for their appearances than they received for their regular first-class appearances. Bagenal was sure he could take the idea further; he was skilled in spotting new money-making opportunities that had escaped the attention of the inert, old order in cricket. He felt that Cavaliers matches on Sundays against each of the counties could be a winner and, above all, a natural for TV. Up until then, the only Sunday games played were benefit matches for retiring players, which might have raised a few hundred pounds. Bagenal's plan was to build on this. My job was to draw up a set of rules for the new format, broadly speaking forty overs each, to be completed in a day, always with a result with no draws or ties. To be sure of getting all the overs in, we restricted the bowlers' run-ups, effectively to reduce the amount of time required per over. The matches had to finish by 6pm, in time for the BBC to broadcast their Sunday evening *Songs of Praise*. The income from the broadcast was important because, although thousands turned up to see the big international stars playing, we weren't allowed to charge for entry to the grounds on a Sunday, although we did inflate the charge for the scorecard, which went some way to making up for it.

More crucially, Bagenal had already identified Rothmans as a likely sponsor. He was currently running a tennis promotion for them and, as a further spur to the idea, cigarette advertising was to be banned on British television from the beginning of 1965, which had left the tobacco companies desperately looking for somewhere to spend their massive advertising budgets. Sponsoring sporting events that would attract long sessions of TV coverage with big audiences of smokers was exactly what they wanted, and the cost, per viewer reached, would be a fraction of direct advertising. Rothmans came on board almost as soon as we'd pitched the idea to them and got right behind it from the start. Denis, Bagenal and I were pleased with what we'd achieved and, while I didn't at the time quite appreciate what a significant milestone this was in the development of cricket, I didn't doubt that it would have an impact. However, I'm not so sure that I would feel comfortable today about encouraging the world's cricket fans to coat their lungs with tobacco tar.

We started arranging fixtures for the Rothmans International Cavaliers right away, squeezing a few into the current year, and planning a full schedule for 1966, mostly against the English counties, but with a number in new, intriguing venues, against obscure ad hoc teams – Oxford University Past & Present, The Duke of Norfolk's XI, Rest of the World XI, JB Statham's XI.

A trunkful of national treasures signed up for the Rothmans International Cavaliers, as well as a few young and hungry. I'm not sure which category I came into, turning thirty in May that year. We had such an amazingly strong side – Sobers, Compton, Graeme Pollock – I was only able to creep in at No. 6. The BBC came on board wholeheartedly, providing extra revenue for the series of games and making imaginative choices of presenters. Frank Bough, also a client of Bagenal Harvey, fronted up a team that included John Arlott and Learie Constantine, with Bough doing interviews with players, prematch, post-match and during play, which hadn't been done before.

The games were nearly always played on Sundays and gave spectators a chance to see a wide range of famous players on their local county ground. In the first full season of 1966, they drew 280,000 spectators, compared with 327,000 on the other six days. A couple of Cavaliers games were scheduled for

1965, versus Nottingham in May, which I played in, and then nothing until the West Indies in September, for reasons which will become obvious.

Meanwhile there was some Test action to look forward to in England that summer. New Zealand were arriving in May for a three-match series, with South Africa coming over for another best of three in July. It was the first time two Test series had been played back to back at home.

Mike Smith retained the captaincy, which I accepted with good grace, recognising that he had performed well in South Africa, and I settled down to enjoy myself. Although the first Test at Edgbaston was played in vile weather and was not much of a spectacle, we won by nine wickets. In one of those quirks of cricket, Ken Barrington, who had made by far the largest score of 137, was dropped from the side because he had taken over seven hours to do it.

The Lord's Test was more significant for me, in that it saw the Test debut of my fine young Sussex bowler, John Snow. Among the fast bowlers he was playing third fiddle to Trueman and Rumsey, but when he came on I stood at mid-on and had a word with him a couple of times an over, encouraging him to keep it simple, to keep a line and a length and let his natural ability take care of the rest. He took two wickets in each innings – not a bad debut to an extraordinary career of fifty-four Test appearances. In our second innings, I scored a pleasing 80 not out, when we won by 7 wickets and took the series.

As soon as the Test was over, I was back at Lord's playing in a Gillette Cup match against Middlesex, who won, knocking us out of the competition for the first time, which depressed me a little. It was a good thing I was looking forward to the next day when I'd arranged to go racing at Newbury with some friends.

There was some good racing, a good lunch with chums, a couple of well-priced winners backed – altogether, a useful, relaxing event after the previous day's effort at Lord's. When the last race had been run, I turned down a tempting invitation to dinner nearby, climbed into my blue Jaguar and set off for home in London.

On the M4 near Maidenhead, I noticed that I was getting short on petrol. After another twenty-five miles I thought I wasn't going to make it to the London end of the motorway; I came off it for a while, failed to find petrol, pressed on and hoped for the best. I was coming up to the Chiswick Flyover when I was sure I wouldn't make it to Finborough Road. The needle was showing empty and I had no idea what the reserve tank held.

I remembered there was a roundabout below the flyover, very imminently, where I was sure there was a petrol station. I drove down from the top deck

and coasted along the old road beneath. Two hundred yards before I reached
the roundabout, the tank was empty; the motor spluttered and coughed, and
the car came to a silent halt.

I cursed myself for my stupidity and climbed out to see what I should do. I
locked the car and started to walk towards the roundabout. I never got there,
though; if I had, the laugh would have been on me. There was no petrol station
at that roundabout, just a car showroom.

But after I'd walked a few yards, I turned to look back and see if everything
was alright. Other vehicles were flooding up from distant traffic lights, driving
into a bottleneck caused by my abandoned car. I had to move it out of their way.
As I walked back, I spotted an open courtyard, a little behind the car, beside the
landmark Martini & Rossi building.

When I reached the car, I switched the lights on to alert the approaching
traffic to what I was doing and started to push it backwards towards the opening,
steering through the open window. It crept gently down the slight incline until
the car was off the road and at right angles to it. I had simply to straighten it out
and guide it down to the courtyard where there was plenty of room for me to
pull it up gently. I knew I was in trouble when it wouldn't straighten; there was
no pressure left in the power steering and it wouldn't respond. The car began
to move down a short, steepish slope towards the locked doors of the Martini
building. There was no way I could stop it now and I realised it was bound to hit
the doors; I stayed with it and tried to restrain it as best as I could. That wasn't
enough. The shapely rear end of the Jaguar hit the doors hard and carried on
straight through them. I leapt to the side, kept my balance and managed to
avoid getting trapped between the car and the doors, but I felt a sharp tug at
my leg.

I looked down; I felt no great pain – that came later – nor was there much
blood. What I could see was a hole in my trousers and a lump of flesh, a good
handful, hanging from my right calf. I had a fearful vision of the consequences
of severed veins, arteries, gangrene, tetanus – all the possible horrors. I was
badly injured and alone, with a stream of traffic rumbling past just twenty yards
away, but I had just enough presence of mind to shove the lump of muscle back
where it had come from, and pulled up my sock to keep it there. I didn't realise
I'd broken a bone as I scrambled and hopped my way up to the edge of the
road, where I lay down and raised my leg to rest it on a convenient low railing.
I started bellowing 'Help!' which didn't carry far over the traffic noise echoing
under the concrete flyover. The stream of cars kept on whooshing past and I
began to despair. Luckily a young lad on a bicycle came riding by slowly enough

to see that I wasn't a maniac screaming for a lift but a frightened, slightly bloody man calling for help. He stopped at once and asked what he could do. I asked him to phone an ambulance as quickly as he could. He asked me if I knew where there was a phone?

I didn't, but begged him to please carry on and find one.

He nodded eagerly and shot off.

There was nothing more I could do but lie back, keeping my leg up above my heart, and gaze up at the flyover and the clear blue sky beyond.

It was 6.30 in the evening of Thursday, 24 June – a date etched in my mind forever.

Trying to stay positive, I began whistling a tuneless jig. From nowhere, it seemed, a small group of people began to gather around me, trying to guess what had happened, while I was beginning to feel quite sorry for myself. Shock had set in and I was shivering uncontrollably. Something was placed under my head and someone covered me up. I remember asking if anyone would turn off the lights of the car, with its back end buried in the warehouse doors. On the far side of the road an ambulance raced by with bells jangling. It wasn't for me; it carried on westward to sort out some other idiot who had come to grief along the Great West Road.

Someone asked my name; they didn't say why.

'Dexter,' I said quietly.

After a pause, the same voice blurted, 'Not *the* Dexter? Not Ted Dexter?'

I owned up to it. They answered with an embarrassed titter, but nothing worse. My body was still quivering like a blancmange, but my head started to clear. I wasn't going to die, but would I be maimed for life? In the end, I felt there was nothing wrong with me that I couldn't cope with. And with that positive thought, an ambulance arrived. The ambulance men tied a bandage round my leg, heaved me onto their vehicle and within a couple of minutes of reaching me, I was on my way to the West Middlesex Hospital.

The young cyclist who had gone to the rescue for me had vanished. I never did have a chance to thank him.

* *

Once we reached the hospital, I was trolleyed straight to the X-ray department where it was established that I had broken my fibula – the smaller of the two calf bones which stabilises the ankle. This wasn't a big problem, I was told, but the other damage to my leg was more complicated. I was cleaned up and wrapped up to stop the shivering, and put to bed, while I gabbled on to the nurses about the importance of legs, especially to someone in my profession. It was essential, I tried to insist, that whatever they did and however long they took, the leg should work properly again.

No doubt to the nurses' relief, Susan soon appeared. It was marvellous to see her and that had an instant beneficial effect. I grinned a lot and cracked a few feeble jokes, she told me afterwards, and said I was taking it all so calmly, she couldn't believe anything serious had happened.

By 9pm I was in the operating theatre where I stayed, unconscious, for two hours. I came round to find a nurse trying to stop me from getting up, until I was shoved back and slumbered again. When I woke, fully conscious, my leg was in plaster right up to my crotch, and, supported from below, raised up above the level of my head. I was feeling it could have been a lot worse.

On Friday, the day following the smash, the dope was still working; I felt vague and disoriented, confused by the faces that kept appearing in my little room at the end of the ward. But I clearly recall a visit from the surgeon who had patched me up the night before. He looked exhausted, having been on call all night, but he did a lot to cheer me that morning with the news that no great lasting damage had been done and that with the right care and a lot of rest, the leg would fully recover.

The press, who love nothing more than prying into a personal disaster, were onto my troubles like rats up a drainpipe. I had a word with the hospital secretariat about keeping them away and issuing bulletins that were to the point and devoid of personal detail. A policeman arrived and, with diffident tact, asked me just what had happened. I told him the ridiculous truth, which he took calmly and wrote carefully in his notebook; I heard nothing on the matter from the police after that.

Bagenal Harvey turned up with a bottle of whisky and a message from my editor, Clifford Makins, full of sympathy but reminding me that he was looking forward to copy for my column in Sunday's *Observer*. This was good for getting my mind back into gear, and on the following morning, Saturday, I turned down the offer of a desensitising jab and scribbled away in a big cash book.

I wasn't at my sharpest, but picked up a theme from a recent comment by Bernard Levin in his *Daily Mail* column, in which he'd described a cricketer as, 'a creature as very nearly stupid as a dog'. To this I added a brief, technical analysis of our defeat by Middlesex in the Knockout Cup.

As a well-deserved reward to myself, I sat up in bed and watched Meadow Court win the Irish Derby on a portable TV set which Susan had thoughtfully brought in for me. *The Observer*, using their privilege as my journalistic employer, sent a photographer who came in and took a snap of me sitting up in bed, and my sister looked in.

Apart from relations, my business manager and my newspaper, all other friends and well-wishers were turned away, including even Gubby Allen, perhaps the most important promoter of my cricketing career, and a man who usually got what he wanted.

Susan, of course, came frequently; she was relieved to see that I was responding well, although undoubtedly worried about how I was going to deal with several weeks, if not months, of recuperation. She was probably worried as much that my fervent fascination with horse racing was encouraging me to gamble more than ever, and that the boredom of immobility would only make it worse. Her worries were not entirely unfounded.

For most of the next week that I was in hospital, I was kept occupied by watching the tennis at Wimbledon on television, irritatingly dominated by Australians that year, including two in the men's final (won by Roy Emerson), *four* in the men's doubles final, and the winner of the women's final, Margaret Smith. Perhaps it was then that I confirmed my earlier thoughts that even if I were fit, I wouldn't go on the Australian tour in the coming winter. In the meantime, my leg started slowly to heal, my mood was bolstered as more visitors were allowed up to see me and I had scores of letters from well-wishers. Despite these enjoyable distractions, I had a lot of time to myself, probably the first opportunity in my life for some serious consideration about where I was and where I was going.

For a start, it was possible that it would be weeks or even months before I could take any active exercise. The rest of the season's cricket was obviously out. In rare moments of gloomy self-doubt, I did think that perhaps I deserved what had happened.

For seven years I had been steaming through life like an express train on amphetamines, playing international cricket, going wherever that took me, trying to keep myself as fully entertained as possible at the same time. While I wasn't doing that, county cricket was almost totally time-consuming, with six days' play in a week. I was squeezing the last drop of my energy resources if I wanted to go racing, buy horses, go to parties, play golf and see my wife and children sometimes. I'd recently begun to think that I might be going a lot too fast and now, here I was, at a dead stop, on my back in bed.

Apart from my cricket I had been an active professional journalist for three years and loved doing it. I'd had real encouragement from the newspaper and felt that my copy was getting better. I enjoyed meeting people from another metier who, besides appreciating sport, saw it in a wider context. Even before I'd had my accident, I had more or less made up my mind not to go to Australia. In the meantime, my journalism and potentially some commentary work would pay the bills. Denis Compton and Richie Benaud were regular commentators now, and even Colin Cowdrey had contributed his views on the 1963 West Indies Tests after he had broken his arm at Lord's. I could see no reason why a broken leg should stop me airing my views in the commentary box too.

I recognised that this spell of incapacity and confinement in the West Middlesex coincided with my own burgeoning dissatisfaction with the direction in which my life was going. I'd always loved playing cricket; I'd done few things as fulfilling in my life as receiving a ball plum in the middle of my bat, and whacking it away with all my strength to the boundary, or over the top of the pavilion. But I didn't love it to the exclusion of everything else. I was by nature vigorously competitive in any of the sports I liked to play. I was also, I believe, hampered by a low boredom threshold. Certainly, lying there in a hospital bed, I was sure I needed to escape the six-day circus of county cricket.

Added to these shortcomings of a full-time cricket career, I was beginning to feel it was time I thought about making some money. While I was well aware from close observation that money doesn't guarantee happiness, I had also developed a few expensive hobbies (besides unprofitable gambling). I was interested in flying aeroplanes, if possible, flying my own plane, and I already had a taste for classic cars, interesting vehicles made by the world's top marques over the previous decades. And, although through my own efforts and my agent's I'd earned a fair sum out of cricket and its spin-offs, I knew I'd get nowhere much by staying with the game until it gave me up.

When my overcrowded schedule allowed, I'd been having these kinds of thoughts for well over a year. Without doubt, my political venture, contesting Cardiff South East for the Tories, was a clear sign of this restlessness, a symptom of my desire to move on from cricket. Since then, I'd been waiting for a lull in the hurly-burly of my existence to ask myself just what was I going to do for the rest of my life? Now I was on the spot; the question had to be addressed and, if possible, answered.

There was no denying that sport had been the mainspring of my life, and I was still absolutely committed to it. I was sure there was the potential for a future for me with an active, challenging involvement in the commercial side of sport. In step with the demise of amateurism in cricket and, ultimately rugby union, this seemed to me to be a relentlessly expanding field. I had already had a couple of speculative discussions with Bagenal Harvey about joining his organisation in some kind of partnership but hadn't taken it further. I also had some nebulous reservations about committing to a closer business relationship with him.

In the meantime, holed up in the West Middlesex, I was doing a little modest, promotional drinking. Martini & Rossi, evidently relaxed about my crashing through their doors, sent me not a bill (that came later), but a case of Martini – six Rosso and six Bianco. Noilly Prat, for whom I'd done the TV advertisements with Susan, wrote suggesting that if I had to crash into anyone's premises, why choose one of their competitors? This reasonable rebuke was accompanied by half a dozen bottles of champagne.

After a couple of days laid up, I was put under a new regime, in which I began to use the leg again. It was essential that I walk on it to get the blood flowing, to help in knitting the bone. To begin with I found the effort of hobbling about really tiring, and after a short stint, I had to sit back down with my leg in the air. But the progress, though slow, proved sure enough, and I was very happy when, once the surgeon had cut off the plaster cast, checked that the leg was repairing alright and replastered it, I was told I could go home. I was just in time to see the start of the third Test, and my replacement in the England side, John Edrich, make 301 on his debut on a pitch as flat as a billiard table. It was deeply frustrating to watch, thinking that at least half those runs belonged to me! I had made 57, 62 and 80 not out in the first two Tests. However, I cheered up a lot when I was allowed out for the first Test against the South Africans at Lord's on 22 July.

If I hadn't been so disorganised as to not fill up the Jaguar when I'd left Newbury races a month before, I would have been playing in the match. However, as I'd been hoping, I did the next best thing when I joined the BBC Radio team in the commentary box at Lord's. At the invitation of Brian Johnston and his colleagues, I sat alongside them and, when prompted, chipped in with my 'expert' view on the playing of the game.

I didn't get off to an auspicious start. Just before the game commenced, I was let in to the box, which was cluttered with commentators, technicians and statisticians with piles of reference books and dog-eared sheets of data. Play started while one of the technicians was giving me a final briefing on how to use the earphones, microphone and accompanying knobs. I was about to turn and sit down when there was a mighty roar from the crowd. I jerked my head round to see Eddie Barlow, the South African No. 1 walking out, bowled Rumsey, caught Barber for one.

I settled into my seat.

'Ted, what did you think of that catch?' Johnston asked.

'I'm afraid I didn't see it,' I replied in a smaller voice than usual.

From then on, I enjoyed the job. I didn't dry up – in fact, probably talked too much – and was absorbed by the challenge of explaining technical detail in a way that would make sense to the viewers. I also discovered what an exacting task the regular commentators had, waffling away into the mic with a producer talking at them through their earphones, while viewing the game through the eyes of several cameras around the ground. It was clear to me that coolness and considerable technical finesse were even more important to the job than expert knowledge.

My stint in the commentary box was wonderful for my morale, but not, as it turned out, for my health. I had a walking plaster on my leg which only allowed me to take short steps and I seemed to be continually clumping up and down the stairs to the box. I tired easily; I had also developed a cold and was coughing up a bit of blood. After what I'd been through I really thought this wasn't fair, even less so when I was told I had pneumonia and had to go back to bed.

I missed my stint in the commentary box for the Trent Bridge Tests, and watched it on TV like a normal viewer, somewhat appeased by the general press consensus that the England team were missing my services as a batsman.

Otherwise this was the start of a bad patch for me. The leg wasn't repairing fast enough, the skin around the wound wasn't healing and I became irritable and edgy. To my miserable dismay, I felt worse and worse, breaking out into sweats and experiencing all the manifestations of the injury as I had in the days after the accident.

Quite abruptly, though, one day – at teatime, I recall – it was all over.

In a few minutes I knew that the shock had run itself out, and I was back in form, a normal human being again. I knew exactly what to do next.

Susan, Thomas and I headed straight for Diana Marina on the Ligurian coast in Italy, where we stayed for ten glorious August days. We lay on the beach, with Thomas pottering about in the manner of three-year-old boys in the sand, while Susan and I swam a little, ate a little, and did nothing much else. The wound on my calf, which had been slow to mend, responded marvellously to the Mediterranean seawater, and began to heal properly. The last remnants of the scab, buried deep in the hole in my leg, finally came popping out like a cork. By the end of our short, lovely sojourn, I was feeling almost fine again.

We were back in England by 25 August, the day before the start of the third and last Test against the South Africans at the Oval. I clambered happily up to the commentary box where I spent a super day with the gang, before going home to file my copy for that Sunday's *Observer*.

**

In September we returned to Italy, this time for the proper holiday we had planned earlier in the year, with fifteen-month-old Genevieve completing the family. We stayed with my brother John at his summer house which had been the lodge of the Villa Lugarna where my family had lived, overlooking the small town of Menaggio, with a breathtaking panorama across Lake Como to the Dolomites.

Despite some beastly wet weather, I managed to get in some golf, and had the unexpected pleasure of winning a local but prestigious tournament, the Targa D'Oro at the Villa d'Este. There were many good international golfers in the field ready to play in the next event, the Italian Amateur. As a result of my win, I was eligible to play in it too, although I was convincingly knocked out in the first round. But I was so relieved to be really active again that I didn't mind much and headed back to England with the family, feeling full of energy and ideas.

I had already told the selectors that I wouldn't be available for Australia; and it was patently obvious to me that simply restricting myself to county cricket without playing Tests was not an option. As soon as I was back I pointed the Jaguar down the A23 to Hove where I met the Sussex chairman, Arthur Gilligan, and politely informed him that I wished to resign as captain, and would not be playing for Sussex in 1966.

I left with the impression that most would miss me, a few wouldn't and one or two understood my decision. Driving away, a little sad, I did feel that I'd had a distinct impact on the fortunes of Sussex since I had become captain five years before. I didn't doubt that there would be aspects of it that I would miss, although it was not unlike coming to the natural end of one's days at school, when the time had come, as it were, to put away childish things...

Although, of course, cricket didn't cease to be part of my life, it would no longer be the prime motivator, but I had little idea of what life after cricket might have in store.

PART TWO

Beyond Cricket

Chapter Thirteen

THE PEN IS MIGHTIER THAN THE BAT

My decision in 1965 to stop playing Test and county cricket wasn't an easy one. All my instincts, unreliable as they could be, told me that after playing in sixty-two Test matches, half of them as captain, in every major cricketing nation in the world, there really weren't any new experiences to be had. My 172 at the Wanderers Test in South Africa the previous winter, and 80 not out in my final Test innings in June suggested that I wasn't yet on the way down, and I'd always planned to leave at the top. County cricket, apart from the one-day knockout games, had been mouldering in the same backwater since the war, while attendances dropped from over two million in 1950, to less than half a million by the time I'd decided to go. My view on what was needed had been well aired, but given the rate at which the counties and their chairmen habitually moved, no changes were likely for decades. Another few years of county cricket without Tests was not even a remote option for me.

On the other hand, top-flight cricket was in my blood; if I were being interviewed about it now, I would probably say it was in my DNA. Whichever, cricket had been the major part of my existence for half of my first thirty years; I was going to miss it like hell; and I was going to miss the adrenalin rush it gave me for a long time to come. In truth, of course, I didn't give up playing cricket entirely, but it did cease to be my overriding raison d'être.

The problem confronting me now was how to fill this great vacuum in my life, and pay the gas bill. At the beginning of 1966, that field was wide open.

One non-playing activity in which I felt I had a future, albeit part-time, was my writing. I was still producing my weekly column for *The Observer* under the rheumy eye of sports editor, Clifford Makins. Earlier in his career, Clifford had been writing the words for strip cartoons in the boy's paper, *The Eagle*, on which he'd become editor. At *The Observer* he had won awards for his sports journalism; he was an adaptable and versatile scribbler who was always up for a new project.

One winter weekday, over a bottle of Krug and plate of quail's eggs in El Vino's, he proposed that the time had come for me to write my autobiography, 'to mark the end of an era' as he flatteringly put it. If I wrote the first draft, he offered to do a bit of editing and fact-checking (not all that efficaciously, as it turned out). We offered Stanley Paul Limited a sniff; they wagged their corporate tail and said, 'Yes please.' Stanley Paul was the sporting imprint of giant publishers Hutchinson & Co, and, with no big send-off in the middle of 1966, let alone a launch party, *Ted Dexter Declares* was let loose on the public.

From a distance of fifty-five years I would say that the book gave a perfectly accurate account of my life as a cricketer – 'I did this and then I did that' – a standard 'end of career' sort of potboiler. I was quite happy with it and, broadly, it still stands as such, although some of the views expressed in it do not entirely reflect the views I hold half a century on. I should add, though, that it was not a source of significant income. It hadn't been my first venture into book-writing – the forerunner having been *Ted Dexter's Cricket Book*, a 1963 collection of experiences and advice – and nor was it my last.

Ten years after the publication of *Ted Dexter Declares,* I was still in sporadic contact with Clifford, but his love of drink had begun to degrade him. As far as I could tell, he was on his uppers and camping with two girlfriends alternately, one in Wembley and the other in Richmond. Ealing was a convenient halfway house. He would get in touch, out of the blue, already fairly well oiled, but still needing another. But Clifford was never a scrounger and always honest about money. In fact, I once gave him £200 in notes to back a greyhound – which lost.

'I knew it wouldn't win,' he told me, and handed back the money.

I had always liked Clifford and I always tolerated his visits even when it was inconvenient but on one of these encounters, he came prepared with an idea – another proposal.

He wasn't the first person in the business to have spotted what an amazing success the former royal jockey, Dick Francis, had had with a string of annual thrillers based around his old sport of steeplechasing, but as far as I know Clifford was the first to suggest a thriller based on cricket. I had listened to his whimsy often enough, just to humour him. But I had had enough.

'Right, you're on!' I declared rashly. 'Come to my office in Ealing next week with a synopsis to show to a publisher, and I'll give you £50 – cash.'

He wandered off, nodding, and, although the idea did have some appeal, I didn't think I would hear anything more about it, until he turned up, surprisingly sober, with the outline of a cricket thriller, to be co-written by us under the title *Test-Kill.*

Test-Kill was published by Allen & Unwin (J. R. R. Tolkien's publisher, no less), on the first day of the first Test between England and West Indies in 1976. It sold well enough to be included in *The Sunday Times* bestsellers list and reissued as a green Penguin paperback, but I don't imagine it ever had the great Dick Francis quaking with fear of the competition. I can't really be objective about the quality of the book, but it did have an interesting quirk which nobody picked up. All the Australian cricketers' names were also the names of Australian towns.

Not long after that Clifford, who must have possessed depths so hidden that I hadn't spotted them, married Nora Beloff, one of Britain's leading female journalists – not any old agony aunt, but a major political writer. In one bound he went from being down and out to living in a penthouse in St John's Wood.

This would undoubtedly have had a positive impact on his finances and I guessed that any more talks about our collaboration were at an end. Nevertheless, Clifford was back after year or so with a plan for more thrillers based on my other sporting interests, first golf and then, less originally, horse racing, already a somewhat overcrowded field.

We got as far as writing a second novel, under the spine-chilling title, *The Deadly Putter*, which was published in 1979, although, after that, we must have run out of steam because nothing was ever said about the racing thriller. Maybe Clifford was back on the bottle because it took our professional reader no time to discover that some of the murkier female characters had somehow appeared twice under different names.

I wasn't often in touch with Clifford in the years after that, but when I did bump into him, he was in good form. Since his marriage to Nora, he seemed less desperate, generally looking a little sprucer and less inebriated. In 1987, he rang to ask if I was going to Bagenal Harvey's funeral. That unsung pioneer of sports commerce had died with less of a send-off from the press than I thought he deserved, and I was certainly going. Clifford asked if I could pick him up in St Johns Wood and take him, which I did. I drove him back home afterwards; he didn't seem particularly drunk but, as he explained, he had no money for a taxi. In fact, as he clambered out of my Bentley, he asked if I could let him have £50. I didn't have £50 but I managed to scrape up £30 which I handed over, and he pottered off.

The following morning I had a furious phone call from the redoubtable Nora Beloff. 'Ted Dexter! How could you do that?'

The police had delivered Clifford back to her penthouse, completely plastered. She had, she explained, been deliberately keeping him short of cash, just to avoid this kind of thing.

God knows, it wasn't my fault, but I understood how Nora felt. As it happens, Clifford didn't last much longer himself; I was at his funeral in 1990. He had died from no obvious illness, but his lifestyle was no recipe for longevity.

** **

I had stopped writing for *The Observer* in the late sixties and within a month was offered a column in the *Sunday Mirror*. I wrote regularly for an appreciative audience in the *Mirror* for over twenty years, during which I covered the 70/71 tour to Australia, having flown myself, Susan and our two children out there in my own Piper Aztec.

Always keen to offer new angles in my column, I also set up a piece for the paper that left a physical bruise on me. The Australian fast bowlers, Dennis Lillee and Jeff Thompson, were in England for the 1975 Ashes series and as a pair they were renowned for being a fearsome attacking force on their team. We conceived the idea of a shot of a batsman's worst nightmare – the two of them running up to bowl on either side of the wicket, coming at the camera at the same time. That worked, but afterwards we thought we should try to get a few good pictures of the kind of bouncers that were raising hairs on the back of some of the England batsmens' necks. We set up some shots of Dennis Lillee bowling bouncers wide on the off side and me looking as if I were ducking out of the way.

As we were ending the session, I asked the photographer if he thought he had the shots we needed. He said that maybe they wouldn't look authentic enough; I agreed and, remembering my stands against the speed of Wes Hall and Charlie Griffith, I reckoned I could handle Thomson. I volunteered to do a couple for real. This was foolish; I'd forgotten how much older I was.

To show Lillee's control and accuracy, the first one not only pitched on the right spot, it seamed back and followed me like an off break. I tried to readjust but I wasn't quick enough and the ball smacked me on the side of my head. It was the first time I'd ever been hit on the head but, as the great Bill Edrich had once told me, it didn't hurt a bit. We got a nice shot of Dennis and me shaking hands afterwards, with no hard feelings, but I did have a quick bout of concussion driving back to London that evening – all in a day's work for a conscientious hack, I told myself.

In that same series, I pulled off my great journalistic scoop. Working for the *Sunday Mirror* again, I was at Lord's when Australia were bowling. I watched them with growing unease and disbelief. The ball was swinging more than I had ever seen before – and not just a little, but maybe fifty per cent more. It was especially noticeable in their medium pacer, Massy.

After the game, I got hold of the England captain, Tony Greig, on the phone.

'What the hell's going on, Greigy?' I asked. 'Why is the ball swinging like that?'

'It's LIPOICE, man.'

'It's what?'

'LIPOICE.'

I took a moment to translate it from his strong South African accent.

He had said, 'Lip ice.'

'What the hell is that?' I wanted to know.

'Lip ice, man. You know – the stuff you put on dry lips. The clear kind. They rub it into their trousers and then polish the ball. The umpires don't seem interested.'

Bloody hell, I thought, I'm interested!

I went straight out to find a chemist and bought every brand of lip cooler they stocked. Only one of them was colourless. I rushed home with it, squeezed some onto a rag and found a couple of well-used cricket balls. Carefully I rubbed each of the balls on one side with my lip-iced rag.

The effect was instant and a swing bowler's dream!

I had never seen a shine like it before. In great excitement I rang my editor, Tony Smith; his reaction was no more than lukewarm. 'But come in and let's talk about it,' he said, mollifying.

I was on my way. With a tube of LIPOICE, a rag and some old cricket balls I was on the Piccadilly line from Ealing within minutes and in Tony Smith's office inside half an hour. I got him to do what I'd done: rag, lip ice and rough old balls. Once again, the effect was spectacular – cricket balls gleaming like freshly burnished red snooker balls.

Tony was convinced. The story leading the sports pages in the next *Sunday Mirror* was a straightforward accusation of cheating by the Australians. I followed it up at once by calling the Australian team manager to arrange a meeting, in which I took the initiative.

'I haven't come to apologise,' I announced.

The manager didn't look surprised.

'Have you read the story?' I went on.

'Yes,' he said, with no attempt at a defence. 'It won't happen again.'

And it didn't. As if miraculously, the balls stopped swinging as if they were going round a bend. And the English batsmen heaved a sigh of relief. Maybe there should have been sackings, suspensions and ministerial outrage. Perhaps it was a gentler age when the colossal media explosion, such as followed the sandpaper scandal, was still in the future. But it did my journalistic career no harm.

As well as pushing news stories when I had the chance, I wasn't coy about campaigning. Although I had played all my Test and county cricket as an amateur, as a journalist I wanted to take a closer look at Test players' remuneration. At that time, in the early seventies, they were only paid match by match, which seemed poor recompense for a seven-day commitment: travelling on Wednesday, playing Thursday, Friday and Saturday, with a rest day on Sunday, playing Monday and Tuesday, and travelling that evening with a county match starting on the Wednesday. I compared the overall percentage of the gross revenue for the Test matches with Open Championship golf, and Wimbledon tennis. This revealed that, whereas the golfers and tennis players received thirty per cent of the gross, the cricketers got only ten per cent. As a campaign it was a long haul, but many years later, as chairman of the MCC Cricket Committee, I was able to persuade the county chairmen to award key players contracts which paid a lot better and offered more job security. Now the whole England squad are on annual contracts running into millions of pounds.

* *

I always enjoyed my journalism, while taking it seriously and professionally, rather than as just something I did on the side. Indeed, I was one of the first cricket journalists to file copy electronically. For a period, I stopped writing for the newspapers when required to as a condition of my being appointed chairman of the England Committee by the MCC in 1989. A decade on, in 1998, I started again, writing a bi-weekly column that I shared with the venerable E. W. Swanton on *The Daily Telegraph*. This continued only until the first month of the new millennium when E. W. S. died, aged ninety-two, one of the best-known sports writers of his century. We cricketers were less enthusiastic; since he often seemed to compare Test cricket unfavourably with, say, a gentlemanly joust between MCC and the I Zingari.

* *

During all the time I was a practising journalist, I did consider myself lucky to have a ready outlet for my thoughts and views on the way that cricket was being run, and I was prepared to be forthright in what I wrote. In the press box, I always enjoyed being part of that traditionally disreputable world and made a lot of friends there.

In 1981, I fulfilled a long-held desire to write a book about the world's greatest batsmen of the previous fifty years. The idea was to analyse their individual style, their approach and the particular qualities that had made them memorable, and thus *From Bradman to Boycott – The Master Batsmen* was published, and still stands, I hope, as a valid textbook in that field.

A year later, I was approached by publishers Arthur Barker (an imprint of Weidenfeld & Nicolson) to do the first of a planned series of books about people who were at the top in one sport, but loved another. I was, as it were, to be the guinea pig. *My Golf* by Ted Dexter, a book about my most favourite pastime, all its joys, all its frustrations and the perpetual challenge the game poses, published in 1982, turned out to be the first and last in the series; it obviously wasn't a bestseller. Most of the heavy lifting was done by a ghostwriter, sports journalist Alan Lee, who was then cricket correspondent for that beacon of truth, *The Sun* newspaper. Lee was a sound, competent journalist, and a good enough writer to sustain a full-length book, albeit with my putting my spoon in the bowl throughout the process, and I was happy with the result. Nevertheless, I was less happy when he approached me after more than a decade (during which he had been upgraded in the Murdoch stable to chief cricket correspondent on *The Times*) to ask if I would co-operate in an official biography of myself. From my perspective, the timing of the request was suspect; I had just stepped down from a five-year stint as chairman of the England Committee at the MCC, during which I hadn't had a particularly good relationship with the British press, in which Lee had not been a notable exception. He asked if he could make a date to come and talk to me. I told him I'd get back to him.

My first instinct was to demur. I realised he would want my views on a lot of other peoples' theories, and ask me to justify all the more controversial decisions I'd taken. I didn't like the idea of being put on the back foot, having to deal with these questions from a defensive position, partly because I couldn't see how this would help anyone. Thinking that in due course, I would have an opportunity to explain my thinking in my own words, and from a distance in time, I declined his request.

'That's a pity,' he said, using an old journalist's tactic, 'because I'm going to do it anyway, but you won't have put your side of the story.'

I shrugged a metaphorical shoulder. 'I can't stop you.'

The book, *Lord Ted, The Dexter Enigma*, was published by Gollancz in

1995. I was surprised to find that in the opening pages, he had somewhat disingenuously thanked me for my co-operation. Other than that I didn't look at it for twenty-five years, until now, in fact, although a few years after it was published a strangely inaccurate piece about me appeared in the MCC monthly members magazine containing some passages which could only be described as utter balls – scurrilous and completely wrong – about my short career in the City. The article claimed that I'd been given a job on the strength of my name, and I spent most of my time in the local bookies. This was during my second session at C E Heath when I'd been taking my professional exams and I wasn't gambling at all. It occurred to me that this disinformation might have come from Lee's book. Although I'd promised myself not to look at the book, I risked opening it and soon identified a passage which had been lifted from it, word for word. The MCC editorial staff, including one with the title, 'chief researcher', were embarrassed enough to publish a retraction, although, as always, it was harder to find than the original piece.

**

Over the next few years after Lee's book came out, various collaborations and cricket compendia appeared with my name on, most recently, in 1996, Bloomsbury's *Ted Dexter's Little Cricket Book*, a collection of inspirational cricketing anecdotes.

In the meantime, I was always ready – some might say too ready – to offer my views on any cricket matters – players' performances, bad decisions, questionable selections – when asked, as well as publishing regular blogs on prevalent topics, up until now, in 2020, as I approach my eighty-fifth birthday.

**

My wife, Susan, and I, thank God, remain reasonably fit. Although I'm still troubled by a knee injury, a hangover from a cartilage operation while still at Radley, exacerbated by one of Charlie Griffith's meteor deliveries at Lord's in 1963, I'm well enough to play a (slow) round of golf and to walk a strapping greyhound a mile or so every day. I'm not yet bereft of marbles, and I'm more or less in control of my Mac, thus it was felt that this was the right moment to look back over the whole span of what has been a pretty full life, with many lessons learned, some triumphs and some disappointments. Looking back on it from this point in my life may not be the most accurate way of assessing my progress through it, but at least it offers the advantage of perspective.

As a result, with the encouragement of Andrew Johnston of Quiller Publishing and son of my old friend Brian, the book you have in your hands came into being.

In the first half of the book, I've tried to give an account of my early life and the cricketing career that placed me firmly in the public domain. I can't say what I would have done if I hadn't been a cricketer. I might, like my brother, have followed in my father's footsteps in the insurance business, but in the brief period I tried, I never felt much affinity for it. It's in my nature to look at things from every angle, to shake out the essence of a subject, analyse it and, where appropriate, improve on it. My penchant for creative ideas in cricket was well known, even the butt of a few jokes – 'More theories than Charles Darwin!' – but in the end, productive. That was to apply, too, in other innovations I pioneered in the presentation and staging of cricket. But there is no doubt that it was the playing of cricket, and, specifically, my style as a batsman, that made me well known and, to some extent, everything I did subsequently was influenced by that renown. So, in this second half, I will be covering the ground with longer strides, less chronologically and in a more thematic way.

Chapter Fourteen

LATER CRICKET AND FAMILY LIFE

My official retirement from first-class cricket in the autumn of 1965 by no means meant that I never played again. The most obvious difference to my former playing career was that now I was paid for it (except, of course, for games played for the Lord's Taverners and other charity matches). Over the next five years, I took part in around fifty games for the Rothmans International Cavaliers, mainly against English counties but also against sides from Jamaica, the West Indies and The Rest of the World as well as a mixed bag of ad hoc teams that were pitched against us. The Cavaliers circuit was undoubtedly a circus but a high-class one which entertained millions of people, live and on television, until they were forced by the MCC to disband in 1970.

Once the county chairmen had finally woken from their slumbers and realised that there was entertainment and money to be had by playing Sunday cricket, the TCCB wanted to stamp their authority on this significant development. In January 1968, their Advisory County Cricket Committee took a decision that they hoped might, as *The Guardian* put it, 'change the shape and mathematics of county cricket forever'.

From the 1969 season onward, they announced that they were introducing a Sunday County League, with matches comprising two innings of no more than forty overs. Their declared intention was to present the county game in a fresh way which, it was hoped, would revive the interest of the millions who had deserted the game, as well as attract a whole new audience through television, while, perhaps, solving the counties' almost overwhelming financial problems. These matches would also, incidentally, give the county players a chance to earn some useful extra money.

The success of the Gillette Cup had undoubtedly influenced their thinking, but it was, above all, the spectacular popularity of the Rothmans Cavaliers that had forced their hand. Other events also had some influence on this change of attitude in inherently conservative bodies like the MCC and the TCCB.

During 1966 in England, the sports pages were dominated by the staging of the football World Cup. This immense event presented the ever-inventive sports agent, Bagenal Harvey, with a bandwagon onto which he could not resist jumping. He conceived the idea of the Rothmans Cricket World Cup and with some help from me and Denis Compton, the concept sprang into life. By the time it was all agreed in March, it was too late for it to be included in the official fixtures list, but dates were set for three days in September at Lord's, following three days of warm-up matches at the annual Scarborough Festival. Naturally, Bagenal had made sure that the tournament would be televised by the BBC, who got involved from the start. Unfortunately, 20 March, the day of the press launch for this potentially exciting new tournament, was rendered ineffective by the far more dramatic news that the football World Cup itself, the Jules Rimet Trophy, had been pinched (although it was found a week later by a dog called Pickles), and subsequent coverage of the forthcoming cricket jamboree was muted, if not entirely drowned out, by the clamour surrounding England's progress in the football tournament.

The cricket World Cup games were run along the lines of the Rothmans Cavaliers matches, with fifty overs each, and were contested by only three teams. As it turned out, the way we planned it, they were genuinely world representative. There were an England XI, a West Indies team and a Rest of the World team. Having decreed that Australia's Bobby Simpson would be skipper of the World team, all the other players in it were selected from shortlists in a public poll organised by the BBC, with ballot papers printed in the *Radio Times*, in an early forerunner, perhaps, of the public vote for Mark Ramprakash in *Strictly Come Dancing*. The Rest of the World team was impressive by any standards; as well as Bobby Simpson it included Graeme Pollock, Colin Bland and the Nawab of Pataudi.

Colin Cowdrey skippered the England XI backed up by, among others, Jim Parks, John Edrich, Basil D'Oliveira and me. The Rest of the World, despite the high calibre of their players, had little combined experience of the one-day game and as a result, England met the West Indies in the final. We batted first, with a total of 217 for 7. Early in the West Indies innings, Colin Cowdrey left the field with a muscle injury. I took over, and drew on my experience of all the Gillette Knockout Cup matches that I'd skippered. I kept the field defensive and put the pressure on, with firm instructions to the bowlers. 'Aim at the stumps, pitch it up, and if someone starts whacking it, pitch it up a bit further.'

I had a couple of ideal bowlers in medium-fast Ken Higgs, who took 4 wickets, and Barry Knight, who took 2, with Snow, Titmus and D'Oliveira taking the other four. The West Indies were bowled out for 150 in the forty-first over. England had won the cricket World Cup for the first and last time, until 2019 when they finished after a spectacular Super Over in a tie with New

Zealand with England winning on a boundary count.

The Rothmans World Cup was played once more in 1967, but after that it wasn't until 1975 that cricket's world body got around to organising an official cricket World Cup, hosted by England with a memorable final between the West Indies (who won) and Australia.

For our inaugural Rothmans World Cup, the TCCB sniffily kept themselves at arms' length, agreeing only to send out the invitations to the matches, while making it clear that they had nothing to do with selecting the teams. When, two years later, the board announced their new counties' one-day Sunday series of matches, they pointedly turned down Rothmans' offer of sponsorship and, perhaps out of sheer bloody-mindedness, handed it to one of their tobacco rivals, creating the John Player Sunday League.

After this, the Cavaliers carried on for a season or so, but the boot was firmly put in by the first-class and minor counties banning their English players from taking part in televised matches without permission (which they were never going to get), prompting the BBC to withdraw their coverage.

Nevertheless, it was clear that far-reaching changes were going to occur in the way cricket was played around the world, and I'm proud to have been at the sharp end of the one-day game with my involvement in the Gillette Cup, the Rothmans Cavaliers and the inaugural World Cup. When international cricket reached a point where limited-overs cricket grabbed most of the world's attention, I did feel a sense of 'I told you so'.

Family Life

In the spring of 1966, while we were preparing for the World Cup and I was becoming more closely involved with Bagenal Harvey, Susan and I had been feeling claustrophobic in our maisonette in Finborough Road. With two small but growing children, we were hankering after a less confined existence. Driving home one evening through the leafy environs of Ealing in West London, we both remarked on how much better suited it would be as a place for our family to live. The big houses in large gardens, the open spaces and acres of greensward, the vast spreading plane trees and the handiness of the Piccadilly line were all attractions that convinced us it would make sense to move west from Finborough Road.

The problem was how to dispose of Finborough Road. I had paid £7,000 for a short lease but there were still a number of years to run. To start with, I went along to talk to one of the dunderheaded estate agents in the Fulham Road who had drawled that leases of the length I was trying to sell weren't worth a lot. None of the other agents showed any interest, the property market at the time was generally fairly flat, so we decided to move out anyway, and let the place for the time being. In the long run, this was a good move, which provided my children with somewhere to live when I encouraged them to leave home.

In the midst of one of the serial recessions that seemed to plague Britain in the late sixties and seventies, the resultant slump in house prices meant we were able to buy a big family house and garden in Warwick Dene, overlooking the south-western edge of Ealing Common, for a modest £14,000. A mortgage of £10,000 and some cash left over from the sale of the Ebury Street flat clinched the deal. Warwick Dene was a short, quiet road of large detached houses, immediately opposite a corner of the common known as Warwick Dene Park.

Number 5 Warwick Dene was no beauty; built at the beginning of the century, it had been the victim of several ill-judged extension plans, involving some ugly white clapboard and a false balcony. The house and the water were heated by a huge boiler which burned anthracite fed from its own coal hole. However, it was very spacious with a large, impressive hall and a lot of rooms. It hadn't been lived in for a while and would need a lot of work to make it comfortable. It also contained a huge end-to-end room on the second floor, which was almost totally dark when we first looked at it. Once we had moved in, we found some large, purpose-built window frames lying on the floor which turned out to be dormer windows planned for the front and back ends of the room. It was the perfect party space and in return for much the hospitality I'd received on tours, I invited gangs of visiting Australians and South Africans for many a shindig.

We were completely undaunted by the prospect of making the house liveable — at least, I was — and in the end, it turned out to be as ideal as we'd hoped. Behind it was a large garden with an expansive lawn, big trees and plenty of shrubs — plenty of room for small children and summer drinks parties. One of our first additions to the ménage was a female golden retriever puppy whom we named Caramella. She was the ideal companion for the children though always short on discipline. She had just one litter of eight puppies, for whom I diligently built a feeding pen with eight stalls. This construction turned out to be a waste of time when the bigger ones simply wolfed their own food before barging in on the others'. With their father a national champion, the pups were in great demand and sold fast, while their mother remained part of our family until years later, with much mourning, she died.

We quickly discovered that we liked living in Ealing; we put down strong roots and were happy there for the next thirty-five years. In 1987, we downsized a little and moved to a newly built Georgian style terrace in Woodville Gardens. Although the garden was smaller, it was curtained by its own trees and those of a neighbouring garden – at least, it was up until the great hurricane of October 87. The following morning, there was a strange lightness in the garden, and clouds of smoke billowing over the fence from the adjoining garden to the accompaniment of a noisy chainsaw. The neighbour, who had been wanting to get rid of two big trees but was having trouble getting permission, was using the hurricane as a cover for chopping them down entirely, although I didn't believe that the wind had damaged them much at all. It is, as they say, an ill wind… but we weren't so happy about it.

**

Ten years on, with the arrival of the new millennium, and our children long since settled in homes of their own, we decided that we were ready to move out of London to more rural surroundings. We bought a large chalet bungalow in a village near Ascot, where Susan could have a dedicated studio of her own to do her painting and I could reach my favourite golf courses in fractions of an hour. The 'garden' we inherited with the house was a featureless paddock and we both enjoyed the art of creating an entirely new garden – a little like painting, although on a larger canvas and a much slower process.

**

Since the early years of our marriage, even when she was still active as a model, Susan had been an enthusiastic artist, and she loved having the space to devote a lot of time and talent to her art. In my eyes, of course, her pictures are all minor masterpieces and a delight. I was immensely proud of her when, after months of hard work in her studio, she held a charity sale of her works at the new house in Ascot. She sold the lot and raised a couple of thousand for our former parish church, St Matthew's in Ealing. We both had a great attachment to the parish and its people and, in a way that we hadn't anticipated, we found we were missing what had become an important part of our lives. This was making us think again about living in Ascot – this and the fact that we both, Susan in particular, had found it hard to extract the deep roots that we had put down around Ealing Common.

We had underestimated the value of the friendships and connections we'd enjoyed in Ealing and, to some extent, we missed the easy availability of the colour and bustle of London compared to the quiet sterility of Home Counties life. At the same time, I was beginning to wind down some of my varied range of business activities, while living in one of the most expensive areas in England didn't make much sense. Returning to Ealing could have been an option, but we were beginning to feel it was time to make a break and try something entirely new. We started to think about the possibility of living somewhere where the climate was warmer, the surroundings more vivid and property less expensive, where we could enjoy a more mellow seniority.

* *

When we first moved to Ealing in 1966, our son, Tom, was just four, and his sister, Genevieve, two. They both immediately took to their new home and the refreshing leafiness of the world around them, and we knew we hadn't made a mistake. Having the wide open space of the common just on the other side of the road gave a sense of being in the country and the traditional shops within walking distance (albeit alongside Macdonald's and Blockbuster) had the reassuring nature of a small English town. We were confident that this would be a good environment in which to bring up our young family.

* *

Susan had chosen to go to St Bartholomew's Hospital to have our first baby because the principal gynaecologist at the hospital was a friend of the Dexter family. He had looked after two of my sisters and one of them had given birth there for the same reason. Although Barts was an old-fashioned Victorian hospital and, in the early 1960s, the wards were still under the reassuring regime of strict, old-fashioned matrons who looked like Hattie Jacques, Susan was comfortable there. However, it was near Smithfield Market and she noticed that a number of the mothers were wives of Smithfield workers, and most of them colossal smokers; as a result, the loos were always full of women puffing away in a haze of acrid cigarette smoke. As the baby was born on a Sunday, I wasn't playing cricket and was able to get to the hospital just before our child was born. I hadn't been in Susan's room ward long before the birth was very imminent and I was shooed out. Despite my absence the delivery went well, and Thomas Edward Dexter was born and weighed in at a solid 9lbs. He had a bigger head than most of the other newborns and was dubbed 'Buster' by the nurses who looked after him and his mother over the ten days they were there. She was not allowed to leave until Tom had regained his birth weight. They would have been lucky to get two days now.

When I drove them home to Venner House, a maternity nurse was waiting whom we had taken on to help Susan for the first month of Tom's life, which helped her to overcome her 'first baby' anxieties. Once the monthly nurse was gone, we did our best to settle him into a proper routine, but he would always have a yell just as we were sitting down to dinner. It was only since the appearance of Doctor Spock's book that people started picking up babies at the first bawl. I was of the old-fashioned school that thought it right to tough it out and let them rip, while stolidly ignoring the racket, and I discouraged Susan from rushing to pick him up. In the end, of course, he did settle down and became a fairly docile baby.

Tom was nine months old when Sue flew out to join me in the MCC's Australian tour at the end of 1962. She hadn't done any modelling since her early pregnancy, and she'd been feeding Tom for his first three months. She'd had to work hard to lose weight and regain the hourglass profile. Peter Lumley had booked her plenty of work in Australia, but after all the ups and downs of that trip, Susan had been quite upset when she got back to find that Tom didn't know who she was. But she soon had other things to think about.

Like many children, when Tom made the transition from pureed foods to a more solid diet before his first birthday, he started showing signs of eczema and asthma, both of which stayed with him for much of his early life. The eczema was apparent in rashes behind his knees, while the asthma was obviously affecting his breathing. When he was about seven, we took him to see Dr Jolley, a brilliant paediatrician who did amazing things for him. He gave Tom some instructions which led to a turning point in dealing with his asthma. He showed him how to induce an attack, then how to deal with it through a series of strict breathing exercises. This put the boy more in control of the condition and gave him more confidence. He also told Tom that all the things about him that we were complaining of were our fault, not his – which may have been true. It certainly gave Tom a boost of self-worth and he walked out of the doctor's consulting room looking six inches taller.

Tom had been just four when we had moved from the confines of Finborough Road, where the closest open space was the somewhat macabre Brompton Cemetery next to Chelsea football ground, to the broad acres of Ealing Common, and our own good-sized garden. He liked his first primary school, Beacon House, and the move to Durston House, a prep school which was only a brisk walk from Warwick Dene. However, he wasn't a great pupil there and was obviously completely uninterested in learning and especially in doing his homework. It was hard for us to see why; if he wanted to do things, he could. His writing was good and he read a lot; he once told me how he had taken a book into the loo with him, and it suddenly dawned on him how to read and what reading was all about; he had even read *War and Peace* before he was eleven.

But these abilities weren't coming out in his regular schoolwork. We got him some coaching at maths and we arranged for him to take an IQ test, in which he performed well. The people there told us that there were no problems at all with his cognitive skills; he simply saw the world in his own unconventional way. The school asked us what we were thinking of doing with Tom for his secondary education. We were hoping to send him to one of the big London day schools but Durston House said he wouldn't pass the entrance exams. We tried everything we could think of to encourage him, but he would sit on his own in the dining room to do his homework with a few simple tasks to complete and when we went back twenty minutes later he hadn't made a mark on the paper; he was sort of frozen in a mental block. Always a dreamer and looking out of the window, he found it hard to concentrate. While he might have scraped through in English if he buckled down to finish a paper, maths was a serious problem for Tom, and he wouldn't get into any good school without a respectable mark in maths.

I wouldn't be writing about these problems if it weren't for the fact that, though the tunnel was long, there was finally a good strong light at the end of it, and I can confidently advise parents facing similar circumstances that you never really know what's at the end, and all you can do is go on loving, trying to understand and doing whatever you can to encourage your temporarily disconnected offspring.

Later in life Tom was working for Rolls-Royce as a highly qualified electrical and electronic principal engineer, with responsibility for electromagnetic compatibility, electronics hardware and systems design. He was also doing some research work for civilian aircraft engine controllers for the Trent jet turbine series used in Airbus and Boeing aircraft. At about that period, I came across one of his old teachers from his prep school days who asked me what Tom was doing. I brought him up to date but was met with a blank look. 'No,' he said, 'I meant Tom, your Tom.'

When he was eleven, we sent him to a crammer, Millbrook House, near

Oxford, to help him with the Common Entrance exam to his next school. When we took him there to board for the first time, we dropped him off and drove away but had to stop around the corner because we were both so tearful – a very soppy couple of parents. But the school was small and looked after their pupils well, to encourage them to work. They gave them good food, plenty of amusements as well as a low pupil/teacher ratio. Tom made some new friends and liked the food. It was a happy time for him and he made progress.

We were hoping to get him into a suitable public school and had made some provisional choices. I hadn't seriously considered Radley – I didn't think it would suit him, and it probably wasn't an option anyway. Friends involved in education, whose advice I'd sought, were sure that it wouldn't be the right choice for him, and I'd written it off as a possibility. But when I was back visiting my old school, I talked to the warden, Dennis Silk, whom I knew well as a former captain of the Cambridge XI. He asked me about Tom, and I explained that we were thinking of sending him to King's School, Bruton, which we and Mr Glazebrook, the headmaster of Millbrook, thought would be right for him. Dennis said he would like to meet Tom. A little surprised but elated that this might be an option, I said I'd bring my boy down, and did so shortly afterwards, when he behaved with great charm. Dennis obviously thought so and was impressed by Tom's interest and ability in English. He said he would welcome Tom to Radley; we happily agreed, and he started there at the age of thirteen. I remembered my early days at the school, which I'd loved, and hoped and prayed that he would feel the same. I don't know why but it didn't really work for Tom from the start. I was called down to Radley two or three times to sort him out. At the end of his second term, we had an ultimatum from his housemaster: unless Tom changed his attitude they wouldn't be able to keep him. We spent the holidays wondering what to do. I wasn't sure; we asked Susan's brother for his views. Perhaps he could persuade Tom to be positive about Radley and fit in more, but Tom wouldn't compromise. We took him away from Radley and, happy to have him at home, sent him to our local state school – an impressive establishment which had formerly been Ealing Grammar School, now Ealing Green School. He settled there well enough, made a little progress and seemed content, although not all the friends he made were helpful.

It was while he was there that he showed an interesting sign of his own persona, when he came home one Friday afternoon and disappeared to his room at the top of the house. We didn't see him all weekend, until we went up and found that he had painted a huge, impressive mural on a very large playroom wall. He was going through a not uncommon teenage period of spending a lot of time in the playroom, with his music and loudspeakers, and it was hard to winkle him out. Other people would tell us about their difficulties with teenage children, and the frustrating breakdown in communications that could happen between them. I didn't know what I should do but it did occur to me that if I could find some kind of activity which we both enjoyed and could spend time together over it, that might offer a way through.

By that stage in my life, in the late seventies, I had owned a series of motorbikes, each a little hairier than its predecessor. Like most things in my life, they appealed to me for the fresh challenges they presented. I mentioned to Tom that I was planning to buy a vintage Vincent bike which I intended to strip down and rebuild to a state of perfect restoration. It was the kind of project I liked, and I had an inkling, from questions he asked about my bikes, that he might too.

The bike came, was perched on its stand in the workshop and we got started. The project was a success from the very beginning. Tom loved the job and was totally engaged. I was immensely elated about this; now at least we had a strong common interest, and I was doing it as much for my own fun as his. I was genuinely impressed when every so often we would come across some intractable problem which I couldn't think my way round. Problem-solving is what distinguishes the mere mechanic from the inspired mechanic, and Tom could think laterally and come up with solutions, a skill that stayed with him ever since.

Over the years that followed, Tom's interest in bikes grew, although he wrote off his 50cc moped by riding it into the side of a car belonging, luckily, to a very understanding local businessman. After that he graduated to his mother's Honda C70. In time, and when I thought he was ready, I agreed to buy him his own first real bike, a 200cc Honda Benly, which he could ride before passing his test. He passed and graduated to a Yamaha XS 650cc, straight off the stand at the NEC Bike Show.

We would go out on road trips together, giving me a good excuse to use whatever big superbike I had at the time. For one memorable trip we crossed the Channel and headed up to Spa in Belgium for the Grand Prix. We had a good time, enjoyed the races and headed back. I'd let him lead the way to Calais but when we reached the border guard post between Belgium and France, Tom didn't slow down; he drove straight through as if it wasn't there. I pulled up and explained to the border police that he was my son, and obviously unaware that he was supposed to slow down or stop. They responded with a grin, and an imitation of firing a machine gun at his diminishing figure. '*La prochaine fois*,' they half joked. I caught up with him and told him. He went slightly pale.

He went a lot paler on the occasion Susan and I arrived back from holiday to find my brand new CBR 1100R hand-built Honda with one side flattened and scraped, after he'd promised me that he wouldn't go near it. He'd obviously been egged on by his mates to give it a try, the road was wet and down he'd gone. Thank goodness he wasn't hurt, though I made sure he learned a lesson from it by taking responsibility for his own actions and making reparations over the damage.

Tom left Ealing Green High School with a handful of modest qualifications and was disinclined to settle at anything while we tried to find a way to help him on. We agreed to send him to Richmond upon Thames College where he completed a year's art foundation course.

At twenty-one and at his request, he went to Bath to do a City & Guilds 389. Here he spent time working on motorbikes, which seemed to give him fresh inspiration. He passed comfortably and made some great friends there. He used his new training to work as a mechanic at a garage in Ealing, which belonged to a friend, where, for a pint or two, he would mend his mates' machines.

After this, though, Tom found himself at a bit of a loose end. He had left home and it was becoming clear that he was suffering from stress caused through living a busy social life by night, and not achieving much during the day. Susan and I were also worried about his health, which seemed to be a further obstacle to his progress. It was additionally frustrating for us as by this stage, we were fairly sure that he had the potential to make real progress in a branch of engineering work, but still lacking the necessary education, he lacked confidence.

When I had the chance, I talked informally to an obviously bright young GP who had joined the local medical practice – an unmarried and good-looking man, reportedly fancied by half the women in Ealing, he was very popular at local parties. I managed to corner him at one of these and told him about our concerns for Tom. He asked a few questions and nodded sympathetically.

'Oh dear,' he said. 'You've got a long haul ahead of you, but it will work its way out. Give him until he's about twenty-eight and then he'll be fine.'

To our eventual relief and joy, it turned out that he was absolutely right.

* *

Tom's younger sister, Genevieve, entered the world, like him, at St Barts Hospital, on 19 June 1964. At 9lbs 10oz, she was even bigger than Tom and, according to her mother, a good baby. Her birth had been overseen by the gynaecologist with the Dexter connections who had officiated at Tom's birth, allowing Susan to be more relaxed about the whole performance, despite her new daughter's large size.

When we told him that we intended to name her Genevieve, he protested that we couldn't name a great big girl like that after a vintage car. We explained that my mother had been Elise Genevieve Dexter, and we wanted to stay with Dexter names.

I was captivated by my new daughter and thought her the prettiest little blonde girl I'd ever seen. However, in the course of her childhood, she did experience a few minor medical problems – some nasty colds when she was still very young, brought on by a perforated eardrum. This must have been troubling to her, but she seldom complained. Her natural disposition was cheerful and positive and I have a wonderful memory of her on top form at her first birthday party, held in a box at Lord's with a cake and one candle, during the second Test against New Zealand (and just four days before I broke my leg on the A4 under the Chiswick Flyover).

As a toddler and small girl, Genevieve loved pottering about among the shrubs and bushes in the garden at 5 Warwick Dene and playing with Caramella, the golden retriever. When the dog nibbled her and the nibbling became too enthusiastic, we could hear her remonstrating vigorously: 'Top it! Top it!' Now, fifty years on, she is a keen gardener and has a lovely dog, Rosie, whom she found abandoned on the street as a puppy.

She was always very curious about everything; she wanted to know what everything was, how it worked, what it did – a trait that hasn't left her in adulthood. One of her earlier experiments was with earthworms, which she tested for edibility. She called them 'werrrrms', imitating our nanny who had a pronounced Scottish brogue. We don't know if she ever ingested a complete worm, but if she did, it did no damage. Could this be an answer to future world food scarcity?

Gen, as we called her, was always bright and quick on the uptake. I wish I had spent more time with her; when I did it was the greatest fun listening to her already quite grown-up chatter. I used to enjoy taking black-and-white photos of the children which I would develop myself. As a pretty characterful child, she was a natural model and she grew up a strong-featured, striking lady, with a big personality, a great sense of humour and disinclined to suffer fools.

She started at a local primary school before going on to Notting Hill & Ealing Girls' High School where she did well academically, although she wasn't always as diligent as she could have been. However, she was certainly sporty, which obviously pleased me. She played tennis for her school and, because she was tall, goal defence at netball. Playing against other schools with very menacing tall girls, they still managed to beat them. Gen also played netball at junior county level for Middlesex. Besides tennis and netball, she was athletic and good at swimming, especially the backstroke. She was only beaten when she wanted to win a silver medal rather than gold because it was her favourite colour. The coaches at the Southall Swimming Club tried to persuade us to bring her in for special training sessions at the pool at 6.30 in the morning, with a view to turning her into a competitive swimmer.

We weren't sure about this and around that time, I was asked to a charity event with a crowd of other sporting notables. At lunch I found myself sitting next to Anita Lonsbrough, swimming gold medallist at the 1960 Olympics. Making conversation with her, I mentioned Genevieve's swimming and the proposal to push her up to another level in the sport. Anita was unequivocal in her response. 'I wouldn't wish the sort of a life I had as a young swimmer on anyone, or encourage them to go through what I did. I would strongly advise you not to let her get involved in that sort of intensive coaching.'

I had to think about this. Although I loved my various sports, I had never felt a strong proselytising urge about them. It seemed to me that if this was something she was desperate to do above all else, we would have been prepared to go some way to supporting her. There are parents who have done absolutely everything they could to nurture a talent in their children. I know, for instance, that Lewis Hamilton's father dedicated thousands of hours a year to his son's early driving career, and there are many similarly dedicated parents around the country who have helped to produce a number of national sporting heroes. I didn't want to kill off any dreams Gen might have had, but I wanted *her* to decide how far she took it. She was thirteen at this stage, but quite capable of knowing her own mind.

Luckily, she enjoyed a lot of different sports – riding ponies, athletics, gymnastics and tennis. I sat down with her and told her that the time had come when she had to choose which activity she wanted to do most. 'You can't do them all,' I told her. 'We can't be driving you all over the place to do everything. You have to make a choice.'

I held my breath, waiting for her answer.

She chose gymnastics, thank heavens, because of her love for the Romanian prodigy, Nadia Comăneci. We were relieved because, as a tall girl, this would be good for her, giving her balance and strength, but with no one lurking in the wings ready to drag her into some punishing juvenile training regime. She also suffered from vertigo, like me, which meant that the beam and bars were always a challenge. She still enjoys swimming and scuba-dives in the Caribbean every year, but she's probably glad to have avoided all the agonies of senior competitive sport.

Another aspect of her nature that emerged at school was a wilful streak in her nature over the matter of clothes. Whatever the latest fad, like platform shoes, she would save up her pocket money and find a way. Because of her height, though, she had to learn to make her own clothes and Susan helped her create a sewing club on the ping-pong table, with some help from Susan's tailor.

As an adventurous and fearless girl, she was inclined to be accident-prone. Starting at the age of four, she badly damaged her fingers by catching them in a folding chair. Her natural inquisitiveness did her fingers further damage when she wanted to know how electricity worked. She had undone the switch on her bedside light, prodded around, and got badly shocked and burned. Luckily for her, she was in bed and comparatively insulated. If she'd been sitting on the side of the bed with her feet on the ground, she might easily have been killed.

We had to take her to the burns unit at Mount Vernon Hospital, where war-damaged soldiers had had their burnt faces repaired with plastic surgery, and they applied skin grafts from her chest and legs to her hands. She had to go back several times to complete the treatment but apart from a few scars on her hands she ultimately came out unscathed. She formed strong friendships with her fellow patients and still corresponds with them. During the process we were given a kitten, which Gen had always wanted, so when we went to see her after a small operation, we thought we'd cheer her up by telling her about it. Already a bit of a cynic, she declared, 'I don't believe you!'

She was only six when the four of us were flying in my Piper Aztec to Australia (when I was covering a Test series for the *Sunday Mirror*). Genevieve was particularly sad at leaving her cat behind, but she seemed to find another at every stage of the four-week journey. We had a stopover in Kuwait where some expat friends had organised a place for us to stay. We were knackered and dying for a drink, which wasn't readily available, until our friends very thoughtfully dropped off a bottle of gin. Tom and Genny went up to play on the roof, as a lot of people use their flat roofs for sitting out on, where she managed to tear her leg on something. We were off again to the local equivalent of the A & E, where a surgeon stitched her up. We only found out he was a cardiac specialist when we saw Susan's family's old GP while we were passing through Calcutta, and he took Genny's stitches out. He said the way the stitches had been sewn showed that they had been done by a heart surgeon.

However, she hadn't learned her lesson, and other accidents occurred. In her early teens she managed to impale herself on some cast-iron railings, thanks to her platform shoes, but once again survived.

A mishap that occurred much later, when Gen was in her gap year and on her way to work as an au pair in Verbier, was, I admit, entirely our fault. Her ferry to France was delayed, her train to the capital very late and she found herself stranded at the Gare du Nord without a proverbial *sous*. She had plenty – hundreds, if not thousands of French francs, which Susan had given her from an ancient stash; unfortunately, they were *vieux* francs, pre-devaluation banknotes which were by then entirely worthless. She was sitting on a bench, aged eighteen, in tears because she had no money to get anywhere or do anything. She was, though, rescued by an angelic lady who took her home so she could ring up the family in Verbier where she was going to work. Her fairy godmother paid for her ticket and made sure she got on the right train. God bless her.

Since she'd been a toddler, Gen had always been gregarious and outward-going, always enjoying her birthday parties and forming strong, lasting friendships, in particular with a girl called Alison who had been one of the few not to shy from holding her hand, despite the unprepossessing skin grafts she'd had at the Mount Vernon. They were netball teammates for many years and are still good friends.

As a teenager she was firmly independent – helped by an outside staircase which led directly to a door to the second floor. She and Tom had their own bedrooms and a bathroom at the top of the house where they could keep themselves to themselves, although they didn't share the same circle of friends. She had a passion for the music of David Bowie, where Tom would be listening to The Rolling Stones. Gen always held strong views, and wasn't coy about expressing them. We always respected this even if sometimes there was quite a distance between her position and ours. As a result, there was never a breakdown in communications that I've seen in other families, sometimes with distressing long-term effects.

Gen left her Ealing school with a reasonable crop of A-levels, though not good enough to get her into her first choice of university, probably because her essays were too forthright, and expressed her own views, rather than the conventional perspective. As often happens, this turned out not to be a bad thing, as she went on to have a stimulating and productive three years at her second university choice.

In 1982 she happily arrived at Sheffield Polytechnic College (now Sheffield Hallam University) to study Modern Languages with Politics.

She found that the teaching and ambience suited her well and she benefitted from the outstanding language laboratories there. During her course she went to Nancy University where she wrote a thesis in French on the scandal of the Sinking of the Rainbow Warrior by French foreign intelligence services, and Turin, where she wrote a paper in Italian on politics and Italian television – featuring the activities of Signor Berlusconi. Both theses helped her a great deal with the languages she was studying, and she graduated with BA Hons in Italian and French to start the next phase of her life.

Chapter Fifteen

SWANSONG TEST AND
THE CHALLENGE OF FLIGHT

After I'd officially retired in 1965, and had gone on to play regularly for the Rothmans International Cavaliers, and, indeed, for the winning England team in the somewhat hyperbolically named 1966 Rothmans World Cup, it was still some while before I completely abandoned active cricket. I was even, for a brief spell of déjà vu, lured back into the world of Test and county cricket. Frankly, I didn't need a lot of luring. I was keeping my eye in with a dozen or so games a year with the Cavaliers, scoring a steady bag of runs, including 104 versus the West Indies at Blackheath in 1967, when Gubby Allen started making noises about the dire need for batsmen in the England team that was struggling against an indifferent Australian XI in the 68 home Test series. Colin Cowdrey rang me to ask if I could put in an appearance for my old county, Sussex, so that I would be eligible for selection. I wasn't as busy as I would like to have been, scratching around for deals with Bagenal Harvey and I was in the right frame of mind for a bit of centre stage, and found myself pawing at the ground like an old war horse at the sound of a bugle.

Sussex weren't in great shape in the Championship, floundering around at the bottom under Jim Parks. Morale was low and there had been murmurs of player revolt early in the season, with the increasingly prominent John Snow said to be among the disgruntled. As I walked into the pavilion to talk about a game, I sensed strongly that they badly needed a bit of a lift. Certainly Snow, and the recent recruit, Tony Greig, seemed pleased to see me. It was agreed that I would play in the next Championship match against Kent at Hastings. A few days later, I heaved my battered old bag into my plane and headed for the East Sussex coast.

I had a good feeling as I walked out with my old brown, lightweight bat to face Derek Underwood, who was bowling on a pitch that should have suited him. Happily, I had a good record against the great Kent left-arm spinner. I had worked out that neither his quicker ball, nor his slower ball really turned. Thus, if I waited patiently before moving (in the manner of the great Garfield Sobers)

I would see some good chances to score – through the leg side for the quicker ones, and off the back foot for the slower balls.

Unfortunately for him, my eye was in, the form was there, and I started scoring runs right away. I was making minced meat of the Kent bowling and reached 100 quite comfortably. I knew that was enough to get me back into the England team and, in retrospect, I should have listened to the warning creaks in my knees and slowed down. But I was on a roll; I was living the moment, loving the glory and I was greedy. In what must have been among my best-ever innings, I carried on until I'd passed the double century, when I was promptly caught for 203. Fittingly, it was off Derek Underwood's bowling, who must have been mightily relieved; I'd hit three sixes and twenty-three fours in five and a half hours.

My selection for the England team was confirmed for the fourth Test at Headingley, at which point Australia were leading the series 1-0. I bowled some overs, without taking a wicket; I was under no illusion that I was as quick as I had been. I'd lost the pace; the zip and the sting had gone out of it, but I did catch the Australian skipper, Barry Jarman, deputising for an injured Bill Lawry. Batting at first wicket down, I made a modest 10 in the first innings, and 38 in the second – helpful but not significant in a game which ended in a draw. I was nevertheless selected again for the last Test at the Oval, having decided in my own mind that this would be my last-ever Test appearance.

England started well in the first innings when John Edrich and Basil D'Oliveira made over 300 between them of a total of 494. The Australians replied with 324. Even after our less impressive second-innings total of 181, they were still left with a target of 352. We were already feeling confident when Bill Lawry opened and was out for just 4. We had them on the run, but after their fifth wicket had fallen for 65, a short violent cloudburst descended and temporarily waterlogged the pitch. When the rain stopped as suddenly as it had started, in the forlorn hope that we might see some play, Colin Cowdrey walked onto the pitch carrying his umbrella, and started prodding the ground, seeing the surface water drain straight off. Without a hint of encouragement from the England captain, within moments the ground was full of volunteers with umbrellas doing the same, until the umpires declared the pitch playable once more. This came as a surprise and cause of disgruntlement on the part of the Australians, who were already at least half-packed and ready to leave the ground for a draw.

The match resumed with Australia needing over 270 with five lower-order wickets in hand. After Basil D'Oliveira bowled Barry Jarman, Derek

Underwood took the last 4 wickets for 15 runs, we'd won the match and squared the series. For me that was some consolation, although my personal celebration was somewhat subdued; my contribution to the match had been 21 and 28, and I hadn't bowled at all. It felt great, though, to be on a winning team against the Australians, when memories of 1963 in Melbourne came flooding back.

Some decades later, watching my musical hero, Frank Sinatra, performing one of his several last comeback concerts on television, I wondered if he felt about the narrowing of his vocal range, and the dwindling strength of his voice, as I had in my batting and bowling in my much earlier swansong.

However, it didn't stop me enjoying my ongoing involvement with the International Cavaliers, with whom I happily continued to play for the next couple of years. This provided two entertaining trips to the West Indies – Barbados in August 69 and Jamaica in January 1970. It was on this second short tour that I met the quietly spoken Scotsman, Gavin Gordon, with whom I started and enjoyed a long business partnership. I would have been quite happy to go on playing with the Cavaliers for at least a few more years, if the ECB's decision to launch the John Player County Sunday League hadn't rendered the whole idea unviable.

Instead, not having played any official limited-overs cricket since the Gillette Cup Final of 1968, I played almost two full seasons of Sunday League cricket for Sussex in 1971 and 1972, also a B&H Cup match in 1972 – all unpaid. After a lull of seven years, I finally played my last competitive game of cricket, aged forty, for Old England v. Lord's Taverners at Rushden – my very last swansong, when I top-scored with 71, and took the wicket of Derek Ufton, the former captain of Charlton Athletic.

Beyond this, though, I turned out regularly for the Lord's Taverners and in response to invitations to play in other charity matches. The Taverners were always fun because half the membership was comprised of cricket-loving actors, while our patron and twelfth man was the Duke of Edinburgh.

The Duke enjoyed his cricket and I had the honour of playing for and against him on several occasions at the wonderfully picturesque ground at Highclere Castle, where the Herberts, Earls of Carnarvon, have staged matches since the 1840s. Lord Porchester, son of the 6th Earl and the Queen's racing manager, was a keen cricketer, as well as a fine host on the weekends Susan and I spent there for various matches. I was, of course, always on best behaviour, although in one match when the Duke was bowling to me – not a bad off-spinner, I recall – I was unsure of the protocol. I quietly patted away the first over. The

Duke was amused. 'You don't have to be that bloody respectful,' he remarked sardonically.

I nodded. 'OK, sir', and whacked the next three balls for 6. I instantly regretted my *lèse-majesté*, but fortunately, he forgave me with a smile.

At another game being played at Highclere (whose pitch has featured splendidly in an episode of *Downton Abbey*) I was sitting beside Her Majesty, chatting as we watched the cricket, when a hard pull shot came bounding across the outfield, directly towards where she sat in an open-sided marquee. Instinctively, I contrived to get myself between the ball and Her Majesty and deflect it before any royal bruises resulted.

This event is recorded in a history of the ground which I recently found online in a piece by the current Lady Carnarvon. I got in touch with her about it and was kindly invited to a match at Highclere this summer (though NOT to play) – an invitation which, sadly, was hit for six by the dreaded coronavirus.

* *

One of the more bizarre promotional games in which I agreed to play was organised by the industrious Reg Hayter sometime in the mid-sixties. He gathered an 'England' team and flew them out of London without telling them where they were going. It was the middle of February; they hoped they were destined for somewhere warm. They landed in Paris, which was as cold as London, where Reg told them he'd been hired by Maurice Gardet – an eccentric French impresario with political ambitions – to stage an exhibition cricket match in Paris as part of a drive to introduce the game to the French. This bizarre event was to be held at the north Paris rugby venue, Le Parc des Princes. Reg's match was to be played by a press team, mostly cricket-related and including some county players, Godfrey Evans and myself, against Reg's own North London cricket club, Stanmore.

Frankly, as a publicity wheeze in non-cricket playing France, it struck me as a non-starter, but a free weekend in Paris in congenial company, with a fee attached, was enough for me, and I agreed to play. Our team, despite being mainly media-related, were reasonably well behaved, apart from ascending the Eiffel Tower and trying to bat a few oranges off the top deck into the Seine.

The day before the game and knowing Reg's lack of attention to detail, Godfrey Evans and I thought we ought to make sure that something had been done about a pitch to play on in what was basically a rugby ground. We went up to the vast stadium to see for ourselves; there was nothing beyond a fairly shaggy grass rugger pitch and, as far as I could see, nothing at all had been organised.

We were put in touch with some British members of an international military outfit known as SHAPE – Supreme Headquarters Allied Powers in Europe, who ran their own cricket team. They rallied round at once with startling efficiency and turned up with a good matting wicket, stumps and balls, and had them all in place in time for the match the next day. It looked like a reasonable pitch to play on.

We foregathered next morning, a little circumspect, and wondering who on earth was going to turn up to watch this match; if it were being staged at Stanmore, we would have been lucky to get more than two hundred, and here there was capacity for forty thousand spectators.

To our astonishment, a crowd of seven thousand appeared, mostly French as far as we could tell. As soon as we started playing, it was clear from their reactions that they had no idea what was happening, but we didn't let that stop us enjoying ourselves. However, when a tea break was called, in a somewhat ham-fisted attempt to parody the Englishness of the event, a butler and footmen dressed in tails and spongebag trousers carried on the tea in bone china pots on a silver tray with sugar bowls and silver spoons. The crowd were bemused and didn't respond at all. We shrugged our shoulders and carried on.

I took the ball – a white ball, for unexplained reasons – and started bowling in a leisurely manner to an eighteen-year-old lad from Stanmore. I pitched up a few nice easy half-volleys for him to hit, but all he did was defend, studiously pushing the ball away. As I was running into bowl for my next over, it suddenly clicked in my head that he wasn't a driver of the ball, but probably a hooker and cutter. Intending to help him, I whacked down a short one to see if he could score off that, but he just looked at it, with his eyes getting wider and wider, until the ball smacked him full in the mouth. He went down like a burst balloon. Stretcher-bearers rushed on, there was blood all over the place and the crowd went wild. They were properly excited; this was what they'd come for! Now they were cheering me on, presumably in the hope that I would cause more harm.

I felt awful. The poor man's injury was, obviously, completely unintentional. It was just one of those unfortunate things that happen.

As a promotion, I can only assume that our match (and don't ask me who won) was not a success; no more cricket is played in France now than it was then, and I don't believe M. Gardet made it into politics – indeed, according to

Wikipedia, he didn't exist. How much Reg Hayter made out of this escapade, I never discovered; for me it was fun and a memorable experience, if not remotely profitable.

The Inner Self

While I carried on playing cricket during the 1970s, albeit with diminishing frequency, I had become more absorbed by my business activities, my journalism, my family, my passion for motorcars, motorbikes, aeroplanes, horse racing, greyhounds and golf. And amidst all that, I had become, with Susan, more aware of the non-material side of life; I had been encouraged in this by my friendship with David Sheppard, the late Anglican Bishop of Liverpool.

I had played cricket with David several times during my professional career, for the last time in the 1962/63 Antipodean tour, with particular memories of the great second Test at Melbourne when he scored a magnificent 113. However, it wasn't until some years later that we became closer. For twelve years David ran an East London mission, the Mayflower Family Centre in Canning Town, catering for the poor, the underprivileged and others abandoned by society. Susan and I visited him and his wife, Grace, there several times, and they came and stayed with us in Ealing; they had a daughter, Jenny, who was the same age as our Genny and they would play together.

What impressed me about David was the utter sincerity of his urge to help those who needed it. He was a tremendous communicator, patient, consistent and tireless. He was steadfast and felt profoundly his closeness to Jesus. Although my family had always been committed Anglicans, I became more involved with my Christian faith when, at David's suggestion, Susan and I went to see the great American evangelist, Billy Graham, preach to tens of thousands at Earls Court in 1967. I was so captivated by what he had to say, I went back again the next evening, when standing at the back of the huge crowd, there were tears in my eyes and a lovely, large West Indian lady put her ample arm around my shoulder, and murmured, 'You're really feeling it, ain't you?'

I wasn't cured of my compulsive tendency to gamble, but I believe my experience at Billy Graham's meeting made me think more seriously about my aims in life – which was a help in itself. If I'd been told then that I would spend seven years of my later life as treasurer of the Anglican Church in Nice, I wouldn't have believed it possible.

However, I came away with the belief that Jesus was a real, historical person, who had chosen to live a life where he could be perceived as the son of God, and that we all have the choice to live as he had. Susan and I became regular supporters of St Matthews, our local parish in Ealing, and good friends with the rector, Peter Watkins. Peter was a quite exceptional man and scholar who, by the time he retired in 2015 at the age of eighty-one, had been vicar of St Matthews for forty-eight years. Before that he had been in the army and had run on the athletics track for Oxford University, which was, perhaps, why he used to enjoy coming with us to the greyhound races at Wembley Stadium on a Saturday night. For all the time we lived in Ealing, from 1966 to 2000, our parish was a key part of our lives and leaving it, when we moved to Ascot, was a great wrench.

I've no doubt that my faith has helped me through the crises that have cropped up in my life, and also with the perennial niggling problem I had with gambling. Certainly David Sheppard talked to me about it with real sympathy and helped me to get it under control. Much, much later I had help in that, too, from an unexpected source, a friend from my earlier days in Ealing, Peter Davies. Peter and his brother were the sons of the owner of a successful shopfitting company who had money to spend, and an indefatigable appetite for fun. The younger of them, Peter, went through a string of mishaps with businesses, as well as his own addiction problems. He was at rock bottom, but responded well to the therapy he sought and received. He began to think that offering therapy was something he could do himself. He trained and qualified, and set up as a counsellor himself.

I met him by chance in 2005. He knew about the gambling problems I'd had over the years.

'How's the punting going, Ted?' he asked without much preamble.

'You know, up and down. No big deal,' I obfuscated.

He wasn't going to let me get away with that. He came up close and looked me straight in the eyes. 'I'm not so sure about that,' he said with quiet firmness. This was a man who'd been through a hell of a lot and come out the other side. If anyone had an opinion on this kind of thing that was to be respected, it was my good friend Peter Davies. Apart from the one bet per annum that I now allow myself, I haven't had a punt on a horse or a dog since that encounter.

It's true to say that I had never allowed this habit to become a debilitating or obsessive problem, but for a long time it cost me money and, more troubling, caused Susan worry. It was a big relief to be free of it once and for all and I'm sure my closeness to Christianity was a factor in overcoming it.

I'm a little sad that my children are less committed than we are, but they are good, thoughtful people and I can see that some Christian beliefs are hard to sustain within the hyper-rational, fact-based attitudes of the modern Western world. At the same time, I sense that people – including many young ones – are searching widely for some deeper insights into the mysteries of human existence, and perhaps there will come a time when at least the basic tenets of Christianity – love, tolerance, compassion, selflessness – will seem more relevant again.

The Freedom of Flight

I have always enjoyed travel by any means of transport, but I've enjoyed it most when I've been driving and navigating myself, allowing me to stop or change direction whenever I've felt impelled. Impulse had been a big factor in my life in all departments – marriage plans, cricketing strategies, business proposals – and my decision to learn to fly was no exception. It wasn't a decision towards which I slowly worked my way after a lot of thought and consideration. It was the simple corollary of realising that during 1967 I had driven over forty thousand miles in my Mini-Cooper S, which I loved, and in which I'd been in two crashes. The second of these triggered my decision to fly. Although I love driving cars (and have owned over fifty different models so far) I figured that there was less traffic and fewer obstacles in the air.

On 4 January 1968, I drove down the M4 to the small airfield at White Waltham, near Maidenhead, for my first flying lesson. Shortly after that I found myself chatting to the legendary spitfire pilot, Douglas Bader, at a London drinks party.

'Have you been solo yet?' he barked. 'No? Then be sure to let me know when you do.'

Ten weeks into my training, on the day I was due to go solo for the first time, Douglas showed up as he had promised. However, as my test was delayed by low cloud, he invited me up for a spin in his Twin Beech, and generously allowed me to take over.

'OK, then,' he boomed. 'You have control now. That's right, my boy; you're doing fine!'

After a quick potter around the Berkshire sky, Douglas reached down to drop the landing gear as the White Waltham grass landing strip loomed dead ahead.

The old ace's gravelly voice crackled through my headphones. 'I say old boy, would you think me an awful cad if I did the landing?' He was a great man and a huge character.

* *

On 15 May, my thirty-third birthday, I was granted my private pilot's licence. It hadn't occurred to me that I wouldn't pass my final test and I had bought my first plane a couple of days before – from a second-hand London car dealer through an ad in a flying magazine. It was a well-used but tidy Beagle Airedale, a good stable platform for a beginner. I was up in the air as often as I could be, thinking of any places I could visit by air. In June I flew to Le Touquet and back; by mid-July I was roaming further afield with a trip to the south of France. As I'd expected, I absolutely loved the incomparable sense of freedom that I found in flying my own plane, and it was joy that stayed with me for many years, and over six different planes.

In the spring of 1969, I acquired my second aircraft when I traded the Airedale for a Falco, a small but dashing Italian two-seater with a retractable undercarriage. The Falco was thirty per cent faster than the Airedale which was fine by me, but made bigger demands on the pilot, who had to see more and think faster. At the same time, I was quickly becoming aware of the constraints of flying in Northern Europe imposed by the climate and prevalence of cloud that made purely visual navigation unreliable. If I wanted to broaden my scope, I would have to get myself an instrument rating.

When I saw an advertisement for a correspondence course offered by the Flying School at Kidlington near Oxford, I signed up immediately and was soon working away diligently, regularly sending back my week's work by return, until the course stopped coming. When I got in touch, they put their hands up and admitted that I'd caught them on the hop by being so speedy with my lessons, and the second half of the correspondence course hadn't been written. They offered a compromise of a short residential course, which I completed in four days, when I was granted my instrument rating.

This freedom to fly brings with it the further responsibility of the pilot to recognise his own limitations. Provided he is qualified and sober, nobody can tell a private pilot not to fly. It is entirely his own decision, but I also thought it would be sensible to learn some basic aerobatics in case, inadvertently, I found myself upside down one day. I became competent but I never managed a loop the loop on my own in all the time I flew. Nor, thank God, did I ever find myself unintentionally upside down.

Towards the end of 1969, I was driving up from Kent, passing close to Biggin Hill, an old wartime airfield just south-east of London which was currently the collecting point for the London to Sydney Air Race due to start that week. I thought I'd drop in to have a look at all the aircraft gathering for the off. While I was in the tower, checking it all out, I overheard a loud, desperate voice on the phone. It belonged to one of a pair of Australian flyers who were short of a crew member as a result of the flu bug that was doing the rounds. They needed an instrument-rated replacement and, true to impulsive form, I volunteered, forgetting to consult anyone at home.

Not long before Christmas, we set off from Biggin Hill and headed out across the Channel through heavy cloud. Gatwick control gave me a new radio frequency for the handover to France but it turned out that the plane didn't have a class 1 radio, thus no contact with French controllers. We had no choice but to turn back for an instrument landing at Gatwick and wait for better weather. We got away the following day and seven hours later landed in Rome to refuel. I went to have a pee and found that my aim was alarmingly haphazard because I was shaking so much. I realised I'd caught the flu from the epidemic that had taken a hold in England. However, knowing that they wouldn't be able to go on without me, I felt I owed it to the Aussies to keep going, even if I was lying in the back semi-conscious for most of the time.

By the time we reached Karachi I was in a very sorry state and I had to call it a day. The two Aussie bush pilots could manage without my instrument skills from there on, and I waved them goodbye with mixed emotions. However, it was the right decision. I managed to get a seat on a BOAC flight and arrived home on Christmas Eve with a solid dose of pneumonia. Susan had been going to her parents with the children but made a quick change of plan and managed to find a frozen turkey and a Christmas pudding at the last minute, while I retired to bed.

* *

The following August, I'd flown myself up to Leeds in my latest purchase, a Piper Comanche, a four-seat retractable, faster again than the Falco, to play in a Cavaliers match. After the game, I was flying to Blackpool for an extra game which had been slotted in and offered a lift to a pair of fellow Cavaliers, Peter Pollock, South African fast bowler, and Derek Murray, West Indian wicketkeeper. It was a fine evening and we were enjoying the view over the empty moorland of the south Pennines when I felt a hefty vibration from the engine. This hadn't happened to me before, but keeping calm, I managed to send a Mayday distress call and then to confirm I was going to ditch the plane. Surveying the landscape for somewhere to land, I miraculously spotted two small grass fields, next to a farmhouse, which I guessed were just long enough for a belly landing.

My passengers seemed to take it all in their stride; they said afterwards that they'd never doubted I would get the plane down safely. I had not shared their confidence, but I didn't tell them.

The farmer in whose field I had ditched came out to greet us, completely unfazed.

'Aye oop! Sorry 'bout the plane! Come on in and meet the wife, and have a cup of tea,' he offered, with an authentic, down-to-earth Yorkshire welcome. 'Oh – and you might want to use the phone.'

He told me that I'd landed at Cowlaughton Farm, Cowling, Keighley. I thanked him profusely and sent him a card each Christmas for the next few years.

* *

Later that year I was still feeling bad about bailing out of the London to Sydney race with the Australians, and knowing that I would be expected to go down under to report the 1970 Ashes tour for the *Sunday Mirror*, I had developed a cockeyed idea that I would fly myself down there, and – even more cockeyed – take the family with me – that is to say, my wife, my eight-year-old son and six-year-old daughter. Before I could start even planning this, though, there were a couple of practical obstacles to be overcome. First, it meant buying a twin-engined plane, then, learning to fly it. I did consult my wife and children on this occasion, as they were part of the risk, and they agreed.

Within a month I'd found and bought a twin-engined Piper Aztec, and immediately set about getting a 'twin' rating. Then I addressed the enjoyable business of planning the flight there and back in a plane with which I had little time to familiarise myself.

Susan's parents, Tom and Heath Longfield, were understandably distraught at the thought of their idiot son-in-law endangering their only daughter and the two grandchildren. However, they knew we weren't going to be talked out of it and Susan's mother implored Tom to do something – anything to lessen the risk. For the first time in years he picked up the phone to an old military friend, a high-ranking officer, General Terence McMeekin. The General sent one signal only down the line which was short and to the point. 'Dexter family en route London to Australia in light aircraft, Piper Aztec G-ASNA; departure date: 19 October 1970. Please offer all assistance.'

The small farewell group that mustered at White Waltham at the start of the trip were not filled with confidence when I had to summon an instructor to help me before taking off. He swiftly pointed out that I had failed to switch on the radio. Minutes later our plane, emblazoned with its new name, *Pommie's Progress*, was taxying to the start of the runway and we were off on our journey more than halfway round the world.

** **

The logistics of the voyage involved some large numbers. The circumference of the earth at the equator is twenty-five thousand miles. The distance from London to Sydney, as flown by a crow, is seventeen thousand miles. At the Aztec's cruising speed of two hundred miles per hour, it could take just eighty-five hours; we expected to take a month. The plane had fuel capacity of four hours, with reserves, allowing flights of eight hundred miles, with about twenty stopovers, including Kuwait, where Gen tore her leg and had it stitched up, and Calcutta, where she had the stitches taken out.

The children adapted remarkably quickly to life on the wing, enjoying it, especially in the intertropical zones, where there was some serious turbulence to bounce the plane up and down like a roller-coaster ride. Susan, of course, was brave, and stoical, rather than ecstatic. But we were all pretty pleased as we prepared for our final leg from Kupang in East Timor four hundred miles straight across the notorious 'shark-infested' Timor Sea to Darwin. I was especially pleased to have two engines that day, and to be helped by an unexpected stroke of luck.

Flight regulations in the UK required the Aztec to carry a long-wave radio and a peculiar trailing aerial. I had tried this radio on each leg of the flight but so far had never made a contact. Once we were airborne and heading for Darwin, as part of my regular routine I tried again.

After a moment, the silence was broken by a clear voice with a strong Australian accent: 'Golf Alpha Sierra November Alpha. This is Darwin. Welcome to Australia!' – the most comforting words we heard throughout the whole journey.

** **

For those who live on our small island, the sheer scale of Australia is mind-boggling. Darwin to Sydney is close on two thousand miles, the same as London to Beirut. Our flight path across the outback was a zigzag as towns with airfields are scarce, and it took us three days from Darwin to Longreach, the last landing before our first big city stop, Brisbane. Longreach is known in modern Australian history as the birth place of QANTAS – Queensland and Northern Territories Air Services. We saw the name emblazoned on the single large hangar as we taxied in. We were to see more of that hangar than we'd planned.

As we prepared to take off for our last leg to Brisbane the next morning, it was so hot the we kept the cabin door ajar while we were taxiing out. We secured the door before take-off – we thought – but we hadn't because it popped open just as we left the ground. That meant flying a circuit round the airfield and landing to shut it properly; all the while the engine temperatures were climbing.

We took off again and levelled out at nine thousand feet, our usual cruising height, and settled down on the autopilot. With Tommy sitting up front beside me, I began to feel my eyes closing. In fact, I was utterly exhausted. I turned to Tom. 'Just keep your eyes on those two gauges, please,' I asked. 'I must just close my eyes for a few minutes. If any of those needles move, just give me a shake, will you?'

It seemed like the next moment that I was woken abruptly by an excited eight-year-old boy yelling at me. 'Dad! Dad! One of the needles has moved.'

I certainly didn't want to believe him, until I noticed a clear loss of oil pressure on the starboard engine. I had to think what to do. 'Mayday' calls are reserved for imminent danger. If you have a problem and want to change your flight plan in any way, you make a 'Pan' call. I made the call at the same time as I was trying to remember how to shut down one engine and feather the propeller to reduce drag.

'PAN! PAN!' I radioed. 'Shutting down starboard engine. Returning to Longreach.'

'OK, that is copied,' came the laconic reply.

To maintain speed and height, I had to increase the power on the remaining engine, and I found myself trying to recall and calculate the single-engined, fully loaded performance figures. I ought to have been able to maintain an altitude of five thousand feet – maybe four thousand, taking the heat into account.

Longreach control on the radio broke into my calculations.

What level would I be at?

Without thinking, I said four thousand feet and happily let down to that height. What I should have said was, 'I'll keep you posted.'

If I had used all my nine thousand feet capacity to drift slowly down, I would have made it easily without frightening myself and my family half to death.

The official figure may have been four thousand feet for a brand-new aircraft and a crack pilot, but my plane was neither new nor in the hands of an ace. And the air temperature was too hot to produce much lift. We drifted gently downwards with still over ten miles to run and I was seriously looking around for a flat piece of the bush for a forced landing.

Our altitude dropped to three thousand then two thousand feet, and our position was looking critical. At 1,500 it was looking desperate, when a small miracle kicked in. As we dropped nearer to the ground, a sudden hot updraught off the land caught us and we sailed home, as if we were surfing on a great wave. They don't teach you everything in flying school.

Landing was no problem but taxying on one engine is only possible as long as the plane has enough momentum. If it has slowed too much, it will go round in circles. Fortunately, it looked as if the controller was aware of this, and he let me roll straight into the cavernous Qantas hangar. I could almost hear a sigh of relief from the overstressed port-side motor as we were approached from the far side of the hangar by a friendly looking, middle-aged man with a broad Yorkshire accent, who turned out to be an aeronautical engineer. He offered to check the engine that had conked out. After a few moments tinkering and clanking, he turned to me with a screwed-up face and some bad news.

'You've run a couple of bearings, by the look of things,' he pronounced glumly. 'There's metal in the oil. You'll definitely need a replacement. If you can get one sent up it would suit me to fit it for you. I was just about to go back to England because the work here has dropped off badly. A week or two earning money before I go would help with the tickets.'

We caught the daily flight to Brisbane on a Fokker Friendship, where we made camp in the local Travelodge. I sat on the phone for a few hours, and eventually sourced an engine from Sydney. It was brought up the long way, by road, to Brisbane; I booked it on the next flight to Longreach and was out on the tarmac to see it loaded. I was verging on the incandescent when the plane moved off, and my precious cargo was still sitting in the middle of the tarmac. Luckily, I was saved from apoplexy by a Samaritan in faded jeans and a battered hat who was relaxing in the cool shade of a high wing Cessna 206.

He ambled across to me and spoke through the side of his mouth in authentic Australian. 'You seem to have a problem, mate.'

'Why did they leave the engine behind,' I asked, not disguising my indignation.

'The pallet's too darned big. But it would fit in my 206. I could take it.'

He offered to do it for less than I was expecting, loaded up the engine right away, and got going. The engine was duly delivered and fitted, all within two weeks of conking out. When it was done, we got on our way in time for me to cover some of the tour games in Queensland and the first Test in Brisbane on 27 November.

For the next three months we criss-crossed the continent, mostly following the MCC tour but with a lot of sightseeing between matches, from Alice Springs to Perth, Hobart, Melbourne, Sydney – twenty-two flights in all. I filed I don't remember how many reports for the *Sunday Mirror*. They hadn't sponsored my flight, but slightly larger expense claims were kindly tolerated. As the third Melbourne Test was abandoned for rain an extra Test fixture was added. England, under Ray Illingworth, won the fourth Test in Sydney as well as the final Test, also in Sydney, clinching the Ashes series 2-0, although sadly not without a certain amount of controversy.

John Snow had just felled Terry Jenner, which prompted a drunken Aussie fan to grab hold of him with some fruity language. The game only restarted when Ray Illingworth's threat to march his team off the field was taken seriously.

On a lighter note, I'll admit to a twinge of schadenfreude when I saw Geoffrey Boycott hurl his bat to the ground after being run out in the sixth Test.

By the end of our stay, I'd had to replace the second engine as well as the first. That meant, at least, that I was feeling confident about the journey home. I was philosophical about the inconvenience and the cost of it, and considered that for both engines to fail so soon after a full engineering check before we set out must have been due to one of two things: outrageous bad luck, or some serious malfeasance and jiggery-pokery between the people who had sold me the plane and the engineers who must have known the potential problems when they signed the plane off. The second scenario seemed to me a lot more likely than the first.

Our last taste of Australia was a marvellous overnight stay in Darwin with Mori Blake, one of the bush pilots I'd set off with from England for my aborted part in the London to Sydney Air Race. While we were there, Tommy disappeared with another boy his age and reappeared carrying a couple of stinking cattle hooves as a trophy to take home. He was bitterly disappointed when he had to leave them behind.

We flew out of Darwin on 15 February 1971 to head back the way we had come. It took us a week less to get home than it had to come out, and I never did work out why.

One of the few incidents on the return journey that stand out occurred on the approach across the Adriatic Sea to Brindisi at night in thick murky conditions. I was startled when I heard a sound, like the rattle of someone kicking a tin. I turned back to look at Tom. 'What are you doing?'

'It wasn't me, Dad, honest,' he pleaded.

It happened again; Tom was blamed again.

It wasn't until the next morning that I saw the paintwork on the outside of the fuselage had taken a pounding, and I worked out that it was from ice flying off the propellers, not Tom after all.

I remember less of the second half of our odyssey, perhaps because I knew what I was doing by then and it was less of a novelty, but I do recall how amazingly green and welcoming was our first sight of England.

* *

Not long after the big trip, the Aztec was sold and I only played around with flying for a while. It was ten years before my interest was seriously revived when an advertisement in a magazine caught my eye. Brand-new Cessnas were being built in Rheims including 206's like the one that flew my engine to Longreach. Brand new, with a three-blade prop and a 300 horsepower, fuel-injected engine, the price was just $100,000, fully radio and instrument equipped to the highest standard. The exchange rate was $2.50 to £1, thus the price equated to £40,000. It wasn't hard to spend that amount on a car and the temptation was too much for me.

A few months later I took my daughter, Genevieve, with me to collect the plane which was everything I'd thought it would be. Cessna liked to call it the 'Sports Utility Vehicle of the Air', and they were just about right. It was a versatile load carrier, a great short field performer, and as comfortable as needed – everything a private pilot could wish for.

I had to update my instrument rating with an annual Air Ministry test flight with one of their top brass – a test which had to be taken seriously. When it was my turn, I was met by a fully uniformed 'tester' with an impressive display of gold braid on his sleeves.

'OK, Mr Dexter,' he said in a deceptively quiet voice. 'I want you to take off to the north, heading 320, climbing to four thousand feet, maintaining an airspeed of ninety and a rate of climb of six hundred feet per minute.'

I set off confidently – I had, after all, hundreds, if not thousands of hours of twin-engined flying experience behind me. I knew that this first manoeuvre would take about seven minutes and, once I was settled in the climb, I dared to start a conversation.

'Do you get much flying yourself, sir?' I asked.

'Yes, I do,' he answered economically.

'And what do you fly?'

'Concorde,' the much gold-braided tester replied, after which the conversation was restricted to his brief instructions.

I was relieved – indeed, chuffed as hell – afterwards when I was told by one of the school instructors what the Concorde pilot's assessment had been, if I may be allowed a quick toot on my own trumpet.

'That Dexter chap of yours is no slouch. He's just done the best Test I have ever taken.'

**

The only problem with the Cessna 206 was that it was quite thirsty and generally expensive to run. I looked around for someone to split the running costs with me and fortunately found a flying club member to take a half share which worked well for both of us. Most of the time, private planes sit around doing nothing, so doubling the usage makes sense, as long sharers don't want to go separate ways on the same day. That was never a problem, and we got a lot of fun from it until we sold it in 1984. Before I was fifty.

In the years that followed, I was working full-time – or as close to full-time as I ever got – on my sport's PR business, Ted Dexter & Associates, and later, in my functions at the MCC . There was little time for recreation, and I was beginning to suffer increasing back problems. By 1995, when I turned sixty, I had relinquished my role as chairman of the England Committee, I had more time on my hands and was looking for some exciting new activity, provided I could do it sitting down. An innovation in helicopters came to my aid.

The recent development of a compact, lightweight petrol-engined machine, the Robinson 22, had effectively slashed the cost of instruction to a sensible level. I made an appointment at the Helicopter School at Denham where I was met by one of the most attractive women I'd ever laid eyes on, cleverly enhanced by a figure-hugging, white cashmere pullover. This is a sales ploy that tends to work with me and I was swiftly won over; two months later

I had a helicopter pilot's licence. It was going to suit me very well. I wouldn't have to *buy* a Robinson because renting was easy and a lot less extravagant than most people realised. Over the next few years I rented one several times, which yielded a couple of memorable experiences.

I always loved going to the Cheltenham Festival every year and in the early days of my flying, it was possible to land a light plane in the middle of the course. The Falco was ideal for that and I arrived there in it several times. When the Cheltenham authorities put a stop to private planes landing on the course, I began a ceaseless search for ways of getting there without sitting around in a car for hours, queueing to get in and, worse usually, getting out.

I tried travelling there by train, by flying in to Staverton and taking a short helicopter hop to the course, by parking a couple of miles away and cycling the last bit on folding bikes, and by motorcycle, which was by far the best. When I arrived on a bike, I simply ignored the parking wardens and carried on straight to the stewards' parking area.

On one occasion when I had an invitation to a box I shot down from Ealing to Prestbury on my latest Honda hotpot simply snaking my way between the queues of traffic crawling towards the racecourse from miles around. I left before the last race and was soon sitting at home with a Scotch in my hand. My host rang to see if I'd got back.

That was self-evident. 'Where are you?' I asked.

'Still at the course, stuck in traffic,' my host growled.

But I had always envied the helicopter passengers sauntering in and out without a care. At the first festival meeting after I'd acquired my licence, I jumped into my rented Robinson, with Susan in the passenger seat, and dropped straight into the middle of the racecourse as I had always dreamed of doing. We had a great day's racing and when it was time to go, relished the pleasure of a short brisk walk through the chilly evening air to the chopper park to clamber into our handy conveyance. We strapped ourselves in, closed the doors and I turned the engine switch. Nothing happened. The battery was as flat as the Bonneville Salt Pan.

We climbed out into the freezing cold and went to shelter in the helicopter control hut, feeling frankly pretty miserable. We both would have preferred to be sitting in a warm car in a traffic jam. We were promised a couple of seats on one of the big twin jet machines but watched them take off one by one without us. We realised we would have to make our own arrangements and set off to walk from the racecourse.

We walked and walked until at last the first pub appeared. We ignored an

Above: Two Captains after Drawn Series, 1963.

Below: A crucial catch at Lords, Gillette Cup Final v Warwickshire, 1964. T. W. Cartwright (Warwick) is caught by Sussex Captain E. R. Dexter off the bowling of J. A. Snow for 7.

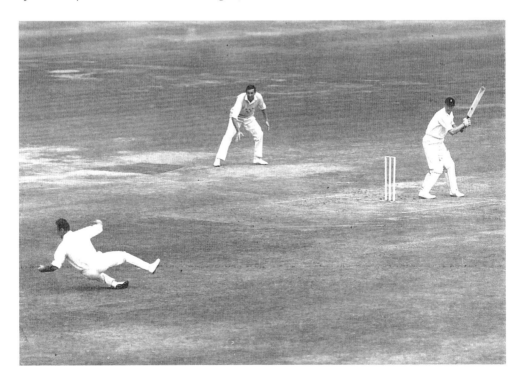

Above: First born, Thomas.

Below: Second born, Genevieve.

Left: Ted's favourite back foot drive.

Below: Ted.

Bottom: Ted's return to the England Team at the Oval, 1968.

The whole family in 1967.

Top left: Keeping fit after retiring from cricket

Top right: Aeroplane GASNA with Ted, Susan, Genevieve and Thomas in Milan, 1970, en route to Australia.

Above: Ted, Gary Sobers and Wes Hall

Left and below: Cricket coaching academy at a township in South Africa with Ali Bacher, CEO SA Cricket in 1988.

Ascot 21631

Sunningdale Golf Club,
Sunningdale, Berks.

January, 1979.

Annual Revision of Category One Golfers

I am advised by the Surrey County Golf
Union that following the Annual revision
of Category One golfers you have been
allotted a Handicap of Scratch.

C.L.Elliott
Assistant Secretary

E.R. Dexter Esq:

Top left: Before injury,
Wentworth Foursomes
Semi-Final and *above right*:
After injury, Wentworth
Foursomes Final, 1965.

Above: Annual revision
of category one golfers,
Sunningdale Golf Club,
1979.

Right: Low score, aged 66,
2001.

OLD COURSE			SUNNINGDALE							S.S.S. 69							
Player A		E. DEXTER (age 66)					H'cap	5	Date June 2001								
Player B							H'cap		Event Len Hattons Day =								
Player C		N.B. 9 holes in 28					H'cap		June 2001								
Marker		− 3 strokes − 25"					H'cap										
No.	Marker's Score	Points	Yellow Tees	Par	Stroke Index	A	B	C	Points	No.	Marker's Score	Points	Yellow Tees	Par	Stroke Index	A	B	C	Points
1			467	5	8	6			1	10			442	4	7	3			3
2			446	4	4	4			3	11			288	4	15	4			2
3			278	4	12	4			2	12			404	4	7	3			4
4			147	3	16	3			2	13			153	3	17	2			3
5			375	4	2	4			3	14			475	5	5	4			4
6			385	4	10	6			−	15			213	3	11	2			3
7			379	4	6	5			1	16			408	4	3	4			3
8			157	3	18	2			3	17			396	4	13	5			1
9			251	4	14	4			2	18			399	4	9	4			2
OUT			2885	35		38			17	IN			3178	35		31			25

DISTANCES ON SPRINKLER HEADS
REPRESENT YARDS TO CENTRE OF GREEN

OUT	2885	35	38	17
TOTAL	6063	70	69	

05110 (9/99)

Marker's Signature ....

Player's Signature ...... E.R.Dexter.

HANDICAP	5	(42)
NET SCORE	64	

TED DEXTER

SUSSEX AND ENGLAND

"CRICKET IS AN ART FORM....
DEXTER PLAYING AGAINST THE CARIBBEAN
IN 1963, AND THE FAST BOWLERS HALL AND
GRIFFITHS - TWO OF THE FINEST YOU COULD WISH
FOR - AT THEIR BEST. AND THEY BOWLED
DEXTER OUTSIDE THE OFF STUMP - AND HE
SENT THEM SQUARE TO THE BOUNDARY
- NOT TOWARDS THIRD MAN - SQUARE -
THAT MEANT HE HAD TO HIT EARLY. AND THEY
BOWLED THE BALL UP TO HIM - AND HE
TURNED AND HIT THEM TO SQUARE LEG.
AND THEY THOUGHT THEY SHOULD BRING
IT UP TO HIM - AND HE LEANED FORWARD
WITH THE UTMOST GRACE
AND THE BALL WENT FLOATING
DOWN TO THE PAVILION
- I RECALL THESE THINGS."
C.L.R JAMES

Wallace

Tex Dexter illustration by C. L. R James.

Left: Ted, after a new hip, with Susan in Nice in 2008.

Below left and right: Genevieve and Thomas.

Bottom left: The grandchildren, Edward and Elizabeth.

Bottom right: Ted.

unwelcoming sign on the door which proclaimed: 'NO RACEGOERS', went in ordered some much-needed drinks and unfroze while we waited for a taxi we'd ordered to pick us up and take us back to London.

After a few days I called the flying school to find out if they had recovered their helicopter. If they hadn't, I proposed that I would go with an engineer to fit a new battery and fly the machine back myself. This was agreed and I set off in another Robinson 22 with a mechanic next morning. The weather was vile as we dropped down over Prestbury Hill and immediately spotted the little helicopter – the only one there – looking forlorn on the edge of the huge empty racecourse. We landed beside it and the engineer jumped out. As soon as he'd opened the housing he realised he'd brought the wrong battery. The terminals were the wrong way round and the power leads wouldn't reach it. We were gazing at it mutely and pretty pissed off when out of the low grey clouds another R22 dropped down to join us – three of us in a row. From it stepped Mr Smith, who owned the flying school.

He looked at the helicopter, and then at me. 'Right,' he said, 'I can give you a jump start. The trouble is, if you have to put down anywhere, you won't be able to take off again. Are you OK with that?'

I shrugged. I'd taken worse risks than that. I climbed aboard and turned on the rotor. I was purposefully running my preflight checks when the door opened and Mr Smith poked his head in.

'To hell with that,' he said, 'just get going and follow me.'

It was a lot of excitement for a beginner as we headed for home through the murk, three in a line.

* *

Our trip down to the Isle of Wight in a Robinson 22 was a lot more enjoyable. It had come about because Susan had asked me what I would like to do for Father's Day. A rental chopper wasn't available until 5pm and had to be back by 8 the next morning, which suited us well.

By 6 in the evening we were moving slowly past the Needles before landing at a splendid country house hotel for a superb dinner.

'Breakfast in your room at 6.30, sir? No problem.'

Our rotor was spinning at 7am, we were back at Denham on the dot of 8, and I'd loved my treat.

* *

Throughout my flying I'd had fun, and only ever got into difficulties as a result of factors beyond my control. I'm not by nature a cautious man, but nor am I completely foolhardy. There is a lesson to be learned from a cautionary tale about the experiences of the great Graham Hill, Formula One driver and world champion, in 1962 and 1968, who enjoyed his flying. An old saying circulates among flying folk: 'There are old pilots and there are bold pilots; but very rarely are there old, bold pilots.' Graham, sadly, was a bold pilot.

My first encounter with his flying style occurred when he gave me a lift back home from Belfast where we had both been taking part in a major charity event. He was flying a Piper Aztec twin, the same model that I was to fly to Australia a few years later. At the time, I was already fully instrument rated and was well up to date on best practice. I was immediately uncomfortable with Graham's tendency to cut corners, disregard some no-go areas and fly wherever he felt like going. I made a mental note not to take airlifts with him again.

My next encounter with Graham as pilot was at Cheltenham Racecourse. I was flying in myself, but had radioed ahead to be told the landing area was waterlogged, and had diverted to Staverton. Graham had flown over, seen a plane on the ground and just landed anyway. What he didn't know was that the plane already there had flown in the previous day, before the rain had fallen. Although Graham's plane wasn't completely bogged down, his wheels were in several inches of mud.

When I saw him in the bar after racing, he asked my opinion on getting airborne again, because he had four passengers who wanted to get home. If he insisted on flying, I suggested, he should send his passengers over to Staverton, a few miles away, by taxi, drain off as much fuel as possible, then fly over to pick up fuel and his passengers. I was alarmed when I saw him still in the bar an hour later.

I had a first-hand account of what then happened from my old friend, Charlie Benson. All the passengers had piled into the Aztec and Graham simply took off from where he was without doing anything to reduce the weight the plane was carrying. Charlie told me that the stall warning hooter was sounding from the moment they got airborne and was still hooting as they barely cleared a copse of trees at the edge of the course. By all normal standards it was a crazy thing to do, but very luckily for Graham and his passengers, they got home that time.

Although I was very saddened, I was not surprised when I heard the news in 1975 that he had crashed his plane on his approach in poor visibility to his home airfield at Elstree, and everyone on board had been killed. In the end, in flying, if you don't respect the odds, that's the downside.

In January 1997, at the age of sixty-one, I made my last flight in the Robinson 22; it was, sadly, the last time I piloted a flying machine of any kind. I had enjoyed almost every minute of my time in the air and, I believe, derived more than my fair share of excitement from it. I'm also aware that I've been a great deal luckier than some other amateur pilots, given the risks I've taken from time to time. On the other hand, I'd never forgotten that the risks were there.

Chapter Sixteen

COMMERCIAL ENTERPRISE: DEXTER & GORDON

The Turf

In early 1970 I had joined the Cavaliers for another congenial tour of Jamaica. Like our last visit in 1964, it involved a couple of tour matches and a first-class game against the Jamaican national team. Sadly, Sir Frank Worrell wasn't there to entertain us as he had previously; he had finally succumbed to the leukaemia from which he'd been suffering and had died three years before, but we thought of him. As always on events like this, there were a number of camp followers – sponsors, agents, media (just called 'press' then) and anyone else who had an excuse for a jolly. Reg Hayter, proprietor of Hayters sporting press agency, who had first introduced me to Bagenal Harvey, was on the island to pursue *his* favourite sport – chasing ladies.

As usual we were farmed out to stay with anyone who would have us and Susan and I were lucky enough to be billeted with a warm and hospitable young married couple, Gavin and Juliet Gordon, along with their quite noisy baby. Getting him to sleep was a nightly performance. One evening I was trusted as babysitter and successfully shushed the child by speaking loudly to him in grown-up language: 'IT'S TIME FOR YOU TO GO TO SLEEP, YOUNG MAN.' Pleased with myself, I left the room on tiptoes and pulled the door to. It scraped the floor with a frightful screech. And I had to start all over again.

Gavin was coming to the end of a three-year assignment as local representative for Rothmans – sponsors of the Cavaliers Tour – and was planning his return to the UK. He was a bright personable young Scotsman with whom I got on well from the start. I found myself chatting to him often over the course of the tour and it became clear to me that his head was buzzing with ideas – a complaint with which I was familiar – and he also had some experience of putting deals together. My relationship with Bagenal Harvey never having been, as it were, consummated, I was open to suggestions.

229

One evening, after a few rum punches, he started to tell me about his newest project. 'In the West now, especially in the UK,' he spieled, 'people have gone mad over health and fitness. Everyone is looking for a way of getting a bit of hard exercise every day without taking them away from the office for too long.'

'Are they?' I asked, puzzled. I was always looking for exercise that would take me out of the office for as long as possible, which was why I loved playing golf. But I listened on.

The answer to this perceived new demand, Gavin explained, was squash – a game that could consume a great deal of energy in a short space of time and seemed to deliver enough of an adrenalin hit to satisfy most busy whizz-kids. And what he had, or was hoping to obtain, was a franchise for marketing the leading, possibly only, flat-pack, prefabricated squash courts in the world.

He told me, looking me firmly in the eye, that he was looking for a business partner with good contacts in the world of sport generally, who would also lend an instant high profile to the company he was planning to form. He suggested that I would be an ideal candidate. I was sold.

Back in London, once we had formed a company, Dexter & Gordon Ltd, Gavin introduced me to Alistair Standring. Standring was an entrepreneurial cattle farmer who had developed a range of prefabricated calf houses which he'd been marketing successfully, and had now segued into easy-to-assemble squash courts. We took on the marketing franchise, with some early success in delivering four-court units (with showers, clubroom and bar), to small flexible units that could be used in deconsecrated churches and supermarket car parks. They were bought and constructed all over the UK, and were exported to Germany, Switzerland and the Middle East.

This kind of activity was bound to attract attention from other quarters, and we were approached by a Japanese firm making sports goods for Dunlop and Slazenger. They wanted to establish their own brand, Starmaster Ltd, in the UK, ideally through a company owned in partnership with an existing suitable British company. We could see that we were at the start of a period of growth in sports brands, and there was in the early seventies a shortage of international brands to feed the market.

Dexter & Gordon agreed to become the UK partner in Starmaster with a good product range but mostly tennis and squash rackets. We made a great start, selling into Lillywhites, Harrods and Selfridges.

On the way back from a cricketing assignment in New Zealand I detoured via Tokyo to meet the Starmaster principals where I was lavishly entertained –

but not without some hesitation on their part. I had insisted that we had our business meeting first, to which they agreed, but obviously reluctantly. The following day, I picked up a small publication outlining the dos and don'ts of doing business in Japan. I had done a 'don't' and broken rule number one: fun first; work second.

Generously they took me off to a huge nightclub with drinks priced according to which of three levels was chosen. We were in the posh bit, drinking beer and each of us enjoying the attentions of a geisha girl – although not in formal traditional attire. I noticed that the young women were assigned to the clients by a tough-looking senior lady perched up high up from where she could survey the whole room. If she saw that there was no obvious rapport, with a subtle signal she would swiftly withdraw the girl, to have her immediately replaced by another. There was no sexual innuendo of any kind but the girls were wonderfully trained to entertain and flatter. I entirely forgot my jet lag and spent the happiest hour or two of my trip.

When I got back to the UK, I was mightily relieved to find that our relationship with our partners had not been damaged in any way by my faux pas. Nevertheless, the Japanese were anxious to expand more quickly and sent an English director, Dick Causton, to join us in 1974, with a brief to speed up the process. Causton was one of those curiosities that pop up in the course of a business life, conforming to no previously known pattern. He was in his mid-fifties when he arrived in London from Japan. He spoke little about his past or, indeed, about anything much. Married to an almost invisible Japanese lady, he seemed surprisingly quiet for a man charged with the aggressive expansion of his bosses' UK market share. He just hung about the office, not really doing anything we could see and was frankly a bit of a nuisance. To our relief, after a few months, he simply melted away, never to be seen again by us in any commercial context.

We did learn more about him, a long time afterwards, and his route to Japan which was distinctly bizarre. Born in London, he went to Dulwich College, and from there to Sandhurst, just as war broke out. In 1944 he was posted as Brigade Major to the Allied Forces in Northeast India, where he had direct experience of the attacking Japanese Army. He remained in the army until 1958, when he went to work as a vice-general manager at Harrods in London. After several years, he left Harrods and was appointed sales agent for Dunhill in the Far East, where he was based in Tokyo. Strangely, given his wartime experiences, he became enamoured of many things Japanese, including Mitsuko, the woman he married. He also developed a strong rapport with Nichiren Buddhism and the Soka Gakkai and became a practising Buddhist. We knew little of this in the short time he was working with us. In 1975, he founded Soka Gakkai International UK and became its first chairman, but it was some years later that I learned he had become the respected leader of this Buddhist sect, with a magnificent central temple, based in a Victorian mansion near Maidenhead. His perks for this eminent role included living in some style with his Japanese wife in a grand house on Richmond Common. In 1995 he published a book on practising Buddhism. Some people find a way; others do not.

By the mid-seventies we were trading well, but being hampered by the external effects of a devaluation in the value of sterling. To stay competitive in the British market and take advantage of the lower pound, we had to look for some genuine British manufactured sports goods with export potential.

Through the time-honoured medium of a classified ad in a national newspaper we attracted the attention of a small fibreglass manufacturer which was producing 'Malibu' surfboards. They looked pretty good to us, although I knew very little about surfing, and nothing about the market. We arranged a speculative trip to a massive sports goods trade exhibition in Cologne in order to gauge the market.

Gavin strapped a surfboard to the roof of his car and drove across Europe to check out the exhibitors for surfboard suppliers, dealers or manufacturers. There wasn't a surfboard to be seen, but Gavin did find a number of exhibitors showing windsurfers – a newish thing – with boards made from a polyethylene material. He persuaded one of the firms he'd met to look at our fibreglass board. Sigmund Petramer, of Petramer and Adamek GMBH, Munich, liked the look of it and the quality. He wanted to see what prices could be achieved if he bought from us, given lower British labour costs and the weakness of the pound against the D-mark.

Gavin quickly returned to Germany, to Hamburg, to pick up a mould for a windsurfer board and bring it back to price it. It was soon clear that to do business with these people we were going to need far greater production capacity, with fibreglass and foam injection capabilities. We had to find other sources of production, bigger than the small firm which had originally approached us. We soon found ourselves talking to JSP of West Bromwich, which had ceased manufacturing Jensen cars in only 1976, as well as a smaller outfit in Kent. We made progress, to the point where the board produced by Jensen won an award from a major German windsurf magazine and several hundred boards were being collected from West Bromwich on a Friday afternoon and delivered to Munich on the following Monday. We had, we realised, a hit on our hands.

Up until that point, I had never been a sailor or a surfer, but watching footage of skilled windsurfers, I could see that there was a thrill to be had, if one could master the thing. A good opportunity to try it arose when I received an invitation from my old friend, John Churchill, to stay in Andratx, Majorca, with the added instruction, 'Bring one of those boards, won't you?'

These early boards were long and heavy and, I checked, a few inches too long to be taken as luggage. But John was insistent that I bring it; I had to take a chance. At the check-in I was asked, 'How long is that board?'

I was economical with the truth, and the board went into the hold. Neither John nor I had attempted to windsurf before, and none of the other people hanging around the beach had ever seen a sailboard, let alone stood on one, so there was no useful advice to be had there. After a lot of tottering about and falling in the sea, John gave up.

Naturally, I persevered until, running before a strong breeze, I scudded off to the harbour mouth. Unfortunately, I hadn't got the hang of tacking back into the wind, and had to swim back, towing the board behind me. Another time, on a flat Scottish loch and clad in a fully insulating wetsuit, I had another go and did manage to master the art (though never in a gale), and found the sailboard a demanding, sometimes painful conveyance, delivering sporadic moments of great exhilaration.

The next windsurf problem we had was that demand from the importer quickly outgrew our production capacity, just as technical problems emerged in the manufacturing operation. But overriding these difficulties, Pertramer and Adamek had come up against major patent problems from the American company that held the patent of the crucial windsurf steering mechanism and a specially designed boom. This meant that the importer could no longer sell the British boards in Germany and had to move his centre of operations to Salzburg in Austria. This triggered some unforeseen disastrous financial consequences for him and, thus, Dexter & Gordon, which resulted in some huge legal fees.

By that time Peter Mills, whom Gavin had also met in Jamaica, joined Dexter & Gordon on a speculative basis as a consultant. A former quantity surveyor, he had the right type of head to provide practical and moral support in resolving the tangle of problems around the windsurf board patent and European distribution. As a direct result of what he'd achieved, we offered him a partnership in the company. He swiftly justified this by introducing another activity to our portfolio – instant printing on sports and leisure garments.

We were able to do this using a machine capable of printing images on small quantities of clothing through a newly devised heat process that didn't need the long print runs required for conventional silk-screen printing. This service attracted significant new business from big companies who went on to become major customers, placing much larger orders, which D&G were able to subcontract. Mars, H J Heinz and National Panasonic were among clients who came on stream and soon Dexter & Gordon was turning over sales of c.£100,000 per month, putting it in a position to clear the residual debts from the windsurfer crisis. This increased business allowed us to buy a small warehouse and a refurbished factory unit on the Slough Trading Estate.

We also identified and moved into the field of branding conventional sports goods with companies' logos and the names of their products – lager, soft drinks, chocolate and electrical goods – being printed on items from footballs and tracksuits to fleeces and even boomerangs. Gavin went out and drummed up business from our many contacts among the sports clothing manufacturers – good cash flow business too, because, for all bespoke printing, we could reasonably demand upfront payment, and no credit.

Almost by chance we forged a successful venture with the German company, Kettler GMBH, who, as any parent who has bought a family ping-pong table will know, manufacture a range of versatile table tennis tables, designed for home delivery and home assembly. The tables were warehoused somewhere in the Midlands and dispatched direct to the customer on instructions from Dexter & Gordon with orders supported by a credit card over the phone. We never had to touch the tables, and the source of all our orders was a simple ad in that great organ of trade, Exchange and Mart. The low marketing overheads meant that we could offer the product at a truly competitive price, making us one of Kettler's most successful distributors. A lovely simple, sound operation which made a steady profit for us over a long time.

Although my presence was by no means vital to the activities of Dexter & Gordon Ltd, I enjoyed being involved in it, and should, in theory, have learned a lot about the commercial pitfalls that lurk around every corner for small and medium-sized trading companies. It operated for nearly thirty years with Gavin at the helm and would have gone under a few times were it not for Gavin's Scottish bulldog tenacity. I was more loosely involved and had to put my hand in my pocket from time to time. A modest cheque came the other way early in the company's existence, in 1970, which I think was swiftly passed to the funds of the needy St Matthew's Church in Ealing.

Nevertheless, when the time came, we were able to pass on the company after thirty years of trading, despite a few roller-coaster moments, sound and in good shape.

Dad and Horses

After living in Italy for four decades my father and mother loved their retirement years in Chichester, where my father's favourite pastime was riding his horse up on the Sussex Downs. Alas, the joy this gave him came to an end sadly, after a visit to our house in Ealing, as a direct result of his being an overzealous grandfather. Using his walking stick as a prop, he was entertaining Tom and Gen with his impression of doddery old TV character, Mr Pastry. In the middle of his 'act', he collapsed abruptly to the floor, and I had to haul him up into a chair. He didn't lose consciousness, but was obviously in a bad way, although he managed to ask me for a large brandy. That kept him going until an ambulance arrived to pick him up.

Dad had suffered a small stroke, but after a short spell in hospital he returned to Chichester with no obvious damage done. However, there were more, similar episodes over the next few years, each one an increment of a slow process which ended with his being laid up and needing twenty-four-hour nursing. There were, though, several good years in between, of which I was determined he should make the most.

My instincts were that it would be a good thing if he and I had a few shared interests, with a view to keeping a healthy dialogue going. I suggested that we might share a racehorse between us, with the aim of winning a hurdle race or two. Dad had often said he would love to own a really good hurdler and, although that description flattered our four-year-old, Ocean Diamond, the gelding did win a couple of races for us.

The first was a modest Novice Hurdle on the Cheltenham course, but following that, a persistently weak leg meant that he spent more time recuperating than being trained. He did run again intermittently but always in company that was too good and, as I was anxious for Dad to have the pleasure of another win while he could still enjoy it, I had a word with our trainer, Peter Chisman.

'What exactly are we trying to do with this horse?' I asked. 'Win the Gold Cup – or what?'

The trainer – in the way racehorse trainers do – gave a non-committal answer.

'Alright,' I asked. 'What is the worst race for which our horse is eligible?'

This turned out to be a selling race at Stratford-upon-Avon some months ahead in the spring. It was agreed that Peter Chisman would get the horse fit while Mum and I would do our best to keep Dad healthy through the cold West Sussex winter.

When the long-awaited day arrived, we drove up to Stratford where I had made special arrangement for a viewing place for Dad in his wheelchair. The horse had arrived and looked happy enough, and the champion jockey, Josh Gifford, was booked to ride him. Ten minutes before the 'off', I had to leave Dad for a few minutes to have a nervous pee; when I got back, the wheelchair was empty. I couldn't think what had happened and searched around anxiously for him. After only a few moments I was rewarded by the sight of a limping figure moving as fast as he could towards the bookies' pitches. He wanted to put a little more money on our 9/4 favourite, he told me.

In a very moderate field, Ocean Diamond stood out and came in first — just. He was clear with two jumps to go when he must have pulled a tendon. Suddenly he was seriously lame, but he managed to struggle home on three legs. As the winner of a selling race, he had to be offered for sale by auction straight after it. He duly hobbled around the ring but, not surprisingly, there were no bidders and the trainer had to take him home. In the meantime, Dad and I stuffed our pockets and made our way to the bar. Dad was more excited than I'd seen him for years, inviting people to dinner, and celebrating so hard that by the time the evening party began, we still hadn't checked in at our hotel; it was midnight before we discovered there was no lift to the bedroom landing. By this stage, Dad was legless, and I had to shove him up the stairs, step by step, with my shoulder under his behind.

I managed to heave him onto the bed, with his outer clothing removed, but still in his vest and pants. Mum and I decided that putting him into pyjamas was too much trouble in the circumstances. We pulled up the bedclothes and kissed the happy slumbering racegoer goodnight. Mum went back to her adjoining room. In the early morning she had a surprise when her husband walked into her room wearing his pyjamas but, bizarrely, with his vest and pants on top. This was a puzzle which was never resolved, but it was not the last time Dad showed amazing powers of recovery after an evening's carousing and a good night's rest.

After that, the gelding's tendon trouble kept recurring, and he never raced again. That was a pity, but I didn't mind; just seeing Dad's jubilation at Stratford-upon-Avon was well worth all the expense and the hassle.

This brief horse-owning episode had whetted my appetite for more, and I managed to talk some friends into two more racing ventures. To start with, we leased a novice hurdler in Nicky Henderson's yard which ran a few times but never won, so we moved up a gear and bought a mature miler on the flat, which we sent to another trainer. We all turned up at Windsor to watch its first race.

We'd been told it would be a trial run, so we kept our money in our pockets, only to see the animal go straight to the front and win. The trainer seemed as surprised as we were until he dropped his guard for a moment. 'Mind you,' he let slip, 'there isn't any of mine that can keep up with him on the gallops.'

* *

Back in Chichester one night, not long after our day at the races, Dad fell half out of bed. My mother simply wasn't strong enough to get him back in and rang me in Ealing. I got dressed, clambered into my leathers and went downstairs to wheel my new Norton Commander out of the garage and ride out into the deserted roads of the middle night. In a little over an hour I was at my parents' house.

I went straight up to help Dad into a comfortable resting position, and he thanked me for coming. Their loyal nurse, Henry, came in early next morning and had just propped his patient up with a cup of tea, when I walked in.

Dad's eyes popped. 'Teddy! What on earth are you doing here?'

* *

Dad's most amazing recovery took place near the end of his life when he was in hospital in London with a lung infection so serious that I was told not to expect him to survive for more than a matter of hours. There seemed to be nothing to do except wait for the end with all the family resigned – except my sister, Ann Woodward, who with great faith in her own GP, Dr Blakey, rang him and described Dad's symptoms. The doctor with a breadth of experience suspected a tropical infection, linked to Dad's wartime spell in Egypt. The hospital gave him permission to intervene, and a specific obscure drug was injected.

The effect was almost instantaneous. Within a matter of minutes, the fluid threatening to swamp his lungs had begun to recede; within forty-eight hours he was giving us a cheerful wave as he was wheeled out to the ambulance that was going to take him home. He was a tough man, brought up at a time when pain and a lot of other discomforts were an accepted part of life, like putting up with the cold and damp of the First World War trenches. Only when my mother, his beloved Elise, died suddenly and unexpectedly of pancreatic cancer did he become less concerned about his own need for survival.

I was very happy when Dad decided to leave his Chichester home for what turned out to be the last few months of his life and moved into our place at Warwick Dene. This meant some adjustments, with the dining room being converted to a bedroom and a bath hurriedly being installed in the downstairs loo. He needed full-time nursing, but he seemed quite content.

Susan remembers fondly that Dad sometimes insisted on her keeping him company and while he talked about his life in a warm and unusually open way. There was another happy moment when I luckily located a specifically modified Hooper-bodied Rolls-Royce, with an electrically driven swivelling rear armchair built for use by an invalid. Buying it was a squeeze; it cost us Dad's Mercedes, plus my S-type Bentley Continental, plus some cash, but it was worth it. That was especially true when Dad felt well enough to be driven up to CARE, Shangton, where his much-loved third son, David, had been in the protected village for some years. As a result of a number of bouts of illness, Dad had never been able to visit before now and it was a joy to me when he pronounced that now he could die happy, having seen for himself how contented and well cared for David was.

Not long after this, I was beginning to look around for a bigger house more suited to our new circumstances. When I mentioned it to Dad, he was firmly against the idea, on the grounds that he wasn't going to be around for long. And so it turned out.

Susan and I had been anchored at home for several weeks when Dad encouraged us to get away for a decent weekend on the small cruiser we had moored on the Solent. While we were away we were contacted by Dad's doctor who told us that he'd taken a sudden turn for the worse and that it might be wise to resist any ideas of resuscitation. He was in favour of allowing nature to take its course, and we agreed.

Dad, the great survivor, was eighty-three when he passed away and can have had fewer regrets than most looking back over his honest and honourable life. His funeral was held in St Matthew's Church in Ealing before he was taken to be buried beside his wife, Elise, in the peaceful churchyard of St Mary the Virgin in Barnham, West Sussex, where my sister, Peggy, was also buried when her time came.

Greyhounds and Trotters

The kind of enjoyment Dad and I had with Ocean Diamond wasn't restricted to the owning of horses. I also had long relationships with dogs, both as pets and as sporting propositions.

When I was fifteen years old, spending a school holiday in England, I visited my Aunt Doreen and Uncle John Kington, with whom I'd stayed for a few months after Norfolk House prep school had gone bust. I'd always liked Uncle John, and I was excited when he asked me if I'd like to go the greyhound races with him at a track near Southampton. I was fond of dogs, and already a little obsessed with speed; greyhounds were a good combination of the two.

I was fascinated by them from the start – so fast, so powerful, elegant and aerodynamic in their pace – and I already liked having a punt. I loved the races and won a few shillings, but I never imagined that this most striking of all the canine breeds would become an important part of my life for the next seventy years. I have had three as pets, including my present companion, Cleenas Mags, a five-year-old pied bitch, who, like others before her, has a lovely nature and deserves all the affection we lavish on her.

I have bred a few, which I can't recommend, as they tend to have large litters and the pups have to be kennelled, fed and watered for at least a year before the emergence, with luck, of a single potential racing animal. All greyhounds are fast but just the occasional one is faster than the others and, sadly, finding homes for the slower ones isn't easy. In my cricketing days my interest in greyhound racing was limited to a traditional Saturday night out after playing at Lord's, at the White City dog track. In Sussex, too, after play I would spend an occasional evening at the Hove stadium. We were always welcomed at the tracks, with a table reserved for dinner from which we could watch the races while we ate.

My first attempt at owning a greyhound was one of the more ridiculous things I have ever done. I'd seen a small ad in the *Sporting Life*: 'greyhound for sale, good racer, no injuries, reason for sale: illness of owner…', and the Dexter impulsiveness kicked in. I blithely made up my mind to do it, parted with two hundred quid, and duly took delivery of the long dog with no idea how to care for, train, or otherwise gain any amusement, value or satisfaction from my new friend.

The whole enterprise fell apart when I persuaded a trainer to take him on, and he sent the dog straight home on the grounds that he had no detectable interest in chasing a mechanical hare – the worst possible flaw in a racing dog.

It took a while to recover from such an asinine episode, but my next attempt was a little more level-headed. I contacted a local trainer and became the proud owner of Westmead Lace, a genuine racing greyhound, a bitch with good parentage, fit and ready to run, albeit in the lower grades.

Our first race was at Wembley Stadium, as White City had closed a couple of years before. One of the Wembley trainers had the unusual surname Dartnall, which was my mum's maiden name. I also noticed that when his kennel put their money down, they had a very high percentage of winners. I went looking for Mr Dartnall, introduced myself and quickly found that our two Dartnall families were a long way apart. This could have been the end of our connection, but my continuing ambition to own a good dog kept it alive.

By this time, our honest toiler, Westmead Lace, was living with us at Warwick Dene. The lovely Caramella had passed away and we needed a replacement. Our beautiful greyhound became well known in the area and was once booked as the celebrity to open the annual church fair; the turnout was larger than usual that year.

In my brief first encounter with Terry Dartnall, I'd suggested to him that if he ever had a potential 'Open' racer in need of an owner, to give me first refusal. The months went by and I assumed he had forgotten all about it. A less honest man would have been on the phone within days with some ostensibly attractive proposition, but we had no such come-on from Terry. When he did get in touch it was with a genuine and exciting proposition.

There was a novice bitch for sale in Ireland, unbeaten in outstanding times and impeccably bred. Her price was five thousand pounds, a lot for a greyhound, though not compared with the price of a racehorse. We flew in the Cessna to Cork where we saw her just beaten after a bit of interference, but I was already sold. I had never seen such a perfect looking athlete. Minnesota Marsha became mine and I never regretted it. She was the fastest bitch in England in her time, without doubt, and notched up some famous victories. However, she did have one glitch: she could be picky about which hares she would chase and which she would not. Up in Glasgow, she won the William King Cup with a thousand pounds to the winner. She was never beaten in four visits to Open Races at Ipswich because she loved their hare.

If this distinction sounds implausible, the truth is that hardly two hares are the same in greyhound racing. Some run on the inside rail, some on the outside. Some are set in a track at ground level, others on a raised rail about a foot above. They can be all sorts of different colours and sizes. What intrigued her so much at Ipswich was that some of the lights around the track were missing which meant that the outside McGee hare at ground level was in and out of the light. She loved it and never let us down. We were intending to breed from her but one sad day on her afternoon walk, she simply lay down and died. Terry called me and I was down at his yard in Stanwell Moor near Staines within the hour. We dug her grave and said goodbye to her with tears running down our cheeks.

Not long after Marsha's demise, another Irish dog was brought to our attention. He was not as expensive as Marsha, and his name was Cordal Jet. I bought him in partnership with another of Terry's owners. He turned out to be the ideal racing machine and, although not quite Derby class, utterly reliable at level 2. He more than earned his keep when we found a major Open race in Glasgow. It comprised three heats on a Thursday, with only the first two in each heat going on into the final on Saturday. The winner would receive five thousand pounds in cash on the track.

Second in his heat, he came in first in the final. The other half-owner of the dog and I agreed how to spend our five grand. Four thousand would buy another couple of dogs, leaving a thousand to pay for a grand party at Wembley. The bill for dinner was over £900; we told the staff to keep the change. We ended the evening on a high point, when we had a nice-priced winner, and all our guests had backed it.

The only time Cordal Jet was beaten at Milton Keynes he stretched a tendon, which meant he would never race again. He came home to Warwick Dene and became a pet called Sam. As a pet, though, he was a challenge and my first job was to retrain him.

To start with, I put a muzzle on him and took him to Gunnersbury Park at 6am. With not a soul around, I let him loose and within seconds, he'd disappeared from sight. I followed where I'd last seen him and rounding a corner, my heart froze. A lady in fine furs was standing rigidly in one spot while Sam raced flat out around her, coursing a poodle in ever decreasing circles until it leapt up into the safe haven of the woman's arms.

I hurried up to her as obsequiously as I could and started to make apologies. Completely in control of herself, and apparently untroubled by Sam's performance, she cut me short. 'This is not my little dog. It is my husband's little dog. I hate little dogs. I love hounds.'

Sam and I were reprieved. However, he continued to chase anything that ran away from him, and I despaired of ever being able to take his muzzle off. One day, though, a small, white three-legged bitch appeared, and Sam fell in love. They were inseparable every morning in the park, Sam stopped his chasing habit and the problem was solved.

His instincts were not entirely abandoned, though, and surfaced in the form of an unhealthy interest in a fox stole which my secretary sometimes wore to work. Another time, an evening we'd left our bedroom door open while we were out to dinner, we came back to find Susan's genuine chinchilla jacket torn to shreds and scattered all over the floor.

We forgave him and slowly he became my constant companion. He came everywhere with me in the car, usually resting his head on my shoulder. When I was playing golf at Sunningdale, he was generally well behaved, but on the tenth tee was always waiting tensely to be released for a 450-yard sprint to the refreshment hut, where there would be a sausage waiting for him.

He added a lot of happiness to my life and was irreplaceable when he died, to the extent that we acquired a pair of Abyssinian cats instead.

Much later, by the time we moved to France in 2003, we had no outdoor space and thus no pets; it was only when we returned to England in 2017 when we once again had a garden that we bought a superb standard poodle bitch called Betty from a local breeder. Sadly she developed cancer early in her life and died.

Our thoughts then turned inevitably to having another greyhound and I phoned my old friend and trainer, Terry Dartnall.

'I've got just the girl for you,' he said, 'just spayed and looking for a home. Come and get her at the weekend.'

We did just that in the summer of 2019, and Mags is now our much-loved companion who takes me out for a good walk every day.

** **

Like dogs, horses in various roles had also been part of my early life. From the time when John and I had saddled up the pony to take to the gymkhanas in Buckinghamshire during the war, to the excitement of going to the trotting races in Milan with my dad, and the thrill of owning our first hurdler, again with my dad, I had always been captivated by horses – their speed and beauty – as well as punting on their performance.

One of my more obscure equine investments was in an Australian trotter. I'd first been to watch the trotters in Sydney's Harold Park Raceway during my inaugural Ashes tour with England in 1958/59. Since going to watch the trotters as a boy at the San Siro, I'd always found it a terrific spectator sport – in some ways more exciting than ridden races because the sulkies introduce another element. (I've always imagined that the great four-abreast chariot races around the Circus Maximus in first-century Rome must have been one of the most exciting things on earth to watch.)

In 1991, I was in Australia with the England team as chairman of the England Committee, and I began to plan the realisation of a long-held dream to have a runner in my name at Harold Park. I knew I would be back there in 1992 and

I wanted to make some preliminary preparations. I took a train from Sydney out to a country meeting, hoping to meet a trainer and get the ball rolling. At the dusty, treeless track, it was ferociously hot and nobody was showing their face outside. Poking around determinedly, I chanced on a young driver lurking in the shade at the back of the stables. A little doubtfully, he listened to me outlining my ambition, before he went off to fetch his boss.

By great good fortune, the boss – his father – was Mr B. P. Hancock, the most famous trainer/driver in Australia, although I didn't know it at the time. I reiterated the spiel about my dream of having a trotter run in my name at Harold Park; he didn't look impressed, but gave me a phone number and told me to keep in touch.

Back in England, I phoned him a couple of times; he said he would call me back but never did. By this time, I had his address and, in an attempt to move things on, I mailed him $1,000 to demonstrate my bona fides. That worked; the next time I was in Sydney in 1992, I was invited down to his HQ. He had a deal set up and ready to go. I was to share in a three-month lease of a novice three-year-old, Malone Man, with a Mr C. Smith. I drove back to Sydney feeling that at last my trotter-owning ambitions might be realised.

I'd also told him that I would like the experience of driving a trotter myself; an old stager was duly harnessed up and made ready. I knew enough to collect the reins, put my bottom backwards onto the seat of the sulky and swing my legs round. I settled myself into the sculpted seat and found myself staring at my horse's backside.

This animal was what was called a 'pacer', as opposed to a trotter. A pacer's action looks a little strange to those who haven't seen it before. They move with an abnormal gait which is a lateral trot, like a camel's, where fore and rear legs on each side move together, encouraged in this by being 'hobbled' with leather straps, as my horse was. This is the norm in Australian and American trotting races, although in France, where it is also a big sport, they use the normal diagonal trot.

A young lad led us to the training track and I asked him if he had any tips. 'Don't worry,' he said. 'He'll show you what to do.'

He let go of the reins, gave the horse a slap on its quarters and we were off.

I loved it; it was like driving an open sports car, with plenty of acceleration and wind in my hair. When the horse broke his trot into a canter, I dropped my hands as I had seen good drivers do on the track. He understood this and immediately dropped back into a trot. A good, long striding pacer can travel up to thirty-five miles per hour, almost as fast as a galloping thoroughbred in the

Derby, at around thirty-seven miles per hour.

We weren't doing that sort of speed, but it was still pretty quick and tremendously exhilarating. However, after a circuit a sudden rainstorm blew up and brought me abruptly down to earth. I was relieved to see the young lad out on the track and pulled up beside him, thoroughly satisfied with my session. He had other ideas, though. He was holding a plastic cape which he threw over my head.

'See you in half an hour,' he chortled.

I realised that the Aussies were having a nice little joke at my expense, but I wasn't going to give them the pleasure of seeing me plead for mercy. Soaked through, I did my half hour and thanked them with a smile, feeling that honour had been satisfied.

Two weeks later Malone Man ran at an out-of-town track and won by a distance, which qualified him to run at Harold Park. I invited a crowd of friends and acquaintances to join me for dinner at the track to witness my triumph and help me celebrate. I even gave a few of them a wad of dollars to back the horse for me just before the 'off'.

Five minutes later the dream was in tatters as Malone Man trailed in at the back of the field. However, that wasn't quite the end of the story.

All the guests had gone home and I had to dig deep to settle the dinner bill. There was one race left. Disinclined, as always, to throw in the towel, I had one last desperate bet on a couple of outsiders to finish first and second. And, astonishingly, they did – at enormous odds!

I walked out of Harold Park with enough cash to cover the cost of the whole evening, including my losing bets. I've sometimes been a very lucky man.

Two or three years later I was back in Australia, sitting in a flight departure lounge, watching some harness racing on TV. To my utter astonishment, one of the runners in the upcoming race was Malone Man – an extraordinary coincidence to see him as I'd barely looked at a trotting race since my Harold Park escapade. Remarkably, too, he was favourite, and even more extraordinary, he won. Sadly, there hadn't been time for me to get a bet on, or for that matter, an adjacent bookie with whom to do it.

Thinking about it afterwards, I reckoned that what shortened the odds against my seeing the horse again was that racing trotters are seldom injured and tend to have long, active racing lives. Nevertheless, it was a heart-warming coincidence.

Chapter Seventeen

A LIFETIME OF GOLF

Towards the end of the sixties, with excellent timing, my dad had decided to pass over a large slice of my ultimate inheritance. He was in his late seventies, his health was already variable, periodically stable, but increasingly troublesome. He decided now to make an early bequest to me under the rule by which gifts made more than seven years before the donor died were free of death duties. This useful piece of unencumbered capital allowed me to look at a broader range of activities and the possibility of buying my way into an existing business or indeed, buying one outright.

How I came to consider fish farming as an investment, I have no idea; perhaps I had enjoyed a good grilled trout in Sheeky's and made a connection when perusing the businesses for sale column in a Sunday paper. However, I do recall wheeling the mighty Honda Goldwing Aspencade from the garage and heading off down the M3 to look at a trout farm. After a fascinating tour around a series of fish ponds stuffed with lugubrious trout, I told the owners I would be in touch.

As I was about to leave, a sweetener in the form of a large box of trout was tied onto the bike's rear carrier. As I rode away, I had a vision of a mangled Goldwing, with my broken body lying nearby among a shoal of dead fish. I took it as an omen that fish farming was not to be my destiny.

I also flew to Ireland to visit a well-respected National Hunt stables with a view to taking up some kind of horse training apprenticeship and, perhaps, having access to some useful insider knowledge. The Guv'nor (or so I thought) met me off the plane with much bonhomie and blarniness, and invited me to join him for two or three pub stops for a few 'whisky and whites' on the way home. We were greeted with frosty circumspection by a fine-looking but stern-faced lady who quickly made it clear that she wore the trousers in that yard. At that time women weren't allowed to hold a trainer's licence so it was not an uncommon arrangement. This created an atmosphere into which I judged it wiser not to enter. I stayed only for a little more blarney before promising to think about the idea and leaving.

More than anything, my dad's timely legacy had given me time to think more clearly about my options. As I was picking my way through the many and eclectic ideas I had been entertaining of how to occupy my post-cricket life, a piece of down-to-earth advice imparted to me by the great Lancashire and England fast bowler, Brian Statham, came to mind. During one of the tours we'd been on together, he'd witnessed me placing a string of losing bets on horses and had observed laconically, 'Only play games you know, lad. Only play games you know.'

That started me thinking seriously about 'games' I knew in which I could profitably participate. Cricket was now in the past, but there was also golf, which was less age-restrictive. I began to wonder if perhaps I should turn pro. I was a highly rated amateur and maybe it wouldn't be too wild a notion that I could move over to the paid ranks.

In the slightly bizarre way in which these things proceed, my father's solicitor's brother ran the Professional Golfers' Association; seeking an audience with him was easy. Mr Bywaters ran the organisation single-handed from a small office at the Oval cricket ground. When I went to see him, he was affable but discouraging. I discovered that the regulations which maintained the gap between amateur and professional were prohibitively stringent in protecting the livelihoods of existing pros. Amateurs could either qualify or get an invitation to play in a professional event but they were subject to a five-year moratorium on making or taking prize money. Around that time Clive Clark, second only to the esteemed Michael Bonallack in the amateur ranks, took that challenge and somehow managed to survive the five-year wait before earning money. He was the only transitioning golfer I know of who achieved it. Mr Bywaters listened to me attentively, gave me a friendly pat on the shoulder and advised me to look elsewhere. I was more disappointed than I'd expected to be.

I've been playing golf since I was ten years old, and I'm still playing it now, seventy-five years later, albeit with the help of one of those buggies which I used to deride. The practical truth is that my arms, shoulders, eyes and hands (up to a point) still work, but the knees and hips are not so good; thus I can still hit a ball over two hundred yards off the tee and in roughly the right direction, but walking eighteen holes isn't an option.

If first-class cricket was in my DNA at birth, then so, undoubtedly, was golf. I have believed from time to time, if it weren't for the insuperable obstacles put in the way by the PGA, I could have had as good a sporting career in golf as I did in cricket, and it would have lasted a lot longer.

My dad, Ralph, was a golfer. So was his dad, Edward, with his name on a handsome silver trophy to prove it. By the time I first played with my father in 1946 at the Menaggio and Cadenabbia Golf Club, he was already in his mid-fifties and fairly rusty after five years of war without golf. He was a nice striker of the ball off the tee but as he approached the green he would be beset by what golfers call the 'yips' – a common nervous affliction in which a player is unable to make short putts because he can't achieve a fluid putting stroke. His speciality was a chip shot where the ball barely moved as the club face got stuck in the turf. He coined a term of obvious origin to describe the disastrous shot a 'gin-stab'. Thus I grew up believing that having to take four or more shots from the edge of the green was a simple fact of life.

While Dad was hard at work for five days a week in Milan, as boys, my brother John and I had plenty of opportunity to explore the great game, not only on our own terms, but by lucky chance, with the wise and experienced tuition of Signor Prete. This charming man and long-retired golf professional lived near the course and was more than happy to coach us. There was, though, one peculiarity in his game which I inadvertently adopted. Signor Prete had restricted vision in his left eye, thus when addressing the ball, he turned his head down sideways to give his right eye a better chance. As a ten-year-old, I naturally tried to reproduce his excellent golf swing in every way – including the peculiar tilt of the head. It didn't harm my game too much, but it stayed with me for a long time before I made a conscious effort to eradicate it.

Five years later as a fifteen-year-old I was in the first cricket XI at Radley College, by definition strong enough to play with the older boys and adults. This precocity was mirrored in my golf, where I could already keep up with most comers for length off the tee. Thus, at the time, Aldo Casera, a professional and occasional visitor to the mountain course at Menaggio, persuaded Dad to let him take me up to Crans-sur-Sierre for the Pro-Am, prior to the Swiss Open.

At the time I wasn't particularly impressed by the other players as ball strikers in a four-ball practice round, even though the opposition were two well-known Ryder Cup players, Eric Brown and Dai Rees. It took me a long time to understand that professionals are only as good as their short game, like Phil Mickelson, the arch-exponent of wedge play and putting.

Generally, my golf in Menaggio was confined to summer holidays while the course was in the process of being restored and partially reopened through the efforts of my father and his partners. It was five summers before the first green fee golfer arrived there, and perhaps another five before a few members joined the club. Gradually a number of Italians started to help the club grow and all the while, until he retired to England in 1963, my dad and a couple of friends were paying for it. In the early years only a few competitions were contested which provided me with the first thrills of winning, albeit at a lowly standard.

At school in England, a handful of the boys played golf in term time although it involved a tough eight-mile cycle ride with clubs on our backs to Frilford Heath Golf Club. John and I contested the school championship, when I chipped in blind from over the back of the eighteenth green to confirm his often-expressed view that I was a 'lucky little so and so'.

There was also one master, Noel Fisher, a good golfer himself, who encouraged us. Given the extent to which the school frowned on individual games as compared with more masculine and character-forming team games, Mr Fisher's support was important to us, and in my last year he managed to excuse me from a corps exercise and sneaked me out for a quick eighteen holes. Since my schoolboy days playing there, I did once return to Frilford Heath for a seniors event to find it altogether grander, with a fiendish rough and a much altered layout, and I've not been tempted back since.

At Cambridge, after putting in a dutiful appearance on the rugger field in my first autumn term, I took to the golf course in the Easter term and was selected as one of two reserves for the annual match against Oxford at Formby There was a quaint tradition attached to this event called the 'dinner match', which was played by the respective reserves to decide which side paid the bill for dinner after the main match. When I played the first nine holes in thirty-two strokes for a 7 and 6 win followed by a similar margin in the afternoon, our captain, David Marsh, rather wished he hadn't left me out of the actual team – especially when the main match went Oxford's way by just a single game. There was, though, a dividend for me in my election to secretary of the university club for the following year. David went on not only to captain the Walker Cup at St Andrews but also famously to hit a three-iron second to the heart of the infamous seventeenth 'Road' Hole to clinch the match for the UK. We have played a couple of times against each other but he claimed a complete mental block over events at the Oxford match in Formby.

It was a peculiarity of Cambridge University golf that all home matches were played not at the nearby eighteen-hole golf club (named, bizarrely, the Gog Magog) but at the more distant Royal Worlington, which has only nine holes. Nevertheless, there were advantages, a principal one being that it is on sandy soil, similar to the links courses that are traditionally selected for the Oxford match. Besides this, the fine, man-sized design of this superior nine-hole course gave us a natural advantage over opponents who had to struggle through the winter mud at their chosen university. I am naturally biased in my fondness for this course; I once played Michael Bonallack there, and beat him 5-4.

We played an away match against clubs most weekends through the winter – foursomes in the morning, singles in the afternoon. In those days eighteen holes were completed in about half the time it seems to take now. It was good training to play a lot of matches 'sight unseen' and, at a time when range finders weren't even dreamed of, judgement of distance by eye was an essential skill to develop.

The following year I played in the first of seventeen President's Putters, the annual Oxford and Cambridge Golfing Society KO matchplay event at Rye, always played in the first week of January. The reason for this potentially risky date is that people are generally at home for Christmas and thus a good turnout is more likely. Another key element in this date and venue is (or was) that the links course is the most suitable at that time of year.

I parenthesise 'was' because there has been a transformation in the terrain at Rye over the years. In the fifties a hooked drive to the left of the eighth hole at high tide could mean a watery lie in brackish rough. Now there is a whole new golf course to the left, as the sea has receded over the years. Sparsely grassed fairways made for tight but fair lies, ideal for the better iron players. The greens were brown and fast but absolutely true, needing a fine touch to get the ball in the hole. The last time I played Rye, I was horrified to find mud on the ball, green grass on the fairways and greens half the speed. I should say, though, that the course retains its special character, with its five short holes, of which the prevailing wisdom is that the result of any round at Rye depends on the quality of the second shot at those intimidating small, well-bunkered targets.

**

Being elected secretary of the Cambridge golf club in my second year meant that I would captain in my last year. The choice of venue for the Oxford match fell to Cambridge that year and I picked Rye without a second thought. We won by a single point. Curiously, a fiftieth anniversary rematch with ninety per cent of the original players took place at The Berkshire and produced exactly the same result.

My record in the President's Putter is flawed, with only two wins from seven finals, but I have a pretext for this. My first two finals were against a leading international, P. H. Moody. He was a top performer but played at a pace slower than I'd ever encountered. I fair better in the ranking as third in the all-time points table, concocted by historian John Littlewood, with two wins, five times runner-up, plus a further two semi-finals.

* *

My golfing life had to be put on hold when I walked straight from university into county cricket, as captain of Sussex, and embarked on a year-round cricketing career at home and overseas. During my cricket years, of course, I played sporadic games of golf, with several notable encounters, including my cherished round with Gary Player while I was captain of the 1962/63 MCC Ashes tour in Australia.

We'd flown into Adelaide and I'd made a date with Gary to meet at the wonderful Kooyonga course, not far from the airport. At the last moment Colin Cowdrey asked if he could come too, but when we got to the course with Gary already set to go, Colin found he hadn't brought his golf shoes and had to pick them up from the hotel.

Gary, always a gentleman, was prepared to wait but suggested that the two of us should play four holes to pass the time. Halving the first in birdies, I then went eagle, par, birdie – two up. The bonus to this was that when Colin finally joined us, Gary was determined to get his head down to show who was really boss. It was a wonderful demonstration, finishing with an 8 under par 64.

Golf only reappeared in my life as a regular option after my car accident in 1965 which led to my decision to retire from Test and county cricket. From that point on, although I was still playing a lot of one-day cricket (and a couple of Tests), golf was my sport, and while I was working hard at journalism and my burgeoning business interests, I always found time to drive down to Sunningdale Golf Club, which became my home from home.

Like golf clubs everywhere during the years after the war, Sunningdale were finding it difficult to keep their finances in balance. One of the decisions made to re-establish the club's former prestige was to offer good young players favourable terms. I was one of those lucky young men. By the time I closed my membership, I had enjoyed the competitive atmosphere, the challenge of the two courses and many friendships for over fifty years. I was captain of the club. My name appears on many of the honours boards, including two Spring Medals and one Scratch Matchplay.

This last result came just at the time when Julian Earl, a leader of the more raffish element of the membership, announced that he had arranged a match in Paris – Sunningdale against the French national team. I was available; I flew over in my own plane, the Falc0, to arrive promptly an hour before play at Chantilly, not far from the beautiful racecourse where I had spent many happy hours.

Having just won the club matchplay event, I was given the honour of playing in the top match. I had no idea who my opponent was to be but, when Julian offered odds of 9/4 on the outcome, I guessed that I was second favourite. Nevertheless, I accepted the bet of his ninety pounds to my forty and set off. By the time I'd got a lucky half at the first, I was already aware that Monsieur Godillot was a cultured and quality player. Had I known that he was probably European number one amateur at the time, I might not have taken the bet. However, weighing up the odds, I concluded that trying to match his quality striking through a tree-lined course was not going to work for me. I decided instead to play to my only obvious advantage, which was superior length off the tee – effectively to give it the full smash and see what happened. It worked. He missed a couple of putts and I won comfortably enough, £90 pounds in credit with Julian Earl.

I was sitting at the bar on my own before any of the other matches came in when Julian put his head around the door, saw me and came over. I didn't tell him what had happened, he assumed I'd lost and, in a spirit of sneaky generosity, he offered me double or quits on the toss of a coin. I accepted his offer but called it wrong. I had some consolation in seeing Julian's face when he realised that I didn't owe him the £80 he was expecting.

Already a member of the Royal & Ancient Golf Club, St Andrews, I attended the autumn meeting most years and won the Bombay Silver Medal (after being runner-up twice), before finally winning the even more obscurely named William IV Medal, the Holy Grail for R&A members. More excitingly, the medal was presented to me by the President of the United States, George Bush Sr, who was the club's guest of honour at the traditional dinner.

I also won the Prince of Wales Cup at Royal Cinque Ports, Deal, finishing 2,3,4,4,3. The birdie at the last did me little credit because, after a good drive, I suddenly realised for the first time that I might win. The resulting second shot was hit nastily thin and skimmed through the back of the green. I thought I'd blown it and, as a result, was fairly casual about the chip, which is probably why it ran so sweetly into the cup. The PoW Cup has an enhanced status because it forms the first half of a major weekend, with the second round played at Royal St George's, Sandwich. The best combined score puts the player's name on a magnificent silver trophy alongside many amateur greats, including, I am fairly sure, the name Jack Nicklaus.

I had an early start time at Sandwich on the Sunday, only to find the course enveloped in thick fog, which led to a long delay. Before it lifted the players were spread round the course to be sure of getting everyone round and I found myself set to tee off out in the country. When the starting klaxon sounded, the mist might have cleared around the clubhouse but it was still as thick as porridge where we were. The first few holes were literally hit and miss, costing me three or four strokes before the air cleared. I did manage to finish in the top half-dozen but I still think ruefully of what might have happened on a clear day.

I had an even greater disappointment when I reached a play-off for the final place in the 1978 Open Championship, won by Jack Nicklaus at St Andrews. My six-footer to qualify had lipped out at Leven Links and the play-off started after 9pm in the evening. There were four of us, the other three all professionals, first man to win a hole outright to qualify. Sadly, it wasn't me.

* *

When the Curzon House Club, an exclusive casino in London's West End, decided to form a golf society, they also instigated a handicap matchplay competition, to be played at the Coombe Hill Golf Club in Kingston. I was a member of the Curzon, although roulette and blackjack never interested me much and I seldom played there, but I put my name down for the match. After I'd gone three or four rounds, I was in the final against Judith Agate, who had some county golf experience, and I was giving ten shots. A small crowd of locals turned up to watch which made it more exciting than I'd expected. It was worth £100 to the winner (c.£500 now).

I was on the tee at the appointed start time but there was no sign of Judith. When she arrived, half an hour late, she apologised profusely but her arm was in a sling. She lived quite nearby and had taken a stroll in her garden where she had been stung on the hand by a bee. She said that she'd felt she owed it to everyone to play and would simply do her best.

It was in the days when putting 'croquet' style with a long putter was permitted, and she holed from everywhere. All square after eighteen holes and off we went down the nineteenth, a short par four and, for me, the green was driveable. I knocked it pin high and chipped it stone dead. Judith was on the front edge for two with a twenty-yard swinging downhill putt which she holed for a half. I scrambled a birdie at the second against her par but was giving a stroke, and we were still all square. I won at the twenty-first hole.

I had borne in mind an old sporting adage – 'beware the injured player'.

Gary Sobers was once uncertain to play against us at Headingley because of a painful whitlow. He did play, I feared the worst and, true to the saying, he made a superb 100.

* *

Over a long time I was regularly asked to take part in charity games, and if I liked what the charity was doing, I generally did. On one occasion I agreed to play at a children's charity golf day at Littlehampton Golf Club with various celebrities, including the comedian Jimmy Tarbuck. I asked the club for permission to land my trusty Cessna 206 on their seventeenth fairway. I had reconnoitred the length and breadth of this straightway par 5 and had no qualms about using it. In an attempt to drum up the maximum publicity for the charity I hired a head-turning costume and wore it in the plane.

Richard Boxall, top pro, turned commentator, gave an account of my arrival.

'I was just an assistant pro in those days but I reckoned I was longer off the tee than most. I saw this guy land, get out of the plane in a gorilla suit, walk straight over to the long driving competition and win the thing.'

That wasn't my only happy memory of the day. At the close of play, Jimmy Tarbuck sat down and simply started telling stories for over an hour to a spellbound audience. This was the affable comic at his best – giving generously of himself and of his time, all for the charitable cause.

* *

I'm glad to say that there have been times when my golfing interests and my business activity coincided, with happy results. One of these was triggered in 1994 by an unexpected call from a Scottish golf journalist I knew only slightly. In 1975, the Carnoustie Links course had been dropped as an Open Championship venue. Now they were offering a year's contract to any sports PR company that could create a framework for the return of the great course to the Open Championship roster.

'I'll do all the work,' he said but he needed an established name to work with. 'I know who's likely to get the contract, but Carnoustie is very close to my heart and I think the particular Glasgow-based outfit is completely unsuitable.'

The journalist and my company jointly put together a proposal to Carnoustie which resulted in our getting half the contract, with the other half going to the Glasgow people. We set up meetings with the R&A, the PGA, the European Tour and potential sponsors we'd identified but came away without a result. Prospects were looking bleak as we drove to Dundee for what we felt would be a decisive last meeting with all the likely players: the Carnoustie Club, Scottish TV, the local council. It was quite a gathering, which included our associate from Glasgow.

Desperately seeking any other last-minute options, our Scottish journalist in the back of my car suddenly suggested that we might try to persuade the owner of the *Scottish* Open to leave its cosy home in Gleneagles and switch to Carnoustie. 'But,' he added, 'it will take a lot of money. The owner also likes a bit of luxury entertainment, which we can certainly provide.'

We agreed that we would be more aggressive at the meeting, making the point that we'd been sent into battle without any guns. What we needed was money. We would tell the meeting that anything less than £200,000 would fail. The Glasgow view was that it sounded like a lot of hot air. 'But,' he added, 'I look forward to hearing you explain this thinking to the meeting, Mr Dexter.'

Once we were all ranged around a highly polished mahogany table in the main clubroom, with portraits of a few dour Scotsmen scowling down on us, I stood up, pushed back my chair and took a deep breath. The assembled company listened to our proposal in complete silence; I feared it had fallen on deaf ears. The chairman looked at me for a moment before speaking in a reedy Scottish brogue; he asked for a ten-minute interval to consider my proposal. I left the room, resigned to rejection. When summoned, I returned to the meeting, took my seat and waited for the formal dismissal. I nearly fell off the chair when the chairman agreed our terms.

We pursued our strategy for bringing back the Scottish Open to Carnoustie with complete success. But we were under no illusions that we had completed our task. This was only a halfway house towards reinstatement on the Open Championship venue rota. Luckily, though, this result had not gone unnoticed.

When the news filtered through to the Royal & Ancient, the then secretary, Michael Bonallack, was alarmed at the idea of a clash with the Open Championship, due to be held at St Andrews in 1995. He quickly got himself over to Dundee to sort out an accommodation. I wasn't part of those discussions, but agreement was reached. The Scottish Open move was delayed one year and the great Carnoustie golf course, with its long history of Open Championships, was restored in 1999 to the list of venues, after a break of twenty years.

We didn't earn much from this outcome, nor were we ever credited with our role in bringing it about, but it has always been a matter of satisfaction to me that I played a part in this happy result for Carnoustie, and I'm glad we persevered until we got that result.

I'm glad, too, that I persevered in my playing of the game I love. I maintained a scratch handicap well into my fifties and later had one of my most successful years at the age of sixty-nine (handicap 5). After that, though, my physical condition began to wane. I had a hip operation and my length commenced a remorseless decline. This was followed by a rise in the yips, both with the putter and worse with the chips, compounded by a botched carpal tunnel operation on my left hand, and a reprise, which left me with diminished strength and feeling in the fingers. Golf, I felt, was slowly passing me by. But I rallied and at the age of eighty-three I got myself going again – enough at least to beat my age, which I'd done every year since I was sixty-nine, though now, admittedly, off the forward yellow tees. Nevertheless, I'm still trying to improve. I putt left-handed (no yips, but hit and miss) and I chip right-handed with my left below right. The end may be nigh, but I'm not there yet.

Chapter Eighteen

IDEAS FOR INNOVATION: TED DEXTER & ASSOCIATES

I am sure there was a careers master at the time I was about to leave Radley but it never occurred to me to seek him out. I simply assumed that I would follow my dad into the insurance business. My brother, John, did (with outstanding success) and which, to a limited extent, I did myself while I was unpaid as a cricketer.

A careers master would probably have perceived that I was too independent-minded to make a reliable soldier beyond my unavoidable stint as a National Serviceman. He would have known that I certainly wasn't going to be an academic, despite my intended tenure at Jesus College, Cambridge, nor would he have suggested entrepreneurial businessman – still a faintly unsavoury prospect for an Old Radleian (although not uncommon).

However, a dozen years later, when it came to my having to choose what to do as an ex-cricketer, it was probably my enjoyment of risk and the unknowable, as well as the gambler in me, that attracted me to the unpredictable field of speculative commerce.

My initial introduction to this murky world had been through Bagenal Harvey, who gave me my first job. His proposal, which I naively accepted, was that I work my way, without pay, into a partnership in his growing business. I've mentioned elsewhere that Bagenal was the first of the sports celebrity agents, his original client having been the easy-going Denis Compton. He had branched out into other areas of sport, including commentating, with well-known names like Frank Bough and David Coleman in his stable. To those too young (or not old enough) to remember David Coleman, he was for many years the principal BBC sports presenter and linkman – a proto-Gary Lineker.

Some of the time I was frankly superfluous to the normal running of Bagenal's business and I found myself in situations for which I was completely unsuited. A good instance of that was a nebulous posting as a general gofer to Jarvis Astaire, the dominant boxing promoter of the time. Jarvis was very much the grande fromage of his field, and a powerful character. He was one of the first in London to have a telephone installed in his Rolls-Royce and I was quickly made aware that it wasn't to be used by me calling Susan at home.

Quite unexpectedly, I did once get the chance to punch above my weight for Jarvis. In the late sixties, recent technological advances allowed for a major boxing match in America to be shown live on the big screen of the Odeon cinema in Leicester Square. I was with Jarvis when we arrived in good time for the event to find a vast crowd outside the Odeon, waiting for the doors to open. Jarvis surveyed the scene with a satisfied nod, while we were let in through a side entrance.

We made our way round to the foyer to greet some of the celebrities who would be arriving, when we were urgently summoned to the projection room. The chief technician was howling with anguish that the feed from the American TV company supplying the transmission had been externally disrupted. He was struggling to find a solution but time was passing, and the crowd were becoming increasingly belligerent as the time for the fight approached.

Jarvis looked like he was chewing iron shards as he tried to discover what was going on. One theory was that it was the equivalent of a modern cyberattack, probably instigated by the BBC, where nobody was taking Astaire's calls. It was looking like a real possibility.

Almost erupting with fury, Jarvis turned to me. 'Come on, Ted! For God's sake, you must know SOMEONE!'

As it happened, I did. Since my attempt to be elected as MP for Cardiff South East in 1964, I had kept in friendly contact with Jim Callaghan, my opponent there. He was now Home Secretary. I told Jarvis.

'Get him on the phone! Now!' Jarvis ordered.

Miraculously, it seemed, a few moments later I was talking to the Home Secretary. After a couple of pleasantries, he asked, 'So, Ted, what can I do for you?'

I told him as succinctly as I could what was happening at the Odeon.

'Leave it to me,' he said, and he was gone.

The live feed was restored within minutes.

I received little recognition from Jarvis for defusing the crisis, but I did find that my use of the phone in the Rolls-Royce was occasionally tolerated. Another bonus was that I got to meet Muhammad Ali in his suite at The Dorchester. Just shaking his huge, strangely soft right hand was quite a thrill.

There was another subsequent spin-off, though not necessarily a bonus; when my dad and I decided to buy our hurdler, we bought Ocean Diamond for £1,000 from Jarvis Astaire.

I was still loosely linked to Bagenal Harvey in 1970 when I met Gavin Gordon and we set up Dexter & Gordon, our sports product business, with all the commercial adventures that spawned. Beyond the mixed bag of projects I shared with Gavin, I was also developing other ideas of my own. These were generally compatible with my interest in cricket and golf, or at least in some way related to them, and I'd been developing an idea for a product – a system, really – for which I'd identified a need when I moved from radio to TV cricket commentary. I'd chosen to carry on working for the BBC because I enjoyed it and it kept me closer to the game. The pay was rotten, which the BBC justified to the commentators on the grounds that it put their faces in front of the public which they could go on and exploit in other ways. They got away with it with me, I presume, because they knew I liked doing it, and they didn't want to waste the licence payers' money. I have noted, though, that they don't appear to take that line these days with their current crop of star sports presenters.

When I was working on the BBC radio commentary team and a question of statistics was raised, it was immediately referred to the 'expert' buried in the back of the commentary box behind stacks of volumes of Wisden and other reference books. Minutes later he would relay the information to the commentator; he never had a voice of his own. When I was moved to the TV commentary box, I was amazed to find the same system as for radio. Data shown on screen was limited to the occasional scorecard with a production process as bizarre as the result. Somebody using Letraset or something similar pressed each individual letter and number onto a large board, before sliding the board down a slot into a hefty machine called a caption scanner. It would appear on the screen, with a bit of help from others in the box. 'It's not straight; up a bit on the right; left hand down a bit!' When it finally appeared it was seldom straight and was grainily superimposed on the outfield as a background. It looked a thoroughly amateurish presentation to me, and I was sure that the appropriate technology could produce a better result. I tackled OB director David Kenning about it, but in keeping with the prevailing culture in the BBC, he was generally unreceptive to new initiatives. After a couple of years, though, he finally agreed at least to consider a more efficient way of displaying data on screen. The other end of the deal was going slowly too. I had been to talk to most of the large computer giants at the time – Hewlett Packard, Sony and IBM – without a response.

I had happily imagined that any of these mainstream computer companies would jump at the chance of showing off their technical capabilities in return for getting their name on the nation's screens throughout the TV cricket coverage, but they weren't. I had spent months of desultory meetings with uninterested and disenchanted middle managers and I was beginning to despair.

I couldn't see what I was doing wrong – it seemed such an obvious application of not particularly complex technology – but I was still looking for a technical partner for the on-screen data project when I heard from Rayner Blanch. I'd met Rayner several years before when we'd been fundraising for handicapped children. He'd had a good settled position then, but at the end of 1977, he rang me to say that he had lost his job and the only work he could find was in Rhodesia. He wanted to know if I would give him a reference. I said with complete honesty that I would be delighted to, and finished the conversation. Within minutes I'd picked up the phone again, to ask him to come and see me before he did anything else.

I wanted to discuss the possibility of his working with me on the on-screen data project. He liked the idea a lot, and together we produced a fresh sales pitch and managed to get a date at Honeywell Information Systems with David Croft, a bright young man, who immediately understood what we were trying to do. He picked up the phone to his technical division, requesting the services of three programmers for a set number of hours for a number of months. He told them what the project was about, and that no knowledge of cricket was needed. Having got a positive response from his technical people, he signed a preliminary agreement with us then and there.

We were able to work out a sponsorship deal with Honeywell whereby they developed and provided all the hardware and software for the system. The BBC were pleased to take on the new system, Honeywell got their name on screen regularly throughout transmission of live cricket, the process improved data presentation enormously and operated for nearly twenty years. I'm sure that the principles involved still apply.

In the meantime, in 1978, I created a single commercial entity, Ted Dexter & Associates to handle the On-Screen Data System contract, as well as a broad spread of sports sponsorship deals and, some ten years later, the World Cricket Rankings, which, with the on-screen franchise provided some two thirds of Ted Dexter & Associates' income in the following years.

I had found a way at last.

* *

I didn't need to take on any partners nor give away a share in the business to anyone. Rayner was my first employee and remained my right-hand man from then on, joined ten years later by his son, Jim Blanch. When I moved out of the house to an office in Ealing, Susan's brother, Ivo, joined the team too.

Rayner was a very enjoyable man to work with although he was somewhat debilitated by a serious balance problem which meant that people often thought he was pissed. 'Sometimes they're right,' he would say, 'but not all the time.'

He was inevitably a little accident-prone. In the 1990s we set up and ran a national amateur golf competition, the Honda Team Golf Championship, in which the finals were held at the stunning Penha Longa Golf Club in Sintra on the outskirts of Lisbon. At one of these, Rayner was sitting in his buggy on the edge of a deep rock-strewn ravine beside the eighteenth green. I was standing nearby chatting to his son, Jim. Rayner waved to us to let us know he was moving on. He put his foot down on the accelerator when to our horror we saw he was in reverse and heading for disaster. With incredible luck, the buggy ran straight backwards into the only tree around and came to an immediate halt, just above the ravine.

In another incident at the 96 finals on the same course, Rayner was talking to Honda's general manager, Ken Kier, by the eighteenth green again when he noticed something on Ken's neck. Thinking it must be some beastly insect he started to swipe the offending 'bug' from Kier's neck. Unfortunately, it wasn't a bug; it was a rather large skin tag attached to Ken's neck but Rayner continued to swipe at it, while it still remained attached, oscillating wildly, like a boxer's punchball. We weren't too surprised when Honda didn't renew our contract.

Rayner's balance problem was severe enough for specialists to have suggested that he would be wise not to plan too far beyond the age of fifty. He is now ninety-three, and still in possession of his full quota of marbles.

* *

Another man who walked through the door of my office in Ealing and into my life was Victor Head from Commercial Union Insurance.

This was the result of a fairly rudimentary campaign I'd instigated to find sponsors for various sporting events – existing and prospective. I'd started down this road initially as an individual who wanted what was best for cricket, in seeking a sponsor for county games against the touring teams. The simple idea was that a decent sum of prize money finding its way into the coffers of any county winning a match would encourage them to turn out their best teams and produce better games for the fans to enjoy. I found an excellent and relevant sponsor for this in Holts Car Care Products.

I'd also been looking for sponsors for our first venture into golf, a junior world championship, to which Victor, on behalf of Commercial Union had responded. The first final was held at St Andrews Old Course where I suddenly set myself, with only half an hour to go, the task of remembering the names of two players and a manager for each of sixteen countries so that I could introduce them one by one at the initial gathering. I had been reading books on memory skills and, as much to my amazement as anyone else's, I was word perfect without looking at a note, even with the Japanese names.

The following year we went to Portmarnock in Ireland, where the weather was atrocious. Rain and a strong following wind off the first tee were playing havoc with some of the drives, until a small Spanish boy made his presence felt. As he addressed the ball with a driver, thinking I was speaking quietly, I murmured, 'Why not a 3-wood to get the ball in the air?'

Still addressing his ball, the youngster exclaimed out of the side of his mouth, 'You think I can't hit a driver downwind?'

He nearly drove the green; his name was José María Olazábal, twice a Masters winner and a winning Ryder Cup captain.

For the third year of the tournament, we were in Atlanta, Georgia, at the Athletic Club, home to the legendary Bobby Jones, where the same young Spaniard birdied two of the last three holes to win the event for Spain. The Commercial Union Junior World Cup produced a good crop of famous US winners and the same sponsors took on our National Under-15 Golf Championship which would identify future stars of the British game.

In line with my sales pitch, CU took the view that they could – indeed did – spend millions on straight advertising and sell tens of thousands of policies off the back of it, but good PR activity would engender loyalty and give policy holders and prospective clients a good feeling about them – a distinct if unquantifiable advantage over the opposition.

By pleasing coincidence, the first series of the CU Under-15 Golf Tournament was won by the then twelve-year-old, and smallest player in the field, Peter Baker, a future captain of England in the 1998 Alfred Dunhill Cup, vice-captain for the victorious 2006 Ryder Cup team, and now the highly regarded professional at my local South Staffordshire Golf Club.

Victor Head was a charming man who had been taken on by Commercial Union to set up a separate PR section. He brought a lot of business our way although, in the end, when they were on the point of sponsoring a major project with us, the directors found that they had mislaid over $100 million from their Canadian operation. Victor's PR department was closed almost as soon as it started.

We worked with a number of other major insurance companies who liked the idea of allying themselves to fresh, innovative sporting competitions, as well as car makers Renault, Honda and Fiat. One area in which I'd always felt there wasn't enough investment was in encouraging new bowlers, so in the summer of 1984, we managed to persuade Webster's Yorkshire Bitter to put up £100,000 with the aim of finding six previously undiscovered fast bowlers by winter. The 'Find a Fast Bowler' campaign attracted hundreds of applications. To narrow the field, it was easy enough to devise simple athletic tests, including power throwing and sprinting, as well as a key cricketing requirement, an ability to catch. It was fun but it had a serious purpose. From a cricket point of view, it was no great success though I believe one newcomer was taken on by a county. Publicity, however, which in the PR business is a prime objective, was excellent. So much so that we were confident of renewing the contract. It turned out that we had been rather too successful. Webster's Yorkshire Bitter had flourished to the extent that they were now major advertisers and didn't need our little sideshow.

However, by far the biggest and most important project undertaken by Ted Dexter & Associates was the World Cricket Rankings. This was a concept that had been lurking in the back of my mind for a long time. It was clear to me that ranking players simply by their averages, both batsmen and bowlers, didn't tell even half the story because it didn't take into account all the other factors that might have surrounded a particular innings or bowling performance.

My interest in finding a way to recalibrate the player ranking process prompted me to telephone *The Cricketer* magazine to ask if they had recently published anything to do with cricket and computers. They pointed me to an article in the August 1986 edition which had been written by a man called Rob Eastaway, who worked for Deloittes, the well-known City management consultants. The article focussed on a computer programme written by his friend Gordon Vince, which Eastaway claimed was a sophisticated version of a dice game called *Howzat!* that young boys had been playing for years.

In Gordon's computerised version the player entered details of two imagined cricket teams, pressed a 'start' button and moments later it produced a ball-by-ball analysis of what looked remarkably like a real match. Eastaway explained that he had rebuilt a version of Gordon's cricket programme on his desktop computer and, out of curiosity, had entered the details of the current England and India teams. He'd then run the programme to see what random match the computer would produce. The scorecard that emerged from the printer looked so realistic that Rob imagined that he was a sports journalist and wrote a report of this fictitious match.

Once he had written the match report, he thought he might as well send it to *The Cricketer* magazine. To his astonishment the editor not only accepted the article but decided to make it that month's lead feature. When I read it and how it had been arrived at, I was transfixed – it seemed to me that this chap's combined interest in cricket and computer programming might well make him the very man to talk to about my own as yet germinal project. I wrote to him that day, asking if he would like to get in touch. His boss at Deloittes had the good sense to let him take a few hours off to come to Ealing to see me.

I was rather surprised when a young man who looked as if he might not be much more than eighteen turned up, before appreciating that if he understood computers, he was bound to be a lot younger than me.

I took him down the road to the Grange pub and over a pint of beer and a steak and ale pie, he excitedly told me about his project and that he was hoping I could help develop it. He looked a little crestfallen when I explained that wasn't why I had asked him to come. I told him that in golf an excellent system for ranking players had recently been developed, called the Sony Rankings. What was smart about it was that it took account of more than just a player's score. It allowed for the strength of the opposition, the status of the tournament and so on. It had occurred to me, I told him, that a cricketer's ability is measured very crudely using averages when what we needed was something more sophisticated, like the golf rankings. Quite apart from that, I was pissed off with Boycott always being at the top of the averages.

Rob was (and is) nothing if not quick on the uptake and was soon looking animated by the whole idea and clearly saw the potential. He told me that when he'd been at school, he'd had an idea along similar lines himself. In 1981, for instance, Mike Gatting had scored several 50s for England in low-scoring matches, which, in context, seemed to be almost as valuable as centuries in higher scoring games. What was needed, Rob felt, was some sort of weighting process that took account of the strength of the opposition and the general level of scoring in the match. This exactly matched my own thinking and I listened carefully to what he had to say.

His first observation was that, unlike golf, cricket was a team game, and he wasn't sure how a team game could have individual player rankings. I pointed out that unlike most team sports, cricket is better viewed as being a series of contests between individuals, each of which is recorded statistically. After all, I said, cricket had thrived on statistics, comparing one player with another, ever since the figures had been recorded.

Rob's other concern was that while he understood the challenges that would be involved and he had a very good understanding of the maths needed to model the cricket, he felt that he didn't have adequate computing skills for a project like this. However, he did know a man who did – his friend, Gordon Vince.

Almost from that moment on, Rob, Gordon and I began working together on a mathematical system to rank cricketers, not by the raw score, as had been done for the last 150 years, but taking every factor surrounding these scores into consideration. For instance, we should take into the calculation whether or not a score had been achieved in a high- or low-scoring match, set against a rolling average since Test matches began. For batsmen, the strength of the bowling would be a factor, and, in reverse, the same for bowlers.

The working title for the project – not my choice – was the Dexter System, but thanks to the vision of the management at Deloittes, who could see the benefit of having their name flagged up every time anyone was talking about a cricketer's performance on TV, on the radio and in the sporting press, it became known as the Deloittes Rankings. As a result of mergers between the big City accountants during the 1990s, the ratings system was subsequently renamed the Coopers & Lybrand Rankings, then the PwC Rankings.

Subsequently the system and all intellectual property relating to it were sold by me to the International Cricket Council in 2003. The beneficiaries of the sale were principally myself, with Rayner Blanch, Rob Eastaway and Gordon Vince each fairly rewarded. As a bonus, I'm delighted to say that Rob and Gordon still operate the system on behalf of the ICC. The system is now known as the Official ICC World Player Rankings, encompassing rankings for Test cricket, One-Day Internationals and T20I, and is a crucial element in the reporting and management of cricket worldwide. And it all started in an Ealing pub, over a steak 'n' ale pie.

* *

Over twenty-five years, since its birth in 1978 until it was formerly wound up before we moved to France in 2003, Ted Dexter & Associates provided PR services and arranged sponsorship deals across a wide range of companies, and instigated a number of new sporting events. It was generally an efficient, effective organisation of which I was proud to have been the essential driving force. I had some of the best colleagues I could have wished for and enjoyed all the challenges with which we were presented, even the fun of it when they didn't always come off quite as we'd planned.

One innovation, a winter golf tournament for pros, was known as the Winter Shell. We'd sorted out a TV contract and were excited as the players were getting ready for the first day's play. It was at this point that a large man descended from one of the TV support trucks and called a halt to proceedings. His superiors had ordered a technicians' strike – end of tournament!

The following year, it all came to a standstill with the onset of a foot and mouth outbreak.

When we did eventually get as far as a final, there was a delay for fog. This meant that by the time the last players came to the eighteenth, with the winner's cheque still to play for, the sun was low in the sky and shining straight into the main camera. All we saw were a few small figures putting, out in the far distance. It seemed that the Winter Shell really was jinxed.

* *

One of our original initiatives, the Honeywell On-Screen Data System, had functioned well and delivered for the sponsors for twenty years, when they renewed for another three years, and reneged almost immediately. At a meeting with their CEO and in-house lawyer, we pointed out the key paragraph committing Honeywell to the contract. The lawyer sniffed. 'In a court of law,' he said, 'that paragraph wouldn't be worth the paper it's written on. I know; I wrote it.'

That contract, along with the cricket rankings, had been a major source of income for Ted Dexter & Associates, and its termination presaged the end of the company. I derive a lot of satisfaction from knowing that our two most significant achievements, the Cricket Player Ranking system and the on-screen data programme, both solid earners for us for a long time, are now embedded as key contributors to the world of international cricket.

Chapter Nineteen

FAMILY LIFE – THE YOUNG ADULTS

I'm not sure that I was entirely aware at the time of all the changes that are said to have occurred in Britain in the 1980s under Margaret Thatcher. While I was kept busy with a wide range of business activities, as well as my journalism, golf and several other outside interests, they weren't much affected by the Big Bang, or the wearing of wide red braces in the City of London or any of the other perceived effects of Thatcherism – apart from one major incident.

In 1982, at a time when my son, Tom, was still a little adrift in his life, I had the idea that I might fund him in some kind of business that would engage his enthusiasm and, with luck, give him a bit of income. In one of my habitual perusals of the business-to-business ads in the back of *The Sunday Times*, I found a proposition for a franchise that might suit.

The idea was that an individual, under the advertising and administrative umbrella of the franchisor, would negotiate with a local council to rent a town-centre multi-storey car park that wasn't otherwise being used on a Sunday. The space would then be temporarily converted into a second-hand car sales pitch. People with cars to sell would simply turn up, hand over a tenner, park in an orderly row with a price written across the windscreen and wait for the punters to come along.

Those wishing to buy a second-hand car without going through the traumas of an auction, or the minefield of used-car sale lots, could come and buy at a good net price with no middleman involved. I went to have a look at an existing site and was impressed by the way it worked. It looked like a good wheeze to me, and something that Tom, with his interest in motors, could easily do and enjoy. As franchisee, all he had to do was pay the council, say, £500 for the use of the otherwise fallow car park, charge a hundred owners of cars for sale a tenner a head, and keep the difference.

Tom was up for it, Peter Mills from Dexter & Gordon came on board to help him get things going, I wrote a cheque to the franchisors for £10,000 and we found a handy car park in Slough. The blurb that came with the franchise indicated that it would take four or five weeks before a new scheme would attract enough cars and buyers (with the help of their advertising) to break even. They even included a graph of the likely sales trajectory.

In our case, for the first two weeks, Tom was close to this forecast, and we began to think that we'd picked the right deal. We were all set up for week three, when Mrs Thatcher declared war on Argentina over the ownership of the Falkland Islands.

The following Sunday, just one car turned up, business dried up at once and for the next few months Britain was glued to the television screen on Sundays and the man from the Ministry of Defence, with glasses and a deadpan voice, reading out lists of casualties and ordnance destroyed. For the time being, at least, that was the end of the business, but the franchise agreement required us to carry on for a minimum of several months. I feared that on top of everything else, they would sue me. Luckily, they didn't, but I had to write off my £10,000 – not my best investment.

It was after this that Tom decided to capitalise on his interest in motorbikes and went off to Bath to do his City & Guilds. Returning to London, we encouraged him to move into the maisonette in Finborough Road which we still owned. While he was there, he suffered a bad and prolonged attack of eczema, from which he developed sepsis and was rushed to the Lister Hospital. He was lucky to survive but as he recovered, he was surprised by the number of people – friends and family – who cared enough to come and visit him. It dawned on him that he mattered to more people than he'd realised and, as a serious hospital experience can often do, it had a far-reaching effect on his sense of self-worth and overall outlook on life. He left hospital a changed man.

At the time he became ill, Tom was living in our place in Finborough Road with a couple of friends. Before he had moved in there, and since we'd moved to Ealing, we had kept the maisonette, trying to deal calmly with all the hassles of letting to young renters – non-payment and damage, as well as the possibility that they might suddenly turn themselves into sitting tenants. In time, though, the maisonette provided a useful base for Genevieve and Tom before they found places of their own. When we had downsized our Ealing house, enough cash was released for us to buy a flat in Swiss Cottage for Gen, and now Tom was keen to get a place of his own.

By this stage, the lease was becoming dangerously short, and if we wanted to realise anything on it, we needed to sell it urgently. Once again, I went and talked to a few vacant-eyed Fulham Road estate agents, which still proved a dead end. However, looking through a London property magazine, an advertisement for an upcoming auction caught my eye. I dialled the number given and had an entirely different reception.

'Put it in the auction? Course we will. Come to think of it, it could go really well.' The man on the other end sounded a bit of a rough diamond, but he exuded confidence. 'No need to put a reserve on it. Trust me. You'll do OK.'

A few days before the auction, he rang me. 'Ere boss, I've had quite a tasty offer – eighteen farsand parnds. But don't you take it!' Shortly afterwards, he rang again. 'OK, Guv'nor, I've had an offer: twenty-three grand, but don't take it!'

This all sounded a bit too good to be true, and I started wondering if he was all talk. But our maisonette was entered in the sale, and I guessed I'd know soon enough. However, just before the auction took place, the man rang once more. He'd had an offer of £28,000.

'Shall we take it?' I asked, tentatively.

'Take it? Take it? Course you take it. Bite his bleedin' hand off before he changes his mind.'

We took it and gave the proceeds to Tom. He put the money into the purchase of a flat in South London, which placed him securely on the first rung of the property ladder.

**

Tom had been developing an interest in electronics in which he was encouraged by the stepfather of his then girlfriend. As a result, he enrolled on a course where he took an ONC in Electrical and Electronic Engineering, which he passed, followed by passes in an HND and then a BEng (Hons) at the University of the South Bank. Now he found himself with a dossier of good, useful qualifications, but no job.

At that point, we had a big slice of luck. I had told a good golfing friend at Sunningdale about Tom's position, and he suggested I speak to another member, Christopher Lewington, then CEO of Tube Investments.

'He's a great guy,' my friend said, 'and will always help anyone if he possibly can.'

However, I was reluctant to ask a favour of a fellow member whom I had never met, until shortly afterwards, by happy coincidence, I was in the club one morning when the only other person around was Christopher Lewington himself. I talked to him about Tom and, as I'd been told, he was more than willing to do what he could. As a result, Tom started his first engineering job in technical support at John Crane UK, Engineered Sealing Systems, on the Slough Industrial Estate.

From that point on, Tom made steady progress in his working life, at one stage boasting a Rolls-Royce business card, identifying him as a Principal Engineer. He was able to reverse the struggles of his youth to such an extent that, for the last twenty-three years he has always had work in his chosen field of aerospace engineering. He moved with his family to Wolverhampton to work at Lucas Varity as an electrical and electronic systems engineer and he is now a director of his own consulting company.

In achieving this, Tom had a lot of support from his wife Catherine, whom he met while they were both studying at the South Bank University. She was a chatty, copper-haired Irish girl, one of eight children in the Clarke family from County Meath, Ireland. Her mother was a senior nurse at the local hospital, well liked and respected in the area. Catherine was by nature a strong, dependable person and when their relationship was obviously becoming serious, Susan and I thought that she would be marvellous for Tom. We were thrilled when she agreed to marry him and knowing how much she missed her seven siblings back in County Meath, we were very happy to welcome her into our family.

** **

Tom and Catherine were married on 1 November 1997 in St Columbanus' Catholic Church in Catherine's home village of Ballivor. It looked to us as if half the village was there, in a wonderful, warm wedding service. After that, there was a tremendous party in a hotel in Kells, which, like most Irish parties, felt as if it lasted a few days. Catherine's mother showed great stamina and by the time Susan and I were completely knackered, she was still alert and sitting proudly upright. I found Tom in the bar, having a breather and a contemplative pint, and suggested he should ask his new mother-in-law for a dance. She loved him for the gesture.

Before they were married, we went to stay with the Clarkes on their smallholding, where they kept cattle and sheep – hands on and hard work. One day, as I was looking out of the window, the rain was torrenting down, creating a quagmire between the house and the cattle shed. Through this, I saw Catherine walking, unfazed and unbowed, towards the barns carrying a pair of feed buckets; she always pulled her weight when she was back home. I was impressed and thought Tom a lucky man to be marrying such a determined and resilient lady.

I think, at first, she was a little wary of me, and must have found me a somewhat old-fashioned and forbidding father-in-law. At the same time, she wanted to show me that she was her own woman, making her own decisions without any help from me, which I didn't doubt for a moment, and naturally admired. In time we learned to know and understand each other; after all we were united in wanting the best for Tom and their children, and she has been a terrific mother.

Once the festivities were finally over, Tom and Catherine left the party riding an almost brand-new, top-of-the-range BMW motorcycle, which I'd happily lent them, and headed off on a tour across Europe.

When Tom was offered his job with Lucas in the West Midlands, he and Catherine, with the proceeds of the sale of his flat in South London, were able to buy a decent house in Penn, an attractive suburb to the south-west of Wolverhampton. While they were there, in 1999, their first son Edward was born. Susan had already driven up to help with all the preparations for the new arrival. So I was on my own in London when I heard the good news. I jumped into the Continental Bentley I then owned, and whooshed straight up the M6 to the hospital in Wolverhampton to welcome our first grandchild – a proud moment for any man.

Subsequently, Tom and Catherine found a house they really loved – solid, characterful, Victorian and pretty ramshackle – in Tettenhall on the north side of Wolverhampton. It was ripe for the kind of imaginative improvement they enjoyed, with the added benefit of a large old-fashioned garden. They had been looking for a house where they would have more room and where they had the potential to do their own thing. They moved there in 2003, shortly before Susan and I left for Nice. They have done an enormous amount of work on the house, aided from time to time by Susan and me, although there wasn't always complete agreement over the way the job should be done. But we willingly put in a lot of our time and some money on the practical grounds that we would have somewhere to live when we came back to England for the summer months. Our contribution when we stayed was in childcare, allowing Tom and Catherine, who had a demanding job in the NHS, to carry on working during the long summer holidays. We also had a base from which to visit the rest of the family in England. However, familiar with the problems of older buildings, we were naturally concerned about the state of the roof. Susan gave them a decent lump sum for the repair, but when we came to stay the following year, they'd spent it all on furniture. We were a little miffed at the time, but seventeen years later, the roof's still there; maybe they made the right decision.

Having worked on the building over the years, what they have now is a really super house which they enjoy enormously. It has been an ideal place to bring up their two children, and their eldest son, Edward, when he's not at university in London, is always glad to come back to it. Edward is not only busy at Goldsmith's College, where he is studying English Literature and Creative Writing, he also sings and plays lead guitar in a band he formed called, inexplicably, Hüds, which gigs widely around the North and the Midlands. In between these two activities, he also had a role to play for a while in his Aunt Genevieve's company in central London.

When we decided to come back from France to live in England, we chose to live on the north-western outskirts of Wolverhampton, a mile or so from Tom and Catherine, close enough to be able to see them and our grandchildren easily, far enough not to get in each other's hair, and it's working very well indeed. We love being near our grandchildren and we're very proud that Tom survived the vicissitudes of his earlier years and came through it with such success.

* *

Meanwhile, Gen's love of travel, inspired by the family's round-the-world trip, encouraged her to make the most of the long university holidays to visit Colombia, Senegal, Thailand, with even longer spells in Japan, post university, learning the language at SOAS when she got home.

She enjoyed university, made a lot of friends, expanded her interests and went to a lot of parties. Unlike me, she was never much interested in cars, although she did borrow Susan's Renault 4 from time to time. She didn't take up driving in any serious way until ten years later, when I gave her a surprise birthday present of a classic Rover 75 Saloon, which I knew she had always liked the look of.

She drove this until her mid-forties, when, with characteristic generosity, she gave it to one of her nieces and decided to treat herself to a car that exactly fitted her needs. Knowing the ridiculous number of cars I'd got through over fifty-five years, she came to me for advice – although there were some specific requirements: it had to be convertible, but with four seats, so she could look in the rear-view mirror and see her dog, Rosie (a rescue Staffy-cross bitch) sitting behind her with ears flapping madly in the wind. Together we found a stylish Volvo Coupe with a retractable hard top for under £10,000. When I tried the roof, it opened and closed with such perfect precision, I told Gen that this superb piece of engineering alone was worth the money. It made me quite sad when recently, after a good ten years, she sold it for a song.

Once she had got her degree, she worked as a volunteer for the Kensington branch of Amnesty International, arranging a huge fundraiser for the 'disappeared' of Argentina in what is now the Bluebird Restaurant in Chelsea. She liked this involvement and applied to work as a full-time employee with AI, but ended up finding a job as marketing assistant at Abacus Software in Pall Mall where she developed her love of all things tech.

After a few years, her deep interest in TV and film led her to apply for a job with an American film production company, where she became involved with film animation, especially for kids' TV. She was busy, talented and regularly promoted. The company liked to do things in style and we were once invited to dinner on their luxury yacht during the Cannes Film Festival; this turned out to be not such a good omen, as the company suddenly went bust. Her subsequent employers fared much better, so well, in fact, that they sold their companies for millions and Gen ended up with a P45.

More significantly, and perhaps giving her the confidence to take a major, potentially risky decision to start up her own business, she met Jerry Harrison. A school friend of hers, Armorel, had taken Gen to a party in Somerset where she met a man whom she fell in love with for the first time in her life. After that weekend, she couldn't understand why she was so worried about him crashing while driving Picassos around Europe for an art shipping company, until Susan told her that's what love feels like! He was also a good musician, writing songs for her and painting pictures. Their love burgeoned, and after two years of a long-distance relationship, they decided to live together in Belsize Park.

As soon as we had met Jerry we breathed a sigh of relief. We hadn't found much to like in any of Gen's previous boyfriends, and were delighted that, now she'd found one we did, she was going to commit herself.

Where Gen had met him in Somerset wasn't far from his birthplace in the village of Blue Anchor on the north coast. The most immediately striking thing about Jerry is that he is an exceptionally large, strong man – not fat, but broad across the chest and shoulders. We soon discovered that he was also thoughtful, soft-hearted, practical and dependable, and we completely understood what Gen had found in him. Quieter than her, and widely read, he was a well of general and historical knowledge, known among his friends to be a walking encyclopaedia. Whenever they wanted information without looking on Google, they would ask Jerry, to the point when once, at a party and not wanting to be bothered, he hung a sign around his neck: 'Information Service Temporarily Suspended.'

What I liked about Jerry from the start was that he was interested in everything and could converse about almost anything, but he had told me that he didn't know a lot about cricket and had never followed it. However, perhaps in an effort to see a little of my world, he asked me if I would take them to watch the touring West Indians when they played at Lord's. He and Gen came, I enjoyed entertaining them, and it wasn't a bad match, but it wasn't long before they'd seen as much as they wanted to. After we'd had some tea, I suggested we might go along to the MCC Cricket Museum for ten minutes, where there were a few things I'd donated. There could have been more, but unfortunately, I had lost – or perhaps I should say, mislaid – a number of old items of memorabilia some ten years before.

A man had turned up at Warwick Dene and told me he was forming a collection for a cricket museum. I had piles of stuff cluttering the house, and as he seemed like a genuine sort, I happily gave him a heap of bats, caps and blazers, although none of the more special items and trophies. In retrospect, it was obvious that I was never going to see him or my things again and that, not for the first time, I'd been a victim of my own naivety. A few months later, someone did buttonhole me to tell me that they'd seen one of my caps for sale in Southall.

The curator at Lord's gave us a great welcome and offered to show us round to see all my things. Genevieve, always eagle-eyed, saw my name written in the labels on a cap and blazer, although below the exhibit, they were described as having belonged to Michael Brearley – of all people.

The curator was most apologetic. 'I'm *so* sorry. We'll get that put right at once. How could that have happened?'

When he showed us a bat inscribed with the names of all the winning counties of the Gillette Cup from 1963, I pointed out that it wasn't the Gillette Cup in 1963. Gillette had sponsored the Knockout Cup only since 1964. I remembered that well enough; Sussex had won the first two tournaments.

I knew that I'd presented the ball with which I'd taken 5 for 8 for the Gents v. Players at Lord's in 1957, and it had been mounted with a little silver shield, but we couldn't find it. The curator was in an abject panic by this stage.

We left feeling a little underwhelmed when he came rushing after us to say he'd found the ball. Poor man – it had turned out a bit of a bad day for him. But I think Jerry had found it interesting.

Soon after that they'd told us they were going to be married, we drove down to Somerset with them to meet the rest of his family. On the way, Jerry suddenly spoke from where he was squeezed on the rear seat. 'I think there's something you ought to know. You know I'm one of three brothers?'

'Yes,' we said, wondering what on earth was coming.

'Well. I'm the small one.'

Given Jerry's own proportions, this was a bit of a surprise, but when we arrived at Blue Anchor, we found it was true: the brothers were colossal. Jerry's mother was a warm and lovely woman, but his father, sadly, had died a year before. Mr Harrison had come from a family of builders, and he had been a man of versatile skills, having been active in the restoration of the Minehead and West Somerset Steam Railway. His grandfather had been a gifted woodworker and was responsible for a most elegant timber gallery in the Luttrell Arms Hotel where we stayed in Dunster.

**

When it came to the wedding, having seen Tom and Catherine married in Ireland the year before, we were naturally keen, and excited, to have it in our own parish church of St Matthew's, which we had attended regularly since we had arrived in Ealing, nearly thirty years before. There was the cricket club where we could hold a large reception, a number of local hotels for guests to stay in, but Gen and Jerry were sure that they didn't want a traditional Church of England service.

On 11 June 1998, after the civil ceremony had been carried out in the local register office, they had arranged to hold their own rite of marriage near the village of Rodhuish, not far from Dunster, in a huge marquee pitched in a field which may have witnessed some defining moment in their relationship. They had found an unusual couple of Buddhist/humanist shamans to lead the ceremony with incantations and ancient prehistoric rituals, in which Gen and Jerry leapt over a log to symbolise their commitment, and they had written their own very moving words as part of the ceremony. It couldn't have been more different from our own wedding, and yet it was every bit as meaningful, and wonderfully original.

The party that followed the wedding was a tremendous, bucolic affair. The marquee was garlanded with wild flowers and greenery, where a band and other musicians played for hours on end, where everyone danced and guzzled gallons of Veuve Clicquot. Near the marquee a large luxury yurt had been erected in which they stayed and friends sat around in great comfort. Naturally it rained, and cars were stuck in the mud, but that didn't matter – it was a lovely, earthy event, with an amazing mix of guests, many from a long way off, and a good gathering of locals. Sitting, surveying the scene, I knew it was going well when two strapping Somerset lads walked by, both well merry and carrying pint tankards of champagne. 'Good stuff, this Veuve Clicquot,' one was saying as he took a large slug of it.

The band was replaced by a DJ and the dancing went on until the birds in the woods and hedges were beginning to twitter, long after Susan and I had left for our hotel, but around 10am the next morning, we came back to find everything very quiet. There was to be a big lunch, a lot of people to be fed, and we wanted to make sure all the arrangements were in hand. We went into the marquee to find it strewn with comatose bodies, evidently lying where they'd dropped. Eventually things slowly came back to life, and an enormous long lunch followed, with more musicians and entertainers.

This marvellous, joyous party finally broke up on the second evening as people drifted home or off to the village pubs where a big football international was being shown on TV.

We drove back to Ealing happily feeling that in Jerry, Gen had made the best possible choice of life partner. He has been a huge support for her – a brilliant chef and wine expert, tremendously practical, with an extraordinary breadth of knowledge. He takes great care of Gen, and must be a useful restraining influence on her impulsive, eccentric nature.

Gen and Jerry were both determined to keep a foothold in his part of the world, and soon found a small cottage in a terrace in Oakford, just off the main road from Tiverton to South Molton. It is in Devon but we all have to shout out 'Somerset' whenever we cross back into Harrison country. Twenty-five years into their relationship they still love each other very much, living between their house in London and the Devon cottage.

**

In 2001 Gen decided to set up her own company, Cake Entertainment, named after her habit of drawing charts to demonstrate shares of finance, equity and copyright in films, an ideal name for a children and family entertainment company too.

This involved sourcing embryo projects and then putting together the finance to turn them into animated films for children. Although she was doing well enough on her own, she became aware of a reluctance in some potential investors to trust a sole female entrepreneur. She took on board a very capable Dutchman and together they grew the business into a substantial enterprise, employing quality staff and working from a smart office in central London.

Heaven knows why, but I was asked one day to take her beloved dog Rosie to the office to say goodbye to one of her senior aides who was leaving. With much fussing and tail-wagging, the dog was trotting round to each desk, all happily, until she came to the Dutchman. Suddenly she bristled, bared her teeth and growled at him – something I had never seen her do before. It was mildly embarrassing. But if her sixth sense detected that something was not quite right with him, she turned out to be spot on. Within months Genevieve caught him with his hand in the till – planning to sell her company from under her feet and to short-change her on the deal.

They obviously had to part company but coming to an agreed settlement was anything but easy. Eventually she plucked up courage to book a day in the high court and came out of it, not only a clear legal winner, but also a serious financial winner.

This was an extremely stressful year of her life but turned out to have been entirely to her advantage. She was known as an outstanding distributor but had always aspired to move more towards the production side and this upheaval opened a window for her. She currently runs two companies so that if something happens to one, she will still have another!

Genevieve has since been highly successful at the heart of the huge world market for animated films for children and family audiences with several BAFTA and Emmy nominations and wins. Though she has no children of her own she has become everyone's favourite (and very generous) aunt in both the Dexter and Harrison families. She is also a kind, considerate and loving daughter.

* *

The other member of the family who still made regular appearances at 5 Warwick Dene and afterwards at Woodville Gardens was my younger brother, David. Although he spent most of his time at CARE, Shangton, where he was quite happy, he wasn't cut off from life outside. He loved coming to stay with us, going out to the pub, playing golf or going to see shows and the singers he loved. He was very keen on music and, like most people with his syndrome, he had a great sense of rhythm. He could be very sociable and loved going to hotels, ringing for waiters, ordering food, enjoying comfort and wearing good clothes – all the things that most of us enjoy. He loved dancing and singing, whenever he had the chance. Everyone who knew him appreciated his warmth and always enjoyed seeing him. Despite the frustrations he must have felt from time to time and the awareness of his own differences, I do believe that David was generally leading a happy life. Susan and I made a point of going to the

CARE Village, Shangton, to visit him as often as we could; I was very glad that I had found the place, and had played a small part in getting it built in the first place. When he came to us at Ealing, Susan was a selfless companion to him, always finding things he liked to do or taking him into London, which he loved.

As a boy, when he had been at school in England, he used to come back to Italy for holidays, just like his brothers, and we would take him to regular golf lessons. Although aiming the right way was never his strong suit, he could certainly hit a good ball over a hundred yards.

Walking back to our home on Ealing Common one day after nine holes with him in Gunnersbury Park, I asked him, 'How do you think you played today?'

'Very well,' he answered confidently.

'What about the times you missed the ball?' I asked.

'So what? I did my best!'

This thought stayed with me for the rest of my golfing life. Whenever I found myself feeling grumpy after a lousy shot, I only had to ask myself, 'Was I doing my best?' to put the problem into perspective.

* *

As David moved into and beyond middle age, he became increasingly unsettled, suffering from what was recognised by his carers as a form of dementia. This became alarmingly apparent in an episode towards the end of his life. Susan and I had taken him out from CARE for dinner which we all enjoyed. On returning to his room he proudly showed us his latest acquisition – a pack of a dozen long and sturdy needles. Where he got them from, we could not imagine, but we felt we should get them away from him; we tried bribery and alternative gifts in exchange, but he only grew more agitated. Suddenly he screamed at us, picked up his chair and hurled it through the large picture window of his room; he had always been physically strong. Naturally it was very distressing for all three of us, but the caring staff came to our rescue and gradually calmed him down.

By that stage, David's life was nearing the end, so we were extra pleased that he'd been able to come to my seventieth birthday party in 2005. When he died soon afterwards, aged sixty-one – exceptionally long-lived for an individual with Down's syndrome – a big turnout of family as well as staff from the CARE village came to honour him at his funeral in the church in Shangton. It was a very sad day for us, but at least we felt he had lived as normal a life as was possible.

Chapter Twenty

CHAIRMAN OF THE
ENGLAND COMMITTEE

In May 1988 I turned fifty-three. I was in a good period of my life, enjoying my work, my sports, my family and social life, while my various business interests and media activity were producing a good income. Tom and Genevieve had both left home and we had recently moved from a large rambling family house in Ealing to a smaller, neater terrace house nearby.

I had organised my time so that I could play two or three rounds of golf a week, go racing and have a punt on Saturdays (when there wasn't a Test match to report). At this point, although I was sitting on various committees to do with the structure and finances of county cricket, I was only sketchily aware of what was going on behind the scenes in the world of Test cricket. In 1988 I was covering the Saturdays of the home Test series versus the West Indies for the *Sunday Mirror*. To my later regret, in one of my reports I had described Graham Gooch, the fourth of four different England captains in the series, as having 'all the charisma of a wet fish'. This does show that I was only on the fringes of the game at the time, offering random views to fill a newspaper column rather than with any thoughts of influencing events. In the turbulent years to come, I came to understand Graham's considerable qualities as a captain and as a man. With an impressive generosity of spirit, he was even man enough to forgive me for the 'wet fish' comment.

The series was over by August to general disparagement over the way the England team had been run, and in November it was announced that after seven years in the job, Peter May really had little option but to resign as chairman of selectors. However, it didn't even cross my mind that I might be considered as his successor; thus, when Raman Subba Row, chairman of the TCCB asked if he could come and see me, I assumed it would involve some tinkering around with the minor committees on which I already sat.

When he asked me straightforwardly if I would consider taking on Peter May's role, I was completely taken by surprise and unprepared. My immediate reaction came straight from the heart: '*No. No way.*'

Remembering how Test selection used to be done in my days as captain, over a cosy chat on a Sunday morning at Gubby Allen's house near Lord's, I was in touch enough at least to know that wasn't how it happened now. Gubby's position of absolute authority at the MCC had placed him beyond criticism or challenge. Peter May had enjoyed no such special privilege; he was a public figure whose reputation as one of England's greatest batsmen counted for nothing. If the England team was losing, as they were in 1988, responsibility for it fell on him and no one else.

At that point, with Subba Row, a friend for over thirty years sitting opposite me, I could have done what my instincts were shrieking in my ears, and turned down what was, undoubtedly, a flattering invitation. However, I always was – still am – a sucker for a challenge. On this occasion, I was just reluctant enough to feel that, if I were to take it on, it could only be on my terms. There were several aspects of the way Test cricket was being run that I had felt for years were in serious need of an overhaul. If I cared enough, this was my last and only opportunity to do something about it. My doubts that I should do it at all only strengthened my resolve in this. And I guessed that Raman would convey this to his colleagues on the TCCB.

I laid out my terms for doing the job:

No more county delegates on a Test selection committee.

In the course of a series, match-by-match selection would be solely in the hands of the team manager and captain, and they would be responsible for tactics.

I would preside, dealing solely with long-term strategy.

There would be area observers to keep us up to date with current form in county cricket.

I would be appointed chairman of an 'England Committee' comprising at least the chairman and the chief executive of the TCCB. The brief would be to consider all matters relating to national teams, including junior teams. Previously the title chairman of selectors meant simply chairing selection committee meetings and little else.

* *

Mine were radical proposals which I would take great satisfaction in seeing adopted. I was aware, though, that a potential stumbling block to my appointment could be the TCCB's insistence that I relinquish my work in the media. I would only agree to that if I were recompensed accordingly.

When I gave them the sum of my existing contracts there was an initial sharp intake of breath. I perceived, though, that this may only have been to show each other that they were careful with the board's money. In fact, I think they were relieved it wasn't more. Either way, we had a deal.

It has been written that, 'The TCCB was already planning that the selection process should be absorbed into a new England Committee.' I believe this was said simply to downplay my role in bringing it about; subsequent conversations with Raman Subba Row and Alan Smith confirmed that there had been no such planning. These were my own proposals and nobody else's.

In February of 1989, after these discussions had been going on for a while, but before a final decision had been agreed within the TCCB, there must have been a leak; the press got wind of the possibility I might be the new chairman of selectors, and were badgering me with their customary persistence. I took the only practical course and called a press conference at the Ealing offices of my PR company to announce that I was getting involved. Although this was warmly received at the time, I was subsequently criticised for doing this before the counties had ratified my position. If there was criticism to be made it might have been better directed towards the board representatives who had effectively hired me without setting any restrictions on my public pronouncements.

As soon as everything had been ratified, and my stipulations conceded, I was eager to get on with the job. The first, most pressing item to deal with was the appointment of an England captain, a position last held by Graham Gooch, for the final Test only against West Indies the previous year. Three other captains had been tried and discarded: Mike Gatting for the first Test, John Emburey for the second and third and Christopher Cowdrey for the fourth. As if this shambles were not enough, there was also the involvement of Gatting and Gooch in the rebel tours to South Africa.

Not so much a shambles, you could say, more a chalice of hemlock.

The only constant survivor of the 4-0 drubbing given by the West Indians was the team manager, Micky Stewart. Standing by my own terms of reference, I asked him for his recommendation for captain. Gooch's position was the most confusing. His selection as captain for the winter tour to India had surprised a lot of people, though that tour had been called off by India who objected to the inclusion of players connected to rebel tours, thus denying us the evidence of his captaincy skills. It came down to a choice between David Gower, previously a winning captain versus Australia, though subsequently and puzzlingly discredited, and Mike Gatting. Stewart favoured Gatting, whom he believed would cope better in a tight corner.

Before a final decision could be made at an England Committee meeting, Gatting's name was splashed across the front of the British tabloids attached to a non-story about his liaison with a barmaid from a Leicestershire pub, whom the saintly hacks judged unsuitable. What business it was of theirs and what it had to do with his ability to captain a cricket team was never clear to me; however, he did have some history, including a famous finger-wagging incident with an umpire in Pakistan. I agreed with Micky Stewart and stood by Gatting, but the TCCB representative at the meeting, Ossie Wheatley, had the right to a veto, and applied it.

It was agreed, nevertheless, that we had only one clear second choice, which was David Gower. He was given the job for the next Test series the following year against Australia at home.

Relieved that we'd negotiated this first contentious issue with a result that suited me, I could begin to plant the seeds of my plans to upgrade England's performance at Test level over the longer term.

The first issue I wanted to address was whether or not the playing of county cricket was an ideal or even adequate way to prepare players for the step-up to Test level. Another question was whether or not the existing Test players were getting the support they deserved, financially and physically. As I saw it, the answer to both was emphatically 'No'. But I knew that improvements in both would need a great deal of thought and perseverance in the months and years of my chairmanship.

It had often been claimed, 'the chairman never goes north of Watford'. This wasn't justifiable in my case; I liked driving up to the more far-flung counties, and besides, I had taken the initiative of appointing key county watchers – one each in the North, the Midlands, the South-West and South-East. My northern spotter was Phil Sharpe, with whom I'd partnered a good innings on his debut on the third Test against the West Indies in 1963. A tubby little fellow, he'd been a great slip fielder for Yorkshire and was an unforgiving observer. When I pressed him for news of fresh talent, knowing that Yorkshire had always produced a few good players, he reported, 'Don't look here for anyone, chairman. There's no one; they're all bloody useless, I'm telling you.'

Nevertheless, I went back to watching county cricket, which I hadn't done much over the twenty odd years since I'd stopped playing it. It had changed, and mostly not for the better. The first thing I noticed was that there was much more movement of the ball off the pitch, despite the fact that they were now playing on fully covered pitches. If a pitch was flat enough to suit the batsmen best, it would lead to a certain draw if there was time lost to rain. Evidence suggested that captains were colluding to produce a run chase on the last day – anything to get a result.

This encouraged a style of batting geared to quick scoring. Players batting first would plan to get as many runs as possible before the unplayable ball came along with their name on it. Towards the end of the match it was being played more like limited-overs cricket today – slam, bam, wallop.

The effect on bowlers was even more damaging. If the ball was doing all the work, all they had to do was put it on a length, and wait. There was no point in a bowler bending his back, striving for swing, changing his pace, changing the point of delivery or varying his length.

Anxious to address every element of the game as it was now played, I managed to get hold of a box of new cricket balls. I wanted to see what changes, if any, were to be found. I picked out one at random and nearly cut my fingers on the over-wide, over-sharp and over-prominent seam – the stitching holding the two half spheres of the leather cover together. I had no doubt that this was creating the problem. The better players are able to cope with swing but random movement off the pitch will always defeat the best of techniques.

I reported my concerns to my committee and arranged meetings with Readers and Dukes, the main ball manufacturers. I wanted to know how and why this change had crept in, and to reverse it. They reluctantly agreed to limit the size of the thread they used.

That was a result, for the time being at least. However, when I saw how the Reader ball was moving around again in the 2019 series versus Australia, I wasn't at all surprised to hear that the manufacturers had again been called to account. Australia's opening batsman, David Warner, had a batting average of 50 before the England series. Against the Reader ball, albeit brilliantly exploited by Stuart Broad, he averaged 10 – including a king pair (two noughts) at Old Trafford.

In 1989, I gained some new insight into the batting problems we were having. As I was watching England's net practice on the Nursery Ground the day before the Lord's Test my concern at the variety of techniques being used must have been written all over my face. A newcomer to the England side, Kim Barnett of Derbyshire, spoke up. 'That's just how it is in county cricket these days, chairman.'

He had made a blistering 80 in short order in the first Test. Ironically, had he taken a little longer, we might have held out for a draw. Sadly his form deteriorated as the series went on and a short Test career came to a close. However, I'd taken on board the point he'd made, and hoped that I'd be able to something about that too. I was well aware that nobody was going to change county cricket overnight and was under no illusion about the importance of a long-term strategy over several years.

One of the first moves in this direction was to send 'A' teams overseas every winter, with two objectives. The first was to shake county regulars out of ingrained experience. At home they enjoyed their regular spot in the dressing room and probably a nice cup of tea at exactly the same time every morning. They understood their home-ground conditions and after a season or two, even the conditions and opponents at away games were familiar.

Overseas touring would put them in an upcountry ground a few thousand miles from home, with limited facilities, a turning pitch and a couple of crafty spinners to face where only the more adaptable would survive. As I was planning this initiative, I knew these tours would be expensive and I wasn't sure that the counties would support me. To give them credit, they agreed, not only to these extra costs, but others in the pipeline. Indeed, I found generally during my chairmanship that I was never denied new initiatives for lack of money.

When I'd asked my predecessor, Peter May, what his biggest problem had been during his term as chairman, he'd cited injuries as number one. I reckoned that having a pool of better-prepared players would add the advantage of there being ready-made replacements when the first team suffered injuries.

Since I'd taken on the job, I'd made a point of getting closer to the players, and hearing them talk. What I came to understand was the financial importance to them of being selected for the tour. There weren't many overseas playing or coaching jobs to be had, and if they weren't selected for the tour they were probably stuck with whatever winter jobs at home they could pick up, maybe repainting the sight screens for a pittance. As a result, it was clear to me that the batsmen particularly were playing more for their place on the tour than for the immediate needs of winning a match, and this undoubtedly added a tension to their play which didn't help.

The way in which Test players were being paid for home series was simple and modest. For their week's work they earned a few hundred pounds. They would travel to the match on a Wednesday, in time for afternoon practice, play Thursday, Friday, Saturday with a rest day on Sunday, play Monday and Tuesday, travel home Tuesday evening/night in time for the three-day county match on Wednesday, Thursday and Friday. They might play a new match Saturday, possibly away from home, turn out for a pal's testimonial on a Sunday, then play Monday and Tuesday.

This was not a way to prepare for a top performance at Test level.

To take the pressure off certain key Test players (for whom an injury could always come along at a bad time) I persuaded the counties to set aside the money to pay for what I termed 'winter contracts' for six or eight of our best players. These were to be selected as early as June/July, and meant for the first time that Test players could enjoy something approaching a year's financial security. Now, thirty years on, Test players are all contracted full-time to the board for sums of money that players then could only have dreamed of, but I am pleased to have at least set the ball rolling.

There was an agreeable and effective example of this new arrangement in the case of a then youngish recruit to Test cricket, Angus Fraser. He had earned his winter contract, but nearing tour selection, he suffered a severely torn hamstring. From personal experience I knew how long the recovery time could be for this injury. I was able to persuade the board that a period of proper rest in a suitable climate was important. I packed him off to the sunny beaches of Barbados for a fortnight. He came back fully recovered with his energy levels topped up and, as far as I know, the injury never recurred in a long and successful career.

A fairly complex side issue of the way county cricket was being played was the dwindling role of the slow spin bowler. They had their place in keeping the runs down – as indeed they still do in limited-overs cricket – but gone were the days when a team needed a couple of decent spinners to take advantage of a drying pitch after rain.

In an attempt to define the most likely candidates to send on A tours where they might find better opportunities for their craft, I made a whistle-stop tour around the counties to see what there was – and more importantly to chat with these somewhat overlooked craftsmen.

Given the importance of powerful spin at Test level, I questioned each of them on the subject of sore fingers. I had a vivid memory of seeing the great spin duo of Jim Laker and Tony Lock after play, gingerly tending the cracks and tears they had suffered in a day's bowling. In the morning they would apply Friars' Balsam or some other sticky substance to reduce the pressure. In the evening the first move was to clean off the gunge, the last move to apply some calming oil to soften their sores and ease the pain, before starting all over again next day.

Knowing this, one of the first things I asked the county spinners was how much trouble they got from their main spinning finger. Did they bleed? Did they develop cracks? Invariably they would tell me that they were lucky enough not to suffer any such problems, which told me what I needed to know about their technique.

Jim Laker was the only orthodox front-of-the-hand finger spinner I played with who rotated a worn ball enough to produce an audible hum. When I fielded close at short leg, I could distinctly hear the ball whirring its way down the wicket. Jim had massive hands with gnarled fingers and one day he showed me the secret.

'You have to hold the ball in the ends of the fingers,' he told me, and showed me how, with a full inch gap between the ball and the web of the fingers. I fear that such advice should come with a health and safety warning: 'Danger! Don't try this at home.' In reality, it was a conjuring trick, to flip it out like a spinning top and land it in the right place.

Jim's successors, John Emburey and Phil Edmonds, certainly had their successes, but it took the arrival of the DRS technology, so brilliantly exploited by Graeme Swann, for orthodox spin to become a force in Test cricket once more. The reason for this is simple enough. Before the technical evidence was available, umpires wouldn't give lbw on the front foot; they weren't prepared to guess.

With DRS today, anyone hit on the pads in line playing forward is a likely candidate for the chop. One effect is greater use of the feet to get to the pitch of the ball. Comparative statistics between John Emburey and Graeme Swann, for instance, clearly demonstrate the effect of DRS: of Emburey's first hundred wickets, less than ten per cent were lbws; Swann's figure was closer to fifty per cent. Regrettably, during my time in charge, we had a distinct paucity of good Test spinners. This was shown up most dramatically in India, when, in a three-match series, the Indian spinners took 30 wickets to our 10.

I was in no doubt that the damaging legacy of three-day cricket on covered pitches meant that changes had to be made. Four-day county games had been vaguely under consideration for years but there were strong financial incentives for keeping the three-day format. Most of the counties had festival weeks at their outgrounds, usually consisting of two matches which were well attended, with some spectators taking an annual holiday to watch them both, which influenced not just the county cricket club, but the local economy as well. Inevitably there was strong opposition to anything that would affect this

Everyone knew where I stood. More than twenty years earlier I had gone on record in recommending the four-day game, not only to provide a superior sporting event, but also to produce players better prepared for the tougher demands of a five-day Test.

Now I was in the driving seat, I needed no pushing to introduce these changes. To start with there were only a few scheduled four-day games. From 1993 onwards, all County Championship matches were played over four days.

From where I stand now, I think that a better option might have been a halfway house: three-day matches with uncovered pitches and four-day games covered. Frankly, these days, with new formats springing up everywhere, you never know, the mix and match approach may still be tried before too long.

**

While I saw my role as creating and implementing a long-term plan aimed at producing better international team results, the media preferred to treat me as a self-appointed supremo with a bit of added arrogance. My view is that what they saw as arrogance, I saw as single-minded focus on the job I had to do. I didn't help myself with my policy of fronting up to the press when things were going wrong, while giving the limelight to the captain and the manager when things were going well.

Not surprisingly, I remember the early Test matches of my time at the helm better than most, although many will recall that England under David Gower immediately got off on the wrong foot when he asked Australia to bat first at Headingley. They went in and promptly made 600!

They had the help of an unexpected and extraordinary change in the weather, which happened within minutes of the toss and Gower's fateful decision, which I had no reason to argue with at the time. The weather, which had been consistently showery for days, miraculously produced a perfect sunny day for batting. Of course, it wasn't just the sunshine that gave them the 600, it was also the increasingly obvious weakness in our bowling. Headingley was the first of a six-match series for the Ashes; it turned into a long hard summer for England.

Over this protracted series, in which we eventually lost 4-1 and had to hand the little brown urn back to a beaming Alan Border, two moments stand out. We had just been thrashed by Australia in the second Test at Trent Bridge in under four days. I didn't think it would look good if we simply packed our bags and went home a day early. We decided that we would stay overnight and come together in the dressing room the following morning at 10am to say our farewells. I was, I think, justifiably annoyed when the only man who didn't show up on time was the captain.

That embarrassment was closely followed by another when, at a press conference, I uttered a verbal juxtaposition in which I referred to bowler Devon Malcolm, after showing his first glimmer of promise on his debut, as Malcolm Devon. The tabloid hacks pounced on the easily committed faux pas like so many vultures on a dying buffalo. It is still referred to, even thirty years after the event, although I'm happy to report that when I last saw Devon at a reception in Birmingham less than a year ago, I greeted him with the words, 'Hello, Malcolm.' He replied with a good-humoured chuckle.

By the time the Australians left, taking the Ashes with them, Gower's unsuitability as captain was beyond doubt and I had to tell him he wouldn't be captain of the West Indies winter tour; indeed, along with a fading Ian Botham who was sure he was going, he wasn't even selected to play. Meanwhile, we'd announced that Graham Gooch would skipper the Caribbean tour.

* *

In the winter of 89/90 I spent some time with the first-ever A team to play in Zimbabwe, captained by Mark Nicholas, planning to go on afterwards to join the main tour to the West Indies, captained by Graham Gooch. I was with Mark and some other team members in the clubhouse at one of their matches, when I was trying desperately to get news over the phone of the first Test in Jamaica, which England looked like winning. By happy chance, we finally got through just as Ned Larkins scored the winning run.

I had planned to go to the West Indies later in the four-match series but it was far too exciting to wait and, this time with Susan, we arrived there to see the second Test in Trinidad. England's good form continued as we dominated the game needing only 150 to win on the last day.

When I drew the curtains in the morning to see a cloudless blue sky there seemed to be nothing to stop us. We were doing fine, until late in the first session when a massive black cloud welled up from nowhere, the rain belted down and stopped play for three hours. After the restart, there was still time to win but the West Indies indulged in some blatant time-wasting, with no intervention by the umpires, thereby scraping themselves a draw. It was a cruel blow. Had we gone two up at that stage we would surely have won the series. As it was, they were able to regroup and won the next two Tests.

It's worth remembering that all 'away' Tests were then umpired by local men. The international umpiring of today was years away. I once asked Don Bradman how much 'home' umpiring influenced away series in his day. 'Always,' he answered. 'Away from home, you needed to be fifty per cent better than the other team to get a result.'

England probably suffered more over the years simply because our own umpires were invariably retired first-class cricketers who knew and respected the game enough to be impartial. That was not the case everywhere else. For instance, when I captained the England XI in India and Pakistan in 1960/61 there were different umpires for every match and some of their lbw decisions were very hard to take. I felt particularly sorry for the left-handed Peter Parfitt who fell foul of Polly Umrigar's gentle off-cutters, bowled from over the wicket. The umpires seemed conveniently unaware of the need for the ball to 'pitch in line'.

For the next three years Gooch's team more than held its own against all-comers, except Australia, and with the advent of One-Day Internationals, England were a clear step ahead in the format. By the time the World Cup was played in Australia in 1991/92, we were firm favourites and played like champions all the way to the final.

I was so confident of winning that I persuaded the ECB to gather all the county chairmen in a London hotel with special facilities to watch the Melbourne match versus Pakistan. It turned out not to be my finest piece of public relations when a session of inspired bowling by Wasim Akram turned the game their way. Trying to rescue the situation as best I could, I persuaded the board to treat our returning team with the respect they deserved at a grand lunch party in London. Each of the players was presented with an expensive, high-quality and specially engraved wristwatch as a valuable memento. Inevitably though, one of the players pressed me over the chances of a cash bonus, dismissing the watches as an obvious act of sponsorship by the company that made them. I saw their point, but a man can always do with an extra watch.

* *

Of the several controversies that dogged my regime, one that should not have been contentious was my appointment of Andrew Wingfield Digby, leader of a group called Christians in Sport, as chaplain to the England XI. As I was known to be an active Christian, this was presumed to arise from my own beliefs, on a kind of evangelical whim. In fact, the idea came from Australia. One morning during the Ashes tour of 1990/91, when once again we were being hammered, I happened to arrive at the Sydney Cricket Ground so early that only one other person was to be found in the pavilion. I introduced myself. It turned out that my new acquaintance was there in his capacity of 'pastoral carer to the Australian team'. His team were doing so much better than ours, I could only view this as a possible contributory factor and decided that we would do the same. And it had its uses.

The availability of a discreet and trustworthy friend for members of the team soon proved its worth. On the Saturday of the Lord's Test versus Sri Lanka in 1991 one of the England team was called to the phone half an hour before the start.

He picked it up to hear the harsh, callous tones of a *News of the World* hack. 'We're running a story tomorrow involving your estranged wife who has been soliciting for purposes of prostitution. We thought it only right that you should know before you see it in the paper tomorrow morning.'

This was characteristic of the destructive ethos of the vile rag that was subsequently forced out of business as a result of their vicious style of journalism. The story, whether it was true or not, was run, for no other reason than the link with a national team, in the midst of a major sporting event. The front-page splash would sell hundreds of thousands of extra copies, which they would cynically calculate would bring in far more revenue than any damages they might subsequently have been ordered to pay. To be on the wrong end of an old-fashioned 'screws' coup could be a horrendous ordeal. And anyone in that position would feel the need to share his problem. To have kept it to himself would have made it impossible to concentrate on his game.

Talking to his captain wasn't an option, or even a best teammate. But a completely trustworthy outsider, who provided an understanding ear, was there to share the burden with him.

After three years in the job, I was reasonably confident that I had made progress in the areas that mattered. I knew I still hadn't won over the county chairmen, but I believed that I had won their respect as someone who had the best interests of all England teams at heart. Indeed, in one ECB committee meeting, when one county chairman complained that all they talked about was the England team, I clenched my fist in pleasure – but out of sight under the table.

When I was offered a two-year extension to my job I took it on with no major qualms although I was aware that there was still resentment in some quarters. It was dispiriting, but sadly, a mark of the insularity of county chairmen, and not to their credit, that I never once received a 'Good luck' message or phone call before a match or a tour.

In return, I did tease one or two of them when they plucked at my sleeve, demanding that I come to watch a particular player in their county team. 'Yes, I'd love to do that' I would answer. 'What does he bowl?'

But, of course, they never brought bowlers to my attention; only batsmen.

The truth is that every county team has a favourite batsman who gets runs every year and commands respect. However, there aren't sixteen batting places on the national team, and when their protégé was not picked the previous winter for the main tour or the A team tour I had to say if he wasn't picked in the top twelve in the country, then he obviously wasn't quite what selectors were looking for. In any case, there was still resentment that Test selection was, as they saw it, out of their hands, until finally they kicked, insisting that a county representative be added to the captain-manager axis of responsibility.

Reluctantly I capitulated and welcomed Dennis Amiss into the fold. But as I sat in on their deliberations, I noticed that Dennis only wanted to tout Warwickshire players. His bias was so blatant that, as chairman, I had to ask him to discuss the merits of players from any county *other* than Warwickshire. That was probably a mistake. Telling a county representative what he could or could not do was not a diplomatic move, and news of it undoubtedly filtered back to those who were, after all, my employers, and the knives started to appear. I still see Dennis socially these days, and we share a passion for golf. Happily, we both honour an unspoken agreement not to raise the issue again.

* *

Several accounts have been written of the weeks leading up to what is politely called my 'resignation'. In truth, I was pushed before I had time to jump, but on the whole, I would probably have gone anyway. The feeding frenzy of the media had reached such a crescendo that it was damaging my relationships throughout the game, including within the confines of the England team; I knew that it was time to go.

Things had started to go wrong over the disastrous 92/93 tour to India. This manifested itself from the very start, even from the moment the outward flight was called for passenger boarding, when it was by no means certain that the captain would be among them. When the team landed at the other end, Air India announced that they were going on strike, condemning our players to days of travel by bus and train, perfect breeding grounds for illnesses to spread around the whole team. On the field our bowlers were having trouble reaching the stumps and making little impact. The unavoidable perception was that the tour was sinking fast, not helped by the British press bigging up a trivial side issue over unshaven players, in which they managed to involve me for my alleged lack of concern.

When I realised the seriousness of the condition of the players, on and off the field, I booked myself a flight to Calcutta, at least as a gesture of support. I quickly had first-hand evidence of sickness when Graham Gooch joined me for dinner and passed out with his head on the table before we had finished the soup. The next morning I was in the dressing room looking out at the murky, polluted atmosphere in the ground, listening to a cacophony of players' violent coughing. I stayed with the team when they travelled to the next match and around the swimming pool of our hotel, I sat and chatted informally with a group of journalists. I mentioned a meeting I'd had in Calcutta with an eminent medical consultant who had described to me, with some alarming detail, the likely effects on athletes of heavily polluted air. I'd made a note to bring his conclusions to the attention of our medical advisers once I was back in England.

Two journalists who hadn't even been present during our discussion, picked up my remarks second-hand, and used them as a basis for headlines proclaiming them as my excuse for England's poor showing on the tour. They presented me as a bumbling figure, obviously at the end of my tether and clutching at straws to defend myself and the team. It was soon clear to me that this was part of a concerted effort to undermine me as an individual, and my role as chairman. This kind of character assassination, because it's easy to write and it makes people pick up newspapers, is a common phenomenon that crops up regularly between the press and those in the incredibly volatile field of managing sport. The tabloids especially seem to relish the opportunity to cluster around an individual like hyenas around a buffalo they've pulled down, laughing and licking their chops. I wasn't unaware of this danger when I took on the job, and I refused to let it affect me... at least, I tried to. When I got back to England, the paparazzi were swarming around outside my home and even my golf club!

* *

When Graham Gooch announced that he was standing down as captain during the 1993 Ashes series, the circumstances surrounding his decision had not been accurately described. The truth is that he had been uncomfortable in the job for a while but Micky Stewart and I saw no benefit in him making a snap decision and he agreed. Gooch gave me a firm agreement that he would finish the series against Australia first, and we wouldn't discuss the captaincy until then.

Yet another home series against Australia had started badly and showed no signs of improving. I went up to Leeds for the first two days of the fourth Test, before returning late to London. Next morning, I had an early call from Micky Stewart. He told me that Gooch was going to announce the end of his captaincy that day. He asked me if I could get back up to Leeds at once. I told him I could not.

If I needed a firm shove over the cliff, that was it.

Chapter Twenty-One

THE 1990s AND THE MILLENIUM

Istepped down from the chairmanship of the England Committee nearly thirty years ago. I've moved on, cricket has moved on, the journalists of the time have moved on. However, although I am not by nature a whinger, even at this distance in time, I still feel irritated about the press's role in my resignation. If I were to comment that when the press were reporting my actions or performance, they consistently and deliberately chose to misrepresent the actuality, I wouldn't be the first to say so.

My crime or, I should say, my error, lay not in what I did but in what I said, in the mistaken belief that I was dealing with a) adults and b) people with senses of humour. Perhaps I was naive in not fully understanding the motives behind many journalists, particularly those of the yah boo sucks faction in the tabloid papers, for whom the attacking of people in the public eye is their most effective sales tool. I recall a quote from a news editor of the now defunct *News of the World*: 'This is what we do, we go out and destroy other people's lives.'

Against that ethos, who stands a chance?

I have no doubt I made mistakes in my four years as chairman; I would be a rare bird if I had not, but if those journalists who were baying for my blood were now asked to pinpoint a *specific* clear-cut wrong decision or error, I think they'd be pushed to do so. Regrettably, the press were also being egged on by a small, vocal group of county chairmen who objected to my initiatives over the introduction of four-day games and other changes to the county game, often for very parochial reasons of their own, often out of sheer distaste for change. They were led quite overtly by Chris Middleton of Derbyshire who was consistently rubbishing my work. Middleton was a discredited figure within his own county and wasn't himself re-elected, but he was prepared to sound off to any sports writer looking for contentious copy.

In practice, I wasn't too fazed by all this – I have a fairly thick skin. But it did make it harder to do my job and – more importantly to me – Susan was beginning to find the constant carping and frankly hurtful criticism of me quite hard to take.

While I was in charge of the England Committee, I took a number of initiatives over the general administration of the game and most of those have stuck. The four-day county game is now universal. Cricketers, especially members of the Test squad, are far more fairly treated and remunerated. The one-day game, which I supported from its very inception, is now an absolute key element of cricket around the world, not least in the finance department.

There were undoubtedly fringe benefits to being chairman; for instance, I very much enjoyed going with the England team to Australia for the 1992 World Cup. England got off to a great start, winning five and drawing one of their first six matches and ending the round robin stage second in points.

The most memorable game for me – perhaps the most memorable of my chairmanship – was the match against Australia in Sydney. Susan was with me and both of us were so nervous that we got up in very good time and arrived at the ground an hour early, sitting in the stands completely on our own in the vast forty-eight thousand-seat stadium. Slowly, the space filled up with spectators and, in the days before the Barmy Army of England supporters had come into being, they were mostly Australians, determined to see a victory. Their boys batted first, when they got off to a good start and at 106 for 3 looked well on the way to winning. Their supporters were in no doubt about it and were raising the roof with their excitement – until Ian Botham found his mojo.

He bowled their skipper, Allan Border, for 16 with an absolute ripper of a ball, leaving them at 145 for 5. When Ian's tail was up and he'd had a sniff of blood, he was fast enough, and he could move the ball all over the place. He proceeded to take the next 3 wickets for 10 runs, putting the home team's score at 155 for 8. It was one of the most magical spells of bowling I ever saw.

The Australians have a good nose for this kind of thing; they were smelling defeat and already starting to lose interest. Their boys were all out for 171. England came out to bat, but by the time Gooch and Botham had put up a 107 between them, before Botham was caught behind, the Australian fans were slinking home.

When England reached 173 for the loss of 2 wickets, there was scarcely a home fan in the Sydney Cricket Ground, and Susan and I found ourselves sitting on our own, enjoying the moment, in the gloaming. We could hear a few Australian stragglers drowning their sorrows in a bar in our part of the stand, about thirty yards away. One of them came out of the bar and walked over to us. 'G'd evening,' he said. 'I know who you are, and I'd like to apologise on behalf of my Australian friends. I'm afraid we just can't take it when we're losing.'

I had another couple of enjoyable moments when I was walking around the back of the stands of the Melbourne Cricket Ground. I'd been recognised by an elderly passer-by who politely stopped me. 'I saw your innings against the Australian XI in 1963, when you hit those straight sixes. I have never seen anyone else hit them so far,' he said, proffering a wrinkled mitt. 'It's nice to shake your hand.' He carried on his way, spawning happy memories for me of that great second Test at the MCG over new year 1963.

I walked on and a few yards later stopped at a small kiosk selling cold drinks, hats and sun cream. A gravelly voice from the dark depths of the stall greeted me. 'You're Ted Dexter, aren't you! You remember you gave a bat to the Victoria Cricket Association, to be auctioned after the match against us? Well, I'm the guy who bought it and I've been waiting for thirty years to get it signed.'

He turned to reach behind him and produced the bat like a rabbit from a hat. It was an amazing coincidence, and luckily, he had a suitable pen for me to apply my moniker to its ageing, slightly discoloured front.

**

Susan and I were walking through Melbourne, taking the lovely, leafy stroll from our hotel to the cricket ground when we saw ahead of us a pair of beefy young Australians carrying between them an enormous 'esky' (Aussie slang for a portable cooler box, no doubt derived from the former, un-PC term for the Inuit inhabitants of the Arctic Circle). Suddenly the bottom of the cooler crashed to the ground, releasing untold numbers of beer cans, most of which started to roll their way down the sloping path and around a corner. The two lads gazed at their departing stock of amber nectar, speechless with horror.

It seemed to us that they had few options. They could gather up as many as they could carry in their arms, in time for the start of the match, and leave the bulk of the cans to the proclivities of passers-by. Or one of them could stand guard over the whole hoard, while the other went off to seek a replacement 'esky'. How they resolved their predicament I have no idea. But what has stayed with me ever since was the eerie silence as the dumbfounded pair surveyed the wreckage of their carefully planned day.

In the end, England did well in the 1992 tournament and lost only two matches in the round robin, making it through the semi-finals to the final, against Pakistan. They lost this game by 22 runs. We could have won, and it was a big pity we didn't. However, after four appearances in the final of the World Cup since its inception in 1975 (excluding Bagenal Harvey's Rothmans 'World

Cup' of 1966, which we won), 2019's victory was very welcome – incredibly exciting, too.

One other thing I was able to get out of my system on the 92 trip to Australia was my bizarre ambition to watch a trotter, owned by me, run at the Harold Park Raceway in Sydney, albeit the horse trailed in last.

**

In the opening years of the new millennium I was still loosely in harness as an administrator of cricket. I was appointed president of the MCC for 2002 – a symbolic, non-executive role, though nonetheless an honour. The presidency lasts one year, although one of the few meetings of any interest over which I presided took place in 2001, when I deputised for my predecessor, Lord Alexander, who couldn't chair it through a conflict of interest. This concerned the continuing membership of the MCC of popular novelist, Jeffrey Archer. He had just been sent to prison for committing perjury during his libel trial against the *Daily Star* in 1987 (in which Robert Alexander had appeared for him) and there was a strong faction within the MCC Committee who wanted him barred from the club to avoid members feeling uncomfortable at his presence. Somewhat to my surprise, the committee was fairly equally divided over the issue. I had no idea how many of them had attended one of his infamous Krug and cottage pie parties in his South Bank penthouse. I certainly hadn't; I can think of few more indigestible combinations.

In the end it was agreed to suspend Lord Archer, but there was further disagreement over the period. After some wrangling, it was fixed at seven years, although, as it turned out, it made no difference; he carried on coming and going into the Long Room and people's boxes just as he pleased without anyone challenging him, protected, I imagine, by a blend of rhino hide and brass neck.

My last act as president of the MCC was the pleasurable one of handing on the role to cricket-loving lyricist, Sir Tim Rice. Meanwhile, from 2001 to 2003, I also served as chairman of the MCC Cricket Committee. I had sat on the committee for decades, but I was glad to chair it for those three years as well as managing to make a few changes while I was there. The most important of these, which I achieved in the face of some irritating opposition at the committee stage, was the complete relaying of the outfield of the Lord's cricket ground over the winter of 2002/03. The task involved removing all the London clay beneath the turf to a depth of eight feet, and replacing it with a layered sand base, providing almost instant drainage to the whole outfield. It was a massive undertaking, overseen day to day by the then Head of Cricket, Australian Tony Dodemaide. Tony's role was critical; he'd arrived at Lord's from Melbourne a few years earlier and had had previous experience of relaying the outfield at the Sydney Cricket Ground. Lord's had an additional, inherent problem, with its nine-foot fall from north-east to south-west. Regrettably, to have levelled it would have involved rebuilding all the stands.

The Lord's relaying cost a lot of money – it took hundreds of forty-ton truck movements just to remove the clay – but that cost was eventually repaid by the number of playing days saved which would otherwise have been abandoned, thereby triggering full refunds to ticket holders. I admit that I find it gratifying that the new outfield is still sometimes referred to within the MCC as 'Dexter's outfield'.

* *

I felt proud, too, that in the 2001 New Year Honours list I was named a CBE for services to English cricket. I was presented with the medal by the Queen herself, who, in a kindly gesture, murmured something along the lines of 'about time too'. We had met in enjoyable circumstances several times over the previous five decades.

Generally, the first few years of the millennium were spent thinking about winding down all my activity and preparing myself with Susan for the next phase in our lives. I was sixty-eight and Susan sixty-five when we started considering the option of going to live somewhere near the Mediterranean. We wanted to be sensible about our assets and their distribution to our children, while I had also to be realistic about my own earning capacity and the limited extent to which that would top up our existing income; certainly the case for remaining in our house in one of the most expensive areas of England wasn't strong. We had searching discussions within the family in deciding what we should do. There seemed little point in keeping a house in England for us when we had two children each with their own places and on the whole prepared to accommodate us when we came back to England for three or four months of each year, as we intended.

We didn't have a firm idea of how long we would want to be in France and our only commitment was to a six months' recce so that we would have time to decide if we *did* want to stay and where exactly we wanted to live.

Given the ghastly circumstances of our introduction to Nice, it could have been a brief sojourn indeed; the trauma of our journey and arrival was real enough. While I'd always been fairly relaxed about the stumbling blocks that life drops in our way to test our resolve – not to say downright gung-ho – even I thought we'd had it a bit rough. We tried to get in touch with Roger Shine and his wife, pre-arranged contacts in Monaco to whom we could turn for help if we needed it, but they were incommunicado on a Mediterranean cruise ship. In fact, we learned later, when they became friends, that they were in a bad way themselves, with their ship being battered by a colossal storm.

Sitting in our little rented flat, overlooking its drab courtyard, we were feeling distinctly sorry for ourselves when we'd had our first phone call from the Englishman who had identified me in church that morning. After a brief chat, he had asked how we were. After I'd given him a frank summary of our position, a kind of expat support system sprang to life. Within ten minutes Frank Slaymaker was in our flat with money, serious concern for Susan and the information we needed to deal with our immediate crisis – the nearest pharmacie, and the nearest hospital.

Although Frank was six years my senior, with great generosity and no hint that he would rather have been elsewhere, he stayed with us for the rest of the day, taking Susan to hospital, buying the medication she needed and giving us some sense that this whole distressing episode would come to an end.

Not surprisingly, Frank is still our best friend in Nice. We share a love of cricket, despite the fact that his expert knowledge of the first-class game ended abruptly in the 1930s. After a spell in the RAF, he had worked as a commercial pilot in Iran for many years, which gave us the chance to swap flying stories as well as tales of cricket.

Susan's injuries from the mugging were severe, with at least one arm fracture, which needed plastering, and led to a series of hospital visits. We were reluctant to borrow any more money from Frank, whom we barely knew and turned instead to Ted Clark, one-time Middlesex cricketer who lived in Fréjus, an hour's drive down the coast; he and I were friends from the County Cricketers' Golfing Society. He readily tided us over with cash until we had our replacement credit cards and had time to set up a local bank account.

Meanwhile, Susan was determined to recover as fast as possible, which with her usual resilience and keen sense of humour, she did. It was at times like this that I realised just how much I owed to my wife.

It can't have been easy being married to someone like me, with my sudden passions, short attention span and a tendency to switch off when other people are trying to tell me things. Luckily for me she never was one of those people who expects their spouse to be perfect in every way. She was always practical, easy-going, observant and, above all, always capable of seeing the funny side.

* *

Besides my great good fortune in meeting and falling in love with Susan, we became lifelong friends as well. One thing that we recognised in each other was that we'd both been born and raised overseas, which meant that neither of us ever had a settled home background in England. Susan had been born in Calcutta, where her pre-school years were normal enough for a first child in a loving family, two years older than her brother, Ivo.

However, her parents, like many others in the colonies, wanted her at the age of twelve to travel to England for the first time in order to go to school there. She set off from Calcutta with her mother on a British troop ship, the *Empire Kitchener*. She was excited to be going to Britain, the wonderful country which was her family's homeland. Her first sight of the home country was of the docks in war-ravaged Liverpool in 1950, which was something of a let-down. She was dropped at school, and didn't see her father again for three years.

She soon learned that she would have to fit in with her Aunt Christine's family of two girls with whom she usually lived during the school holidays. She only returned to Calcutta twice while she was at school, and not again until she and I visited it together decades later, when her family connections with cricket in that city were manifest. She survived her time at boarding school, St Margaret's in Hastings, with resigned acceptance, lightened when her mother came over from India for a few weeks a year, when they lived in a rented cottage in Bosham, a lovely village at the top of Chichester Harbour. She would set up her easel and paint by the quay, or filled her days with sailing in the vast spaces of the harbour.

In the early 1950s, teenagers hadn't been invented, and gap years and Eurorail Passes were things of the future. For a young woman the aim was to find a job that wasn't too stultifyingly boring, although the options for females were still very narrow in those days. However, Susan, lucky girl, had beauty on her side. One day she was a schoolgirl and the next she was dressing like an adult, working as a top-of-the-range fashion model in London. Living alone in a bedsit with no friends nearby must have been tough, while she quietly jockeyed her way up to become house model at Hardy Amies. Meanwhile, fortunately for me, Susan's underlying ambition was to be married and raise children.

When we were married and living in our first little flat in Pimlico, I wasn't being paid to play cricket and my income from the insurance company who employed me simply wasn't enough to live on in any kind of style. However, Susan gamely carried on working as a model, with the added help of some better-paid photographic work. It's true to say she enjoyed the work; she had found great camaraderie in the model room and among the other girls in Peter Lumley's agency. It was Susan who suggested to the future top model, Bronwen Pugh, that she should take up modelling. She became friends with Bronwen, and with Virginia Wynn-Thomas, who went on to marry publisher, Peter Blond. In those early modelling days she made a number of friends who were in touch for years afterwards.

At home, money was, nevertheless, in short supply and a not very new, stand-alone gas cooker was the best I could offer in an otherwise bare kitchen. I cleaned the thing until it looked and worked like new, although it wasn't the dream set of appliances she might have expected. But she tolerated all the shortcomings of our underfunded early married life as serenely as she always has handled any crises throughout our sixty years of marriage.

For instance, during my motorcycling days Susan was always ready to ride pillion – on one occasion to a ball at Arundel Castle and, on another, to the Epsom Derby, when she squeezed her very snappy outfit into a backpack and took a chance on finding somewhere to change when we got there. In the racecourse car park at Epsom, a chauffeur in charge of a particularly spacious Rolls-Royce took pity on her and offered her the use of his limousine as a discreet changing room.

Perhaps the most dramatic and memorable of her pillion rides occurred when I was trying to beat the traffic to get to a 7am appointment at the breast cancer clinic at Guy's Hospital in South London; it was only for a check-up, but even this can cause moments of anxiety. By 8am she was declared 'all clear', which demanded a celebration. After a twenty-minute dash across London, we were at the side door to the Ritz, tipping the braided doorman to watch out for the bike and sauntering in for breakfast in that most elegant of dining rooms, still in our bikers' gear.

In the same way, when I started flying, she took it all in her stride. Even when I was trying to learn aerobatics and suggested we might do a slow roll, she just laughed from the passenger seat: 'Go on then. What are you waiting for?'

In contrast to Susan's obvious drive and determination in her work, she was not inwardly a confident person. It became a basic tenet of our relationship for me that I should offer to help her in everything she did. My father in his wisdom had reinforced my commitment by making me promise always to look after her.

It took a while, for instance, to persuade her to learn how to drive, for she was instinctively fearful of the possibility of accidents. Once she got going, she was absolutely fine and passed first time. She even bought her first car before I did, a small Ford, which she let me borrow now and again. I eventually repaid this by buying her second car, after a trip to Newmarket.

I had got to know some of the trainers there as a result of playing in various charity cricket matches. These were sometimes staged by Stan and Gladys Joel, one of whose daughters married trainer Harry Thomson Jones. At these cricket gatherings there were always tips for likely winners flying around, although I'd learned by experience to be fairly circumspect about them. However, on this occasion there was a stronger than usual whisper from the Jones stable about a Newmarket-trained runner, Mighty Gurkha, in the Lincoln Handicap, the first big race of the Flat season. I backed it with £40 to win at 20/1, and the £800 win bought a decent medium-sized Ford Estate for Susan.

In the first seven years of our marriage, we moved house twice, with Susan doing most of the hard work in settling in to new areas, while I was flitting in and out wherever cricket and business were taking me. We were in Ealing for thirty-five years and in the early days, Susan was still modelling, so we always had a living-in au pair. This incidentally also allowed her to go to painting and drawing classes in Ealing – the start of a lifetime interest and commitment to her art. Over time, her skill and technique developed to a point where people wanted to buy her paintings and commissioned portraits, for which she charged tens, rather than hundreds, of pounds with all proceeds, less the cost of materials, being passed on to St Matthew's Church. Susan became a warden of the church and built up a strong circle of friends, who, in turn, became an invaluable support network when she went in to battle against a proposed alteration to the North Circular which was threatening to take a large slice off the edge of Ealing Common.

A further responsibility came her way when her parents landed themselves in quite dire financial straits. Tom Longfield was the most scrupulous of men and had taken his compulsory retirement from India with adequate funds. They bought a charming cottage near Bracknell where Tom loved his garden, while maintaining other interests. He had a small business in the new field of computer software with a partner, and, as a former county cricketer himself, he also took on the job of secretary of the County Cricketers for a while.

It was a cruel twist when his business partner swindled him, at a time when rampant inflation took a hold in Britain – up to fifteen per cent at one stage – which combined to severely slash their income. Tom didn't cope well with this setback and started drinking heavily, though luckily, I was in a position to help. I bought them a decent ground-floor flat just a few hundred yards down the road from our house in Ealing, allowing them to sell the cottage and stabilise their finances. They were settling down well, when Susan's mother, Heath, finally succumbed to several illnesses and sadly died before her husband.

Tom again struggled and Susan committed a lot of time to caring for him, while he found a small bar in the High Street where they enjoyed his company and poured him doubles for the price of a single. Walking down to the bar was easy enough for him, but walking back less so, often requiring the assistance of outside agencies to complete his journey. It caused Susan some anxious pain to see it happen, but she was, of course, loyal to the end.

When we left Ealing for Ascot at the turn of the millennium, Susan continued going to art class every week and had her own, purpose-built studio in our large, rambling bungalow. Naturally when we arrived in Nice, given the generations of great artists who relished the translucence and vivid colouring of the region, we thought that finding a group of like-minded artists for Susan to join would have been easy. But although Matisse had lived and worked only a stone's throw away, and Picasso painted just down the coast in Antibes, while Cézanne, Susan's favourite, spent years engaged with the lovely Mont St Victoire, less than an hour's drive towards Aix-en-Provence, she never found the group she sought. Nevertheless, she settled down to working on her own, and was soon in demand again for portraits. All the proceeds of her sales of work went to the church, although now, the Holy Trinity Anglican Church in Nice, of which for seven years I was treasurer.

With more time than she'd had in England, Susan indulged herself by setting out most mornings to nearby busy markets, packed with fresh Mediterranean produce, to buy the ingredients for our main meal of the day – usually lunch. This allowed her the pleasure of experimenting and extending her already creative culinary skills, of which I was the principal and grateful beneficiary.

One of our original reasons for choosing Nice as, possibly, our final roosting place was that it was a vibrant city with character and purpose beyond that of merely catering for doddering expat Anglos. Our first six months there convinced us that despite some slightly scary aspects of the city it was somewhere which made us feel alive and invigorated and we made up our minds to stay.

We flogged round dozens of estate agents in the city, but it is a common trait among French tradespeople that they are impatient with foreigners, even when they speak the language. Although we explained quite clearly that we wanted a place down on the level part of town, we were constantly sent to addresses on the steep slopes away from the seafront. We had told them we didn't care about having a sea view, nor did we wish to pay the thirty per cent odd premium for the privilege. After chasing quite a few wild geese, we did find a three-bedroomed apartment that we liked in a handsome period block in the Ave du Maréchal Foch, a smart street about twenty minutes' brisk walk from the Promenade des Anglais and the seafront.

One of our reasons for the move to Nice was to slow down our pace of life and with it, the cost of living, so it was that, for the first time in over fifty years, we had no car. For more strenuous journeys, I did have a big fast Honda scooter; however, this attempt at leading a greener, more frugal existence didn't last long because I found that my chronic aches and pains eased so much in the balmy climate that I started to play golf again, and the course I favoured was thirty kilometres away, which meant that I started buying cars again.

But before that, in fact, the very day we moved into our new apartment we had a phone call from Tom which distressed us very much; Catherine's second baby, a boy named Hugh, had been stillborn. We caught the next possible flight to England and drove straight to Wolverhampton where we could offer love and support to the grieving parents. Nevertheless, seeing the tiny coffin placed in the ground at the funeral, no words could express our anguish and that of all the family.

There was a memorable sequel in the local Catholic church where the parish priest offered to honour the baby boy's memory during the next Sunday's mass. Catherine was a regular member of the congregation so the family accepted this, but not without some reservations from the older generation. What followed showed us how wrong we were to have any doubts.

Much of the service was given over to the memory of Hugh whose life had ended so suddenly without apparent cause. The thought that he would be with the angels was so fulsomely expressed by the priest that his older brother, Edward – just four – stood up in his pew, spreading his arms wide as if to fly along beside him.

Catherine was in her mid-thirties by then, with the prospects of a new pregnancy somewhat diminished. As grandparents, Susan and I were desperately hoping for a little sister for Edward. Back in France, in our travels around the country, we took to visiting churches along the way, lighting candles and saying prayers for Tom and Catherine, never having done that before, and not even knowing whether or not they had another baby in mind.

Inevitably, then, we were overjoyed three years later when we heard the news that they were expecting another child. In the event, Catherine's baby girl arrived so early that she needed all the resources of the neonatal unit at Wolverhampton's New Cross Hospital. Elizabeth not only survived, but grew healthy and strong with lovely curly red hair, like her mum's.

From then on, it was no hardship for Susan and me to spend a few months of the summer holidays looking after Edward and Elizabeth while their parents worked. There was room for us in their house and, for people of strong opinions, as we all were, we got along pretty well.

* *

In the meantime, we were settling down to life in Nice and deriving a lot of enjoyment from it. Over the last fifteen years or so, the city has been greatly improved by clever restoration and sympathetic innovation. A lot of thought, care and investment has gone into restoring some of the older parts of the city as well as the installation of an elegant new tram system and the reordering of parks and green areas that are an important part of the city. To start with, though, we had to get used to the reality that Nice could be a more violent place than we were used to, certainly compared to Ealing.

When we first arrived, Nice was suffering a noticeable crime spree, most visible in a ruthless gang that followed expensive cars into underground car parks, where they jumped the occupants as they got out, grabbed the keys and exit card and drove away. Pickpockets were everywhere, too. I had three hundred euros gently removed from my hip pocket in a bus so packed that I couldn't even move my arms. At the next stop, I watched helplessly as the little thief barged his way off the bus and ran.

After a few years, the new mayor Christian Estrosi's zero-tolerance policing regime was having some effect. The car gang had been caught and sentenced, pickpockets were effectively dealt with and, for our part, we never suffered personally from crime in the next twelve years. However, I was a front-line witness to a shooting incident and was nearly run down by one of a pair of jewellery thieves driving a high-powered scooter. The other thief lay dying in the gutter, having been shot by the man they'd robbed. The jeweller had been beaten up but left with just enough strength to pull out his gun and fire it. He was subsequently prosecuted for manslaughter and sentenced. In the end, justice prevailed and he was released on appeal, though, sadly, his charming little shop never opened its doors again.

I'd simply been ambling home with my English newspaper when I witnessed this nasty incident, and a hundred yards further on I turned into the most famous street in Nice, Jean Médecin, with its canopy of trees and broad pavements. Once again, I missed injury by a narrow squeak from a young woman on a scooter weaving her way at high speed through the pedestrians on the pavement. Next thing, she had clipped the walking stick of an old lady, bringing her crashing to the ground. Instinctively, I rushed to help the startled woman, offering a hand to pull her up onto her feet. I was momentarily shocked when she screamed at me to leave her alone. It was a few minutes later that I understood she must have thought I was going to rob her.

It was only a few days since we'd returned to Nice after a holiday. When I got home I told Susan about my adventures and my temporary misgivings. 'I'm not sure I'm ready for the wild west this early in the morning,' I grumbled.

Although in theory retired, Susan and I found that, thanks to the climate and our excellent Mediterranean diet, we were both in good health and able to enjoy all that the south of France had to offer. We made several trips up to the two nearby skiing areas, no more than two hours out of town. We found a charming, sheltered and uncrowded beach down the coast at Théoule which we looked forward to every autumn when we got back from what little summer Wolverhampton had offered while we'd been caring for our grandchildren. And there was always the Italian border, only a matter of minutes away, beyond which, I, for one, rejoiced at hearing the Italian language again.

* *

Happily, in spring 2005 I was given the opportunity to revisit some of the sites of my Italian childhood, courtesy of *The Daily Telegraph*. One of their journalists, Simon Hughes, a former county cricketer who, as it happened, had known our family for years, suggested that as a prelude to my imminent seventieth birthday he might take me on a short tour of these places as the basis for a profile in his paper. It was a very agreeable short tour, starting in Milan outside La Scala, where I had been to listen to Wagner with my father and brother some sixty years before. This was followed by a visit to the Duomo, with photographs outside, and beneath the magnificent glazed octagon of the famously elegant Galleria Vittorio Emanuele II, I was snapped again, pirouetting on one heel on the testicles of the bull set in the mosaic floor – a traditional fertility rite frankly irrelevant in my case. From there we walked a few yards to a table at Savini, one of Milan's oldest and smartest restaurants, where as a boy I had sat with my father. I remembered clearly his ordering a glass of champagne followed by bangers and mash.

After a quick turn around the Giardini Pubblici near our family's old apartment, we sped up to Lake Como, looking particularly lovely in early May as we zigzagged up the steep slopes to visit the picturesque old Villa Lugarna where I'd spent so much time as a child. My father had sold the place in 1963 when he had retired to live in England; the people who had bought it had done very little since by way of upkeep, and the once pristine gardens had been allowed to run feral, although they were still very beautiful. Sadly, my brother John who had bought and restored his own large property in Cardano, only a mile away across a valley, had died suddenly of an aneurism, fourteen years before in 1991, while I was still chairman of the England Committee. His widow Annie was still there, though, and we had tea on the lawns with her.

On the way up from Milan, talking about the Menaggio and Cadenabbia Golf Club, I had told Simon how I had been asked by the American impresario Jerry Weintraub, a good golfing friend, to arrange membership for George Clooney. On the grounds that one good turn deserves another I thought that a Clooney membership might be of equal value to him as a new roof for the lakeside Anglican Church would be to us. Regrettably, the club president beat me to it: so the church roof is still prone to leaks. The more I talked about the place, the keener Simon became to have a look. I was growing more excited myself as we drove up the winding lane to the clubhouse. The course was looking as lovely as ever – lovelier, really. Since the Roncoroni family had bought the club when my father left Italy, they had done a great deal to improve the layout and the already spectacular landscaping. Simon could hardly believe what he was seeing in the extraordinary panoramic views of the lake and mountains from almost every point. For his piece, he wanted a shot of me driving so I faked a few shots for his photographer in front of the clubhouse. Then I thought perhaps I should just have a proper swing. I dropped a ball on the tee to play the tenth, a tight par three, and watched the ball pull slightly, into the trees. I'd just had another go, and done the same, when I heard a golf cart pulling up behind us. Guiltily, I turned to find the club pro, Mark Hood, a very likeable Scot whom I knew well.

'Let's take a look at that swing o'yours,' he said.

I hit a three iron just to the left of the green.

'You're playing off the back foot,' Mark growled. 'This isn't cricket! Turn into the shot; transfer your weight.'

I did as I was told. The ball soared through the air and landed 210 yards ahead, eight feet from the pin.

'There y'are, sorted!' the pro said.

I was happy; I could scarcely believe what a colossal joy it was to be playing up on the Menaggio course once again.

It was a lovely trip, and I vowed to myself I'd be back.

Chapter Twenty-Two

SEVENTY AND COUNTING:
COMING HOME TO ROOST

Apart from our regular extended trips back to Britain every year, we also returned in 2005 to celebrate my seventieth birthday. Although I was feeling generally in good shape, I've always felt it wise to allow for unexpected turns and, before it was too late, I wanted to mark the end of seven decades by acknowledging the friendship of those people who, in many varied ways, had been important to me. Knowing this, and as a special birthday present, Susan proposed that we hold a party for which she would pay the bill from her own funds. What a woman! It was tremendously generous of her and I was delighted also to be given permission to hold a lunch for fifty people in the president's box at Lord's. A National League round four match was being played between Middlesex and Hampshire, then at the bottom of the order, who put on a magnificent show for us, making 353 for 8 in 45 overs. Kevin Pietersen, in a great knock, scored 80 in fifty balls, including six sixes!

Susan drew up the guest list to reflect the eclectic nature of my life (so far). The party included family – my only remaining sibling, David, my brother John's three daughters, my own children and grandchild, and Susan's brother, Ivo; England and county cricketers – Jim Parks, Ian Thompson, Alan Oakman, Peter Richardson and Raman Subba Row; school friends – Clive and Bella Carr, John Scott and his wife; business colleagues and some of our new friends from France. I thought it was a terrific party, with some wonderful entertainment on the field; I hoped that our guests enjoyed it too, and I looked forward to the next one.

To be seventy is not to be old these days, and life can still be enjoyed, with a bit of wisdom and a little luck. Nevertheless, it is a time when doors begin to close that will probably not open again, although that doesn't mean there will be no fresh apertures through which to venture. I didn't feel too old as we headed back to our winter roost in Nice after what had been for me a celebration of all the activities into which I'd thrown myself on a whim, a wing and a prayer during my first seventy years.

Now, with a slight change of emphasis, I became more involved with the church. The community around the Anglican Church of the Holy Trinity in Nice had shown themselves, since the horrors of our first arrival, to be good and loyal friends, and in an attempt to repay some of the goodwill I'd found there, when the role of treasurer for the parish became vacant, with Susan's encouragement, I put myself up for it.

It was, perhaps, the last thing a former action man like myself might have been expected to do, but I'd always had a good head for figures and, despite occasional bouts of scattiness, an orderly mind. I was glad to help and to become involved in the physical legacy of the church and the historic relationship between the British and the city.

As early as the second half of the eighteenth century, members of the English aristocracy started arriving to spend their winters in Nice, then part of the Kingdom of Sardinia. These early expats especially liked the panorama of the long curve of the Baie des Anges and cultivated the habit of taking scenic walks along the coast. In 1820 after a more than usually harsh winter inland, Nice filled up with poor people and beggars from the rural hinterland, desperate for food and work.

The Anglican Church had by then built up a large congregation and wanted to help. In the practical spirit of the nineteenth century English, they devised a vast job creation scheme, on the grounds that, instead of offering handouts to these poor people, they should be allowed the dignity of working for a living. The Brits produced a plan to construct and pave a permanent way for some two or three miles alongside the seafront where they loved so much to promenade. This scheme was entirely funded by the members of the Holy Trinity Church and their vicar, the Reverend Lewis Way. The resulting route became known as the Camin deis Anglés in local dialect, later renamed Promenade des Anglais after Nice became part of France in 1860. Since then the town has taken responsibility for it, extended and developed it.

Holy Trinity Church, first built in 1862, had deteriorated to such an extent by the turn of the millennium that the Mairie of Nice gave notice that one of the decorative spires was unsafe, and threatened to close the church until it was secured. Extensive investigation of the rest of the structure revealed a great deal more damage in need of urgent attention. This triggered a complete *ravallement* of the church exterior, estimated to cost more than €1 million, a lot more than the church had in its coffers.

We were encouraged to look for subsidies not only from the Mairie, but from both regional and national funds. As the restoration progressed, surprisingly large sums became available from the top two tiers of funding, but not from the Mairie, with whom historically the church had a special relationship. We were still €200,000 short.

Without any preamble we were suddenly told that Mayor Estrosi planned to visit the church. Although we didn't know the reason for his visit, we gathered up as many as we could from the congregation to give him some kind of a welcome. He arrived with his entourage and quickly arranged to deliver a speech on the church steps, as politicians do. Normally they would like a large public audience, rather than a handful of parishioners but the mayor delivered an impassioned address on the city's traditional and valued links with the British community. He spoke briskly and concisely before announcing the decision of the Mairie to contribute €200,000 to the restoration. And, in a flash, he was gone; and we were jubilant. It was a graphic demonstration of the way Estrosi had achieved so much in the overall reordering of his city.

My last memories of Holy Trinity Church are rather more complicated, not to say alarming. Our Australian priest was coming to the end of his tenure when he suddenly disappeared, leaving a trail of problems behind him. A room in the presbytery for which he claimed to have lost the key turned out to be knee-deep in unopened mail, uncashed cheques and unread letters. The upstairs private rooms were filthy.

The man had almost certainly suffered a slow burning breakdown. We had no choice but to pick up the pieces and pray for better times. Our prayers were answered in the most practical way when a retired builder and loyal parishioner, Geoff Treloar, gave up a year of his life to restore the presbytery beautifully, making it ready for the next incumbent.

**

When not eating, drinking or helping the church, I was playing a lot of golf. This hadn't been part of our Nice retirement agenda, but because I found I could play, albeit buggy-powered, I couldn't deny myself. As well as the amenable climate and a fine physiotherapist, I'd also been encouraged by Roger Shine, who had been in the great Mediterranean storm when we needed him. He made up for that by providing the introductions I needed to get me started at Cannes Mougins Golf Club. While there was a plethora of golf courses around Nice, all of which I played at, Cannes Mougins was by far the best.

I might have felt a pang of guilt about once more deserting Susan for the game, but she kindly claimed it suited her well, because it gave her a chance to paint and draw without interruption.

There was no shortage of colourful, cultural events around Nice which we could enjoy, but which contrasted with our more muted summer activities in England. Although a few friends looked a little squiggly-eyed when we told them we stayed in Wolverhampton during the summer months, we loved being there with Tom and his family and we have become fond of the area and the outstandingly warm, genuine people.

Nevertheless, special highlights continued to pop up in our lives. In 2012, for instance, we were invited over to Calcutta (or Kolkota as it should now be written) to celebrate the fiftieth anniversary of a great Test match in 1962 between England and India, when the sides had been captained by me and Nari Contractor respectively. Nari had flown over from Mumbai, where he was then based as a principal national coach. He and I took part in a lively Q&A session, which was fun but stretched the memory box to its meagre limits. It was a marvellous event, much enriched by nostalgia sauce, and a great pleasure to see Nari once again after so long.

I saw many more blasts from my past in 2015, when Susan, this time with Genevieve's help, again stepped in to host a party at the clubhouse of the Menaggio Golf Club to celebrate the completion of my eighth decade.

As Susan and I drove up from Nice the morning before my birthday, I didn't know what to expect. I guessed we would be billeted at a modest outhouse with little more than two beds and a loo, just down the road from our former home, the Villa Lugarna.

Genevieve had instructed us to meet her at the gates where she would give us the keys. When we arrived, she simply took me by the arm, walked me up the fifty-yard driveway to the villa itself, and out onto the veranda. Half of my family were already there to greet me. Tables were laid for lunch with many a bucket cooling the champagne. They had decided to start the celebrations a day early which seemed like a great idea once I'd got over the initial surprise.

After lunch I was shown to the principle suite in the house, which really impressed me. I'd never been in that part of the house before and I felt truly spoiled. It turned out that my lovely wife and daughter had been able to rent the place for the week, though I didn't dare think what that might have cost.

This party, with its spectacular location, had attracted even more family and friends than my seventieth, ten years before at Lord's – several from our last dozen years in Nice. I was very proud to be able to show them all my favourite childhood haunts, despite the inevitable changes of the past sixty years. It had been planned to hold the pre-dinner drinks al fresco, with an added Italian flavour of some popular arias to be sung by an operatic soprano and a tenor from La Scala. But true to the unpredictable nature of the lake country, we were treated to a magnificent downpour and the whole party was moved indoors. Even inside, though, through a vast, north-facing picture window, there was still a spectacular view of the length of Lake Como to the snow-topped peaks of the Engadine beyond. It was a very special evening for Susan and me, although I don't think I was the only one who had forgotten what an astonishing volume operatic voices can produce, especially in a confined space.

I went to bed happy in my beautiful room to sleep happily and soundly. In the morning I was hustled by my daughter, Genevieve, to get a move on, to be sure of getting a parking place by the Anglican Church in Cadenabbia in time for the Sunday service. It was unlike her to fuss about religious observance; however, I did as I was told and scuttled off.

As soon as I'd gone, an army of caterers arrived to set up a second surprise lunch party at the villa. With over eighty guests it was even bigger than the one the night before – another magnificent and totally memorable event. I wished I could be eighty more often.

**

During our short stay in the Villa Lugarna, I spent a little time with my brother's widow, Anne, who still lived in their very large property across the valley which John had converted into a comfortable villa for his family. I found myself worrying not so much about her state of health as her state of mind. She had never been the easiest of people with whom to communicate, but her attitude now seemed worryingly negative. She was by then beginning to find it difficult to run the house, which, in any case, was too large for a single old lady. She was regularly visited by her three daughters, my lovely bright nieces: Lucy, Julietta and Camilla.

Lucy de Nardi married a charming, anglophile Italian, who sadly died young; she now works for Prince Charles and lives with her two children in Kensington. Julietta Dexter followed her father and me to Jesus College Cambridge, shortly after women were first admitted to the college. She went on to work in advertising until my brother John's early death at the age of fifty-six, when she felt driven to found and grow her own highly successful PR company, the Communications Store. The artistic Camilla started her own interior decorating company.

By 2016, the year after my eightieth, the sisters had recognised that their mother was finding it too hard to organise her own affairs and they finally persuaded her to move back to England, where they found an ideal retirement home for her near Newbury. The pleasing effect of this was that Anne, who had always seemed a little dissatisfied with life, completely altered her outlook and demeanour. Although still a little inclined to behave like a headmistress, she has become very much more sympathetic and I think is a great deal happier than she was. I know that John would have liked to have seen her like that, and he would be delighted to know that his three daughters still keep the villa where they grew up in the family.

** **

After spending most of the summer of 2015 in England, where we had one or two more octogenarian gatherings and an enjoyable visit to Lord's, we were happy to return to Nice, still pleased with the decision we'd taken to live there. Soon afterwards, though, our perspective altered sharply as a result of the misfortunes suffered by some good friends, John and Dawn Nicholls. They were the same age as us, but their health was deteriorating, and they were becoming anxious about it. They were talking about going back to England, when John succumbed to a stroke and never came out of hospital and, soon afterwards, Dawn had a fall and was taken to hospital where she was diagnosed with cancer. She didn't survive long.

The Nicholls had two daughters with young families, one in London, the other in Los Angeles. As their parents were dying, they were both flying into Nice frequently for meetings with doctors and afterwards to make funeral arrangements. They had to come back again to deal with their parents' finances and to sell their flat. Susan and I did what we could to help but really could only sympathise with the two girls who were having their lives so sadly disrupted. We were surprised and alarmed by the complexities of dealing with these things from a distance and were sure that we didn't want to expose our own children to the same experience, which led directly to our own decision to leave France while we were still standing, and return to live full-time in England.

Home to Roost

Once we had made up our minds about coming back to England in principle, we had to deal with the question of where we wanted to live. We certainly wished to be near one or other of our children. We didn't want to live in London, nor could we afford the property prices, so we felt we would be more use as grandparents in Wolverhampton. We already knew the town well, through having stayed there with Tom and Catherine over the previous twenty years, and we began to look for suitable houses in the more attractive areas of that formerly industrial city.

We found exactly what we wanted – a small, efficient house, recently built, without inherent problems and easy to run. Having witnessed the difficulties that the Nicholls' daughters had to cope with in Nice, within days of moving into our new house, we had bought ourselves a burial plot in the local cemetery. With great efficiency, we also planned and paid for our funeral and cremation arrangements. The children know where to find the contracts – so all they need to do when the ambulance arrives is to say, 'He/she is with the Co-op', turn up at the church and make sure there's good champagne served at the after-party.

The house with its small garden is a mile from Tom and Catherine's big Victorian house and, as we wanted to have a dog again (after fifteen years without one), we had made sure that we were within easy walking distance of some good open spaces. There is also a first-rate golf club nearby, the South Staffs, where I play regularly and have known the pro, Peter Baker, for a long time. At the age of twelve, he won the Commercial Union young players' tournament which I'd organised some thirty years before. Between golf and greyhounds, I'm packing in all the exercise I need. As I was getting close to finishing this book, I received an entirely unexpected present – an Honorary Membership of the South Staffordshire GC.

Susan and I love walking together but she has also been able to fulfil her love of art. In contrast to the lack of amenable painting companions in Nice, in the far less obvious milieu of Wolverhampton, Susan found just the group she'd been missing there. A bonus has been hearing her new mentor telling the others that her work is what they should be aspiring to. On the top floor of the house, Susan has a light and airy studio, where she is enjoying drawing and painting as much as ever.

To keep myself usefully occupied, as well as to amuse myself and protect my brain from atrophy, I have acquired the habit of sitting down to write most days. I hadn't been involved in regular journalism since I'd written for *The Daily Telegraph*, up until just after the millennium, but in 2010, while I was in France, I started publishing sporadic blogs on www.teddexter.com which gave me the chance to air my views on the current state of cricket and golf. The latest, posted in May 2020, looks at the appearance and development of cricket helmets – something I never directly experienced, which, of course, does not preclude me from holding views. Since returning to live in England, I have also started writing extensively about some of my cricketing experiences, golfing moments, misadventures and family memories.

Through a good friend from Nice, Johnny Stevens, who also lives part-time, not far from us, in Much Wenlock, I met a number of other people in the area whose company I enjoyed and with whom I found I had much in common. I also believe that it's never too late to make new friends and through one of them, I was encouraged to look at all the writing I've done over the years and to consider the possibility of putting together a full-scale autobiography. It has been a longish haul, taking the better part of a year to complete it all, but it has also been an immensely enjoyable process, revealing and, in many ways, reassuring. Indeed, the very process of regressing one's mind to past times can unleash some unexpected memories. At the same time, a lot of detail was quite hazy until I looked for written confirmation. For instance, I'd completely forgotten about the Rothmans World Cup of 1966 until I was checking a few facts on Bagenal Harvey. I've also come to the conclusion, in looking back over my career as a player, administrator and entrepreneur, that I achieved about as much as I had it in me to achieve. I'm reminded of my late brother David telling me, after I'd questioned the style of a wayward golf shot, 'So what? I did my best.'

I believe I can make some claims for decisions and initiatives of lasting impact on the game of cricket, as played here and around the world:

The wholehearted encouragement of the limited-overs game, and writing the rules for the International Cavaliers, which some say rescued the game from the doldrums, and ultimately converted it into the multimillion-pound business that it is today. Paving the way for the formation of the now influential MCC World Cricket Committee.

Resistance to the introduction of 'new' bat designs – including metal and honeycomb insets – and insisting that the blade 'shall be made entirely of wood'.

A complete rewrite of the 'Laws of Cricket', not so much to make changes as to provide clarity.

The relaying of the Lord's outfield.

The granting of the first-ever contracts between ECB (TCCB) and England Test players.

An insistence on regular annual 'A' team overseas tours, now labelled the 'England Lions'.

The revision of regulations relating to the manufacture of cricket balls.
Dispensing with the old Test Match Selection Committee.
The introduction of four-day county cricket.

Failed initiative: A campaign to have the former Crown & Triple Lion insignia returned to England Test cricket outfits – not over yet.

**

Beyond all that, in the end I believe that the most important thing to consider isn't what I have done, but where I am now – whether or not I am content within myself, and offering all I can to ensure the well-being and fulfilment of my offspring and their families, as well as the happiness of my spouse of sixty-one years – and my best friend.

In all these things, I'm certainly trying my best. With Susan, it helps that we have always had so much in common. In most things we have the same tastes: we like the same films – not too violent, and certainly not spooky (we leave those to the grandchildren). We still prefer the old ballads with the clever, subtle lyrics – Cole Porter, Sinatra, Noël Coward and Hutch. We read the same newspaper, we have the same catholic taste in food – from Indian curries to French and Italian cuisine and of course, good old Rosbife. However, we have found that it helps to have two TV sets – a somewhat prosaic requirement, but if that's what it takes to stay together for sixty years, so be it.

Finally, once our sex lives, inevitably though sadly came to an end, we agreed, instead, always to have a proper *hug* before going to bed. I recommend it.

ACKNOWLEDGEMENTS

My thanks go to all the Dexter family for their support during the whole of my life but principally to Mum and Dad who so often demonstrated their unstinting love and also, of course, to my ever-loving wife Susan.

I remain grateful to all the coaches, captains and lifelong cricketing friends for tolerating my often-erratic behaviour and for taking me at face value, which I always hope was someone that they could trust.

I offer condolences to all those who, for whatever reason, chose to try and belittle or upset me. Their failure was my gain.

Without the enthusiasm and the sheer hard work of Peter Burden, who revitalised and organised my own written efforts into a coherent story, this book would never have seen the light of day. My thanks also to those at Quiller Publishing who have been quietly supportive throughout.

Thanks also to Benedict Bermange, the Sky Sports cricket statistics wizard, for supplying additions and corrections to sometimes off-beat cricketing facts and figures. Benedict spent his first day of work experience in my Ealing office in 1991.

INDEX OF NAMES

323